THE RISE OF THE RUSSIAN NOVEL

The Rise of the

RUSSIAN NOVEL

Carnival, Stylization, and Mockery of the West

David Gasperetti

NORTHERN ILLINOIS UNIVERSITY PRESS

DeKalb 1998

© 1998 by Northern Illinois University Press
Published by the Northern Illinois University
Press, DeKalb, Illinois 60115
Manufactured in the United States using acid-
free paper
All Rights Reserved
Design by Julia Fauci

Library of Congress
Cataloging-in-Publication Data
Gasperetti, David Wayne, 1952–
The rise of the Russian novel : carnival, styl-
ization, and mockery of the West / David
Gasperetti.
    p.   cm.
Includes bibliographical references and index.
ISBN 0-87580-230-3 (alk. paper)
1. Russian fiction—18th century—History and
criticism. 2. Russian fiction—19th century—
History and criticism. I. Title.
PG3095.G37   1997
891.73'009—dc21   97-11768
                            CIP

Gasperetti's "*The Double:* Dostoevskii's Self-
Effacing Narrative" from *The Slavic and East
European Reiview* 33, no. 2 (summer 1989):
217–34, is used with permission, has been
slightly reworked, and appears as Chapter 8.
Gasperetti's "The Carnivalesque Spirit of the
Eighteenth-Century Russian Novel" from
The Russian Review 52 (April 1993): 166–83 is
used with permission and incorporated into
various portions of this book.

CONTENTS

Acknowledgments   *vii*

Notes on the Text   *ix*

Introduction: The Literary-Historical Importance of the
Eighteenth-Century Russian Novel   3

PART ONE   Context and Theory

Chapter 1. Reluctant Imitators: The Cultural Context of the
Early Russian Novel   *11*

Chapter 2. The Carnivalesque Spirit of the Eighteenth-Century
Russian Novel   *29*

PART TWO   Textual Analysis

Chapter 3. Approaches: Historicity versus Fiction   *71*

Chapter 4. The Limitations and Possibilities of Voice and Rhetoric   *86*

Chapter 5. The Social Order   *113*

Chapter 6. Characterization   *134*

PART THREE   Stylization: A Metaliterary Strategy of the 1840s

Chapter 7. A Theory of Stylization   *161*

Chapter 8. Slowly Fading into Nothing: The Self-Effacing Stylization
of *The Double*   *174*

Conclusion: Emin, Chulkov, and Komarov and the Rise of the Russian Novel   *188*

Plot Summaries   *199*

Notes   *211*

Works Cited   *235*

Index   *245*

ACKNOWLEDGMENTS

During the course of my work on the eighteenth-century Russian novel, I have been fortunate to receive the insights, assistance, and encouragement of many people. I would like to thank my colleagues at the University of Notre Dame, especially Jonathan Boulton, Randy Klawiter, Martha Merritt, and Tom Marullo, for their helpful suggestions and moral support and also express my appreciation to Mary Lincoln, the director of Northern Illinois University Press. Mary's faith in this project and the patience she and her staff have shown in seeing it to completion have made the riotous voyage through carnival all the more enjoyable. In the profession at large I would like to extend a special acknowledgment to Gitta Hammarberg, Ronald LeBlanc, and Marcia Morris, three scholars whose interest in the less-traveled paths of Russian literature has both encouraged and challenged me. Their expertise in pre–golden age Russian literature has had a decisive influence on my understanding of the problems detailed in this study. I am also indebted to Gitta and to Caryl Emerson for a meticulous reading of the manuscript. Their numerous constructive comments have greatly improved the final form of this book. I, of course, accept full responsibility for whatever mistakes and shortcomings still exist.

Grants from the University of Tulsa, the Institute for Scholarship in the Liberal Arts of the College of Arts and Letters at the University of Notre Dame, and the Social Science Research Council have facilitated the completion of this project. I am deeply grateful for the release time and other opportunities their support has made possible.

Special thanks go to my parents, whose encouragement, understanding, and unconditional support have been a constant throughout my studies, and to my children, Claire and Matthew. They serve as a daily reminder of why I have chosen the humanities as a profession and consistently give me practical insights into the positive power of laughter.

My greatest debt of gratitude belongs to the many talented teachers who guided and encouraged me in the study of Russian, including Mel Strom, Sonia Gotman, George Smalley, and especially Peter Hodgson. Peter's kindness, generosity, and intellect have been a constant source of inspiration. From the day of our first meeting in his class on Turgenev, he has shown me what it means to be a caring teacher and an enthusiastic scholar. It is to him that I dedicate this book.

NOTES ON THE TEXT

Transliteration follows the Library of Congress system, with the exception of given names, which are frequently simplified or rendered in an English equivalent. Endings have been modernized throughout, and unless otherwise noted, all translations from Russian are mine.

The Rise of the Russian Novel

INTRODUCTION

The Literary-Historical Importance
of the Eighteenth-Century Russian Novel

Most critics of Russian prose fiction dismiss the second half of the eighteenth century as an inferior and derivative period that is not worthy of the in-depth analysis accorded subsequent epochs. With the notable exception of the sentimentalist writer Nikolai Karamzin, the initiators of the Russian tradition of prose fiction have been relegated to the status of curiosity pieces whose work represents nothing more than a false start in the modern history of their craft.[1] For this reason monographs devoted to the pioneers of the Russian novel—Fedor Emin (1735?–1770), Mikhail Chulkov (1743?–1792), and Matvei Komarov (1730?–1812)—total less than a handful.[2] On the one hand, such critical indifference is understandable: from the standpoint of conception, execution, and intellectual substance the early Russian novel pales before the long list of masterpieces that begins with Pushkin's *The Captain's Daughter* and Gogol''s *Dead Souls*. On the other hand, Emin, Chulkov, and Komarov do merit greater scrutiny because they stand at the threshold of a literary tradition, and no interpretation of the development of the novel genre in Russia will be complete until the beginning of the process is fully understood.[3]

Despite their eclecticism and unevenness the first Russian novels reflect the cultural dynamism of their day. Historians have long recognized that the pivotal issues that shaped the nineteenth and twentieth centuries emerged in embryonic form during the reign of Catherine the Great. The formation of an independent intelligentsia committed to improving the material, moral, and spiritual well-being of the country; the discovery of a uniquely "Russian soul"; and the beginnings of the Slavophile/Westernizer debate that would eventually erupt in the 1840s all trace their initial articulation to the second half of the eighteenth century. As an integral part of this cultural ferment, the novel also laid the foundation for later developments in its genre. Just as the intelligentsia framed the questions that would occupy their heirs in the next century, Emin, Chulkov, and Komarov began to respond to problems that would find much more cogent expression in works like "The Overcoat" and *The Double*. Thus, focusing greater attention on the first Russian novels not only illuminates a body of unjustly overlooked fiction, but also increases our appreciation of works that have already received a well-deserved share of the critical spotlight.

In addition to providing a fuller picture of the development of the novel genre in Russia, an in-depth analysis of the prose fiction of Emin, Chulkov, and Komarov also helps to correct an inaccurate assessment of the role of Western culture in the empire of the tsars. The accepted interpretation argues that in the eighteenth century Russia became a virtual cultural colony of its neighbors to the west, especially France and England. Unable to match the rich literary traditions and achievements of Western Europe, would-be Russian writers, especially novelists, are supposed to have indiscriminately imitated a vast array of foreign models that made their way to Moscow and St. Petersburg. This study takes a new approach to the problem, as it underscores a more circumspect response to Western culture that was also frequently expressed in early Russian prose fiction. Without denying that figures like Emin, Chulkov, and Komarov appropriated foreign literary norms to create some of Russia's first novels, I focus instead on the many ways in which they attacked these conventions as being incapable of representing Russian cultural reality.

The rise of the Russian novel in the second half of the eighteenth century took place within the context of a complete reorientation of society. Recognizing Russia's backwardness in everything from military affairs to ode writing, rulers such as Peter the Great (1682–1725), Elizabeth I (1741–1762), and Catherine the Great (1762–1796) encouraged the wholesale adoption of foreign models as the quickest means of catapulting their country into the first rank of European nations. In the area of literature the Russians chose to emulate the paragons of French neoclassicism. Starting around 1750, the works of Corneille, Racine, and Molière were held up as the standard to be met, and the principles of Boileau's thesis on literature (*L'Art poétique*) were transcribed into Russian. Within a decade a host of Russian writers was turning out tragedies, comedies, odes, and epics in the neoclassical manner. By the 1760s a wave of Anglomania coupled with the advent of the literary aesthetic of sentimentalism added the novel to the list of preferred models. Translated excerpts from Swift, Defoe, Richardson, Fielding, Smollett, and Sterne became the common fare of literary journals, and the publication of their novels in Russian also dates from this time. As with verse and drama the appearance of a large number of first-rate foreign models engendered an immediate and overwhelming response. By the end of the 1760s Russia had not only produced its first original novels, but the genre itself eclipsed verse and drama to become the most popular form of literature in Catherine's realm.

Given the history of its formative stage, it is no surprise that the early Russian novel contains a host of conventions popularized in French and British literature during the preceding one hundred years. Typically, the introductions in Russia's first novels announce that the following tale is designed to improve the morals and expand the knowledge of its readers. If the work happens to be an adventure tale or rogue's novel, the author dutifully proclaims that his goal is to denounce vice by exposing its fatal allure. The stories themselves abound with informative discourses on geography and education, and monologues on the ideal traits of an enlightened monarch are virtually de rigueur. The glorification of country simplicity, the denunciation of urban intrigues, and the wayward heroine à la Moll Flanders all play a prominent role in the genre as well. From individual devices to its very raison d'être, the eighteenth-century Russian novel confirms the conventional wisdom that it is a faithful imitation of Western literary models.

While acknowledging the imitative base of the first Russian novels, this monograph rejects the conclusion that uncritical acceptance was the Russians' only significant response to the onslaught of West European literary norms. It argues instead that writers like Chulkov and Komarov actually parodied not just the conventions but the very world view that prevailed in the foreign-inspired literature of their day. By birth Chulkov (a court lackey and actor) and Komarov (a manor serf) were not part of the social and cultural elite that promulgated the standards of official literature, and they did not share its system of values. Moreover, as the genre with the least number of formal constraints, the novel offered them the perfect forum to mix a variety of styles and sources. While paying homage to a foreign literary convention on one page, they could ridicule it mercilessly on the next. The goal of this study is to identify and analyze these instances of parodic transformation. How do certain early Russian novels negate the intent of their civic-minded dedications? When is the didactic monologue made to sink under the weight of its own bombast? How does the "Russian Moll Flanders" differ from her English predecessor? These are the questions informing close readings of the complete novels of Emin, Chulkov, and Komarov that constitute part 2 of this study.

Novelists like Chulkov and Komarov found it quite natural to ridicule the officially sanctioned literature of neoclassicism and sentimentalism owing to their close association with the literary subculture. Consisting of an eclectic combination of folklore, carnival entertainment, the pulp fiction known as *lubok*, translated lowbrow literature imported from the West, and even the novel itself, the eighteenth-century Russian literary subculture served as an effective counterweight to the seriousness and didacticism of officialdom. While critics acknowledge that these forms did provide some of the central building blocks of the first Russian novels, they generally fail to appreciate the greater motivation behind their use. They usually point out isolated reflections of the subculture only in order to illustrate how the pioneers of Russian prose fiction failed to completely assimilate a foreign model. The primary contribution of the present monograph to this area of study consists of defining the subculture as an integrated system and showing how it functions in the early Russian novel as a positive defense against foreign cultural hegemony.

The critical approach employed to elucidate this problem is based on Mikhail Bakhtin's conception of the carnivalesque. In his classic work on Rabelais Bakhtin proffers the European Renaissance carnival as the emblem for an extensive and historically long-lived cult of folk humor. According to this theory the folk employs the carnival and such related forms of laughter as comic feasts and banquets, parodies of church rituals, and the buffoonery of marketplace spectacles as a defense against the inflexibility and authoritarianism of church and state. During the carnival itself, for example, the suspension of everyday laws and restrictions and the crowning of a pauper as king temporarily turn the world upside down. Authority is ridiculed, and the common folk ascend to a position of preeminence. In like manner the artistic forms of the Russian subculture assert the supremacy of a Russian cult of folk humor. In this antiworld anything that is serious or that strives to impart an inflexible, didactic view of the world is fair game for the mockery inherent in the fantasy of folklore, the facetious humor of the carnival, and the satire and eclecticism of *lubok*.

In addition to animating the creative core of figures like Chulkov and Komarov, the festive humor of the subculture also helps to establish their niche in Russian literary history by underscoring the important connection between their work and certain classic texts of the next century. While usually bestowing the title of the cradle of the Russian novel on the mid–nineteenth century, most scholars would concede that such a theory seems rather abrupt. Granted, between 1836 and 1852, the "forties," Pushkin, Lermontov, Gogol´, Dostoevskii, Turgenev, and Tolstoi all made significant contributions to the genre. Each of these figures has passed the test of time, and the fiction they wrote at that time still engenders a lively interest among critics and readers alike. From Pushkin's *The Captain's Daughter* (1836) to Tolstoi's *Childhood* (1852) this group of authors grappled with the question of how to assimilate the basically foreign genre of the novel. By the early 1850s, after a decade and a half of experimentation with historical novels, picaresques, and epistolary forms, the tradition of the realistic novel was firmly established. The question remains, however, how Russia could produce so many first-rate authors in such a short span of time if it had virtually no tradition of prose fiction that could nurture them. It is as though the golden age of Russian literature arose out of nowhere. The simple answer is, of course, that earlier generations had indeed prepared the way.

The importance of the 1840s for the development of Russian prose fiction notwithstanding, this period represents the continuation of a process that had begun at least seventy-five years earlier. The literary and cultural backdrop of the latter half of the eighteenth century presented the same sort of challenges to Emin, Chulkov, and Komarov as the 1840s did to

Gogol´ and Dostoevskii. In both eras Russian writers found themselves in danger of being overwhelmed by foreign literary traditions. In the eighteenth century the movements of neoclassicism and sentimentalism posed the greatest threat to native means of artistic expression; in the 1840s this role was taken over by French naturalism. Although both periods turned out writers who were mostly content to imitate imported norms, they also produced figures who took a more circumspect view of foreign culture. For Komarov, and especially Chulkov, the writing of novels meant amalgamating a variety of sources, both foreign and Russian. In the often incompatible mix of elements that marks their work a uniquely Russian voice based on the mocking humor of the subculture resounds just as clearly as the familiar refrains of imitation. Similarly, metaliterary commentary also plays an important role in the prose fiction of Gogol´ and Dostoevskii, although it often takes a more subtle form than in the work of the first Russian novelists. Instead of using the rather crude mockery of the subculture to ridicule the West, it frequently embodies a type of parody that I term *stylization*.

The conception of stylization developed in this monograph springs from insights provided by the Russian formalist critic Iurii Tynianov. In his article "Dostoevskii and Gogol´: Toward a Theory of Parody" ("Dostoevskii i Gogol´: k teorii parodii") Tynianov defines stylization as a *nonhumorous* subtype of parody that seeks to neutralize not just the specific elements of a particular author's work, as parody does, but rather entire literary schools and trends. Unfortunately, Tynianov's exposition of this topic is so brief that it actually raises more questions than it answers. The goal of this monograph is to fill in the gaps in this provocative idea and turn it into a working critical methodology. The most important part of this undertaking concerns the dynamics of reader response. Unlike parody, which encourages us to join with the author in laughing at a flawed literary performance, a stylization actually puts its readers and their assumptions about literature in the center of the critical spotlight. To show how this process works, theory is illuminated by a close reading of Dostoevskii's short novel *The Double*. In this dense and convoluted narrative stylization functions as an artfully conceived, well-orchestrated attack on Russia's infatuation with the literature of Western Europe. Moreover, by highlighting a well-known text that showcases one of the ways in which Russian authors of the nineteenth century encoded their criticism of the West, it becomes easier to see that writers like Chulkov and Komarov had the same metaliterary ends in mind, even though they went about them in a more fragmented and less-sophisticated manner.

In conclusion, I wish to emphasize that this is not an "author" book that attempts to treat selected writers in an exhaustive manner. Although it does analyze the complete prose fiction of Emin, Chulkov, and Komarov as well as their backgrounds and the society that produced them, this monograph is first and foremost a study of the historical and cultural importance of the first Russian novels. The figures investigated here were extremely popular, yet unpolished, writers whose work, from an artistic point of view, is far from flawless. Their novels do turn out to be a cache of undiscovered gems, however, when the question turns to the Russians' creation of a unique national identity in the modern period. As the experience of Emin, Chulkov, and Komarov indicates, a culture that borrows material from a more sophisticated source establishes a complex relationship with it. The mere fact of looking to a foreign culture for models does not turn the borrowing culture into a passive recipient. Along with imitation, the borrowing culture can strike a more critical attitude toward its target as it attempts to employ and defend native values. In this regard the story of the first Russian novels sheds light on any number of intercultural collisions, from the development of prose fiction in the golden age of Russian literature to the fate of postperestroika Russia as it tries to assimilate Western institutions and practices.

Part

ONE

CONTEXT AND THEORY

Chapter

ONE

RELUCTANT IMITATORS

The Cultural Context of the Early Russian Novel

THE TRADITIONAL APPROACH:
IMITATION AND THE EIGHTEENTH CENTURY

The misguided tendency to dismiss the formative stage of modern Russian culture as second-rate and derivative had its origins in the eighteenth century itself. With the imposing figure of Peter the Great looming over Russia's entrance into the modern age, scholars and commentators from the 1700s to the present have tended to see a critical paradigm grounded on imitation as the most logical approach to the period. From edicts on dress and behavior to the modernization and reorganization of church and state, Peter supposedly forced his fellow citizens to become modern-day Europeans by virtue of his indomitable will.[1] After Peter's death an imitative critique of eighteenth-century Russian culture became just as firmly entrenched in the arts. In keeping with the gist of Peter's reforms, the Russians were thought to have appropriated their literature from abroad: first from Germany, then from France, and finally, toward the end of the century, from England. Looking back from the vantage point of the mid–nineteenth century, Vissarion Belinskii articulated this interpretation, which has held sway for the past two hundred and fifty years, when he wrote that "Russian literature is a transplanted rather than indigenous growth. . . . Its history, especially up to Pushkin (and even partly up to the present [1843]), consists of a constant striving to renounce the results of an artificial transplantation, to take root in a new soil, and to fortify itself with new juices" (Lotman and Uspenskii, "K semioticheskoi tipologii," 260). Adapting foreign forms and ideas and making them suitable for a Russian context is generally considered to be the function of the eighteenth century in the progression of Russian culture.[2] In the conventional assessment of the 1700s not until the very end of the century did Russia finally emerge "from her period of foreign tutelage . . . [to] boast the beginnings of an independent culture, nourished and enriched, but not stifled, by foreign influence" (Lentin, 120).

Of all the genres of Russian literature that could be tagged with the label of imitation, none was more susceptible than the novel. Churned out in relatively large numbers to meet the demand for a literature of adventure and exoticism, Russia's first novels were often nothing more than translations of foreign texts. Even when there finally were some works that could be deemed original, they often revealed a strong reliance on a multitude of well-known sources. For example, Viktor Shklovskii has painstakingly traced the inspirations for Matvei Komarov's literary output. As he points out in his monograph on Russia's first best-selling writer, *The Adventures of the English Milord George* and *Nevidimka* are replete with incidents from *The Thousand and One Nights*, characters and devices out of Russian folklore, and allusions to classical mythology. Komarov's first novel, *Vanka Kain*, closely follows the folk legend of this famous eighteenth-century brigand as contained in an anonymous manuscript version of the same name, and his last work, *Various Written Materials*, is a compilation of literary and pragmatic works republished from a host of important journals of the day. Although Fedor Emin was a far more sophisticated writer than Komarov and therefore more skilled in covering up his literary appropriations, he too relied heavily on imitation. The man who could lay claim to the title of Russia's first novelist revealed an astounding command of literary convention, both past and present. From the quasi-autobiographical *Inconstant Fate, or the Adventures of Miramond*, written in the style of a Byzantine adventure novel, to the sentimentalist epistolary novel *The Letters of Ernest and Doravra*, which is modeled after Rousseau's *La Nouvelle Héloïse*,[3] Emin proved to be an adept student and prolific practitioner of imitation.

The most telling example of the use of imitation as *the* preferred approach to early Russian prose fiction can be found in the critical reception accorded Chulkov's novel *The Mocker, or Slavic Tales*. Although this rambling and eclectic work is first and foremost a parody of literary convention, critics generally prefer to view it as a sincere imitation of foreign influences and models. From popular tales of exoticism and adventure to eighteenth-century English burlesque poetry, they have uncovered a wide array of intertexts in the five volumes that constitute Chulkov's first essay into the novel genre.[4] Like *The Thousand and One Nights*, *The Mocker* is itself divided into nights and, as Garrard points out, is indebted to it for much of its plot (Čulkov, 49–50) and for the many descriptions of palaces, statuary, and gardens that fill its pages ("Prose Fiction," 18). Moreover, Garrard compares the stories told by the narrator Ladon to the heroic literature of seventeenth-century France (Čulkov, 55) and sees the influence of a poem like John Gay's "The Fan" (1714) in *The Tale of the Taffeta Beauty Patch,* a novella that runs through parts 3, 4, and 5 (94–95). In his article "The Transformation of Folklore into Literature" Felix Oinas traces the theme of child murder in "A Bitter Lot" ("Gor´kaia uchast´"), a tale from part 5 of *The Mocker,* through the Brothers Grimm and Sicilian folklore to the work of the third-century writer Claudius Aelianus (578–80). Unable to pin down the actual source of the tale, Oinas nonetheless insists that Chulkov must have been following some sort of Western model.[5] Did Chulkov "read a version of this story . . . in some West European publication?" or had he seen a picture of the tale? (580). Although Oinas cannot answer either of these questions affirmatively and even admits that no Russian print of the story exists, he still maintains that Chulkov must have followed a model when composing "A Bitter Lot." Such is the allure of an imitative mind-set with regard to eighteenth-century Russia that even Chulkov's most openly metaliterary and mocking piece of prose fiction is scoured for examples of foreign literary models while its parodic essence is all but overlooked.[6]

The Effects of Imitation Attenuated: Cultural Dynamics and the Influence of Nationalism

Despite their lack of literary sophistication and, as in the case of Komarov, literary imagination and ability as well, Russia's first novelists could claim quite impressive cultural credentials. By the time Russia produced its first original novels in the 1760s, imitation had been a dominant cultural imperative for almost a thousand years. As a result of this experience the Russians had also fine tuned a mechanism for mediating the impact of foreign culture. Beginning with the Varangians in the ninth century, Russian society absorbed one wave after another of intense and far-reaching foreign influence. The onset of Christianization in the late tenth century, Russia's relationship with Byzantium and the Third Rome Doctrine, and the seventeenth-century rift between the Old Believers and Patriarch Nikon's reformist tendencies were all profound stimuli that forced the Russians to confront their relationship to the West long before this became an issue for Emin, Chulkov, and Komarov. When it was their turn to deal with the latest onslaught of foreign dominance in the mid–eighteenth century—this time in the form of the literary aesthetics of neoclassicism and sentimentalism—Russia's first novelists came up with a variety of responses. To be sure, as most critics claim, imitation or, at best, Russification figured prominently in their work. On the other hand, given a well-developed mechanism for coping with outside influence coupled with the powerful stimulus of nationalism, it certainly follows that skepticism and even outright rejection also played a crucial role.

Iurii Lotman and Boris Uspenskii's binary model of Russian culture helps to explain what they call the "internal contradictoriness" of Russia's relationship with the outside world in the eighteenth century.

> A semiotic polyglotism, which is built on a model that can be traced back, in the final analysis, to the Church Slavic–Russian dualism, is peculiar to Russian culture of the eighteenth century. The semiotic dualism of the initial cultural model turned out to be such a stable organizing principle that the subsequent change of concrete languages in the culture had no influence on the dual nature of the model itself. ("K semioticheskoi tipologii," 264)

In this model the most crucial characteristic of the Russians' relationship to the West is their inability to see shades of gray. Beginning with Christianization, "the basic cultural values (ideological, political, and religious) of medieval Russia were distributed in a bipolar field and divided by a sharp boundary without an axiologically neutral zone" (Lotman and Uspenskii, "Binary Models," 31). For example, in the West, life after the grave is divided into heaven, hell, and purgatory, and therefore earthly life is viewed as holy, sinful, or neutral. In the Russian conception of the afterlife there is only heaven and hell, and therefore earthly life is either holy or sinful, but never neutral. Thus, without an axiologically neutral zone, Russian culture tends to categorize all phenomena in a series of binary oppositions, such as "old" versus "new," Russia versus the West, Christianity versus paganism, and knowledge versus ignorance (33).

As a result of such a starkly polarized view of the world the survivability of archaic and "defeated" elements of Russian culture was virtually guaranteed. At first glance, 988 would seem to mark a decisive break in Russian culture: a once pagan country accepts the faith and symbols of Christianity. As Lotman and Uspenskii remark, however, the break was not as clean as it would seem: "New historical structures in pre–nineteenth-century Russian [sic] invariably include mechanisms that regenerate the culture of the past. The more dynamic the system, the more active are the mechanisms of memory which ensure the homeostasis of the whole" ("Binary Models," 31). With Christianization the Russians began to view themselves as a "new" people. In order to do so, however, they needed to keep alive a notion of what was "old." As Lotman puts it, Vladimir "did not simply accept a new system of values, replacing the old with the new, but rather wrote the old into the new—with a minus sign" (34). Creating an artificial pagan pantheon, transforming the pagan gods into devils, and even privileging pagan rituals as a proper type of antibehavior at certain times of the year were all ways in which the binary dynamics of Russian culture preserved the old.

Turning to the eighteenth century, Lotman and Uspenskii push this argument even further by uncovering ways in which "the shift brought about by 'Europeanization' (or what was perceived as Europeanization) [actually] enhanced archaic traits in Russian culture" ("Binary Models," 61). For example, the term that epitomized Russia's new Western orientation—Enlightenment—was in fact generated by an archaic semiotic model. In the medieval Russian Church "to enlighten" meant "to effect a holy baptism"

(54). The use of the term *Enlightenment* to describe the Age of Reason in Russia was therefore not a neologism, but rather a conventional application of the word. During Peter's reign Enlightenment referred to Russia's rebirth as a secular state. Feofan Prokopovich denounced those who opposed Peter's reforms as sorcerers and pagans while he transformed Peter the Enlightener into the new Prince Vladimir (55–56). Later in the century even the Russians' perception of geographic space betrayed a pre-Petrine view of the world. To the opponents of Enlightenment and reform the West was a sinful and destructive place worthy of anathema. On the other hand, the proponents of modernization considered the West a new Holy Land and frequently made pilgrimages to Paris, its new Jerusalem (61–63).

By analogy with what was taking place in the culture as a whole, even though the eighteenth-century Russian novel was generally dismissed by the reigning literary elite, it could still maintain a viable position within society by functioning as a type of officially sanctioned, or at least tolerated, antibehavior. The fantasy, adventure, eroticism, and mocking sense of humor that formed the hallmarks of the early Russian novel banished it to the margins of the literary scene. Like the pagan rituals of pre-Christian Russia, most novels were considered "old," non-Western, and full of frivolous, even dangerous material. As such they were not suppressed altogether but rather tabbed, as Lotman and Uspenskii would put it, with a minus sign. On the one hand, an incorrigible imitator like Emin tried to make the best of the situation by turning out works that might be acceptable to the arbiters of the neoclassical aesthetic. Even though he was ultimately unsuccessful, his frequent recourse to the commonplaces of Enlightenment thought was an attempt to gain the approval of figures like Lomonosov and Sumarokov. On the other hand, Chulkov used his position as an outsider to comment on the official literature of his day. Centuries of historical precedent had set the stage for such a response. Foreign ideas had overrun Russia before, yet traditional ways of viewing the world not only survived but flourished. Instead of blindly imitating the latest influx of foreign culture, Chulkov followed the time-honored pattern of playing the antipode to it. With the mocking humor of a native-inspired subculture he undercut the very system that had tried to brush him aside as being of no consequence. Ironically, it was also the same system that provided him with a raison d'être.

In addition to a cultural dynamic that counterbalanced a fascination for things foreign with a tendency to maintain the status quo, the Russians had a second powerful reason to look skeptically at the West: nationalism. In the second half of the eighteenth century the Russian intelligentsia was more than ready to chart its own course as the quest for a national identity superseded its previous infatuation with the West. Moreover, in the figure of the empress Catherine the movement to establish the merits of native culture had the most powerful defender possible. For instance, in her journal, *All Sorts and Sundries (Vsiakaia vsiachina)*, she openly sanctioned such an endeavor when she proclaimed: "Oh praiseworthy virtues of our ancestors, to you I address myself, show yourself to the world; stop those who slander you and yet do not know you; spread your fame . . . and set an example which is worthier of imitation than a foreign one" (Rogger, 70).[7] Of all the intellectuals who would rise to this challenge during Catherine's reign, none worked more diligently than Nikolai Novikov. In his journals of the late 1760s and early 1770s and in writings that spanned his entire career, he constantly argued against the false allure of foreign culture. For example, in the introductory article to the first issue of *Morning Light* (*Utrennii svet*, September 1777) Novikov attacks the assumption that Russian readers can appreciate or even want the best of foreign literature and thought. Explaining that he is drawn to the journal owing to a patriotic desire "to do something for the good of his compatriots," he staunchly defends the common sense that makes up such a substantial part of the Russian national character: "Those readers who have fallen under the spell of certain foreign writers, with their tinsel glitter, will soon recover if they see their dream beauties, like snowflakes that sparkle in our air in winter, melting away at the rising of the sun of truth" (63). Led by the most prominent figures of the day, Russian society as a whole was becoming more and more uncertain about the wisdom of uncritically imitating West European Enlightenment culture just as the first Russian novels were rolling off the presses.

In the last quarter of the eighteenth century one discipline after another—from folklore, to literature, to history—took up the question of Russia's national identity. Collections and writings on popular mythology, superstitions, riddles, folk tales, proverbs, and songs by, among others, Popov, Chulkov, Levshin, Kurganov, Trutovskii, and Prach exemplified an increased interest in Russian popular culture.[8] In belles lettres the genre of the comic opera railed against the barbaric stupidity of Russia's Francophile aristocracy while at the same time championing the common sense and sincerity of the peasantry. Chulkov's *The Comely Cook* and Komarov's *Vanka Kain* feature the wit, humor, and ribaldry of Russia's boundless lower classes, and in Fonvizin's comedy *The Minor (Nedorosl')* the hero, Starodum, espouses an ideology that is about the exact opposite of the foreign-inspired code of conduct that flourished in the 1770s. Moreover, in the nascent discipline of history Prince M. M. Shcherbatov was one of the first to air in writing a dissenting opinion concerning the benefits of Westernization. In "On the Injury of Morals in Russia" ("O povrezhdenii nravov v Rossii") written in the 1780s Shcherbatov claims that on balance Peter's reforms had done more harm than good (Papmehl, 25–26). Catherine Dashkova expressed the same sentiment even more vehemently, calling Peter "a brutal and benighted tyrant who sacrificed excellent established institutions, the laws, rights, and privileges of his subjects to his own ambition . . . to change all things without distinction, be they good, bad or useful" (26). In virtually all intellectual endeavors the Russians were actively rethinking their position vis-à-vis the West.[9]

Whether it was a cultural dynamic that counterbalanced the tidal wave of new influences, pure nationalism, or the disenchantment arising from unreal expectations, the Russians were not transformed into the Parisians of the East. A thin layer of feebleminded gentry represented by Fonvizin's Ivanushka may have convinced themselves that their "soul belong[ed] to the French crown" (3.i), but few others did. To educated Europeans who knew the concomitants of Enlightenment, Catherine's empire was almost totally lacking the elements needed to transform it into a modern, progressive Western nation. Lord Macartney, a British trade negotiator who won the esteem of Catherine herself, found few similarities between the Russians and the enlightened peoples of Western Europe. In February of 1766 he wrote: "Our error with regard to them is in looking upon this nation as a civilized one and treating them as such. It by no means merits that title, and notwithstanding the opinion that persons unacquainted with it may have conceived, I will venture to say that the kingdom of Thibet [*sic*], or the Dominions of Prester John, might as justly be honored with the same appellation" (Dukes, 176). To Diderot, who visited the northern capital in the winter of 1773–1774, "Petersburg [was] just the court: a confused mass of palaces and hovels, of *grands seigneurs* surrounded by peasants and purveyors" (Wilson, 196). An anonymous English visitor to late eighteenth-century Russia seconded this opinion. He was shocked at the Russians' inability to carry on a conversation. Instead, they needed what he considered a rather crude form of entertainment to break the ice. He noted one episode in which the imperial ambassador had a carnival ice mountain constructed in his room, which "was built with boards, and rendered slippery by means of soap and water. . . . Here it is positively necessary to have some such invention, to supply the place of conversation" (Cross, *Russia under Western Eyes*, 249). According to the testimony of one foreign observer after another, Enlightenment in Russia was just a superficial gloss. Its effects were not felt by the broad masses of the people, and it never penetrated into the lives of the rural gentry. Even those few intellectuals who were inspired and transformed by its ideology remained alienated from a society that either did not know or did not care about what they were doing. Despite the strides they would make toward becoming the equals of their neighbors, the Russians simply could not transform themselves into mirror-image Europeans. Thus, even as late as the mid–nineteenth century the marquis de Custine could be appalled by what he considered the defining characteristic of Russian society: "a real barbarism scarcely disguised under a magnificence which is revolting" (Lincoln, 685).[10]

From the manner and amount that the Russians genuinely imitated Western models, it is apparent that they were less than perfect students. In tracking the Russians' relationship to Enlightenment thought and literature, the ways in which they ignored or rejected Western innovations are even more telling than their appropriation of them. It is as though they imitated Western sources of inspiration, such as the French, just well enough to make their ambivalent and at times even hypocritical cultural dualism a tempting target for a finely honed parodic talent like Chulkov. Of all the incidents that underscore this ambivalent attitude toward Enlightenment thought, none is more striking than Diderot's visit to Petersburg in the winter of 1773–1774.[11] Soon after the philosophe's arrival in St. Petersburg on October 8, 1773, "he was seeing the Empress daily, with a standing appointment for a lengthy personal interview, beginning at three in the afternoon" (Wilson, 176). During these meetings Diderot tactfully presented his views on topics ranging from free competition, the structure of government, and the legislative commission to luxury, usury, and divorce (180). Diderot's method was to draw up notes for a presentation, discuss them with Catherine, and afterward rewrite them as memoranda for the empress's perusal. While this working relationship greatly increased Catherine's reputation as a liberal-minded reformer, Diderot soon realized that his goal of "convert[ing] Catherine II to the philosophy of the Enlightenment, or at least reinforc[ing] what there were of her liberal convictions" was a near impossible task (180).

Although Diderot had come to Petersburg at Catherine's request, the empress all but ignored his advice. Even more so than with her celebrated backtracking on Montesquieu's *Spirit of the Laws* (Lentin, 103–4; Dukes, 183), she never really gave Diderot a chance to influence either her or her country. Catherine kept her conversations with the Encyclopedist so confidential that even her closest advisers were not privy to them (Oustinov, 122).[12] Moreover, at least in private, Catherine evinced the sort of disdain for the philosopher that hardly accorded with a frame of mind that was open to innovation and reform:

> I frequently had long conversations with him, but with more curiosity than profit. Had I placed faith in him, every institution in my empire would have been overturned; legislation, administration, politics, finances, all would have been changed for the purpose of substituting some impracticable theories.
>
> However, as I listened more than I talked, anyone, on being present, would have supposed him to be the commanding pedagogue and myself the humble scholar. Probably he was of that opinion himself, for after some time, finding that he had not wrought in my government any of those great innovations which he had advised, he exhibited his surprise by a sort of haughty discontent. (Wilson, 189)

Apparently Diderot soon realized that he was involved in a losing cause. By December 5, 1773, less than two months after his arrival and a full three months before he would depart Russia for good, he gave up writing his memoranda for Catherine (Wilson, 188).[13]

Just as Catherine and her court gave the cold shoulder to the famous philosopher, the Russians' reception of French literature was also less than overwhelming. Without a doubt, Russian writers beginning with Kantemir looked to the French neoclassical tradition to provide them with a template for a modern literature of their own. By midcentury Sumarokov had issued two epistles on language and literature that modified Boileau's *L'Art poétique* for a Russian context, and French masters had clearly been set up as models of emulation. The panegyrical odes of Malherbe, the verse satires of Boileau, and the epic and tragedy as practiced by Voltaire became the Russians' self-selected standard-bearers (Segel, "Classicism," 49). Yet a literary aesthetic can rarely be cobbled together by fiat. While a thin layer of gentry society responded positively to the genres of Russian neoclassicism, most readers were not so deeply touched by them. As Raeff points out, readers were generally interested in this new literature for the entertainment it provided rather than the seminal Enlightenment arguments it might contain ("Enlightenment in Russia," 37–38). Vladimir Lukin, who as a writer of comedies in the early 1770s had a first-row seat to observe this phenomenon, "complained that the public wanted only to be amused and did not care whether the play it saw . . . bore any relation to Russian reality" (Rogger, 56). Harking back to his education, the erudite writer and translator A. T. Bolotov revealed a "blissful unawareness" of the literary polemics that raged about him in his youth (Rice, 29). The man who would write hundreds of articles and philosophical treatises and translate over a dozen novels admitted that in his youth he was less than fully prepared to grapple with the literature of the Enlightenment. Books were hard to come by, and his reading was eclectic at best. By the time he was twenty-one, Bolotov could not boast of an education that had him thirsting for the latest publications of belles lettres, either Russian or foreign. Instead, "he pursued chiefly the taste for novels which his haphazard Russian upbringing had fostered" (19).

The Russians' lukewarm acceptance of the spirit of neoclassical literature is also borne out by their ambivalent treatment of some of the movement's cardinal figures. Given that Russian neoclassicism put a premium on short, didactic genres, the maxims of La Rochefoucauld should have garnered a wide following. Self-contained and focusing their wit on contemporary society, they seemed ready-made for the type of social engineering that was encouraged by an author like Sumarokov. Contrary to expectations, however, they made their appearance on the Russian literary scene stillborn. First of all, apparently no one was clamoring for this sort of material. Russian-language versions of La Rochefoucauld's maxims never were published in the halcyon days of Russian neoclassicism in the middle of the century; the first Russian translation, by A. F. Malinovskii, was not issued until 1781. Second, even when they were finally made available to the Russian reading public, the translator did not seem up to the task. Malinovskii "certainly didn't know how to achieve the stylistic level of the original maxims. In his translation there are mistakes that greatly distort their sense. Certain complicated thoughts remained inaccessible to Malinovskii, who was insufficiently acquainted with the milieu that La Rochefoucauld's discourse reflected" (Shreder, 186). Third, and most damning of all, the Russians showed little long-term interest in this author. The word *maksim* (maxim), which the Frenchman's writings introduced to the Russians, never took root in the language and entered few dictionaries. Moreover, there was apparently little desire among the literati of Catherine's reign to assume the mantle of the "La Rochefoucauld of the North," for "continuers of his genre are basically unknown in Russia" (184–85).

The uneven reception accorded Molière's plays provides yet another clear example of the Russians' ambivalent attitude toward the West. The first translation of Molière to be printed and published was undertaken by Trediakovskii in 1734 when he fashioned an intermediia (comic interlude) entitled *The Bourgeois Gentleman (Posadskii dvorianin)* from *Le Bourgeois Gentilhomme*. Apparently at the outset of the modern period of Russian literature Molière's name had virtually no drawing power, for Trediakovskii did not see fit to cite it in connection with this work.[14] By midcentury, however, Sumarokov praised Molière's comedies in his 1748 *Epistle on Poetry (Epistol o stikhotvorstve)*, and foreign touring companies began to stage them (Lojkine, 86–87). *L'Avare, Tartuffe, L'École des maris*, and *L'École des femmes* were performed in 1757 and published together three years later by the press at Moscow University (87). Novikov's Typographical Company reprinted this work in 1788 (87–88), and by the end of the century about half of Molière's plays had been translated into Russian.[15] Despite this rather impressive publication record, the Russians' fondness for Molière should not be overrated. On the one hand, as with La Rochefoucauld, they had a hard time appreciating him fully. The first translations of "literary worth—as distinct from scenic effectiveness—had to wait until the early XIX century when N. I. Khmelnitsky . . . translated *L'école des maris* (1819), *L'école des femmes* (1821), [and] *Tartuffe* (1826–1828)" (89). On the other, Molière never really took Russian society by storm; the plays that were translated into Russian more or less corresponded to his most famous works (88). The Russians did not become connoisseurs of Molière seeking out absolutely everything he wrote, but rather enjoyed those pieces that an infatuation with French culture brought their way. As with their response to the Enlightenment as a whole, they absorbed just enough to become faltering imitators or, as frequently happened, inviting targets for writers like the first Russian novelists whose tastes were more lowbrow than serious.

In addition to the Gallomania that plagued the early years of Catherine's reign, Russia's nascent prose culture also had to contend with the ambivalent impact of yet another prominent incursion of foreign influence. Just as its first novels were coming off the presses, Russia was overwhelmed by such a powerful wave of Anglomania that it prompted Novikov to write: "The English have replaced the French: nowadays women and men are falling over themselves to imitate anything English; everything English now seems to us good and admirable and fills us with enthusiasm. But we, unfortunately, are so addicted to things foreign that we frequently consider even their vices virtues" (Cross, "The British," 232).[16] At a superficial level enlightened Russian society tried to look and act like the English. "English houses, furniture, gardens, carriages, livery, and dancing now come into vogue, and we now find the fashion journals praising the simplicity of the newly adopted English style as superior to the ostentatious French dress" (Simmons, 83). To be considered up-to-date, the Russian nobility acquired

English horses and dogs (Cross, "The British," 246–47), and an English-style garden with streams, paths, and sculpted bushes was de rigueur.[17] In a more substantial way the English also had an impact on intellectual life, as the Russian masonic movement was first organized according to the English system. In June of 1771 the Lodge of Perfect Union was granted a constitution by the British Masonic Grand Master (241), and over the course of the last third of the century its membership included such influential figures as Sumarokov, Kheraskov, Novikov, Radishchev, and Karamzin (Baehr, 90).

If the Russians' interest in British culture was just as intense as their previous bout of Gallomania, it was also just as erratic and ephemeral. Limited to the very thin stratum of the educated elite, it underscored the Russians' unwillingness or inability to be mere passive recipients of another way of life, no matter how impressive it might be. In the area of literature, specifically narrative prose fiction, the British would not fare much better than the paragons of French Enlightenment culture had done. For a few decades British novels, short stories, and essays would be all the rage in Russia, but they were fated to have an impact that was much broader than it was deep. Following the pattern laid down by the work of such luminaries as La Rochefoucauld and Molière, the best of British letters was destined to be both template and target for novelistic pioneers like Emin, Chulkov, and Komarov.

British literature first came to the Russian reading public via literary journals. *Monthly Writings for Use and Enjoyment* (*Ezhemesiachnye sochineniia, k polze i uveseleniiu sluzhashchie*, 1755–1764) headed a long list of publications that borrowed freely and frequently from British sources.[18] *Monthly Writings* took as its model Addison and Steele's *Spectator*, with roughly twenty of its articles coming directly from this archetype of the genre (Levin, 78–80). Apparently such a strategy found an appreciative audience, for it quickly engendered a series of imitators. Between 1759 and 1764 there appeared in Russia no fewer than a half dozen journals whose pages were filled mostly with translations from foreign languages, especially English,[19] and a book that was issued at about the same time, *The Amusing Philosopher* (*Zabavnyi filosof*, 1766), also offered translations of the finest essays and moral tales taken from English periodicals (92). In the following decade British literary culture was to find an even more prominent sponsor in Catherine herself. She not only patterned her journal *All Sorts and Sundries* after the *Spectator* but also used her commanding position in society to cajole other would-be journalists to follow her lead. Thus, editors from Emin to Novikov were indebted to English models for the tone, style, and often even the content of their publications.[20]

In terms of content Russian journals presented a sharply focused reflection of British literature and thought. From character types to the genre of the Eastern tale to the all-important Enlightenment theme of reason the journals provided Russia's first writers of prose fiction with an abundant supply of elegant, and mostly didactic, models (Levin, 44, 75). Bacon, Locke, Gibbon, Robertson, and Hume were well represented in Russian periodicals, and a special prominence was achieved by Pope. His "Essay on Man" became one of the most often published works in eighteenth-century Russia. First translated into Russian in 1754, it was reissued no less than five different times over the next fifty years (Simmons, 120). Partial translations of Shakespeare's *Hamlet, Romeo and Juliet, Henry IV,* and *Henry VIII* appeared in the last quarter of the century as did Milton's *Il Penseroso* and *L'Allegro* (129), and Swift's popularity in Russia began in 1758 with a translation of "Esquire Bickerstaffe's Most Strange and Wonderful Predictions." "Other translations followed, and Swift became something of a permanent adornment in the journals of the later eighteenth century" (118). The journals also regularly printed excerpts from eighteenth-century British novelists, although these authors gained the lion's share of their fame in Russia through the separate publication of their work.

Promoted by reviewers for their didactic value, English sentimentalists such as Richardson, Fielding, Sterne, and Goldsmith came into favor with the Russian reading public beginning in the 1770s. Among this group of novelists, Fielding enjoyed the greatest publishing success. *Tom Jones* was issued in 1770 and again in 1787; *Joseph Andrews* was published in 1770, 1772, and 1787; and editions of *Jonathan Wild* appeared in 1772, 1783, and 1787.[21] Goldsmith and Sterne were represented by individual editions, *The Vicar of Wakefield* coming out in Russian translation in 1786 and *A Sentimental Journey* in 1793. Although Richardson could not rival Fielding in the number of times his books were published in Russian, he too fared quite well. If the reading public found him a bit stodgy, critics loved him. In 1782 a reviewer for the journal *Morning (Utro)* wrote that "I would be surprised if one book, such as *Clarissa* or *Grandison,* did not provide the attentive reader with finer and nobler feelings than a whole library of moral works brings to the learned" (Simmons, 141).[22] Russian imitations of *Pamela* (Russian translation 1787), *Clarissa* (1791–1792), and *Sir Charles Grandison* (1793–1794) confirm Richardson's popularity. Nikolai Emin's *Roza: A Half-True Story (Roza, poluspravedlivaia original'naia povest'* [1782]), Lvov's *A Russian Pamela, or the Story of Maria, a Virtuous Village Girl (Russkaia Pamela ili istoriia Marii, dobrodetel'noi poselianki* [1789]), and Karamzin's *Poor Liza (Bednaia Liza* [1792]) directly reflect some aspect of Richardson's novels, from the epistolary form to the characterization of an impregnably virtuous heroine and Lovelace-like rake (113, 144–45).[23]

Despite its rather impressive publication record during the formative years of modern Russian literary culture, the English novel never sank deep roots. By the end of the eighteenth or, at the latest, the beginning of the nineteenth century, Defoe, Richardson, Fielding, and the others were eclipsed by new favorites who once again generally came from France. The impact of the British writers lasted for just twenty to thirty years, and, except for Richardson, few left any trace in the literature of the period. Moreover, in addition to being short-lived, the Russians' support for even the paragons of British fiction could at best be described as superficial. Oftentimes commercial rather than aesthetic or literary concerns determined what the Russian public would have the opportunity to read. Editors of Russia's literary journals were more interested in filling up space with timely and provocative material than in transmitting to their readers a thorough survey of eighteenth-century English letters.

> Translations were made not to satisfy an established demand for certain types of literature, but merely to fill up space when originality was lacking. It was rare when any well-defined method of selection obtained. We are not to suppose that these editors or the occasional contributors had a thorough knowledge of English literature and combed the fields for works which should meet a standard of taste or supply a popular demand. (Simmons, 124)

As with any business, profitability was of paramount importance. Where belles lettres was concerned, publishing was an extremely risky business in eighteenth-century Russia, and more often than not it ended in failure. Given this context, publishers were just as apt to print an author owing to his or her earning potential (which usually corresponded to the liveliness of their plots) as they were to select writings based on intellectual merit.

A desire to capitalize on the meteoric success of the most popular British authors counterbalanced a deep appreciation of their fiction to such a degree that it often led to some rather questionable, and at times unintentionally humorous, practices. In the hope of boosting sales, booksellers frequently ascribed an author's work to a more popular writer. Such was the fate that befell Tobias Smollett. Upon first appearing in Russia, Smollett's novels *Roderick Random* (Russian translation 1788) and *Humphrey Clinker* (1789) were both attributed to Henry Fielding. By the late 1780s Fielding's reputation in Russia was secure, and his name on the title page of a book was sure to attract readers in a way that the newcomer Smollett's would not (Simmons, 149–50). Interestingly enough, this subterfuge went unnoticed even by the reviewers, who were supposed to guarantee the quality of the entire process. Writing in the *Moscow News* in 1788, one reviewer lauds Fielding's narratives for being free of the emotional excess and improbabilities that plague so many novels and goes on to recommend Fielding's *Roderick Random* to his readers (Martynov, 36–37). The reviewer's mistake is doubly indicative of the low level of appreciation of foreign literature in eighteenth-century Russia. On the one hand, he does not know enough about the current state of literary affairs in England to unmask the hoax perpetrated by the bookseller. On the other, he lacks the skill to distinguish the rollicking optimism of Fielding from the misanthropic pessimism of Smollett. If eighteenth-century Russian reviewers had such a low level of literary competence and awareness, one wonders just how much ordinary readers could appreciate the classic texts that came to them from the West.

In eighteenth-century Russia English literature turned out to be more of a cultural phenomenon than a literary model. As Simmons points out, "young men and women affected the attitudes, actions, and occupations of their favorite heroes and heroines." Although they were unable to distinguish Fielding from Smollett, "they tried to live the idealized life which they found in the sentimentalized variety of the 'English' novel, and pure love, an admiration for nature, and ready tears were the characteristics of the sensitive youth of the day" (158). British novels, tales, and essays appealed to the reading public because they were new, sophisticated, and entertaining, but Russia's first novelists looked at them in a more circumspect manner. While certain conventions of British and French literature appealed to them as the starting point for the novel genre in Russia, they made no wholesale commitment to them. On the contrary, they were just as apt to reject the world view that such conventions promoted for a host of reasons, ranging from their lack of literary sophistication to nationalistic fervor.

THE COMELY COOK: A "RUSSIAN MOLL FLANDERS?"

Chulkov's parodic masterpiece *The Comely Cook* is perhaps the best example of the refraction of foreign influence in the early Russian novel. Besides being one of the most famous representatives of the genre, it is also quite closely associated with a specific foreign model. Based on the amorous adventures of a first-person female narrator, Chulkov's novel has frequently been labeled a Russian *Moll Flanders*.[24] At first glance there is much that supports such an interpretation. Like Defoe's heroine, Chulkov's Martona is a mature woman of the world who, looking back from the vantage point of advanced age, delivers a running commentary on her riotous former life. Both stories focus on the underclasses of their respective societies, with adventure, lawlessness, and the allure of sexual promiscuity serving to hold the narrative together. Beyond these rather general comparisons the two novels also reveal a rather uncanny similarity at the level of specific motifs and even episodes. Worldly vanity, materialism, the pitfalls of poverty, and the failure of society to provide for the weak and defenseless play prominent roles in both works. At the level of incident Martona frequently finds herself in the same predicaments as her supposed literary model. Both heroines fall inadvertently into the clutches of a woman who, "though she did not keep an ill house, as we call it, yet had none of the best principles in herself" (Defoe, 117), and eventually embark on a life of prostitution. When Martona is forced to choose between two men who desire her attentions, her predicament echoes Moll's decision to keep her options open with two possible suitors. Moll's admission that "I made no scruples in my thoughts of quitting my honest citizen, whom I was not so much in love with as not to leave him for a richer" (146) catches perfectly the spirit of Martona's early dealing with men.[25]

Despite frequent similarities in plot structure, characterization, and incident, however, the two novels have contradictory aims. The mocking, whimsical tone of *The Comely Cook* has little in common with the blatant, overbearing didacticism of *Moll Flanders*. Whether or not Chulkov knew Defoe's masterpiece, his novel serves as an excellent parody of it, not an imitation. Even before we read the first page of Moll's adventures, Defoe sets the guidelines for interpreting them. Whatever transpires on the following pages, the author assures readers that they can turn it to their advantage: "There is in this story abundance of delightful incidents, and all of them usefully applied. There is an agreeable turn artfully given them in the relating, that naturally instructs the reader, either one way or the other" (29). Foreseeing that some readers could be offended or confused by the ribald story of Moll's life, Defoe reassures them by adding that "there is not a wicked action in any part of it, but is first and last rendered unhappy and unfortunate" (30). Although Moll's life covers a fair part of the spectrum of what was considered vice-ridden activity in eighteenth-century England, Defoe makes it quite clear that the novel is directed at those who possess a rather firm moral character. More than anything else, "all the exploits of this lady of fame, in her depredations upon mankind, stand as so many warnings to honest people to beware of them" (30). Throughout the body of the novel Moll continuously reinforces Defoe's announced intention in writing the work. Either through the dire circumstances that result from Moll's activities or via direct moralizing by the narrator herself, readers find that Defoe's promise "to lead [them] by the hand" (31) is carried out on page after page. The author's plan is so transparent that he frequently seems unable to maintain any distance from his heroine. When, late in her narrative, Moll entreats: "Let the experience of one creature completely wicked, and completely miserable, be a storehouse of useful warning to those that read" (254), her words could easily be transferred to the author's introduction without causing even the slightest shift in tone.

In his short introduction to *The Comely Cook* Chulkov makes it quite clear that didacticism is the furthest thing from his mind. Lacking Defoe's conviction regarding the instructional value of literature, he writes that even he does not know the "value of the book I have written" (157). Moreover, he concludes that not just his novel but all books are of dubious value. Like everything else in the world, books and their authors "exist for a while, finally decay, disappear, and vanish from memory" (157). Such a flexible, nondidactic approach to the written word leads Chulkov to treat readers completely differently than does the author of *Moll Flanders*. Whereas Defoe flatters readers by implying their intellectual and moral superiority over a person like his heroine, Chulkov plays with his readers. In the introduction to *The Comely Cook* the mock reader becomes the *mocked* reader. Chulkov finds his readers superior in their own way, but, instead of elevating them above the debauched elements of society, he facetiously juxtaposes them with the animal world. In a jesting piece of doggerel he proclaims that he has sought out his readers because

Neither beasts nor livestock understand the sciences,
Neither fish nor reptiles know how to read,
Flies don't argue about verse among themselves,
And neither do all the flying spirits.

(Ni zveri, ni skoty nauk ne razumeiut,
Ni ryby, ni gady chitati ne umeiut,
Ne sporiat o stikhakh mezhdu soboiu mukhi,
I vse letaiushchie dukhi.)
(158)

Chulkov's proclamation that he has left the animal world behind to address man the "reader, doer, and writer" (chtets, delets, pisets) rings with mockery. Rather than seeking out a select group of lofty thinkers and sober moralists, the author has chosen his readers almost by default.

Chulkov writes that if readers wish to appreciate the whole of his skill in *The Comely Cook*, they will need to read it upside down (158). In this light-hearted, parodic work eighteenth-century Russia's premier literary jester turns the world view of a novel like *Moll Flanders* on its head.[26] The shadow of the gallows never hangs over any of Martona's deeds, and the themes of incest, abortion, and child abandonment that so torment Moll never make an appearance in the world of Chulkov's free-spirited heroine. When Martona confronts the grim possibility of starving to death or loses all her possessions, she shields herself from harsh reality with a pithy proverb and sets off on the road to a new adventure. On the contrary, when the prospect of starvation presents itself to Moll, she admits she could become desperate enough to join a ring of counterfeiters, even though, if caught, she would suffer the horrendous fate of being burned at the stake (Defoe, 242). As earthy and as sensual as she is, Martona never finds herself in such a menacing world; she just seems to tread above it all. Her life and her commentary on it virtually negate all that is serious and judgmental. Time and again Martona proves that humans are quite fallible and that they can have quite a lot of fun as a result of their innate "shortcomings." Those who come to Chulkov's novel looking for a condemnation of immorality or an explication of the type of life that is to be avoided will be sorely disappointed. Morality and intellect are powerless in Martona's world; they have been soundly defeated by the promiscuity of a heroine whose credo is "just give in to your vices for they will always seem more pleasant and nicer than virtue" (Chulkov, 174).

Nowhere is the rift between the literary orientations of the two authors more evident than in the treatment of the theme of sex. Ironically, the aspect of each novel that supposedly creates the grounds for comparing them—both Moll and Martona fall into a life of prostitution—shows just how different they really are. Although Moll is not immune to the power of sensuality, she considers sex out of wedlock to be an illicit undertaking. Time and again she refers to her sexual relations with men to whom she is not legally married as a crime and, at least in the first part of her adventures, is deeply concerned about being considered nothing more than "a

mere cast-off whore" (Defoe, 74). In what would seem a direct denunciation of the type of life represented by Chulkov's heroine, Moll claims that
she "was not wicked enough to come into the crime [of prostitution] for the
mere vice of it" (117). Later, when she does find herself straying from society's mores, she calls herself an utterly wicked person, "forsaken of God's
grace, and abandoned by Heaven to a continuing in my wickedness" (132).
Even when Moll gets to the point in her life where she supposedly uses sex
freely to make her way in the world, she cannot help but moralize about it.
After an episode in which she succumbs to the advances of a gentleman
and then robs him of most of the possessions he has with him, Moll compares such victims to the biblical oxen being led to the slaughter:

> There is nothing so absurd, so surfeiting, so ridiculous, as a man heated by
> wine in his head, and a wicked gust in his inclination. . . . His vice tramples
> upon all that was in him that had any good in it. . . . Such a man is worse
> than a lunatic; prompted by his vicious, corrupted head, he no more knows
> what he is doing than this wretch of mine knew when I picked his pocket
> of his watch and his purse of gold. (218)

Although his novel is rife with sexual encounters that readers might indeed
find provocative, Defoe always makes sure to interpret them in a suitably
moralistic manner.[27]
   In contrast with Defoe's heroine, Martona never considers sexual indulgence a crime at all and actually finds the life of a prostitute romantic and
liberating. Taken in by the madam of a Kievan bordello just two weeks after
her husband is killed at the battle of Poltava, she quickly strikes up a relationship with a gentleman's servant and never looks back. Neither regret
nor self-condemnation ever enters the picture as Martona rejoices in her
ability to translate her personal beauty into tangible, material rewards. She
joyfully recounts how in practically no time at all she has the income to become a regular customer of the local merchants and is able to add to her ac-
quisitions almost "by the minute" (Chulkov, 159). Giddy with her increased
status and sense of self-worth, she even hires a servant, dresses and acts
like a lady, and flaunts her new position for all to see. As she moves from
one lover to another, Martona shows none of the self-loathing and reluctance so common to Moll Flanders. In virtually every instance the motivation for Martona's change of companions is monetary. Whenever a more lucrative suitor comes along, she is ready and willing to heed the call. Her
experience of living as the kept woman of an aged colonel provides an uncanny contrast with Moll's "leading the ox to slaughter." Shortly after moving in with the colonel, Martona is attracted to the young and handsome
Akhal´. Though Akhal´ has little money, Martona agrees to go with him because he proposes to rob the old man and then run away with her. All goes
according to plan: the old man is hoodwinked, Akhal´ and Martona run off,
and the free-spirited heroine feels no remorse for her actions. Thus, Martona has duped a foolish old man, just as Moll did, but she gets to keep the

ultimate prize: her young lover Akhal´. When misery calls Martona to account, it is not because of any guilt she feels, but because she too has been made to play the fool. Turning the tables on Martona, Akhal´ absconds with their ill-gotten loot and leaves her to suffer the consequences alone. When the old man dies as a result of Martona's treachery, she sheds not one tear for him, grieving only for herself when she is incarcerated for the crime.

If *The Comely Cook* is a Russian *Moll Flanders*, the emphasis must definitely be on the word *Russian*. To be sure, Chulkov's selection of a first-person female narrator keeps his novel in the mainstream of eighteenth-century European literary convention, and the many similarities between the two novels appear to be more than just coincidence. It is just as undeniable, however, that Chulkov's literary orientation serves as a virtual parody of Defoe's. In Chulkov's version of the "fallen woman" motif an earthy humor and nonjudgmental view of the world displace the conventional conceptualizations of authority and morality that lie at the heart of *Moll Flanders*. Moreover, placed in a broader context, *The Comely Cook* encapsulates the struggle of the early Russian novel and even eighteenth-century Russian society as a whole to come to grips with the power and allure of Western culture. Frequently unwilling, and in many instances unable, to be mere imitators, Russia's first novelists established a dynamic, vacillating relationship with the literature of the West. Like Novikov and the empress Catherine, they were dazzled by the cultural achievements of the West, but they remained far from convinced that these applied to the Russian experience. In their refraction, transformation, and even outright rejection of the foreign literature that made its way to their native land, the pioneers of Russian prose fiction left enduring written testimony of Russia's first attempts at self-definition in the modern period.

Chapter

Two

THE CARNIVALESQUE SPIRIT OF THE EIGHTEENTH-CENTURY RUSSIAN NOVEL

BAKHTIN, CARNIVAL, AND THE RUSSIAN LITERARY SUBCULTURE

In order to distance themselves from an uncritical imitation of West European culture and to establish native means of literary expression, writers like Matvei Komarov and especially Mikhail Chulkov turned to the ethos and conventions of the carnivalesque. Although the chief theoretician of the carnival, Mikhail Bakhtin, never applied this concept to the eighteenth-century Russian novel, his writings virtually guarantee the success of such an undertaking. In major studies such as *The Problems of Dostoevsky's Poetics*, "Discourse in the Novel," and *Rabelais and His World* Bakhtin shows a predilection for illuminating his theories with two types of primary text. Within Russian culture he concentrates on Gogol´ and Dostoevskii. When dealing with the prose fiction of Western Europe, his attention is most frequently drawn to writers who stand at the beginning of the tradition of novel writing. The monograph on Rabelais and numerous references to Cervantes take him to the very inception of the genre, and his interest in Fielding, Smollett, and Sterne focuses on the modern incarnation of the novel in eighteenth-century England. At the confluence of these two lines of inquiry stands the work of figures like Chulkov and Komarov. Preceding Gogol´ and Dostoevskii by less than seventy years, these writers helped to lay the foundation of the novel in Russia. Bakhtin may have overlooked them, but their historical and cultural lineage strongly suggests that a carnivalesque appreciation of the written word lies at the heart of their frequent subversion of Russia's literature of Enlightenment.

Bakhtin's conception of the novel emphasizes the tendency of this form to refract and challenge the dominant discourse of its day. In "Discourse in the Novel" he associates this approach to language and literature with what he terms the "second line" of the novel. Beginning with Rabelais's *Gargantua and Pantagruel*, its practitioners include, among others, Cervantes, Lesage, Sterne, Dostoevskii, and Dickens. In each instance these authors use the open-ended structure of the genre to expose the spurious motivations and self-serving goals of any language that represents "the *going point of view* and the going *value*" (301–2). From Rabelais's carnivalesque mockery of the sententiousness of church and state to the competing chords of polyphony in Dostoevskii, Bakhtin views the novel as a direct assault against any discourse that claims to be the sole purveyor of truth— precisely the definition that affords the most promising means of analyzing the significance of Chulkov and Komarov. In the latter half of the eighteenth century the "going point of view" promulgated by the arbiters of Russia's foreign-inspired literary aesthetic was frequently every bit as narrow and inflexible as the petrified conventions of the sixteenth-century romance or the Natural School in the 1840s. No less than Cervantes and Dostoevskii, Russia's first novelists were forced to confront well-established principles of authority, truth, and utility. Although they lacked the artistic ability, intellectual breadth, and stylistic genius of a Rabelais or a Sterne, functionally Chulkov and Komarov fit in quite well with the writers of Bakhtin's second line.

Like the author of *Gargantua and Pantagruel* more than two centuries earlier, Chulkov and Komarov grounded their work on the antiauthoritarian wisdom and whimsicality of a carnivalized subculture. In his study of Rabelais Bakhtin groups the eclectic genres of a historically long-lived cult of folk humor under the rubric of carnival. Along with such related forms of laughter as comic feasts ridiculing church rituals, oral and written parodies, and the buffoonery of marketplace spectacles, the ribald celebration of the Renaissance carnival was employed by the folk as a means of liberating itself from the inflexible and repressive hierarchies of church and state.[1] As opposed to the centripetal discourse of officialdom, which seeks to unify, consolidate, and maintain the status quo, carnivalesque laughter acts as a centrifugal force upon entrenched values and norms. Utilizing the "merry" weapons of excess, hyperbole, and comic reversals as its stock in trade, the carnivalesque creates "a parodic inversion of the official world with its intricate network of social definitions and claims to authority" (Anchor, 240). Under the benign rule of an idiot crowned king, carnival was a time for overturning conventions, breaking taboos, and even suspending certain laws. Food and drink were consumed in abundance, and, especially during carnivals held after Lent, sexual activity increased dramatically as well. By its very nature the carnival also broke down the most fundamental hierarchies of life. Instead of offering presentations for visitors to watch, the spirit of the carnival invited everyone to become an active participant, to play the role of king, fool, or madman. In the extreme example of the diableries, paupers dressed up as devils ran wild in the streets and, with the aid of the temporary suspension of the law, turned the situation to their personal advantage by robbing whomever they happened to encounter. From the bloated belly to the idiot king, the words and deeds of carnivalgoers actively challenged any type of structure, whether it belonged to the political, social, or even natural order of things.[2]

Transferring the language, images, and spirit of the carnivalesque mentality to the printed page, Rabelais stood the official world on its head. In *Gargantua and Pantagruel* the high are laid low and the "merry truths" of excess, fecundity, and pleasure supersede the lifeless platitudes and exhortations of officialdom. Characters deflate the self-important, ethereal discourse of religion as they swear by parts of Christ's anatomy and freely canonize such irreverent saints as Sausage, Mamica, and Goblet (Bakhtin, *Rabelais,* 191). In an episode targeting the highest ranks of secular society, Rabelais envisions hell as a merry banquet in which Alexander the Great toils as a sock mender and the great Persian king Xerxes hawks mustard in the street (381–86). For a work imbued with the mentality of the carnival, the pursuit of enlightenment ceases to be a solitary act relegated to the study or cell and instead becomes a communal celebration of joyous thanksgiving. In *Gargantua and Pantagruel* real philosophizing occurs around a "groaning board," where all are pleasantly satiated, and in the prologue to book 1 Rabelais himself admits to writing while eating and drinking. The subversive power of folk humor is so potent that Rabelais is able to make a virtue of traditionally offensive topics. Despite the negative connotations urine and feces have in most contexts, the author endows them with a decidedly positive meaning. In *Gargantua and Pantagruel* excrement is associated with new life through fertilization, and Pantagruel's urine creates the warm medicinal springs of France and Italy.[3] Even such abuse as wishing the gout or venereal disease on someone rings with comic affirmation. In the topsy-turvy logic of folk humor these illnesses were considered "merry afflictions" that resulted from a healthy, full-blooded indulgence in the material world. From beginning to end the wisdom in Rabelais's grotesque novel is generated by a deep appreciation for life's more pleasurable moments.

By emphasizing literary and philosophical systems rather than political or social relations, Bakhtin's approach to the carnival translates quite nicely into the experience of the eighteenth-century Russian novel. In the 1760s, 1770s, and 1780s Russia's first novelists also wrote against the backdrop of a well-developed carnivalized subculture. By the time of Catherine's ascension to the throne carnival entertainment, *lubok* (crude broadsides and pulp fiction), folklore, translated literature, satiric tales, and even the novel itself functioned as a lighthearted, subversive counterweight to the sober moralizing favored by Russia's Western-inspired literati.[4] While the officially sanctioned genres of the tragedy, epic, and ode appropriated the value system of Enlightenment culture and subscribed to narrowly defined linguistic, thematic, and characterological norms, the novel, by virtue of its noncanonical status, was able to modulate a duality of languages. On the one hand, Russia's first novelists often strove to meet the standards of official literature. Philosophical monologues, edifying commentary on geography, politics, and education, and the sharp delineation of virtue and vice are all staples of the genre. On the other, the discourse of virtue, progress, and civic responsibility had to compete with the antiauthoritarian voices of the subculture. In the hands of a master like Chulkov the comic patter of the *balagur* (carnival sideshow barker) and the earthy realism of folk proverbs deflate what Bakhtin calls "the weighty seriousness . . . [of] ideological discourse" at every turn ("Discourse," 309). Even the work of a lesser writer like Komarov turns established hierarchies upside down. The carnivalesque crownings and uncrownings that attend his morally ambiguous adaptation of Vanka Kain's rowdy biography might lack the focus of Chulkov's tour de force, yet the eclectic nature of his sources assures the collision of incompatible value systems, more often than not to the detriment of seriousness, didacticism, and inflated conceptions of self-importance.

THE COMPONENTS OF THE RUSSIAN LITERARY SUBCULTURE

Carnival: Emblem of the Subculture

In Russia the roots of carnival, which serves in Bakhtin's theory as the most dramatic expression of a broad-based cult of folk humor, can be traced back to the ancient summer spectacles known as *rusalii*. In these ritualistic celebrations the common folk *(narod)* expressed themselves via dramatized performances, songs, satiric jokes, and popular sayings (Kuznetsov, *Iz proshlogo russkoi èstrady*, 22). These genres, and the spirit of mockery that informed them, eventually became part of the impromptu itinerant performances of the *skomorokhi*. Dating back at least to the eleventh century, these boisterous and often lawless roving minstrels managed to attain a permanent and even indispensable presence in Russian society by the beginning of the 1700s (21). Comprising groups of up to fifty singers, dancers, jesters, mockers, and comedians, they adopted one of two approaches to their craft: some, known as wandering *skomorokhi*, traveled from village to village and town to town,[5] while others took up permanent residence in villages and suburbs, formed themselves into artels, and often attached themselves to the court of a boyar or a prince. It was from the artistic and social milieu of the *rusalii* and *skomorokhi* and with the same emphasis on mockery, satire, and parody that the tradition of the Russian carnival arose.

Carnival in Russia became a well-defined event by the end of the sixteenth century. At that time one was held in Moscow each May 1 to celebrate the tsar's departure from the city after his winter residence there. Over time the carnival became a popular means of celebrating a variety of occasions, from national holidays (a coronation or royal birth) to traditional rites (the coming of spring) to church holidays (Shrovetide and Easter). Although it was often associated with the most solemn of official celebrations, the carnival maintained a singularly antiauthoritarian identity as a time devoted to release, chaos, and mockery. As one foreign observer noted, as soon as the priest proclaims, "Christ is risen," at the Easter Mass, "riot and debauchery instantly break loose [and] drinking, dancing, and singing continue through night and day" (Shoberl, 2:49–50).

In the eighteenth century carnival could be found throughout the length and breadth of Russia. According to Pavel Svinin, the author of the official guide to St. Petersburg (1816), it was the Russians' "most important amusement" (Kuznetsov, *Gulian'ia*, 8), a fact that would appear to be borne out by the locations reserved for it in the two capitals. *The Historical and Topographical Description of the First Capital City of Moscow* (*Istoricheskoe i topograficheskoe opisanie pervoprestol'nogo grada Moskuv*, 1796) devotes an entire section to the carnival, citing more than twenty locations that were set aside for the staging of this event, including such prominent sites as the Moscow River near the Kremlin, Maiden's Field, and Novinskii Monastery (Kuznetsov, *Iz proshlogo russkoi èstrady*, 35). In St. Petersburg the carnival was well established not long after the city's founding, and though not as lavish as the spectacles in Moscow, it became a permanent part of the northern capital's social life by 1730. The booths, swings, and ice mountains of the carnival appropriated such choice locations as Tsaritsyn Meadow (Mars Field), Admiralty Square, Palace Square, and the frozen Neva River opposite the Winter Palace (Kuznetsov, 36–38). Nor were such celebrations limited to the cities. In the countryside Shrovetide witnessed, as one observer noted, the construction of ice mountains "in just about every hamlet" (Kuznetsov, *Gulian'ia*, 8), and even in the remotest pockets of civilization one could count on the carnival to break up the monotony and boredom of daily life. Despite their rather torpid existence in the sparsely populated hinterlands, Pushkin assures us that Tatiana's family in *Evgenii Onegin* managed to maintain "the customs of dear bygone times" (45), which included a passion for the Ferris wheel.

Starting with its material presence, the Russian carnival constituted a world unto itself, with its own boundaries, atmosphere, and look. From the rides to the stages and booths used for performances, it consisted of a miniature city of temporary structures that were erected for the festivities, used for a brief time, and then disassembled and stored away for the next celebration. At the symbolic heart of the carnival stood the rides, notably the Ferris wheel and the long, sloping toboggan runs known as ice mountains.[6] In the shadow of these fixtures visitors could find several rows of barnlike bast and board buildings called *balagany*. Strung out in one or more rows, they housed a lively, varied, and colorful array of entertainers. Describing a scene depicted in a late eighteenth-century lithograph of Moscow, Kuznetsov comments that "the carnival at Novinskii Monastery was distinguished by its grand scale. In the middle of a wide boulevard the . . . *balagany* stretched out in a long line. On their fronts it was possible to make out under [the distorting effects of] magnifying glass posters advertising jugglers, acrobats, tightrope walkers, horseback riders, and charmers"

(*Iz proshlogo russkoi èstrady*, 35). Although evidence concerning the structure of the eighteenth-century *balagan* is virtually nonexistent, the memoirs of a nineteenth-century carnival entertainer provide a great deal of insight into the question. Aleksei Alekseev-Iakovlev recalled that the biggest and best *balagany* of the St. Petersburg carnivals of the 1870s contained a stage of four to five hundred square feet, an orchestra pit for from twelve to fifteen musicians, and several types of accommodations for the audience, from standing room to open boxes. With each performance lasting about thirty or forty minutes, a carnival entertainer gave about eight shows a day and played before up to sixty thousand spectators per week (Kuznetsov, *Gulian'ia*, 47–50). It is hard to say how these figures correlate to performances given in the eighteenth century, yet they certainly confirm the great appeal of the anti-world known as the carnival.

The strange mix of entertainment distributed among the tents and makeshift theaters of the carnival testifies that satire, grotesquerie, and a bawdy sense of humor reigned within its precincts. While strolling down the lanes of *balagany*, carnivalgoers were apt to meet entertainers such as the one who advertised himself in the following manner:

> A simpleton peasant from Tula
> Spins his head, waves his arms,
> Says a million words a minute,
> And when he has to, even dances.
>
> (Tul'skii muzhichok—prostachok
> Golovoi vertit, rukami mashet,
> Mil'ion slov v minutu,
> A gde nuzhno—i spliashet.)
> (Kuznetsov, *Gulian'ia*, 28)

This lighthearted, jesting sensibility so dominated the carnival that it even pervaded the adaptation of foreign elements. Among the wide array of animal acts, puppet shows, automata, and dwarfs, giants, and bearded ladies that came from the West, the commedia dell'arte and the harlequinade stand out as prime examples of the carnival consciousness. Framed by the crimson curtains of the stage, the presentations of the commedia dell'arte appealed to a section of the Russian public that had a less than refined sense of humor. Tradesmen, apprentices, and merchants dressed as clowns and buffoons performed before an audience that paid no more than five kopecks for admission. Given such a foundation, the decorations, costumes, acting, and self-deprecating humor of the commedia dell'arte tended to be coarse and lurid. Also quite in keeping with Bakhtin's analysis of the Renaissance carnival, the harlequinade treated viewers to a nonstop series of grotesque costumes and sudden transformations. With little variation from one performance to the next, Harlequin would start out as a dead man who suddenly comes back to life as he dons another person's clothes. In rapid succession he poses as a woman, gets fired across the stage as a human cannonball, is hanged on a gibbet, buried, and finally reborn as a giant (Burgess, 111).

Among the many attractions at the carnival, the single most important representative of subcultural humor was the *karusel´nyi ded*. Working from the balcony of a *balagan* or a perch atop a carousel, the *ded* entertained viewers during breaks in nearby performances and encouraged them to patronize as many attractions as possible. In both appearance and demeanor the *ded* exhibited the merry contradictions and turnabouts associated with the grotesque. Outfitted in a tattered, dirty coachman's coat, worn-out hat with a paper flower tucked in the brim, leg wrappings, and bast shoes, and wearing a fake beard of combed string and ribbons, he gave the appearance of someone who was unlucky, or at least unsuccessful in life.[7] In the context of the carnival, however, misfortune was something to be laughed at. The *ded*'s routine included the ironic topos of his downfall in the world of official culture. Once the servant of a rich family, he was dismissed from his position owing to his lack of knowledge and had become a pickpocket. Cast down from the relative security of official society, he was now very much like the pauper who had become king. Despite a lowly station in life, both figuratively (the fiction of the pickpocket) and literally (most *dedy* came from the ranks of retired soldiers), the *karusel´nyi ded* ruled the carnival. From his position above the carnival grounds he commanded the attention of the crowds and elevated the discourse of the subculture to a position of preeminence.

Even more than his appearance, the *ded*'s routine epitomized the type of humor that was the hallmark of the subculture.[8] Since the *dedy* were not considered actors, they were able to comment on and even satirize contemporary events and personalities. With the aid of a shill in the crowd below, the *ded* engaged in comic dialogues that took a less than reverent view of the important issues of the day. More often than not, however, the *ded*'s routine consisted of a nonstop comic chatter that catered to a particularly lowbrow aesthetic taste. Far from having any real point or message, the *ded*'s discourse emphasized the nonreferential qualities of language. One of the *ded*'s standard devices was the fake auction. Promising listeners a contest in which they could not lose, he awarded the winner an imaginary teapot: it had no top or bottom, just a handle. At other times he would augment his patter with a crude caricature of an ugly woman, spice it with obscene double entendre, or join in a grotesque dance with several beautiful women or a trained bear. Rude, deceptive, and offbeat, the *ded*'s performance was the antithesis of the decorous behavior and seemingly transparent discourse required in official society.

If the *karusel´nyi ded* embodied the mocking sense of humor that ruled the carnival, the structure and function of its major rides symbolized the dynamism of this frenetic world. Sitting atop a carousel, the *ded* was perched as though in the eye of a storm. Beginning with the spinning swings of the carousel itself, everything that surrounded him appeared to be in constant, chaotic motion. The undulating reflection of signs distorted by magnifying glass, the clamor of the crowds, and the cacophony of *bala-gan* entertainers competing for attention combined to overwhelm the senses. Looming above this joyous whirlwind during the winter months, the ice mountains stood as a constant reminder of the unbridled energy of the carnival.[9] For a nominal fee adventurous souls could plunge down an ice ramp on a small sled from a starting point some fifty feet above the ground. Hurtling down the ramp, especially at night in the eerie glow of mica-colored lamps, must have been an exhilarating yet disorienting sensation. After racing along the track for several hundred yards, the sleds would run up an incline and, when their momentum was exhausted, slide back down it. At least for the duration of this wild ride, directionality and order became moot questions. Up and down, forward and backward lost any sense of permanence as they constantly, almost instantaneously, redefined themselves. In summertime ice mountains gave way to the Ferris wheel as the chief icon of the liberating forces of the carnival.[10] The rise and fall of its compartments, in which "some swing up to the heighth [*sic*] of a windmill [while] . . . others fall near as low to the ground" (Miege, 55) epitomized Bakhtin's theory of grotesque reversal. At the carnival high and low were not separated by an impenetrable gulf, but rather were constantly overcome to the accompaniment of laughter. For a mere five kopecks accepted realities and laws could be joyfully circumvented, at least for a short time. When common folk referred to the carnival as "under the mountains" or "under the wheel," their words, like the ironic discourse of the *karusel'nyi ded*, were laden with more than their literal significance.

Like its Renaissance counterpart in Western Europe, the Russian carnival was saturated with grotesquerie. The costumes of the harlequinade and commedia dell'arte, the ramshackle assemblage of luridly decorated *bala-gany*, and the behavior of the carnivalgoers themselves all spoke of spontaneous revelry and the transgression of boundaries. Appropriately enough, the honor of leading the way in this convivial chaos as the nominal king of the carnival was reserved for the most grotesque figure of all. Early in the nineteenth century one observer wrote that

> the carnival . . . is frequently represented by a Bacchus escorted by satyrs and bacchanalians. They parade through the streets with a chariot built for the occasion in grotesque style. The principal personage is in general a buffoon or clown, who displays various sleight-of-hand tricks to amuse the people. Music and grotesque dancing are sometimes introduced and add much to the variety and pleasure of the entertainment. (Shoberl, 1:111–12)

In addition to the rather extreme standards established by Bacchus and his cohorts at any given carnival, a celebration in 1754 witnessed several particularly memorable displays of grotesquerie. On that occasion the empress Elizabeth ordered a parade of the various ethnic groups of her empire. Forty different nations were represented, as they rode or were pulled by a motley assemblage of dogs, reindeer, camels, oxen, and elephants. Amid this procession Elizabeth's court jester and his bride made their way to the famous ice palace, where they retreated for their wedding night. Everything in this structure was like a parody of a real palace, right down to the wedding bed, which was also carved from ice.

If tongue-in-cheek humor, constant motion, and grotesquerie were the essence of the carnival, alcohol was the fuel that kept it running at a fever pitch. To help revelers get into the proper spirit, special food and drink, such as *zbiten´* (honey tea) and *buza* (buckwheat beer) were readily available,[11] and the vodka tent, which was conspicuously marked with a waving flag and curling fir tree, served all who were thirsty. As one Englishman, who resided in Russia for nine years, noted: "In the carnival before . . . Lent, they give themselves over to all manner of debauchery and luxury, and in the last week they drink as if they were never to drink more. Some drink *aqua-vitae* four times distill'd until it fire in their mouths, and kindle a flame not unlike that of *Bocca di inferno*, which issues out at their throat; if they have not milk given them to drink, they presently die" (Collins, 22). One foreign visitor after another expressed shock at the degree of public drunkenness in Russia, especially during carnival. Vodka conferred a sense of release on carnivalgoers, as any sense of propriety, restraint, or even self-preservation was washed away in a sea of spirits. A member of the Austrian legation to the court of Peter the Great remarked that "the Russians call the week that precedes the Lenten fast Maslenitsa. . . . With more truth would I call them bacchanalia, for they give themselves up to debauchery the whole time. Then they have no shame of lust, no reverence of God, and the most mischievous licentiousness is the order of the day" (Burgess, 96–97).[12]

In the promiscuous environment of the carnival sensuality and disorderly conduct increased and were even encouraged. For example, dances that normally aroused little passion were transformed into brazen provocations when performed under the spell of the carnival. Shoberl noted that the *barina* was usually characterized by restraint and stateliness, but that in the right circumstances it could be staged quite provocatively: "Never was displayed more ferocious licentiousness by voice and gesture. The male dancer expressed his savage joy in squeaks, contortions, and sudden convulsive spasms, that seemed to agitate his whole frame; sometimes standing still, then howling, whining tenderly or trembling in all his limbs to the music, which was very animating" (2:72–73).[13] From the amorous to the combative, passions also overflowed their quotidian limits in the form of mass mayhem known as *kulachnyi boi*. Coming together in great numbers, young men would square off on opposing sides and wage a sort of mock war with fists or cudgels. More than just a sporting event, these battles reached such a fever pitch that casualties could always be counted on. Atkinson and Walker even claim that it was "not unusual for it to be fatal to someone or other of the party" (3, plate 7). Like the drunkenness of the masses, the often obscene entertainment, and such other chaos-inducing occurrences as wild bears raging through the crowd,[14] fistfights were the practical embodiment of the carnivalesque spirit of excess and transgression.

The antiauthoritarian impulses of the Russian carnival did not go unnoticed by the representatives of official culture. From the very first comments about the *skomorokhi* in the *Primary Chronicle (Povest' vremennykh let)* the Orthodox Church considered popular spectacles a direct threat to the smooth functioning of a proper society. Under the year 1068 in the *Laurentian Chronicle (Lavrent'evskii letopis')* a scribe complains that churches are empty because the devil is tempting people with singing, dancing, and other forms of entertainment at carnival-like gatherings (Kuznetsov, *Iz proshlogo russkoi èstrady*, 21).[15] Throughout the Middle Ages church and state accused the *skomorokhi* of ribaldry and sedition, and, in the case of the traveling *skomorokhi*, their unsavory reputation often induced authorities to ban them from entering a community altogether. In fact, the anti-authoritarianism of the carnival posed such a threat to the guardians of social morality that the great church council of 1551 (the *Stoglavnyi sobor*, or Council of a Hundred Chapters) specifically denounced this sort of "satanic spectacle" as antithetical to church teachings (27–30). A century later the *Zemskii sobor* of 1648 (a consultative assembly consisting of nobles and merchants), which was convened with the specific aim of bolstering the position of Orthodoxy in the land, called for the eradication of the *skomorokhi*. Tsar Aleksei Mikhailovich wrote a letter in which he singled out the carnival for special criticism and demanded that all musical instruments be broken or burned, with those found in violation of the decree to be beaten or exiled (30). As the carnival became an ever larger part of Russian life in the eighteenth century, the government continued to campaign against it. With the exception of the *karusel'nyi ded* and the comics known as *raeshniki*, carnival entertainers were forbidden to stage any sort of theatrical presentation. As crude as these popular performances most often were, their power to influence people is evident from the role they played in the Revolutionary movement in the late nineteenth and early twentieth centuries. In response to worker unrest the government prohibited the construction of *balagany* on Mars Field in 1897 and placed all popular entertainment under the jurisdiction of Count Witte, perhaps Nicholas II's most powerful adviser. Not to be outdone, twenty years later the fledgling Soviet government co-opted the *gulian'ia* in order to stage political mass theater before as many as eighty thousand persons at one time.

Beyond its literal manifestation as a temporary event in Russian society, carnival also takes on symbolic importance as the emblem of the subculture as a whole. While each mode of artistic expression in the Russian subculture—*lubok*, translated popular literature, and folklore—represents a distinct means of expression, all of them are infused with a carnivalesque spirit. Like the carnival, *lubok*, translated literature, and folklore sought out the lowest common denominator for their audience. They enjoyed such success in eighteenth-century Russia because they expressed the values of the common people, of the peasant and the barely educated urban dweller, in a language that they understood. Even more important, all three modes of expression employed comic inversion and a carnivalesque mixing of voices as a dominant operating principle. The values, ideas, and forms of official culture made their way into *lubok,* translated literature, and even folklore, but, recycled for a new audience with different aesthetic standards, they frequently fell prey to the subculture's irreverent disregard for any type of serious discourse. In this respect the most emphatic and consistent attack on the values of polite society came from the burgeoning pulp fiction industry, known in Russia as *lubok.*

Lubok

The form of fiction known as *lubochnaia literatura* (*lubok* literature), which coalesced in the second half of the eighteenth century, arose out of the earlier tradition of *lubok* broadsides. The process of printing crude pictures from carved wood boards made its way to Europe by the twelfth century (Rovinskii, 2–3), and the oldest extant Russian *lubok,* which comes from the Ukraine, is dated between 1619 and 1624.[16] Like its European counterpart, the *lubok* of seventeenth-century Russia focused on religious topics. Many of the early prints were issued by Pamva Berynda's Kiev-Lvov Typography and were used by the Ukrainian clergy in their battle against the Uniate and Catholic Churches. In addition, the first wave of *lubok* works included Berynda's seven-thousand-word dictionary and a Bible (1645–1649) by the monk Iliia (Ovsianikov, 7–9). By 1647, just twenty-five years after the appearance of the first prints in the Ukraine, the demand for this didactic art was so extensive that it warranted a regularized trade near the Spasskii gate in the Moscow Kremlin (9).

From its origins as an inexpensive type of religious art *lubok* quickly established itself in the marketplace of secular literature. Offering readers everything from didacticism to satire and farce, the trade in prints was soon distinguished by the sort of whimsical eclecticism so common in the artistic expression of the subculture. V. A. Kiprianov's founding of a *lubok* printing house and free lending library in 1709 and the closing of the government printing house in 1727, which forced many engravers to find jobs in the manufacture of *lubok* (Rovinskii, 11), greatly increased both the amount and the types of works that were made available to the public.[17] In the first half of the eighteenth century the interested buyer could find a wealth of images that directly celebrated the life of the subculture. Buffoons and jesters modeled after Callo's Punchinello, *kulachnye boi* (carnival fistfights), representations of grotesque and extraordinary happenings, and, in a fittingly Rabelaisian touch, the "famous glutton and merry drunkard" Gargantua were all brisk sellers. Borrowing freely from the literary tradition of the subculture, *lubok* engravers turned out eight- to twelve-page booklets depicting the sort of vulgar stories that so infuriated the paragons of official literature. Reduced to a series of pictures accompanied by just a few lines of explanatory text, *lubok* editions of chivalric romances like "Bova Korolevich," "Eruslan Lazarevich," and "Peter of the Golden Keys" ("Petr zlatykh kliuchei") paved the way for the development of a *lubok* literature (Ovsianikov, 20–24).[18] On a more sober note there was also the *Biography of the Famous Fabulist Aesop* (*Zhizneopisanie slavnogo basnotvortsa Èzopa*, 1712) and the practical *lubok* of maps, charts, and calendars fostered during Peter's reign. By the 1760s *lubok* lampoons of court fops and dandies as well as the stories "Ersh Ershovich" and "Shemiaka's Court" ("Shemiakin sud") mimicked the movement toward satire that marked the literature of high society.

Early in the reign of Catherine the Great *lubok* ceased to consist solely of simple pictures that might also include a brief caption and expanded to include a wide range of genres. Spurred on by a rise in literacy, *lubok* publishers turned out collections of verse, songbooks, bastardized editions of belles lettres, and even original works of fiction that were entirely text, the only picture being an often crude illustration on the book's cover. In the realm of literature *lubok* versions of Levshin's folktales and, later in the century, Karamzin's stories continued the tradition that started with an edition of Sumarokov's fables.[19] At the other end of the literary spectrum Matvei Komarov pioneered the *lubok* novel; tales such as "Bova Korolevich" and "Peter of the Golden Keys" were issued as complete texts; and "amorous lubok," often bordering on the improper, also secured a niche in the new subliterature. Although these texts were printed just as the odes, tragedies, and epics of official literature were, they came to be known collectively as *lubok* literature because of their many similarities with the preceding tradition of pictures. Like the broadsides, they were printed on thick, inexpensive paper much like dime novels and pulp fiction in England and America, thus making them significantly cheaper than books devoted to legitimate literature.[20] Produced in huge quantities, *lubok* publications were also aimed at the same barely literate audience: the print was often large, the language simple, and the subject matter rarely rose above the adventure story.

The rapid rise of *lubok* literature was made possible by the development of a printing industry that could support a voracious demand. The 1760s mark the success of the publishing house of Akhmet′ev, which began printing picture supplements for the *Moscow News* in the 1750s (Ovsianikov, 19) and then expanded to include twenty presses that were employed in the production of all sorts of *lubok*. Later in the century the firms of Reshetnikov and Ponamarev profited from printing the nascent genre of the *lubok* novel, including at least a dozen editions of Komarov's works prior to 1800. By the end of the eighteenth century the subliterature of *lubok* had become so popular that printing houses in Moscow and Kiev were issuing 150,000 different types of pictures, prose, and verse (Ovsianikov, 32–33; Rovinskii, 18–20; Sokolov, 600).

Available in large quantities and offering a carnivalesque blend of didacticism, irreverence, and farce, the literature of *lubok* struck a vibrant chord with a wide range of readers in late eighteenth-century Russia.

Although the lubok was the traditional literature of the Russian peasant, it subsequently became immensely popular with the newly literate groups, such as merchants, military men, clerks and members of the gentry. Lubok editions were not entirely unknown to the upper classes either, although their members officially frowned on such tales. In fact, the first printed editions at the end of the eighteenth century were most likely aimed at consumption by the nobility. Because of the mixed readership that cut across class distinctions unlike any other form of prose writing in Russia, lubok editions were thus the true literature of the masses for at least 150 years. (Schaarschmidt, 428–29)

Since this new subliterature appealed to such a broad readership, it was relatively easy to set up a distribution system. Not relying solely on the standard booksellers and journal subscriptions that limited the dissemination of official literature, the publishers of *lubok* used a more practical approach that helped them reach an audience that was flung across the length and breadth of European Russia. Works like "Bova Korolevich" and "Peter of the Golden Keys" were "sold in the streets of Moscow and distributed widely in villages, fairs, and bazaars by wandering booksellers called *ofeni* . . . or *korobeiniki*, named after the basket (Russian *korobka*) in which they carried the books" (Schaarschmidt, 427). From its inception in the latter part of the eighteenth century until its suppression shortly after the Bolshevik revolution, *lubok* literature satisfied the aesthetic demands of the broad masses of Russian society better than any other form of literary discourse.

The popularity accruing to works like "Bova Korolevich" and the novels of Komarov was significantly enhanced by the virtual absence of standards for this type of fiction. Just as the subculture constantly appropriated and altered the artistic components of various genres and stylistic levels, there were no sacrosanct beliefs about what constituted the proper realm of the literature of *lubok*. Individual works were continuously being modified in order to appeal to the widest possible audience. As Schaarschmidt points out, "everybody was reading Bova: the nobility, the military, the merchants, the emerging middle class, and, most of all, the peasantry" (430). This sort of reader response was, at least in part, occasioned by the malleability of the tale itself. "As the popularity of the novel grew, each social class would leave its imprint on both the style and the content of the story. Thus, the versions written for the nobility came to resemble more and more the translated foreign adventure novels, while the more popular versions gradually acquired the features of the Russian heroic folk-tale" (430–31).[21] Supported by the subculture's whimsical disregard for boundaries and limits, the early Russian novel was able to adapt itself to the reading public in a way that the novels of legitimate literature never could.

In addition to a rather loose commitment to the concept of textual integrity, the mocking spirit inherent in the subculture sanctioned outright fraud and distortion as a means of increasing the appeal of a work. When Chulkov and Popov compiled dictionaries of Slavic mythology, they did not allow a dearth of source material to stand in their way. The two authors managed to create their own Olympus populated with Slavic equivalents of Greco-Roman gods and goddesses by frequently inventing figures that had no basis in the rich tradition of Russian folklore.[22] In the realm of prose fiction the subculture moved even further in this direction by failing to recognize either the primacy or the rights of an author. Even when dealing with one of its own, it remained unimpressed, or at least unconcerned, with who wrote a particular book. After Komarov's death, for example, not one edition of *Milord George* listed him as the author (Shklovskii, *Komarov*, 122). Subcultural publishers and readers were looking for a particular type of work rather than the stylistic or thematic imprint of a particular person. The many novels of Russia's eighteenth-century subculture with

> their cheap printings, their covers with suggestive or heroic graphics, their exotic or alluring titles (often with no mention of uplifting lessons or morals on the title page), and their indifference as to the author, whose name either appeared incidentally or not at all, clearly emphasized the point that an amusing or exciting story was contained in the pages. Indeed, their popularity may have arisen largely from the attractiveness of the titles, especially those that mentioned adventures, maidens, or the appellations of otherwise anonymous or mysterious European nobility such as "lord," "contessa," or "viscount." Publishers, at any rate, clearly perceived that titles such as these, rather than authors' names, would attract the widest attention. (Marker, 119–20)

In the chaotic world of the subculture where laughter reigned as king, mere authorial intention was never allowed to mitigate the visceral appeal or money-making potential of any novel.

Nowhere was the subcultural distortion and modification of texts more evident than in the reception accorded official literature. Even though such respected authors as Sumarokov and Karamzin found their way into *lubok*, the producers of subcultural literature were hardly concerned with faithfully capturing the essence of their work. The serious and didactic side of neoclassicism and sentimentalism did not interest them as much as the possibility of capitalizing on a literary trend or the name of a prominent author. For example, the beginning of *Vanka Kain* reveals a familiarity with the ideological orientation of the trendy English sentimentalist novel, yet Komarov eventually subordinates this foreign component to an adventure tale about a Russian folk hero. In *Various Written Materials* Komarov treats serious readers to a selection of odes, sonnets, idylls, and instructions by the most renowned authors of his day. Their luster is more than partially dimmed, however, by their placement alongside "how-to" articles on preserving fruit and eradicating cockroaches and mice. This sort of irreverent treatment of official literature in the world of *lubok* continued to gain momentum in the first half of the nineteenth century. Starting in the 1830s, the *lubok* industry churned out edition after edition of Russian classics. As was the case in the eighteenth century, the original work rarely survived intact.

Many literary classics entered the world of *lubok,* but the relationship to the literary text in this environment was most unceremonious. Most of all, publishers abridged texts without restraint, striving to keep the work inexpensive. Sometimes these abridgments even destroyed the unity of the work. Moreover, the language was ceaselessly "retouched" with the aim of making it more understandable, accessible, and "enticing" for the simple reader. A large role was played by the competition of *lubok* publishers, who tried to entice the reader with loud titles that promised many things. For example, the names given to Gogol´'s *Taras Bulba* are characteristic: *The Robber Taras Chernomor, Taras Chernomorskii,* and *The Adventures of the Cossack Ataman, Urvan.* (Sokolov, 602–3)

The degree to which *lubok* plagued the guardians of official culture is documented in its struggle against censorship. By 1674, just a half century after the first *lubok* prints were produced in Russia, the medium itself came under fire from the church. Dismayed by the large number of *lubok* icons that were being turned out by "ignoramuses," the Patriarch Ioakim prohibited further production of such cheap religious images. Ioakim maintained that *lubok* prints on religious subjects fostered a careless attitude toward icons, and, in addition to outlawing new works, he demanded the destruction of existing copies as well as harsh penalties for those who circumvented his edict. Apparently this law had little effect on stopping the tidal wave of *lubok* prints, for similar decrees were issued by Peter's Holy Synod in 1721 and by Elizabeth I in 1744 (Rovinskii, 30–33). By the last quarter of the eighteenth century *lubok* literature officially fell under the purview of the censors. The censorship law of January 13, 1783, included *lubok* under the category of printed books and decreed that all such materials must have the approval of the Council of Decency. In 1826 Shishkov's censorship statute reiterated this position by permitting the printing of only those books that were moral and useful, and *lubok* editions of folktales were outlawed in 1839. As the record makes clear, however, *lubok* remained virtually untouched by official prohibitions. Tolstoi's partnership in a *lubok* publishing house and his attempt to write an adapted version of *Milord George* in order to reach the common folk who had become his new audience testify that the *lubok* industry was doing better than ever right through the latter part of the nineteenth century (Schaarschmidt, 428).[23]

Translated Literature

Although the foreign literature that was translated into Russian in the seventeenth and eighteenth centuries did not have as great an impact on the novel as did *lubok,* it does offer a direct insight into the reading sensibility of the period. Focusing on high literature of the eighteenth century, Marc Raeff writes that the Russians simply borrowed what was already latent in their culture. While acknowledging that "French literary, artistic, and social models dominated the scene in Russia from the middle of the eighteenth century," he downplays their impact on the "more basic aspects of Russian culture and thought" ("Enlightenment," 37).[24] Pavel Berkov takes much the same tack in constructing a theory of intercultural relations. Berkov scraps the notion of literary influence, of one literature that is more developed shaping the course of another, and supplants it with the term "contact." In this scheme the borrowing literature remains the chief benefi- ciary of the relationship, but it is not viewed as the vulnerable and in- finitely malleable target of a superior culture. Instead, Berkov insists that the borrowing literature simply appropriates those elements of a second lit- erature that express an already established, but perhaps insufficiently artic- ulated, world view of its own ("Russkaia literatura," 12–14).

From the works the Russians chose to translate during the formative stages of their novelistic tradition, it is evident that the spirit of the subcul- ture played a leading role. Some of the literature that came to Russia was, to be sure, didactic in nature, yet the vast majority of it would more easily fit under the rubric of carnivalesque. By and large Russians favored works that were eclectic, entertaining, and alive with aphoristic density. Verbal play and sudden shifts in the story rather than ponderous lectures on morality captured the attention of the reading public. This was especially true in the fledgling genre of prose fiction. "Translated collections of stories of various designations—didactic and entertaining—brought into Russian literature a multitude of diverse plots and cultivated a taste for rapid changes in the action and a witty aphoristic dialogue, which often was the very essence of the story itself" (Adrianova Peretts, "Siuzhety," 12). Primed by the carnival and by the growing influence of *lubok,* Russian translators and their readers made a "preselected" choice of the material they im- ported from their western neighbors.

To open up the literary heritage of the Western world, Russian transla- tors relied on a series of intermediary languages. Since few Russians were fluent in English, French and German acted as a bridge to bring the best of the eighteenth-century British novel to the empire of Elizabeth and Cather- ine II. Fielding's *Joseph Andrews* and *Jonathan Wild* and Smollett's *Humphrey Clinker* were translated from German, while French versions of *Tom Jones, Robinson Crusoe,* and *Pamela* were employed in rendering these classics into Russian. In the subculture Polish functioned as the predominant intermedi- ary language that made available everything from recent Polish religious poetry to bawdy miscellanies originally compiled in Latin. First tapped in the 1500s, this pipeline was running smoothly by the following century with the translation into Russian of a host of prose works, including both individual adventure tales—"The Story of Attila," "The Story of Tsar Otto," "Peter of the Golden Keys"—and the great medieval compilations— *The Deeds of the Romans (Rimskie deianiia), The Great Mirror (Velikoe zertsalo),* and the *Facetiae (Fatsetsii).* Of the seventy-five literary and scientific works that came to Russia via Poland prior to the eighteenth century, the majority were destined for lower- and middle-class readers.

> It is clear that translations from Polish were primarily in the areas of artis- tic "mass" literature, history, . . . medicine, geography, etc. It is characteris-

tic that the new (for that time) Polish artistic literature (with the exception of Jan Kochanowski's psalms) did not attract the attention of Russian translators. Conforming to the circle of their interests, they basically translated into Russian those Polish works which in their turn represented reworkings of widely known examples of medieval European literatures. (Berkov, *Russko-pol´skie literaturnye sviazi*, 11)

Bolstered by the emergence of a broad-based subculture, the mocking and often bawdy humor of the seventeenth-century compilations pushed the translated literature of official culture to the margins of the literary scene.

The title of the most eclectic, the most carnivalesque, and the most popular of the seventeenth-century compilations belongs to the *Facetiae* (1680). As was common in the subculture, the process of selection played a key role in the translation from Polish with only 70 of the 170 available stories, which were originally written in Latin, French, and German, finding a place in the Russian version (Kukushkina, 181). Often called a collection of rogues' tales, the Russian edition of the *Facetiae* set out, as Likhachev explains, "to entertain and amuse readers, but by no means educate them" (180). In the true spirit of the subculture material was taken from whatever was at hand. To the original stories that came through the Polish translation, Russian compilers added complementary tales from *The Great Mirror*, *The Deeds of the Romans*, and *The Decameron*. Russian folktales and the satiric narrative "Ersh Ershovich" were also worked into the mix. Forged by the demands of the subculture, the *Facetiae* went through many metamorphoses. For the eighteenth century alone investigators have catalogued twenty-five collections. Ten of these collections contain the full complement of seventy stories, four do not, and eleven are adulterated with other tales or material taken from other compilations (Kukushkina, 181–82). Throughout this chaotic mixing of sources and voices the hallmarks of the subculture—adventure, satire, and the machinations of the rogue—reign supreme.[25]

By the time the first Russian novels were being written in the 1760s, the secularized collection of tales had become one of the most popular forms of literature among Russia's expanding reading public. What had begun in the seventeenth century as a trickle limited to a handful of works turned into a tidal wave in just eighty years. Kukushkina outlines the eclectic content of one of these satiric collections (191–92). In addition to the stories gleaned from previous compilations and satiric tales of Russian origin, readers found the comic poems "On Prokhor and Boris" and "On Fomushka," which were taken from the world of *lubok*. Next to these prime examples of Russia's carnivalized subculture, there were placed poems, epigrams, and epistles by the paragons of official culture Sumarokov and Lomonosov. The collection ends with an alphabetical listing of proverbs, 175 riddles, and some carnivalesque *pribautki* (facetious sayings). The prime allure of collections such as this one was their often satiric tone and their ability to be everything to everybody. Like a minicarnival compressed between two covers they promised

many "fine words, wise plans, quick answers, proper mockery, and pleasant adventures of noble men of times both ancient and recent"; "usefully
amusing sayings"; "pleasant and decorous jokes, witty and intricate
speeches and humorous stories"; "short, but understandable anecdotes,
rapturous stories, and histories with sufficient sentimentality to encourage
us to be honest and virtuous."[26]

From the didactic tales that dominated the first compilation to come to
Russia (The Great Mirror), the genre had developed into an amorphous pot-
pourri more reminiscent of the carnival ded's comic routine than of a
church sermon.

The recombination and proliferation of facetiae and various eclectic collections of prose fiction found an appreciative audience in eighteenth-
century Russia, but it did not completely satisfy the demands of the market. As the subculture continued to grow, it warranted the translation of
more recent works. One such example, The Adventures of Sovest-Dral
(Pokhozhdeniia . . . Sovest-Drala), reflects in microcosm the irreverent spirit
and casual approach to literature inherent in the subculture. Immensely
popular, Sovest-Dral came out in a minimum of five editions in the last
twenty years of the eighteenth century, including at least one counterfeit
version (Berkov, Russko-pol´skie literaturnye sviazi, 28).[27] The Adventures of
Sovest-Dral is a translation of the Polish Sowi-Zrzal, which is in turn based
on the Till Eulenspiegel stories. As with other works that had come to Russia via the German-Polish connection, the translator/compiler did not
leave the German version intact. Only sixty of the ninety-two stories of the
German original are included in Sovest-Dral, and "the Russian translator's
attempt to Russify the German Eulenspiegel and Polish Sowi-Zrzal is notice-
able in several insertions [into the text], a song, and the changed names"
(Guberti, 3:601–2). Moreover, stories are added and subtracted from one
edition to the next, and overall Sovest-Dral exhibits the motley blend of elements that appealed to the readers of the subculture. Richly interspersed
with verse, anecdotes, and sayings, the picaresque tale of the title character's rowdy adventures and love intrigues forms the core of the collection.
With little regard for continuity the compiler even stirred in a dash of neoclassical morality by including a translation of The Spendthrift (Mot, ili rasto-
chitel´, from the French Dissipateur), a play concerning the evils of dissipa-
tion by the didactic French dramatist Philippe Destouches.

In one way or another virtually every aspect of the subculture contributed to making Sovest-Dral a best-seller among the common people. The
influence of the carnivalesque is so pervasive in this work, in fact, that it
has left its imprint, quite literally, right on the cover. The Russian title
Sovest-Dral (the conscience fighter) is not a literal translation of the Polish
Sowi-Zrzal, which, following the German Eulenspiegel, means "owl's mirror," but rather a folk etymology. In addition, the cover is adorned with a
coarse, lubok-like engraving, and the title is rendered in the rhymed prose
so common in lubok and the carnival. It reads:

Pokhozhdeniia novogo i uveselitel´nogo shuta
i velikogo v delakh liubovnykh pluta
Sovest-Dral Bol´shogo Nosa

(The Adventures of the New and Entertaining Fool
And, in Affairs of the Heart, the Great Rogue
Sovest-Dral the Big Nose)

In assembling an eclectic array of materials, the compiler of *Sovest-Dral* selected stories from a classic of the subculture, Kurganov's miscellany
Pis´movnik, and may even have included works of a far humbler cast.
Berkov writes that "it is quite possible that popular works of Russian 'low'
literature, taken in part from *lubok* pictures and in part from manuscript
and even printed 'folk' books, were included in the translated text"
(*Russko-pol´skie literaturnye sviazi,* 31). Whether or not this compilation contained fiction taken directly from the subculture, the basic plot of *Sovest-
Dral* was sure to strike the right chord with Russia's lower-class readers.
The title character's escapades, love affairs, and unpunished lawlessness
were favorite themes among a segment of the population that found its
most cherished release in the turnabouts of the carnival and that made
Vanka Kain the first best-seller of Russian literature.

Folklore

Although the early Russian novel was not as strongly influenced by folklore as were the adventure tales of the seventeenth and eighteenth centuries,
this fund of material still played an important role in its development.[28] To
be sure, folklore was not always informed with the irreverent spirit of the
carnivalesque, yet it did endow early Russian prose fiction with a heavy dose
of native wit, wisdom, and whimsicality that served as an effective antidote
to the foreign-inspired literature of official culture. For example, Chulkov relied on the creativity of the folk to such an extent that Oinas maintains "there
is hardly another writer in Russia whose works are as saturated with folklore
as [his are]" (580). Mischievous "merry devils" of the type mentioned by
Bakhtin in his monograph on Rabelais play central roles in several episodes
of *The Mocker,* and Martona, the prostitute heroine of *The Comely Cook,* relies
on folklore not just to frame her vision of the world, but also to keep her safe
from the crushing, judgmental morality of official society. Whether she is rationalizing giving up one lover for another or salving her bruised ego after
having been thrown out by the angry wife of one of her clients, Martona constantly sees the world through the eyes of a proverb or a witty, folksy saying.
She may be penniless and cast adrift without any means of support, but for-
tifying herself with such flippant remarks as "I was outfitted only with patience and the dress on my back" (Chulkov, *Comely Cook,* 165), Martona
soon leaves her gloom and ill fortune behind. No matter how much proper
society tries to make her conform, Martona's confidence in the flexibility
and resiliency of folk culture insures not just that she survives each threatening situation, but that she actually prospers on her own terms.

The fiction of Matvei Komarov offers another prime example of a body of work that makes extensive use of folklore to mock the values of official society. On the one hand, Komarov is indebted to folklore for the very idea of *Vanka Kain,* his "biography" of a countercultural hero. Although the title character was a real person, Komarov's treatment of his life depends more on the folkloric legend surrounding Kain than on authentic sources. On the other hand, Komarov's second novel, *Milord George,* exemplifies the practice of creating an "original" work by splicing specific incidents borrowed from folklore into an adventure tale plot. In the case of *Milord George* Komarov adapted an anonymous manuscript version of the story that is heavily interspersed with material from *The Thousand and One Nights.* The novel begins with George walking into an enchanted forest and happening upon the castle of a princess. In true folktale fashion George and the princess profess their love, are separated by the power of an evil curse, and then spend the rest of the novel overcoming incredible odds before they are eventually reunited. In a later work entitled *Nevidimka* Komarov again appropriates many incidents from other sources, this time borrowing from Russian folktales and the fairy tales of Hans Christian Andersen. Secret treasures, evil sorcerers, and formidable monsters, all elements that were antithetical to the literary aesthetic of official society, abound in a work that Komarov himself called both a short novel and a "string of simple folktales" (*Nevidimka,* iv).[29]

AUTHORS, READERS, PUBLISHERS, AND THE FIRST RUSSIAN NOVELS

The Pioneers of the Russian Novel

By temperament and experience Russia's first novel writers were well positioned to exploit the antiauthoritarian impulses of the subculture. As David Budgen writes: "Prose in Russia throughout the eighteenth century . . . was a bastard, outlawed and orphaned literary type, and the novel which constituted its greater part was more often than not written precisely by bastards, outlaws and orphans" ("Concept," 65). Given their social and educational background, the pioneers of the Russian novel found it difficult to comprehend the subtleties of West European literary models. Not only were these models part of a complex system of foreign values, but writers like Emin, Chulkov, and Komarov were not from the thin layer of Russia's educated and cultured elite that was best prepared to assimilate them. A sound knowledge of folklore, *lubok,* and the adventure tale did little to prepare them for the complexities of Enlightenment thought or the world view of the sentimentalist novel. On the contrary, if it did anything, it provided them with an effective frame of reference for exposing the shortcomings contained in such systems.[30] Moreover, writers infused with the spirit of the subculture were more than willing to bend the truth or distort a source if they thought it would enhance the appeal of a story. This approach to the written word hardly accommodated the imitation of the literary aesthetic and social code that—through the application of either the intellect or the emotions—were devoted to the pursuit of truth.

Often called the first *lubok* novelist, Matvei Komarov is perhaps the best example of a writer whose subcultural background militated against the facile imitation of sophisticated Western models. Although his personal life is enough of a mystery to make the determination of his social status difficult, it appears that Komarov was a manor serf who gained his freedom well after he began his career as a writer, probably some time in the mid-1780s.[31] Whatever his origins, Komarov readily admitted that he was not a product of polite society. In the introduction to *Nevidimka* he confesses: "I myself am among that number of persons of low condition and am not learned in any kind of science except Russian grammar" (ii). He adds that his education began with the reading of religious works and ended when he progressed to secular ones, but, unfortunately, he fails to list specific titles (iii). These rather severe limitations notwithstanding, Komarov worked in a progressive household and managed to become conversant enough with the norms of official literature to write a poem in iambic pentameter praising his owner's son-in-law for his enlightened attitudes (Shklovskii, *Komarov,* 21–31). Moreover, his inclusion of literary and publicistic works from such up-to-date journals as *The Society for Lovers of the Russian Word (Sobranie liubitelei rossiiskogo slova)* and Novikov's *The Twaddler (Pustomelia)* in his compilation *Various Written Materials* certainly confirms that he had a working knowledge of the literary culture of neoclassicism and sentimentalism. Despite this familiarity with belles lettres, however, the overwhelming evidence of Komarov's oeuvre bears out that the texts he read and knew the best were most likely folktales and *lubok*.

Komarov's subcultural orientation is confirmed by his success among lower-class readers. With their coarse paper and large print, his folkloric novels and grotesquely eclectic miscellany were directed not at the habitués of the salons but rather at the denizens of the shops, markets, and streets. Komarov managed to remain a best-selling author among such a readership for almost 140 years because he was what might be called a literary pack rat. As his work bears out, he loved to compile a wide array of material that would appeal to the most divergent tastes. He did not worry about adhering to a particular literary aesthetic or dignifying the high calling of a man of letters, a title that he freely abdicated (*Various Written Materials,* ii). At times a chronicler and historian, at others a novelist and teller of folktales, Komarov was perfectly in tune with the spirit of ignoring established boundaries that defined the artistic sensibility of the subculture. In fact, he was so adept at expressing the values and concerns of his fellow citizens of low estate that only the concentrated efforts of twentieth-century totalitarianism could stifle his influence among them (Shklovskii, *Komarov,* 16).

Of the three major figures of the early Russian novel, Mikhail Chulkov had the closest connections with official literature. Poet, prose writer, journalist, and neophyte ethnographer, he displayed an interest in the very undertakings that formed the core of official literary culture. Despite his association with the world of writers like Lomonosov and Sumarokov, however, Chulkov could never completely embrace the prevailing literary aesthetic. While adhering to the prescribed genres of neoclassicism, he remained a loner who kept the literary establishment at arm's length: "Chulkov's literary development, demonstrated by his selection and treatment of themes, is not one of linear progress. In his prose fiction Chulkov was in many respects an isolated figure, with neither fellow authors nor critics to support and guide his efforts, and unable to create a school of like-minded writers to continue his work" (Garrard, "Prose Fiction," 26). Even though he could boast of powerful friends and his intellect and artistry far outstripped the meager abilities of a figure like Komarov, it is interesting to note that Chulkov defined his literary persona in much the same way as Russia's premier *lubok* novelist did. In *The Mocker* Chulkov refuses the mantle of author (1:vii) while explicitly making light of his abilities as a writer (3:i), and in week 1 of his journal *Both This and That (I to i sio)* he notes: "However, dear reader, don't expect lofty and distinguished designs from me, for I myself am an unimportant person and I can say, without bothering my conscience, that I am similar to the most insignificant animal" (Zapadov, 96). Playful, sly, and self-deprecating, Chulkov's attempts to define his station in life are a far cry from the confident self-image of an arbiter of enlightenment and morality propagated by his onetime friend Sumarokov.

Chulkov's reluctance, or perhaps inability, to fully accept the neoclassical literary code of conduct can at least in part be traced to social and economic considerations. Not being of noble blood, he found that his personal background was a definite stumbling block to financial and even vocational security. Although his social standing allowed him to spend two years at the gymnasium for *raznochintsy* attached to Moscow University, his education opened few doors.[32] Upon leaving the university around 1758, Chulkov only managed to obtain a series of jobs that kept him on the fringes of official society. At first he joined a troop of actors attached to the court theater in St. Petersburg, where he was obliged to try his hand as a wig dresser before being given the opportunity to perform on stage. Around 1765 he received permission to leave the theater and became a court lackey, a position he maintained for just a year or two before entering the field of literature. As a journalist and poet, Chulkov practiced the prescribed genres of neoclassicism, but his efforts in the love lyric, ode, elegy, and burlesque poem won him little in the way of personal recognition. Despite such attempts to accommodate the neoclassical aesthetic, he never could break into the inner circle of established writers.[33]

Chulkov's distance from the literature of official society and the resulting tendency to poke fun at it were exacerbated by monetary concerns. To add insult to injury, he not only never achieved the exalted status of a Sumarokov or Lomonosov, but also was unable to support himself via the profession of writing. For example, three years after the publication of his *Short Mythological Dictionary (Kratkii mifologicheskii leksikon)* in 1767 he still

had not paid for its printing (Garrard, Čulkov, 24). Moreover, if any one aspect of Chulkov's mocking banter in works like *Both This and That* and *The
Comely Cook* rings true, it is his concern for material stability. Although few
writers turned a profit from their work in the eighteenth century,
Chulkov's obsession with the subject denotes the important role it played
in his life. His glib and sarcastic treatment of this theme in week 48 of the
journal cannot mask the sense of urgency and perhaps even desperation
that runs just beneath the surface: "Am I not justified in hating the Muses,
Apollo, and all of Parnassus for being the cause of my unhappiness? I
loved them, and would love them forever, if they had only been a bit more
generous. But sometimes I am overcome by the feeling that I would sell all
of Parnassus along with the Muses and Apollo for fifty cents" (Zapadov,
97–98). Earlier in the journal Chulkov expresses his sense of frustration and
disappointment even more pointedly. Stripping his discourse of its lighthearted, mocking tone, he openly declares that even thieves are better respected in society than writers are: "Here's how just fate is: he [the crimi-
nal] is much more depraved than I am, but rich; stupider than I am, but at
peace; deserving of contempt, but extremely happy" (96). Throughout
Chulkov's literary career financial insecurity and the bitterness it aroused
were never far from his mind.

Denied the fame and fortune of his profession, Chulkov rarely passed
up a chance to taunt the literary establishment. Whether it was a broad assault on the ethics of his fellow writers, a detailed lampooning of a specific
figure, such as his archrival Emin, or simply indulging in farce and buffoonery, Chulkov reveled in a carnivalesque sense of humor. Perhaps the
best introduction to this side of Chulkov is "Verses on a Ferris Wheel"
("Stikhi na kacheli"). In the opening part of this mock heroic poem, which
is the first low burlesque in Russian literature, Chulkov deconstructs the
reigning literary aesthetic. With little regard for tradition or rank, he transforms the inhabitants of Parnassus into coquettes and dandies and dissects
one canonized genre after another, from the love lyric and pastoral elegy to
the panegyrical ode as practiced by Lomonosov and Petrov (414–20). In a
fine example of carnivalesque turnabout Chulkov then reverses the lens
through which he views his age in the second part of "Verses on a Ferris
Wheel." Leaving behind, at least for a moment, the type of satire and parody practiced by his fellow Russian writers, he more openly expresses the
subcultural basis of his writings. Despairing that he will never be able to attain glory for himself in the prescribed genres of neoclassicism, the poet-
hero decides to write about the Ferris wheel that functions as the center-
piece of an Easter carnival (421–33). In this part of the poem Chulkov
switches to the high burlesque and describes the rowdy folk, or *narod*, who
are celebrating the holiday as classical gods and heroes. Amid "clouds of
wine" (423) a drunken Phaëthon lies in the mud, struck down not by Zeus
but by an overindulgence in the fruits of the carnival (425). An "inebriated
Mars" (421) pesters a group of women who are rescued by a country
knight (*bogatyr´*; 421–23), and several mass fistfights (*kulachnye boi*) break

out involving, among others, a "country Achilles," "fat Mars," and even many of the women who are present (423, 430–32). As in all carnivals, however, things end on a positive note: there are kisses all around, and everyone rests up for five weeks before doing it all again (432). Brief and lighthearted, *Verses on a Ferris Wheel* epitomizes the methods of the inveterate mocker who put together the first collection of Russian riddles, employed the pithy folk proverb as the building block of his fiction, and crowned the prostitute Martona the carnivalesque queen of all she surveyed.[34]

Of the three pioneers of the Russian novel, Fedor Emin represents the most colorful character. Unlike Komarov or Chulkov, Emin exploited a savvy born of the subculture for the purpose of ingratiating himself with the literary and cultural elite. At first glance his life and literary career connect him with the upper echelons of Russian society and with an imitative approach to the calling of author. Having arrived in St. Petersburg in 1761, Emin quickly established himself as the most prominent Russian fiction writer of the early years of Catherine's reign. Between 1763 and 1766 he turned out six original novels, and if the nineteen volumes he penned before his death in 1770 are not some sort of unofficial record for productivity in such a brief period of time, they do represent a remarkable achievement. No matter how talented Emin was, however, or how little quality was demanded by a reading public greedy for novels, Russia's most popular prose writer of the 1760s could not have been as prolific as he was if he had not relied heavily on well-established models. Perhaps more than any other Russian writer of prose fiction in the late eighteenth century, Emin exploited the literary conventions of his day in an attempt to win both the allegiance of the reading public and the acceptance of the reigning arbiters of literary taste. From the Enlightenment theorizing and didacticism of *Inconstant Fate* (1763) to the sentimentalist excesses of *Ernest and Doravra* (1766), Emin rehearsed just about every literary and ideological cliché of his age.

Despite his claims to noble birth and the felicity with which he appropriated timeworn conventions, Emin was powerfully influenced by the subculture and the outlaw status of his profession. A prime example of this attitude is his manipulation of the strange twists and colorful incidents that have come to be called his "biography." During Emin's lifetime his biography was at best confusing, and now, over two hundred years later, it is hardly any clearer.[35] What is certain is that Emin came to Russia in 1761 and settled in St. Petersburg with the intent of making his fortune there. In order to obtain a job as a government translator, this man without a past had to account for his actions prior to arriving in Russia. Complying with the government's request, Emin submitted his autobiography to the College of Foreign Affairs, but, in keeping with the subcultural side of a nature that would have him playing the role of plagiarist and charlatan, his life story changed substantially at least three times in the next quarter century. In his original petition to the government Emin claimed that he was the son of a Turkish governor and himself a bey. By the late 1760s he altered this story and maintained that he had been born in either Poland or Hungary (depending on the version consulted), studied with the Jesuits, and eventually traveled to Constantinople, where he was conscripted as a janissary. In the fourth version of his life, which is appended to his religious tract *The Path to Salvation* (*Put' k spaseniiu*, 1784), the biographer mentions a former friend of Emin, who alleges that the subject in question was actually a Russian and that they studied together in the Orthodox academy in Kiev.[36]

If one thing is clear in the imbroglio of Emin's life story, it is that his machinations were consciously undertaken for personal gain. When he arrived in St. Petersburg, Emin was forced to live on a government stipend of fifty rubles a year and whatever incidental earnings he could acquire via teaching and translating (Beshenkovskii, 192–94). Finding this a relatively meager income, he hoped to appeal to the charitable instincts of the nobility by acting as though he were one of them—thus his original claim to the title of Turkish bey. This facade served him well until about 1768, when Russia went to war against Turkey. To dispel any doubts about his loyalty to his adopted country, Emin renounced his Moslem ancestry and changed his biography to read that he was actually a Christian of European descent who had been forced into service in Turkey (versions 2 and 3; Beshenkovskii, 195). As if to confirm this newfound lineage, Emin took a virulently anti-Turkish stance in his 1769 publication *A Brief Description of the Ancient and Modern Condition of the Ottoman Porte* (*Kratkoe opisanie drevneishego i noveishego sostoianiia Ottomanskoi Porty*). After his death his biography was altered yet again to placate the sensibilities of his readers. By the early 1780s *The Path to Salvation* had been published several times, and readers of this popular religious tract had a hard time believing that a recent convert to Orthodoxy could speak with such power and authority about their faith. To satisfy their doubts, in the 1784 edition of *The Path to Salvation* an anonymous biographer, who probably never knew his subject personally, changed Emin's story to make him Orthodox from birth (Beshenkovskii, 198).[37]

In addition to the political and religious motivations behind the distortion of Emin's biography, the author's manipulation of his life story also had a directly literary connection. Even though he strove to be taken seriously, Emin had no problem overlooking his "commitment" to the task of enlightenment if in so doing he could boost his career. After all, he started churning out prose fiction only because he thought it would be more lucrative than living off a government stipend or working as a translator.[38] During Emin's brief run as a novelist the public favored stories they could read as histories: works that included eyewitness accounts of real events, descriptions of distant countries, and the lives of important personalities were the big sellers (Budgen, "Concept," 67). By manipulating the alleged facts of his biography, Emin hoped to create a literary persona that would allow him to capitalize on this trend. If readers were convinced that he actually experienced the foreign adventures reflected in his writings, his novels stood a greater chance of being read as histories. With this in mind, Emin began his literary career with a novel and a biography that mutually supported one another. In *Inconstant Fate* he recounts the hair-raising adventures of the title character, Miramond, son of the bey of Algiers, whose lineage, rank, and travels throughout North Africa and the countries of the Mediterranean call to mind the figure described in the first version of his autobiography. In the chaotic world of eighteenth-century Russian prose fiction just a few strokes of the pen separated the mockery and facetiousness of the subculture from the loftiest of goals.

The Reading Public in Eighteenth-Century Russia

Emin, Chulkov, and Komarov were able to achieve the success they did largely because the demand for prose fiction, especially when it a had a subcultural bent to it, continued to increase throughout the eighteenth century. Already by the mid-1700s Ivan Shishkin, a translator and early supporter of the novel genre, could claim that one of his sponsors "reads the works of all famous writers so assiduously that if he were able to suddenly see all their works in Russian, he would not mind using half (if not all) of his wealth in order to get them" (Berkov, "Shishkin," 56). While Shishkin's statement is no doubt tinged with hyperbole, it does capture the intensity with which Russians turned to reading. By the end of the eighteenth century only a small fraction of all adult Russians were literate, yet the notion that reading was useful and enjoyable was firmly entrenched in Russian society.[39] Primers and grammars represented some of the most popular and widely circulated printed books in eighteenth-century Russia. In an era when multiple editions of a work were rare, the Academy of Sciences printed Lomonosov's grammar seven times between 1755 and 1799, and Kurganov's *Pis'movnik*, a miscellany of folklore and stories that was often used as a primer, was issued six times in Catherine's reign alone (Marker, 195). With the government acting as the prime advocate of literacy, reading became an ever increasing phenomenon among virtually all strata of Russian society. By the time the first Russian novels made their appearance on the literary scene, the "reading public had become large enough to provide an audience for nearly every kind of book for which a market existed in the West" (202).

Precisely how large the Russian reading public was in the second half of the eighteenth century is almost impossible to know. Sales figures for the eighteenth century are rare, and even the business records of the Academy of Sciences have been lost. From a wide array of circumstantial evidence, however, it is possible to conclude that readership continued to expand, in some ways quite impressively, throughout the 1700s. Gary Marker believes that Catherine's passage of the Free Press Law was in response to market demands for more books (108–9), a fact that would seem to be confirmed by the steady growth in the number of booksellers, both in the two capitals and in the provinces (158–64). Moreover, sketchy sales figures also paint a picture of a small but ever growing reading public. From 1770 to 1790 the *Moscow News* went from selling about five hundred copies per issue to between four thousand and six thousand, and the *St. Petersburg News* increased from six hundred to twelve hundred copies per issue in the 1760s to twenty-five hundred copies in the 1790s (202–3).[40] Compared to the corresponding period in the history of British literature—the beginning of the eighteenth century when the tradition of the modern novel was coalescing—these totals do seem small. Watt concludes that in 1704 English newspapers sold over forty-three thousand copies per week (36). The Russians do quite a bit better, however, when the subject turns to prose fiction. For example, Russian versions of Lesage's *Gil Blas* went through seven printings in the latter part of the eighteenth century. With print runs of between six hundred and twelve hundred each (Marker, 203–4), approximately five thousand to eight thousand copies of this translation were sold. Though modest in and of themselves, these figures are quite impressive for the times. In Britain very few secular works sold more than ten thousand copies during the period that encompasses the rise of the novel, and virtually all of those can be classified as topical pamphlets (Watt, 36).

Following a trend that had begun in the seventeenth century (Likhachev, 36; Baklanova, 161–63), the reading public of Catherine's reign was swelled by an infusion of readers of rather humble background. Although the upper classes of Russian society also supported the novel, it was the merchants, clerks, petty bureaucrats, tradesmen, and manor serfs of Moscow and St. Petersburg who, by their sheer numbers, made it the most popular genre of the day. In the introduction to *Nevidimka* Komarov maintains that interest in novels like his cuts across class lines: "At the present time [1789], not only noble society, which has been enlightened by science, but also people of every rank are much inclined to take up reading" (i). This interpretation is borne out by the marginalia found in the novels themselves. After checking inscriptions in *Milord George,* Shklovskii notes that many of Komarov's readers were merchants and noncommissioned officers (*Komarov,* 90). Moreover, the second half of the eighteenth century witnessed an exodus of peasants from the countryside to the cities. By 1778 there were up to fifty thousand of the so-called trading peasantry in St. Petersburg alone (Shklovskii, *Chulkov i Levshin,* 30). In addition to complicating the life of the traditional merchantry, these "urban peasants" frequently brought a hunger for reading to the two capitals. From the catalogue number in one of the eighteenth-century books in his possession, Shklovskii concludes that the peasant who originally owned the work had a library consisting of at least two hundred volumes (*Chulkov i Levshin,* 32).[41]

The practice of the best-selling novelists of the period confirms that the reading public was dominated by people with the simpler tastes of the subculture. In *Nevidimka,* for example, Komarov virtually admits that he is seeking out a barely literate audience. In the introduction he promises that he has written this novel "in a simple Russian style which does not make use of rhetorical eloquence" (v).[42] Moreover, Komarov's recourse to footnotes and appendices also indicates that he patronized less-educated readers. In *Nevidimka* he deems it necessary to explain that Stambul is the capital of Turkey and that it was formerly known as Constantinople (69). He appends a mythological dictionary to *Milord George* to help out those who are not conversant with the classics, and in *Various Written Materials* feels his readers would not be familiar with Copernicus and Aristotle so he inserts brief footnotes to identify these two world-famous figures (176–77).

Even though Emin was a far more sophisticated writer than Komarov and harbored pretensions of legitimizing the genre, he perceived the need to accommodate a diverse and generally unsophisticated readership. As David Budgen notes, his novel *Inconstant Fate* has much in common with works like "Peter of the Golden Keys," "Bova Korolevich," and "Vasilii Koriotskii." Miramond's adventures upon leaving his father in order to seek an education, and the exoticism, seduction, cannibalism, incest, and role accorded destiny in the novel all recall specific tales from earlier periods of Russian literature (Budgen, "Emin," 68–69). By using the components of seventeenth- and early eighteenth-century adventure tales as the models for his work, Emin made a direct and ultimately successful appeal to an ever growing lower-class reading public.

Despite the neoclassicists' denunciation of stories like "Bova Korolevich" this type of work was a perfect match for the tastes of a reading public swollen by the lower ranks of society. As Watt would put it, the social and literary dynamics of the time were a perfect match.[43] Whereas Novikov found it difficult to sell 200 copies of Sumarokov's plays in ten years, the first Russian edition of Goethe's *The Sorrows of Young Werther* sold only 125 copies, and even such well-liked English novels as Fielding's *Amelia, Joseph Andrews,* and *Jonathan Wild* had Russian press runs of only 300 each (Marker, 204–5), the printed literature of the subculture more often than not came out in one edition after another. For instance, between 1763 and 1792 three separate publishers offered versions of Emin's magnum opus, *Inconstant Fate,* and Chulkov's sprawling five-volume novel *The Mocker* fared even better. Even though it was an ongoing project that was not completed until 1789, it was issued three times in just over twenty years. As successful as these novels were, however, the real best-sellers of the late eighteenth century belong without a doubt to Komarov. Led by the novels *Vanka Kain* and *Milord George,* which were published a minimum of seven times each in the eighteenth century alone, Komarov's works appeared in at least thirty separate editions right up to the end of the Romanov dynasty.[44]

The Rise of the Novel and the Business of Publishing

The marriage between an expanding reading public avid for novels and a new breed of authors ready and willing to exploit this market might never have come about if it had not been for the rise of a publishing industry. Both facilitating and verifying the Russians' growing fondness for reading, the increase in the number of publishers in the second half of the eighteenth century was spearheaded by eight new institutional presses that opened their doors between 1752 and 1774. In addition to the famous publishing house of Moscow University, which began operations in 1756, the Naval Corps (1752), Infantry Corps (1757), and Artillery and Engineering

Corps (1765), among others, began to play a role in the book trade in Russia (Marker, 76). Along with the already well-established presses run by the Academy of Sciences, the new scholastic enterprises accounted for almost three-fourths of all titles published in Russia between 1756 and 1775 (78). Meeting an obvious demand for printed material, the new businesses grew rapidly. By 1760 Moscow University had eleven presses and employed seventy-eight workers, and by the mid-1760s it was issuing forty books per year (83). The Academy publishing house fared even better, expanding from eleven presses in the late 1750s to seventeen by 1770 (89). As one of the largest publishing concerns in all of Europe, by the mid-1760s it employed thirty full-time translators in an attempt to open up the world of foreign literature to Catherine's subjects.

Although some "intellectual" publishers, such as Novikov, did offer adventure tales and romances as a way of trying to stay in the black, in general the institutional presses were reluctant to make novels the central focus of their operations. By and large "the literati . . . were dismayed by the growing popularity of such books, and they looked with disillusionment upon a reading public that reduced reading to mere entertainment rather than using it for the loftier purpose of inculcating respect for Russian culture and individual moral improvement" (Marker, 120). As the flagship of the publishing industry in Russia, the Academy of Sciences showed the way in upholding the ideals of the Westernized cultural elite: "In its day it was probably the leading voice for the French Enlightenment, since it published over a dozen separate selections from the *Encyclopédie*, along with individual works by Corneille, Mobly, Montesquieu (including *The Spirit of the Laws*), Voltaire *(Candide)*, and Rousseau" (92). The literature and thought of the Enlightenment also served as the focus of Moscow University Press. In 1757 Kheraskov was appointed censor and overseer, and particularly as regards the content of some of Russia's first literary journals, he confirmed his allegiance to the Enlightenment credo of defending virtue, prosecuting vice, and, at the same time, entertaining readers (86). The publication of excerpts from the *Encyclopédie* (1767; 3 vols.) in conjunction with the Academy of Sciences was one of the first projects undertaken at Moscow University, and numerous translations of Voltaire, Rousseau, and Molière were also issued. For the most part, the Infantry and Naval Corps presses concentrated on works in which "morals could be told through rather light tales of adventure and romance," yet they also published Voltaire's *Zadig* in 1765 and Molière's *Amphitryon* in 1761 and *The Sicilian* in 1776 (Marker, 79–80).

Confirming the contention that the reading public was more in tune with the tastes of the subculture than with the Westernized literary aesthetic broadcast from above, the publishing of Enlightenment literature and treatises was almost always a losing proposition. In its first five years of operation Moscow University Press ran up a debt of twenty-five thousand rubles (Marker, 84–85), and, despite its prominent position, even the Academy of Sciences reeled under the burden of the many works of highbrow literature

that were foisted upon it in the 1770s by Catherine's Society for Translating
Books. Marker notes that the Academy considered these titles "white elephants" and often sold them at a loss just in order to be rid of them (168).
Even in the 1780s, when the publishing industry in Russia had a history
that could be tracked, an astute and dedicated entrepreneur like Novikov
could not overcome the obstacles inherent in the profession. Following his
heart rather than his head, Novikov de-emphasized the publishing of adventure tales and romances to concentrate on works that promoted learning
or the development of personal virtue. First as the overseer of Moscow University Press and then, after 1785, as the head of his own Typographical
Company, Novikov found himself awash in a sea of red ink. There never
seemed to be enough money on hand to meet operating expenses, and he
was continually forced to solicit the support of patrons or devise new
means of streamlining his operations and raising cash. Despite all his efforts, by 1784 he was still losing from twenty to sixty thousand rubles per
year (130). After his arrest in 1792 Novikov's assets were sold, but the
money raised from them was not enough to cover his debts. In 1818 one of
Russia's staunchest defenders of enlightenment and progress died in obscu-
rity as a virtual pauper.[45]

If Novikov and, to a certain degree, most of the institutional presses
were hindered by the belief that publishing was not so much a business as
a "social service and philanthropic activity" (Marker, 130), the book market
quickly opened up opportunities for entrepreneurs of a more practical
bent. In July of 1776 two German-born printers, Johann Weitbrecht and Johann Schnoor, became the first individuals to acquire the right to publish
Russian books. By 1783 three more publishers had secured the privilege,
and in the late 1770s institutional presses began to rent facilities to private
individuals (104–5). The floodgates burst open in 1783 when Catherine permitted private citizens to own and operate a press without obtaining the
prior consent of the government. Moving quickly to take advantage of the
opportunity, private publishers were issuing four hundred titles a year by
the mid-1780s and would account for almost 80 percent of all books printed
between the formal decree in 1783 and the reimposition of censorship in
1795 (105). Freed from the red tape and restrictions imposed by the government, the ranks of the newly constituted private publishers were filled by
men whose primary concern was to make a profit. Some private publishers, like Novikov, Bogdanovich, and Reshetnikov, were members of polite
society, but by and large the new breed consisted mainly of merchants and
artisans whose main goal was to exploit a burgeoning market for a particular type of reading. From undistinguished backgrounds, but usually with
some experience in the book trade, men like Schnoor, Matvei Ovchinnikov,
and the Ponomarevs used their business savvy and profit-making instincts
to find a secure niche for themselves where the more famous "literati publishers" had failed. As Marker points out, the "merchant" publishers
proved their mettle by surviving in the business long after their upper-class
competitors had fallen by the wayside. Although they were also prone to

falling into debt, their pragmatic approach to the profession usually got them back on their feet. Of the thirteen eighteenth-century Russian publishers who were still operating in the following century, twelve came from the new wave of profit-oriented entrepreneurs (113–14).

Just as Novikov had turned to adventure tales and romances to prop up his beleaguered enterprises, merchant publishers as well as an institutional press like the Cadet Corps managed to stay in the black by concentrating on the lower genres. From 1763 to 1775 translated novels were the bread and butter of the publishing industry. In this period Russia produced very few original novels but offered readers a selection of over 120 novels in translation (Marker, 101). A decade or two later private presses descended even deeper into the subculture and churned out a steady stream of *lubok* literature. Marker writes that

> they warmly embraced the apparently burgeoning market for the popular adventure stories and romances that collectively came to be called *lubochnaia literatura.* . . . The earliest volumes of this kind appeared in the 1780s and 1790s. Loosely bound, they contained large print and engraved illustrations. They often ran to 300 or 400 pages, quite long for the Russian reader, but their simple subject matter and language and their decidedly lowbrow style had broad popular appeal. All of them were brought out by experienced publishers. An example of the type was [Komarov's] notorious . . . *Adventures of the English Lord George.* (118–19)

The advent of a group of publishers like Reshetnikov, Schnoor, and Ponomarev, who put business before sentiment, provided a true test for the early Russian novel. With the support of a reading public clamoring for literature infused with the values of the subculture, it passed quite easily.

NOVELS HIGH AND LOW

The Official Literary Aesthetic and the Subculture

Despite an exceedingly slow start in the first half of the century, the novel quickly established itself as the dominant literary discourse of the 1760s, 1770s, and 1780s. During the first thirty years of the eighteenth century virtually the only new prose fiction the Russians could claim were the four manuscript stories known as the Petrine tales, and even up through the year 1754 only five novels had been issued by Russian presses. Starting in the late 1750s, however, the genre captured the imagination of the reading public, and over 1,100 editions of 839 works classified as either novels *(romany)*, novellas *(povesti)*, or tales *(skazki)* were published prior to the turn of the century (Goodliffe, 126). The onslaught of the upstart genre certainly made a deep impression on the preeminent literary figures of the age, who made no secret of their irritation concerning the competition it provided for "serious literature." Sumarokov dryly remarked that "novels have multiplied so much that it is possible to compile half of the world's library out of them" ("Pis´mo," 350) while Novikov complained that "nowadays many of the best books are translated from various foreign languages and printed in Russian, but they are not bought even a tenth as much as novels" (Serman, "Stanovlenie," 82). Even when the hyperbole surrounding such statements is taken into account, they still seem to be an accurate assessment of the situation. Writing two centuries later, the critic I. Z. Serman would conclude that "the new standard setter of the [eighteenth-century] book market" (52) "began to push out those genres that validated the authority of the prevailing literary theory" (83).

The novel enjoyed such immediate and resounding success in Russia because it mediated a wide array of sources and points of view. In addition to the lowbrow genres of the subculture the early Russian novel accommodated the latest innovations in West European literature and thought. The mixing of high and low, of the crude caricatures of *lubok* prints and the facile stereotypes of civic virtue, of carnivalesque buffoonery and sentimentalist didacticism informed the heteroglossia of the genre. By embracing such a mix of voices, Russia's first novelists expanded their options. On the one hand, they could use the discourse of official culture to cast a broader net among a diverse reading public; on the other, they could play one discourse off against the other or, as Bakhtin would term it, "internally dialogize" the genre. As practiced in Russia in the second half of the eighteenth century, the novel became just about all things to all people. While the norms and values of high literature were often forced to serve a new master, the discourse of virtue and civic responsibility also secured a niche in the newly transcendent genre.

In spite of the contempt they evinced for novels in general, the arbiters of the official literary aesthetic did not write them off completely. Given the great flexibility inherent in the novel form, certain works won the unqualified support of even the most stalwart opponents of the genre. Lomonosov and Sumarokov encouraged readers to plumb the knowledge and moral wisdom available in Cervantes's *Don Quixote* (1615), Barclay's *Argenis* (1621), and Fénelon's *Télémaque* (1699), and in 1766 Trediakovskii published a translation of Fénelon's political novel. Tellingly, he opted to transform this prose romance into verse form, thereby matching its elevated subject matter with a suitably elevated style.[46] Fifteen years earlier Trediakovskii had also translated Barclay's "deep" and "difficult" *Argenis* into what the title page calls an appropriately high-minded "Slaveno-Russian" style. The original work was held in such esteem that Trediakovskii himself admitted he would have considered it impertinent to undertake such a weighty task if he had not been ordered to do so by the president of the Academy of Sciences (Guberti, 1:119). Further justifying his selection of this novel, he noted that "in [Barclay's] final composition there is nothing vulgar, low, or popular [narodnyi]; everywhere everything is most glorious, distinguished, excellent, and worthy of a regal superiority" (1:119).

The dynamic that fused Enlightenment ideals and the medium of prose

fiction reached its zenith in the eighteenth century in such philosophical/
political novels as Novikov's *Kalisfen* (1786) and Kheraskov's *Cadmus and
Harmonia* (*Kadm i Garmoniia*, 1789) and *Polydorus, the Son of Cadmus and Harmonia* (*Polidor, syn Kadma i Garmonii*, 1794). The last two novels are particularly important in this regard because they are steeped in the philosophy of
Freemasonry, the movement that had such a profound impact on the cultural elite of the time.[47] Counting such important enlighteners as
Sumarokov, Maikov, Lukin, Kheraskov, Novikov, Radishchev, and
Karamzin among its members, Masonry privileged the mind and wisdom
over the body and pleasure, a proposition that was completely antithetical
to the ethos of the subculture (Baehr, 90–99). As opposed to the cyclical
rhythms of the carnival Masons compared life to the ascent of a mountain
summit. Members rose slowly through a series of degrees with the aid of an
authoritarian master who knew how to capture and express truths that neo-
phytes could only vaguely intuit. The Masonic system also conceptualized
the prime task of the individual as a quest for knowledge. Viewing life as a
linear, nonrepeating experience with a coveted prize awaiting the traveler at
the end, this scheme totally contradicted the tendency of the carnival to
ground participants in the here and now. Where the carnival called for
chaos, Masonry counseled order; to the democratization of society offered
by the subculture, Masonry answered with hierarchies and elitism; and
while the carnival indulged in a full-blooded lust for life, Masons sought enlightenment through transcendence.

   Kheraskov's *Cadmus and Harmonia* is a virtual primer of an anticarniva-
lesque approach to life, in which the author explains the intricate symbolism of Freemasonry and describes in detail the quest for knowledge, obedience to a venerable master, and recourse to mysticism that form the core of
the movement. Blinded by the surface of things, Cadmus loses the throne
of ancient Thebes and sets out to seek inner peace. The ensuing struggle to
reestablish his authority takes him along a labyrinthine path that he can ne-
gotiate only with the help of different masters. By degrees he comes to a
clearer appreciation of life and eventually finds the Masonic (and anticarni-
valesque) ideal of order and balance in the person of his future wife, Harmonia. After a series of initiations in the Egyptian pyramids,[48] Cadmus is
transformed into a new man, Kadm Admon. As Baehr explains, this is an
anagram for Adam Kadmon. In the Jewish cabala Kadmon represents a
prefiguration of the biblical Adam, a pure spirit who was the first emana-
tion of light from God and thus the closest mortal form to the supreme being (108). Purified and at peace, Cadmus finally attains paradise among the
Slaviane (Russians). Needless to say, the land Kheraskov has in mind for
his transcendent hero is not the Russia of ice mountains, ribald comics, and
lurid *lubok* broadsides.

   In addition to its concretization in a small number of uncompromisingly
didactic texts the discourse of official culture found its way into virtually
every novel of the late eighteenth century. As I. R. Titunik notes, many

writers of the new prose fiction sought to legitimize their work by grounding it in the functions of art declared proper by the neoclassical canon, that is authority, logic, and morality ("Komarov," 352). This sentiment was so well developed that it even shaped the literary outlook of a shady character like Emin. Dismissed by the reigning literati as a producer of second-rate romances, Emin nevertheless incorporated a broad range of topics into his fiction that would have appealed to the staunchest defender of Enlightenment. His *Themistocles* (1763) is the first original political novel in Russian literature, and even in *Inconstant Fate,* a work replete with adventure and love intrigues, the author constantly expounds on the central concerns of enlightened society, from philosophy to military affairs. Moreover, despite the lack of esteem generally accorded the novel, Emin held to a view of the author's calling that was every bit as civic-minded as the position espoused by Trediakovskii, Lomonosov, and Sumarokov. In *Ernest and Doravra* he intones the common refrain that society is the master and an author its servant who is duty bound to use his talents for the master's benefit (part 3, letter 4). Elsewhere in his final novel and in the journal *Hell's Post (Adskaia pochta)* Emin confirms his commitment to this ideal by going on the attack against one of the pillars of the literary establishment. Impatient with Sumarokov's superior air, Emin claims that the "Boileau of the North" is more concerned with inflating his already bloated reputation than with serving the needs of society (Gukovskii, "Emin," 82–89). Through a series of oblique references he vilifies his rival as an unconscionable hater of society who cynically writes only for money and praise.

Besides appropriating the ideology of official culture, Russia's first novelists also cultivated specific rhetorical ploys that were designed to help legitimize their genre. Following the lead of certain West European authors, the pioneers of the Russian novel turned to various forms of first-person narration to enhance the sense of immediacy and "truthfulness" in their writing. For example, Chulkov's *Comely Cook* fits right in with the tradition of the confessional autobiography as exemplified by *Gil Blas* (1715–1735), *Moll Flanders* (1722), and *Manon Lescaut* (1732) (Garrard, "Narrative Technique," 554–55), and Emin's six novels contain just about every conceivable type of first-person narration, including monologues, interior monologues, laments, and letters. Of all these forms, the last one was probably the most effective at establishing an immediate connection between the world of fiction and its readers. As Budgen writes, "the secret, confidential and private nature of the letter and its estrangement from the surrounding text guarantees authenticity of expression and represents an opportunity for the characters of fiction to discard their assumed roles and worldliness" ("Concept," 69). Just as Richardson had capitalized on a new rhetoric of feelings in his epistolary novels (Watt, 191–96), Emin turned to the letter as the surest way to gain his readers' confidence. It is probably no coincidence that he ended his career as a fiction writer with *Ernest and Doravra,* a lengthy four-part work comprising the correspondence of four friends. As the subject matter of his previous five novels attests, Emin continuously sought to enlighten readers, to guide them to the "truth." In his sixth and final novel he pushed this approach to the limit with the openness of expression offered by the epistolary form. Apparently even this innovation left Emin less than completely satisfied, however, for after finishing *Ernest and Doravra* he abandoned literature altogether and concentrated instead on the writing of religious tracts, such as *The Path to Salvation*, to express his vision of the world.

In the new prose fiction of the 1760s, 1770s, and 1780s the fight for literary legitimacy often centered on the notion of the author's presence in the text. Common in the work of an intrusive author like Emin, this device was even employed by Matvei Komarov, the most self-effacing of the pioneers of the Russian novel. For the most part Komarov was nothing more than "a literary professional 'adaptor' [who prepared] materials for printed publication, often supplying prefaces and notes and sometimes revising or even completely rewriting the material itself" (Titunik, "Komarov," 353). In the extreme case of *Various Written Materials* his role was limited to compiling a hodgepodge of works consisting of informational pieces, folklore, and the prose and poetry of contemporary authors. In the "documentary" novel *Vanka Kain*, however, Komarov takes a more active approach and does project an authoritative persona directly into the text. While staying close to the extant source material on the life of his subject, he takes every opportunity to analyze the events in the story for what appears to be maximum didactic effect. As one nineteenth-century observer remarked, Komarov's commentary almost overshadows the "facts" of the Kain tale itself: "Kain's life story, which has been written by Komarov, abounds with the author's own discourse and boring raisoneurism. As a consequence of this, his book has gained in volume, but not in the interest the story holds. The facts that have been collected in it are no greater than in Kain's short autobiographies" (Guberti, 2:27).

Seeking to legitimize his novel, Komarov employs what Titunik calls an "image of author" to bring a serious tone and sense of purpose to the unruly, first-person accounts of Kain's adventures. Based on the unreproducible comic patter of the subculture (doggerel, facetious sayings), an often tangled mix of special languages (dialects, thieves' cant, chancellery language), and even such orthographic tricks as apparently purposely misspelling words (Titunik, "Komarov," 355–56), the first-person version consulted by Komarov lacks an organized moralizing presence. For the Kain tale to be accepted as a work of high literature, many of these traits would have to be modified, transformed, and in some cases deleted entirely. Komarov's response to this dilemma was to put himself at the center of the text. Among other things, this included the addition of a third-person narrator, which allowed him to motivate, analyze, and evaluate the actions and characters in the story. He also decreased the use of dialect, slang, and argot; distinguished the dialogue from the narration; and regularized the text with respect to orthography, paragraphing, and the procedures for reporting speech (357). With these changes Komarov created a "stage manager" for the novel, a figure who could draw a lesson from every situation and who at times allows himself to slip off into a moral digression (359–60). When Komarov's narrator addresses readers, it is with the intent of telling them what he wants them to know. This approach to crafting a narrative helps to give *Vanka Kain* the look of a typical eighteenth-century satire. The issues of virtue and vice are clearly drawn, and the author offers the reader little choice but to side with his interpretation.

Despite the rather widespread reflection of Enlightenment norms in the early Russian novel, the reception accorded this genre by the literary establishment confirms that its dominant voice definitely came from the subculture. Most critical debates of the time simply dismissed the novel, and two hundred years later many scholars still maintain that the prose fiction of the eighteenth century "occupies a position of secondary importance in Russian literature" (Moiseeva and Serman, 40). Except for the sanctioned form of the *slovo*, a speech constructed according to the rules of neoclassical rhetoric, prose fiction usually met with a stinging rebuke, condescending ridicule, or at best a deafening silence from the practitioners of high literature. With the already noted rare exceptions for such didactic works as *Don Quixote, Télémaque,* and *Argenis,* Sumarokov expressed nothing but contempt for the novel, and Lomonosov refused to acknowledge it in his treatise on the three stylistic levels of the Russian language.[49] Moreover, the genre hardly fared any better when mentioned in specific literary texts. In Fonvizin's comedy *The Brigadier* (1769?) the slow-witted and unjustifiably self-satisfied Ivanushka proudly asserts that his character has been formed by reading nothing but novels. Summing up the Enlightenment attitude toward such matters, his fiancée, Sophia, immediately snaps back with an aside: "And that is why you are such a fool" (1.i).[50]

The literary establishment's dismal view of the novel can at least in part be explained by what Budgen calls "the primitive and age-old identification of fiction with falsehood and the activity and profession of 'creative writing' with lying—a kind of epistemological doubtfulness as to the very status of fiction writing within the institution of literature" ("Concept," 65). Sumarokov found that when the frivolous trappings of the novel were pared away, very little, if anything, that could be considered instructive remained. He claimed that "novels are written by ignoramuses, and they teach readers an affected and deformed outlook on life and lead them away from what is natural. . . . They weigh a ton, but don't contain a pound's worth of essence" ("Pis′mo," 350). Lomonosov pushed this complaint even further, maintaining that in addition to being a complete waste of time, novels were simply immoral.

> Fairy tales [*skazki*], which the French call novels, cannot be put in the class of works that employ pure imagination because they do not contain any moral instruction. Sometimes they differ from a fairy tale, such as the one on Bova, only in the matter of style. In essence they are so much rubbish

invented by people who spend their time in vain and only serve to corrupt human morals and imprison mankind in luxury and carnal passions. (*Kratkoe rukovodstvo,* 223)

In addition to leading readers astray, novels were anathema to Russian enlighteners because of their carnivalesque tendency to denigrate even those few fine sentiments they did contain. During the special periods given over to carnival, the process of debasement was acted out by standing convention on its head: paupers were crowned king, prostitutes became the Madonna, and language unleashed its ironic and multivoiced potential. In the eighteenth-century Russian novel carnivalization is realized through the related process of recycling. The high and low of the literary world are not only inverted but also constantly juxtaposed and mixed in new and ever stranger combinations. Within the subculture folklore, carnival, manuscript literature, *lubok,* and the novel itself freely interchanged their fund of types, themes, and language. When the novel struggled to gain acceptance in the literary culture of official society, it also added the values and conventions of this milieu to its repertoire. Thus, at its inception the Russian novel comprised a witches' brew of everything from magic rings and Moroccan pirates to nobly born characters of unflinching principle and philosophical monologues on the dangers of a neglected education. This is in keeping with Bakhtin's assertion that "the novel as a whole is a phenomenon multiform in style and variform in speech and voice. In it the investigator is confronted with several heterogeneous stylistic *unities,* often located on different linguistic levels and subject to different stylistic controls" ("Discourse," 261). Given the sources that constitute its building blocks and the historical and cultural conditions that governed its development, the early Russian novel is like a hothouse experiment in heteroglossia. In its eclecticism and disregard for one authoritative, organizing principle, it rings with a multitude of frequently competing voices.

The literary impact of a carnivalesque mixing of voices in a given text depended upon the interests, talent, and circumspection of the author manipulating them. While the eclecticism of the genre was laden with the potential for mockery, the first Russian novelists did not always exploit it. For example, Emin consistently refrained from developing the comic tension inherent in a dissonance of voices. In his haste to capitalize on the popularity of a new and fashionable genre, he managed to dash off six novels in just over three years primarily by copying and integrating whatever literary models happened to be at hand. From *Inconstant Fate* to *Ernest and Doravra* Emin's preoccupation with enticing readers through the use of familiar material leaves little room for metaliterary play. With few exceptions, therefore, the forms and ideas taken from the adventure tale, folklore, and carnival do not function any differently in his fiction than sentimentalist heroines or Enlightenment philosophy do. When the titillation of enslavement in a Moroccan harem comes too close to a proposal for an ideal government, a humorous response is triggered by the blatant discrepancy in tone and content. Although such an infelicitous juxtaposition can undermine an individual monologue or impassioned meeting of lovers, however, it does not negate the serious intent of the novel as a whole. For the most part Emin's grab bag approach to literature puts his wide array of sources in the service of winning at least a measure of legitimacy for the novel.

The metaliterary possibilities inherent in the eclecticism of the subculture were only realized in the early Russian novel when the barriers separating different voices were systematically removed. The rhymed prose of *lubok*, the bawdy humor of the carnival, and characters taken from folklore do not lie dormant in the novels of Chulkov and Komarov, as they do in Emin, nor are they merely adjuncts to the West European conventions that accompany them. On the contrary, the subcultural components in their work frequently affirm a native propensity for antiauthoritarian discourse while attacking a literary outlook that subjugates the written word to the demands of utility and moralizing. Writing about Villon, Rabelais, Sorel, and Scarron, Bakhtin maintains that "we see the ground being prepared here for a radical skepticism toward any unmediated discourse and any straightforward seriousness, a skepticism bordering on rejection of the very possibility of having a straightforward discourse at all that would not be false" ("Discourse," 401). In most respects Chulkov and Komarov cannot be compared to a genius like Rabelais: they lack his broad scholarly mind, keen intellect, and stylistic originality. In a functional way, however, they can be mentioned in the same breath with the great French writer, for their fiction does harness the mocking spirit of the subculture to challenge an uncritical acceptance of the authority of the written word.

Starting with the title pages of his major works, it is obvious that Chulkov bases the operative dynamic of his oeuvre on the deliberate collision of high and low. During the period of neoclassicism Russians satisfied their taste for the literature of the Enlightenment with journals like *Idle Time Put to Use, The Industrious Bee,* and *Monthly Writings and News about Learned Affairs*. Chulkov countered the pretentious names—and goals—of these journals with works whose titles seemed whimsical if not downright heretical. *The Comely Cook, The Mocker, Both This and That,* and *The Trinket Dealer of Parnassus* are motivated by the sort of playful spirit that is implied on their covers. In *The Trinket Dealer of Parnassus,* for example, Chulkov takes on the solemn image of the man of letters in the age of neoclassicism. Irritated at what he considers inferior versifiers masquerading as bards of world renown, he stages a mock auction in which a dramatic poet is sold for one ruble, eight grivna, and a pompous lyric poet, whose work is as yet unknown to the public, goes for free. Showing, in true carnivalesque fashion, that he does not exempt even himself from such lighthearted mockery, Chulkov also adds his name to the ranks of "excess" authors (Garrard, *Čulkov*, 86–90). Whimsically auctioning off his own writings, he transforms a conventional satiric harangue into farce while at the same time challenging the Enlightenment credo of literature as the agent of social change.

Chulkov's denigration of the lofty goals and standards of official literature reaches a climax in his two major novels. Of the many characters who contribute to this assault, it is Martona, the saucy prostitute heroine of *The Comely Cook*, who leads the way. Whenever the opportunity arises to fall back on a cliché or gloss over a seamy reality with glib "literary" discourse, Martona delights in exposing the conventions that inform her genre. If the situation requires high-minded sentiment and reflection, she can always be depended upon to respond with earthy folk sayings and risqué innuendo, and to those who call for self-sacrifice and nobility of purpose, she answers that self-interest will always prevail over altruism because people are most of all concerned with saving their own skins. Given her station in life, it is no surprise that Martona espouses such an unorthodox philosophy, but even in *The Mocker*, with its lengthy chapters devoted to the fantastic adventures of epic-like heroes, Chulkov carries on the same sort of self-conscious battle against the official literary culture of his day. He openly proclaims that literature does not reflect objective, unchanging "truths," as a novelist like Emin would have us believe, but rather creates its own version of events as the need arises. Readers are invited to peer behind the scenes when the narrator promises to continue the novel "if I don't get too bored with telling stories, and the author deigns to continue with this book; but he is not yet bored, and the more he writes, the greater is his desire to continue these tales" (3:184). Moreover, throughout *The Mocker* Chulkov's narrator is unusually eager to admit what he cannot or will not do. Whether coyly refraining from certain subjects that might offend his readers' sensibilities, or holding something back because it strikes him as boring or taxes his knowledge, he emphasizes the willful and often whimsical nature of literature.[51] Viewing the world through the funhouse lenses of the carnival, *The Mocker*, like *The Comely Cook* and many other early Russian novels, consistently turns the premises of authoritarian discourse upside down.

Part

TWO

TEXTUAL ANALYSIS

THREE

APPROACHES

Historicity versus Fiction

The fundamental distinction separating the type of novels written by Emin from the carnivalesque fiction of a writer like Chulkov lies in the artists' opposing conceptions of literature. Whereas Chulkov revels in the creative freedom afforded the novelist, for Emin the genre serves first and foremost as the perfect platform for "telling the truth." For all of the often far-fetched adventures that make up the fabric of his novels, Emin consciously strove to meet the requirements of the reigning literary aesthetic. Most of all he was interested in convincing readers of the applicability of his tales to their daily lives. In the introduction to his novels as well as in the text he underscores the "real" nature of the people and events represented on the written page. Unlike the capricious and often farcical behavior of Chulkov's heroes and heroines, the virtuous and upright conduct of Emin's characters is presented as being worthy of emulation because it is generated in a world that is serious, detailed, and historically verifiable. In short, it is supposed to be believable. Emin employs several strategies, from lengthy narratives that resemble travelogues to the metacommentaries of supposedly firsthand observers, to reassure us that his novels are based on something far more solid than mere imagination. As opposed to the mind-set of the carnivalesque, which openly recognizes the value of fantasy, Emin's novelistic oeuvre emphasizes prose to the detriment of fiction.

Right from the beginning of his first novel Emin promotes the historical credibility of his writings. On the title page of *The Garden of Love, or the Insuperable Constancy of Kamber and Arisena* he informs his readers that the work has been translated from a Portuguese original. Even though Emin is in fact the author, he perpetrates this deception in order to increase the believability of his story. In mid–eighteenth-century Russia the concept of the translation functioned much like a literary seal of approval. If another culture had found this work worthwhile and if an educated translator had taken the time to render it in his own language, then its contents should amply reward the reader's investment of time and energy. In his second novel, *Inconstant Fate, or the Adventures of Miramond,* Emin takes an even more direct approach by simply proclaiming that his three-part tale is indeed true. In the first sentence of the preface he writes, "I was an eyewitness" (i) (of Miramond's numerous misfortunes) and then several pages later reiterates that "this little book includes Miramond's true adventures as well as my unfortunate travels" (iv).[1] After all is said and done nearly one thousand pages later, Emin returns to the motif that no matter how strange Miramond's travels might seem, they are all true. In a direct address to his audience he states: "Forgive me, benevolent reader, and don't think that the story of Miramond's adventures has been made up. There is no reason to wonder that he has had to endure such strange adventures. The world is the same as it always has been; it has never been without evil occurrences and it never will be" (3:353). Virtually from the first word of his novels to the last Emin consistently fosters the illusion of the realistic basis of his fiction.

Although Emin provides an excellent example of an author dedicated to the principle of historicity, he is far from unique. The eighteenth-century "Russian novel is in general well-garnished with allusions to contemporary events, appearances of personalities socially or politically celebrated and heroes participating in real wars. Historicity not only suggest[ed] authenticity, but [was] also seen as liberating the novel from the hideous thralldom of low romance" (Budgen, "Concept," 67). Perhaps the greatest example of a novel that employs factual material to elevate an inherently low subject into the realm of proper literature is Matvei Komarov's wildly successful "documentary" *Vanka Kain.* To justify the title of a "detailed and reliable history," Komarov takes great pains to outline the sources of his criminal biography. He begins in the preface by mentioning his extensive prison interview of Kain in 1755, his perusal of a "register" of Kain's deeds that appeared to be either written or dictated by the bandit himself, and several conversations with Kain's close associates (v–vii). Komarov then supports these claims in the text itself with a level of specificity rarely matched in the early Russian novel. The work starts out with a document-like recitation of Kain's early life (place and date of birth [1]), contains lists of his criminal activities that in their terseness resemble a police blotter (108–16, 134–76), and abounds throughout with references to real people and places. We are told not only that Kain haunted Moscow and its environs, but are also given the names of exact streets, gates, and monasteries where he made his headquarters. The novel is also strewn with dozens of references to actual people, from Kain's confederates (Mikhail Zaria, Kamchatka) to august representatives of the power structure (Count Chernyshev, Prince Kropotkin, and Baron Ivan Ivanovich Cherkasov). Moreover,

Komarov is particularly adept at imbuing his story with an aura of authenticity through the judicious use of footnotes. Whether it is confirming
Kain's fame by referring readers to popular songs appended to the novel
(6) or admitting that his sources are inconclusive when it comes to the correct spelling of a victim's name or the outcome of a particular crime, Komarov constantly reinforces the premise that his novel is in fact a history.

   In addition to footnotes and reflections of reality, admitting the limits of
the narrator's knowledge is another common device in the literature-as-
history ethos of the early Russian novel. When utilized in even the most
contrived situations, it implies that an event really took place. For example, when Kain ties a peasant to the shaft of a burning cart and then star-
tles the horse, readers are left with the image of the helpless victim being
carried into the distance to meet a potentially deadly fate. At this dramatic
moment in the text, however, the narrator falls silent: he cannot tell us
what happened to the peasant because his sources do not include this information (42–44). The unspoken subtext is that a novelist could supply
the ending to this episode, but the writer of a documentary must remain
faithful to the facts at hand.[2] In less dramatic fashion, but with the same
intent, Emin's narrators frequently stop short in their descriptions of a
character's state of mind. In *Constancy Rewarded, or the Adventures of Lizark
and Sarmanda* the narrator would have us believe that he is somehow giving an on-the-spot report of a meeting between the hero and heroine. He
knows they are in love, notices the furtive glance that passes between
them, but is unable to decipher its complete meaning. As he tells his readers: "Lizark threw her a glance, which, either out of a sense of propriety or
fear, without which love never exists, when it was met by the Princess, remained hidden under her lashes. I don't know what sort of effect this
glance produced in the hearts of the lovers. I only know that Izida felt remorse for the torments that Lizark had undergone, and Lizark, seeing the
Princess, rejoiced over his past sufferings" (67). Although he does not say
it, Emin's intent in this passage is quite clear. Through the device of the
reticent narrator he tries to convince us that nothing less than the limitations of historical accuracy prevent him from fully revealing the young
couple's state of mind.

   In keeping with Emin's direct exhortations to accept his novels as history and Komarov's intensive use of local detail in *Vanka Kain*, Russia's
first novelists also created an air of verisimilitude by frequently setting
their work in recognizable foreign cultures. While the geography in the
novels of Emin and Komarov might sometimes be inaccurate or even
made up, the numerous references to actual cities, countries, and natural
landmarks are no doubt included to inspire confidence in the veracity of
the text. For instance, Komarov's Milord George sets off for Italy only to
end up amid the velvet, brocade, and ivory of the sumptuous and deca-
dent court of the Moorish queen Musalmina (*Milord George,* 59–72). After
escaping the queen, George travels to Cartegena and Toledo (127–95) and
eventually ends up in Venice at carnival time (195–213). Three of Emin's

novels—*Kamber and Arisena, Inconstant Fate,* and *Lizark and Sarmanda*—make extensive use of Egypt as a backdrop for their action, and the cities of Memphis and Alexandria as well as the countries of Morocco and Algiers play prominent roles in his prose fiction. *The Marquis de Toledo (Gorestnaia Linbov' Markiza de Toledo)* is one of Emin's more peripatetic novels as it opens not far from Gibraltar in San Rocco, Spain, only to swiftly transfer its hero first to England (75–88) and then to North Africa. The geography of the Mediterranean world given in *The Marquis de Toledo* is reliable throughout the novel, and Emin's accounts of the seafaring life have a ring of authenticity about them. Despite the Marquis's larger-than-life personality, Emin's careful construction of the geographical backdrop coupled with his eye for detail encourages readers to view this novel as a plausible representation of reality.

No matter how mobile Milord George and the Marquis de Toledo might be, they come nowhere near matching the incredible adventures of Miramond and his companion Feridat in *Inconstant Fate.* In depicting the exploits of these two characters, Emin moves the action of his novel to what must be at least half of the countries of three different continents. Just about every twenty pages or so readers are invited to journey to yet another area of the globe, where they are informed about the customs, manners, and morals of its inhabitants. *Inconstant Fate* opens in Istanbul as the young Miramond is setting off for Italy to learn the ways of international politics and diplomacy (1:1–6). Before even 1 percent of this three-part novel has elapsed, however, he is shipwrecked and on the way to what seems to be an interminable string of (mis)adventures. Captured by raiders, Miramond spends some time on Malta before his freedom is purchased by an English merchant (1:14–28). In rapid succession the hapless hero finds himself in Portugal, Spain, and England before finally making his way to Cairo where he is allowed to find peace and stability, at least for a while (1:99). Before long he again takes to the seas and finds himself making a brief unscheduled stop in Algiers (1:200–210). When Miramond reaches the fictitious kingdom of Zhirie (1:210–11), his travels in part 1 are mercifully brought to a close, but then in part 2 they are surpassed by Feridat's impressive adventures. In the more than two hundred pages it takes Feridat to recount his life story, he introduces readers to dozens of identifiable geographical locations scattered throughout the Middle East, Europe, and Asia.[3] In part 3 no one figure can match the arduous journeys undertaken by Miramond and Feridat, yet various characters manage to bring such locales as Ligorno, Albania, Montenegro, Bulgaria, America, Sicily, and the Holy Land into their narratives. By the time Emin is finished, *Inconstant Fate* reads like a roll call of the states and natural landmarks that would be part of an educated Russian's consciousness, a ploy no doubt intended to impart an air of authenticity to the novel.

If it were limited to the recitation of toponyms, Emin's use of geography would sound rather hollow. What makes this approach work as an effective means of creating the illusion of historicity is the erudition of his narrators. In all six of Emin's novels they are more than willing to enlighten readers about the nuances of virtually any setting, no matter where their characters might happen to be. A good example of this technique is provided by the narrator of *Inconstant Fate*, who seems to know just about everything concerning the numerous lands his heroes travel in. Among many other colorful insights, he explains the shipboard treatment for near-drowning victims (1:13; they are rolled inside a barrel), unmasks the origin of the famed Maltese falcon (1:15), and describes the organizational structure of the Jesuit order (1:61). He also comments on Egyptian wedding and funeral processions (1:159–60), notes that in the Islamic world it is considered a mark of great respect to lower one's eyes when speaking with someone of superior social status (2:107–8), and even expounds on the culinary habits of the Moors (2:185–86). When Emin deems it appropriate, such brief commentary is often expanded into full-blown sociological analysis. As Miramond enters Cairo for the first time, the narrator takes sixteen pages to introduce this exotic city (1:100–116). Beginning with the importance of the ebb and flow of the Nile, he vividly describes such topics as the climate, social structure, military training, agriculture, modes of transportation, and most important of all, the politics and internecine strife of this paradise-like metropolis. Without exaggeration, it is fair to say that Emin temporarily suspends the progress of the narrative and transforms it into a documentary or travelogue. As proof of the importance of this technique in developing an atmosphere of historicity, Emin returns to it many times during the course of the three volumes that make up *Inconstant Fate*. As he comments on everything from the physical charm of Turin ("the flower of Italy"; 2:247) to the magnificent factories of Paris (2:292), the narrator continually instills readers with confidence in the historical value of his tale.[4]

Besides making extensive use of distant locales and foreign cultures in his prose fiction, Emin himself figures into one of the most interesting episodes of historicity in the early Russian novel. Midway through Komarov's *Milord George* the narrative is interrupted so that a young traveler named Martsemiris may recite his turbulent life story. Even though this sort of interpolated tale is common in eighteenth-century Russian novels, it still obtrudes in the text, for its opening scenes are nothing more than a thinly veiled biography of Russia's most popular author of the 1760s (83–89). Like Emin, Martsemiris is an orphan who grows up among the Turks and enters the sultan's service, first as a counselor and later as a military leader. The sultan promotes Martsemiris to the rank of vizier after an impressive victory over the Romans, but his fortunes change dramatically when his Janissaries are routed in a battle against the Persians. Fearing the sultan's wrath and cursing "inconstant fate" (86; the title of Emin's "autobiographical" novel), Martsemiris abandons his post in order to secure his future elsewhere. Much like Emin, he has the intuition that he is actually Christian and so he makes his way to Europe (88), where the rest of his tale unfolds. Notwithstanding the fantasy that colors the later parts of Mart-semiris's story, Komarov adds an element of historicity to *Milord George* by exploiting Emin's many attempts to establish the veracity of his colorful biography.

As opposed to the preeminent position accorded truth, authority, and incontrovertible facts in Emin's prose fiction, a novel like *The Comely Cook* is based on the concepts of constant change and comic reversal. In the first, or prose, preface to this work Chulkov emphasizes that we should not take life too seriously. No matter how hard you try or how earnest you might be, you always end up just where you began: "A human being is born into this world in order to behold glory, honor, and wealth, to taste joy and pleasure, to experience misfortune, grief, and sadness" (157) and eventu-ally to die. Applying this "from-nothing-to-nothing" approach to his own writing, Chulkov admits that in time it will seem just as though *The Comely Cook* never existed: "This book has come into the world so that it will re-ceive some shadow of praise, controversy, criticism, indignation, and abuse. All this will come true, and in the end it will be transformed into dust, just as the person who either praised or defamed it" (157–58). In Chulkov's view of the world there are no lasting values, and anything that might be considered serious, "true," or "real" is just grist for the mill. In his carnivalesque fiction the character who enjoys riches one day is a pauper the next, and the most sacred of principles can be overturned in the blink of an eye to secure personal gain. Mirroring the unfinished and facetious na-ture of the carnival, Chulkov's novel envisions life as a constant—and hu-morous—state of flux.

Chulkov's carnivalesque approach to life leads him to a relativistic ap-preciation of the written word. Whereas Emin would have us believe that words should be placed in the unwavering service of truth, Chulkov ac-knowledges their creative potential. In the opening paragraph of the prose preface to *The Comely Cook* Chulkov admits that he is more interested in the aesthetic appeal of words than in their ability to convey a particular mean-ing or re-create an edifying event. Referring to his anonymous dedication of the novel, he declares that "the title of 'Excellency' adorns a human being, and for that reason I used it for the embellishment of my book; however, I didn't want to color it with excellence, but just with the letters from which this word has been culled" (157). In the story itself Chulkov's heroine Mar-tona also reveals a ready appreciation for the flexibility of verbal expres-sion. While living as the kept woman of a retired septuagenarian colonel, she uses a ruse to pass off her young lover Akhal´ as her sister. The colonel accepts the story, but is a bit perplexed: Why had Martona never before mentioned that she had a sibling? Just like a carnival comic, Martona con-cocts such a story that before long she has the old man's head spinning. She gleefully notes, "I told him so well about my family that neither he nor I was actually able to make out just what my origins were" (173). Not satis-fied with this subterfuge, Martona uses her verbal dexterity to turn the tables on the colonel. Instead of letting him worry about this unexpected visit, she teases that *she* is really the one who ought to be jealous. After all, her sister is a beautiful young woman, and she warns, "I am afraid that you will be seduced by her and throw me over" (173). By putting her aged lover on the defensive, she not only squelches any suspicions he might have, but also manages to validate the "truthfulness" of her contrived story. In Chulkov's world truth is at the service of the glibbest tongue.[5]

Whereas Emin contrives situations (a document is found, a world-weary traveler recites his story, an eyewitness corroborates events) in order to create an aura of historicity in his novels, Chulkov has no qualms admitting that his fiction is simply contrived. *The Mocker* in particular is full of metaliterary commentary, from ruminations on the author's intent to the narrator's constant reminders that he must temporarily stop the story because his auditors are falling asleep. When the monk, who is the second narrator in the novel, begins his lengthy *Tale of the Taffeta Beauty Patch*, the creative foundation of the novel is completely laid bare. Just as Neokh, the hero of the tale, is about to embark on what seems to be a promising adventure, the narrator interrupts to inform us the following story has little to do with actual people or events. He openly proclaims that Neokh is "a character in this novel, which the writer has considered to be in his best interest to write. Neokh is now completely in his power, and he will order him about just as though he were his slave" (3:169). Responding to an Emin-like approach to writing, the narrator says that a novelist can make of the hero whatever he wants, no matter how strange a figure he might create:

> If it pleases him, he will give him a scepter and place him on a throne. Having deposed him from the throne, he will throw him in prison, give him a lover and then take her away, change his appearance, and even send him above the clouds toward the sun. If, however, he loses his mind, as is the custom with novel writers, he will then turn the earth upside down and make of his hero some sort of mythical god, because anything is possible with a novelist. (3:170)

Even though the anonymous monk quickly interjects (duplicitously as it turns out) that he "will continue [his] story without any extravagant embellishments" (3:170), Chulkov's message is clear. Like the improbable novels alluded to above, *The Mocker* is ultimately under the authority of a writer. Neokh's serpentine adventures confirm time and again that Chulkov may do as he pleases with his characters. Chaotic though they may be, Neokh's escapades are every bit as significant as the travels of a Miramond or a Marquis de Toledo; the only difference is that their import is literary rather than social or political.

Toward the end of part 3 of *The Mocker* Chulkov pointedly ridicules the idea that an author is nothing more than a scribe armed with historical hindsight. As he laughingly demonstrates, it is just the other way around: authors have the gift of clairvoyance. With the aid of a wily peasant Neokh makes his escape from a life-threatening situation (3:230). Now out of danger, Chulkov's hero has the entire world at his disposal. Where will he go, and what will he do? The narrator will not say exactly, but he does assure us that whatever happens to Neokh, he will tell us everything down to the most minute detail. In what seems to be a none too veiled dig at the Feridat persona of Emin's *Inconstant Fate*, he says, "As far as Neokh is concerned, even though I didn't follow him around, I still know his every intention and what will happen to him in the future. Although these words aren't a riddle, there is something about them that, to tell the truth, even I myself don't understand" (3:230–31). True to his word, the narrator follows this pronouncement with a detailed outline of the adventures that await Neokh in the last two parts of the novel. How could the monk know Neokh's movements, much less his intentions, without actually accompanying him on his journeys? No matter how unsophisticated Chulkov's readers might have been, they should have had no trouble understanding that eighteenth-century Russia's premier literary jester made up everything, right down to the wayward student's very thoughts.

Whatever tactical purpose Chulkov's metaliterary comments serve in their specific contexts, they all support an approach to literature that emphasizes process over product. As opposed to an author like Emin, who constantly indulges his urge to sum up a situation and draw a lesson from it, Chulkov has little interest in enlightening us about distant lands or sophisticated moral and social philosophies. Throughout lengthy novels like *Inconstant Fate* and *Ernest and Doravra* Emin bombards readers with literally hundreds of conclusions, from the observation that the Christian Maltese are far crueler than the Moslem Turks to the solemn justification for awarding all government positions solely on the basis of merit. Chulkov, on the other hand, is interested in just one thing: maintaining the entertainment value of his text. Episodes do not have to be realistic or even make a lot of sense as long as they give the readers what they want. This is the literary motivation for the anonymous monk to abruptly end a chapter when one of Neokh's drunken revels gets out of hand. He has no objection to the drinking, dancing, and promiscuous sex in the scene; he is only worried that the participants might kill themselves in their overindulgence and thus bring the story to a premature end (*Mocker*, 3:163–64). In an even more direct treatment of this theme Chulkov uses the preface to part 3 to discourage readers from seeking any sort of closure in the novel. Without apology, he gets right to the point by simply stating: "In this part I didn't write an end to the evenings, because it seemed to me that such superfluous and unnecessary material would take up valuable space" (3:i). In the self-effacing style reminiscent of the narrator of *Gargantua and Pantagruel* Chulkov openly announces a freewheeling approach to novel writing that attributes little value to the notion of completion.

In addition to delaying the denouement of a story line for as long as possible, Chulkov was so focused on enjoying the literary process itself that on several occasions he simply gave up altogether trying to bring a work to a close. Textual evidence suggests that he probably never intended to write a second part to *The Comely Cook* despite labeling the extant version part 1 (Levitsky, 109), and there is a twenty-year hiatus between the last two parts of *The Mocker* even though we are promised on the next-to-last page of part 4 that "the fifth part follows on the heels of this one and will soon make its appearance" (4:249).[6] This sort of literary jesting also lies at the heart of *The Tale of the Taffeta Beauty Patch,* which begins in part 3 of *The Mocker,* is continued in part 4, and concludes, if that is the right word, in part 5. In true Chulkovian style the monk who narrates this tale makes almost no effort to enlighten us regarding the issue raised in its title. He begins by facetiously maintaining that those people who have compiled a register of beauty spots have provided a greater service to society than such illustrious thinkers as Aesop, Homer, and Virgil (*Mocker,* 3:151). At first denigrating his talents, he agrees to undertake the task of explaining the genesis of the beauty patch, but then does nothing of the sort. Instead, he introduces the destitute student Neokh and recounts several of his often risqué escapades (vol. 3, evenings 46 and 47). Finally, in evening 48 the monk promises that "it's high time I got to my real task and show that which is the essence of my tale" (3:167). Fortunately, what the monk considers the goal of his story has absolutely nothing to do with its title. Through the remaining eight evenings of part 3 (167–236) the monk concentrates on Neokh's entanglements, and not one word is mentioned about any beauty spot whatsoever. Part 4 presents more of the same as over the course of ten evenings and more than eighty pages the monk refuses to say anything even remotely enlightening about the origin of his supposed subject. Most of his time is dedicated to following Neokh on his bawdy and often illegal adventures, with several chapter-long digressions thrown in to mislead readers even further.[7]

In the final part of *The Mocker* the monk continues *The Tale of the Taffeta Beauty Patch* with the promise that he will now explain the mystery he first brought to our attention so many evenings (and years) ago (5:156). Despite this assurance we are still led through an elaborate set of events in which Neokh falls in love with a mysterious woman during a nocturnal tête-à-tête (5:170–73). After they part, he desperately wishes to know the identity of his lover, whose face he could not make out in the dark, so during their next rendezvous he leaves an indelible spot on her cheek by touching it with a hell stone. When all the women of the kingdom are invited to a ball, Neokh's anonymous lover decides to conceal the unsightly mark left by the hell stone with a piece of taffeta, and in no time at all the well-born ladies of the kingdom are emulating her fashion ingenuity (5:182–84). Finally, after twenty-two evenings and about 190 pages, the monk clues us in on the origin of the taffeta beauty patch. Of course, when we get to it, we realize that this rather hollow ending has absolutely nothing to do with the many colorful escapades the monk has recited for our enjoyment. The most delightful aspect of *The Tale of the Taffeta Beauty Patch* is not to be found in the promised revelation of the origins of the object in question, but rather in the circuitous manner in which readers are brought to this "conclusion." Much like the garrulous Tristram Shandy, Chulkov revels in not taking the straight line to any destination. Since he is never in a hurry to reach a particular goal, tidy endings and informative interludes are usually the furthest thing from his mind.[8]

Appropriately enough, Chulkov saves his most complex and efficient subversion of the concept of closure for his final novel, *The Comely Cook*. In the last few pages of this work there is, at least at first glance, a proper settling of accounts wherein evildoers are punished and a hardworking, though decidedly far from virtuous, heroine is rewarded. On the one hand, the deceitful Akhal', who abandoned Martona to the authorities for a crime they both committed and then tried to kill her lover Svidal' in a duel, lies at death's door after poisoning himself. On the other, Martona, who began the novel as one of society's castoffs, has succeeded beyond her wildest dreams. Having worked long and hard for love and financial security, she now has both: a penitent Akhal' wills his estate to her, and the handsome Svidal' has become her dedicated paramour. Even though Chulkov never issued a part 2 to *The Comely Cook*, the body of work he called part 1 would appear to stand complete. Or so it seems until we take a closer look.[9]

When viewed from the perspective of the carnivalesque, the ending of *The Comely Cook* actually parodies the attempt to neatly tie up something as complex as a novel. Virtually without exception, the "conclusions" to be reached in this work are all somewhat skewed, either morally or logically. For instance, Martona does triumph over society by becoming a landowner, but she achieves this station in life through foul means rather than fair: no doubt the estate bequeathed to her by Akhal' includes the property the pair swindled from the septuagenarian colonel who once served as Martona's sugar daddy. Turning from rewards to retribution, Akhal''s attempted suicide is also morally unjustified, for he certainly does not deserve to die for a murder that never took place. (Unbeknownst to Akhal', Svidal' survived the duel unscathed.) Moreover, there is no way we can be certain that Martona will ever have the opportunity to enjoy her newfound wealth. Given the number of times she has been catapulted from the nadir of despair to the summit of happiness and back again, chances are she will lose everything and be forced to begin anew in a different town and most likely with a different lover. After all, Akhal' is not dead; he may recover and recant the will that has transferred all his earthly possessions to the woman who both betrayed and deceived him. Then again, how can we be sure that the entire spectacle is not a setup? The use of poison and Akhal''s crazed behavior strongly recall an earlier staged assassination that ended happily for the supposed victim.[10] Has Akhal' planned the entire affair in order to draw out Svidal' and have his revenge on Martona? We will never know the answer to this question, but finding one is really beside the point. The true purpose of the ending of *The Comely Cook* is to cast just such doubts in the reader's mind and to forestall any attempt to obscure the narrative richness of this work by summing it up with a glib didactic platitude.

In every one of Emin's novels geography and foreign culture are called upon to create an illusion of historicity. Although references to foreign lands also crop up in novels infused with the ethos of the carnival, they function in a completely different manner. Instead of creating a solid "factual" foundation for the text, they serve as a form of literary name dropping. Distant locales inserted into a work without even the slightest attempt to "bring them to life" are exploited merely for the aura of exoticism they impart. Whereas Emin attempts to enlighten readers as to the social, political, and cultural bases of a given region, Chulkov and Komarov use foreign culture mainly as a key word for mystery and adventure. For example, the action of *Milord George* opens in England, but as far as readers can tell from the complete absence of any particularizing detail, the story could be set almost anywhere. Later in the novel Komarov's reticence remains intact as he sends his heroes to Sardinia, Holland, and Italy. Martsemiris lives in The Hague for four years (113–19), and Ferdinald resides in Genoa for three years (137–60), yet for all intents and purposes their stories could be set in Moscow or Kiev without changing anything besides the names of the cities involved. In his last novel, *Nevidimka*, Komarov expands his horizons by referring to Morocco, Babylon, India, and Persia. Once more, however, readers never learn a thing about the manners, morals, or milieu of the people inhabiting these areas. Functioning much like chapter headings, these place names merely cue readers to expect a precipitous and exciting change in the action.

A carnivalesque disregard for historicism is also underscored by the inconsistent, and even contradictory, way in which time and place are utilized in the novels of Chulkov and Komarov. *Milord George* begins with the explanatory note that it is set "in times gone by when all the peoples of Europe had still not accepted the Christian faith and several of them lived in legendary pagan idolatry" (1). As though confirming this statement, George soon meets a woman, the margravine of Brandenburg, whose title existed as early as the mid–twelfth century (*Brockhaus,* 607), a time when isolated pockets of Europe had still not been converted to Christianity. Later in the novel this chronology is completely undermined when Martsemiris recounts his adventures in Istanbul (88). Given that the Turks did not conquer this city, the former Constantinople, until 1453, the adventures of Milord George, Martsemiris, and Friderika Louisa do indeed take place in a thoroughly, if at times reluctantly, Christianized Europe.[11] Most Russian readers of the 1780s would have been aware of this discrepancy, so it seems obvious that Komarov was not trying to impress anyone with his knowledge of foreign culture. On the other hand, moving the action to Brandenburg or Istanbul would be acknowledged as the provocation for further danger, disappointment, and misadventure—in other words, the basis of a captivating story. This motivation no doubt also underlies the inconsistencies in the fictional world of *Nevidimka*. As the novel opens, we are told that Fets is a kingdom whose capital is the city of Vigo (1–2), yet toward the end of the story Fets suddenly becomes the capital of Morocco (240). This confusion is compounded by the apparently impossible actions of the two heroes of the novel, Arides and Polumedes, who flee Fets by boat only to take shelter by landing in another city that is also called Fets (261–62). Whatever the problem is here, one thing is certain: unlike Emin, Komarov is not at all concerned with objectively depicting the geography of the Mediterranean world. Any city, country, or region will fit his purposes since his goal is to entertain rather than convey "the truth." Even Swift's fictional land of Lilliput serves as the setting for several episodes in *Nevidimka*, which attests to the preeminence of the literary over the historical in Komarov's work.[12]

If the use of time and place in Komarov's novels can be described as outlandish and chaotic, critics would like to think that Chulkov's final attempt at the genre incorporates these elements in a much more rational manner. More than for any other early Russian novel, the critical literature devoted to *The Comely Cook* stresses the "historical context" and concrete, often gritty details that supposedly form the foundation of this work. Echoing the rhetoric Belinskii's school used to describe the literature of the 1840s, I. Z. Serman writes that "Chulkov does not try to subject Martona's life experiences to any sort of moral law; he sees as his goal only the truthful exposition of his heroine's actions. Depicting life 'as it is,' Chulkov, like Defoe *(Moll Flanders)* and Lesage *(Gil Blas)*, is the creator of the novel of everyday life" (Moiseeva and Serman, 59).[13] Taking the same approach, Garrard asserts that "Chulkov has managed to create a viable fictional world; he persuades the reader of its reality, or at least of the possibility that it could exist" ("Narrative Technique," 558). He points out that Chulkov's second novel clearly eschews the use of magic, separate tones, and interpolated stories that defines *The Mocker (Čulkov, 138–41)* and surveys the great number of specific details that create an aura of reality in the novel. *The Comely Cook* takes place in definite Russian locales (Poltava, Kiev, Moscow), establishes a reliable time frame (Martona is nineteen when she is widowed in 1709), and constantly seeks to fix credible spatial relationships (six versts separate Sveton's house from the house of his brother's friend) (*Čulkov*, 118–20).[14] Martona's no-nonsense approach to life, her aversion to covering up its seamy realities with an avalanche of high-sounding rhetoric, and the high degree of specificity found in her narration are consistently underscored as some of the first Russian reflections of a "realistic" approach to literature.[15]

Despite the consensus regarding the realism of Chulkov's literary technique, *The Comely Cook* is not much more historically sound than *The Mocker*, or even Komarov's *Nevidimka*. In a groundbreaking study Alexander Levitsky correctly asserts that any attempt to find realism, morality, or extraliterary significance in the novel is bound to come up short for it would be "incommensurate with Chulkov's own views and with the explicit meaning of the text itself" (97). If some sort of "Russian reality" does form the backdrop of this story, it is riddled with a series of glaring anomalies. For example, being one of the small number of people who constituted the bourgeoisie in eighteenth-century Russia, Martona is far from representative of society as a whole, and even within these narrow confines the melodrama she calls life with a host of hopeful suitors seems anything but genuine. Concerning this aspect of the novel, Levitsky writes that "it was hardly likely in early Petrine Russia that prostitutes should call their lovers Adonis, 'my Mercury' or 'my Jupiter,' or fight duels over them with unloaded guns; nor were the inhabitants of Russia ever commonly named Sveton, Akhal', Svidal', Oral or even Martona" (101). Moreover, even though the tale is supposedly anchored in time by a reference to the battle of Poltava, Levitsky notes that certain other "facts" undermine any attempt to establish a reliable chronology. At one point in the story Martona maintains that she heard someone recite one of Lomonosov's odes in the year 1709. Unfortunately for the cause of historical accuracy, this would have been impossible since Lomonosov was not even born until 1711! From evidence in the text it becomes apparent that the scattered details of time and space in *The Comely Cook* are not milestones on the way to a new literary movement, but rather the misdirections of a jester whose agenda is literary rather than social or political.

Although a less than reverent treatment of the coordinates of reality is common in the early Russian novel, the strongest counterbalance to the principle of historicity is provided by an extensive use of fantasy. Excluding *The Comely Cook* and *Vanka Kain*, the novels of Chulkov and Komarov abound with mysterious temples, visions of paradise and the underworld, and the chicanery of wizards, genies, and various enchanted creatures. In the extreme case of *Nevidimka*, Komarov's self-proclaimed string of fairy tales, paranormal phenomena even serve as the very raison d'être of the work. The basic premise and motivation of this novel come from the folkloric legend of the *shapka-nevidimka*. This special cap, which is given to Arides by a snake that transforms itself into a beautiful sorceress (8–13), makes its wearer invisible, and, in the context of the novel, sets the stage for several humorous tricks and cliff-hanging adventures. Later in the story, when the *shapka-nevidimka* has no active role to play, fantasy continues to shape the course of events. In the interpolated tale of Abdel Dimers, for instance, readers are confronted by flying horses, disappearing magicians, and a magic tablecloth that, when opened, proffers a sumptuous meal to its owner (124–77). Although *Milord George* is more restrained in its recourse to the irrational, magic is also essential to the unfolding of this narrative. The title character's quest to regain the love of Friderika Louisa begins when he loses his way, stumbles into an enchanted forest (5–10), and then is forced to take the eighteenth-century equivalent of truth serum (46–47). Echoing George's plight, the young wanderer Martsemiris finds that the occult, enchanting though it may be, wreaks havoc with his life, too. He acquires a wondrous flute whose music causes fountains to flow, birds to sing, and fruit to fall from the trees (95), yet the major impediment to his happiness is an evil spirit who enslaves his wife and can only be controlled with the aid of a special ring (96–122). By virtue of such frequent manifestations of fantasy, works like *Milord George* and *Nevidimka* openly acknowledge that imagination and creativity, rather than historical observation, lie at the heart of the carnivalesque novel.

Whereas Komarov almost unconsciously scatters reflections of the supernatural throughout his novels, Chulkov's predilection in *The Mocker* is for lengthy passages describing utopias, the nether regions of the universe, and the abodes of gods and goddesses. Like a magical mystery tour of sights, sounds, and actions, these interludes function as the perfect antithesis to the documentary style of a work like *Inconstant Fate*. As opposed to Emin, who finds it edifying to expostulate on the social, economic, and political structure of Cairo, Chulkov is far more fascinated by the splendors of a procession of divine beings. In part 3 of *The Mocker* King Alim sneaks into a hidden grotto and spies on an incredible parade of mythological creatures (3:26–38). Tritons, naiads, and sea horses precede Neptune into an amphitheater, and he is followed by Saturn; incarnations of the seasons, natural elements, and continents; the nine Muses; a host of minor gods; and finally the King of Olympus, Jupiter himself. The emphasis here is not on enlightenment, nor even on reinforcing our knowledge of classical mythology. To the contrary, this fourteen-page passage is inserted as a colorful distraction to keep our interest from flagging during the more serious parts of *The Mocker*. Functioning as an ideal reader of the novel, Alim confesses that "all the magnificence that I had seen did not reduce my curiosity, but rather led it to new heights" (3:39).

Of all the passages that make significant use of fantasy in Chulkov's oeuvre, the most striking one describes Siloslav's visit to what can only be viewed as a vision of paradise (*Mocker*, 2:66–99). Stunned by a mysterious cloud while on the field of battle, the heroic knight awakens to find himself in a garden of earthly delights. A pond of bubbling mercury, trees that burst into flame to light his way, and statues holding pots of aromatic herbs introduce Siloslav to temples of marble, crystal, and gold that contain vaults of the stars, a throne brighter than the sun, and pictures that float in the air. And this is just the beginning. Siloslav is taken to a mountain of ivory, a valley of peace and harmony, and a temple that is adorned with "living" emerald statues. To make this astonishing visit complete, he is finally conducted to the temple of Lada, the Slavic goddess of love: "Siloslav . . . entered the temple and found that, devoid of anything earthly, only a heavenly beauty resided there. In the middle of the temple the naked goddess Lada, clothed only in a mysterious belt woven with astonishing mastery, sat on what appeared to be a transparent white cloud resting on an elevated, crimson-colored throne" (2:92). As Siloslav wanders through this mysterious and enchanted world, there is little attempt to make sense of what he sees. He simply passes by most of these fantastic sights without comment, and the narrator rarely interrupts to interpret the significance of the passage. The most incredible images float by for page after page without any apparent rhyme or reason, and their succession is too disordered to form any sort of symbolic system or allegory. About the only direction that is given in the entire passage comes from the narrator when he says: "Everything played for and tried to comfort Siloslav" (2:71). No doubt these words apply as well to Chulkov's readers, who are both overwhelmed and delighted by the sensory overload contained in the fantastic episodes interspersed throughout *The Mocker*.

Even when Chulkov's fanciful descriptions focus on the darker side of life, they still function as a carnivalesque antidote to the windy documentary passages so common in Emin. For example, Siloslav's adventures continue when he is guided into a second valley that must surely represent the environs of hell (2:96–98).[16] While ostensibly serving as a warning of the harsh punishment awaiting evildoers in the afterlife, this segment eschews outright moralizing in favor of compiling a series of striking images. Readers follow Siloslav through an ice-covered, smoke-filled valley that is perpetually shrouded in winter. Zombielike creatures stalk this depressing landscape, and broken skulls, bones, and weaponry are scattered about. The valley is guarded by a grotesque giant who with his bloody mouth, poison-dripping tongue, and snake-infested head seems to be lifted straight out of the author's worst nightmare. As incredible as these images are, however, they do not provoke a fearful reaction. Instead, they are somehow beautifully and alluringly distant: there are no cries for mercy here, and we never actually see anyone suffering.[17]

The same sort of reaction is provoked later in the novel when the archvillain Askalon is guided through the underworld by Satan's surrogate, Gomalis (4:22–31). A nonstop compilation of grotesqueries, the nightmare world revealed to Askalon is more breathtaking than it is terrifying. Gomalis appears in fluid form—expanding, contracting, and changing shape at will—and then accompanies Askalon to an interminably long underground chamber built of marble, crystal, and sparkling precious stones. Within this hall Askalon finds an assortment of distorted human beings: some have the heads of animals, others one leg and many arms, and still others have eyes upon their chests, to mention just a few of the oddities he observes. Overcome by the sumptuous and grotesque surroundings, Askalon is forced to admit: "I am seeing things that in my entire life it has been impossible to see and that are even beyond my ability to imagine" (4:26). Virtually the same words are repeated many times over in *The Mocker* by many different characters, and the conventionality of such a response hints at Chulkov's larger goal with respect to his readers. In a clear example of the text guiding the way to its interpretation, the narrator notes that while in the middle of this subterranean wonderland, "Askalon became dumbfounded, and instead of a great fear an even greater sense of wonder took hold of him. In fact, he was so astonished that he was forced to come to a stop" (4:25–26). Leaving overt moralizing and dusty documentaries to writers like Emin, Chulkov appeals to those readers who are more interested in exercising their sense of wonder than adding to their knowledge of the world. As a true representative of the subculture, he shows that entertainment, rather than authority and truth, lies at the heart of his literary aesthetic.

Chapter

FOUR

THE LIMITATIONS AND POSSIBILITIES
OF VOICE AND RHETORIC

VOICE: AUTHORITARIAN CONTROL VERSUS BENIGN NEGLECT

With their opposing conceptions of the nature and goals of literature Emin
and Chulkov differ greatly in the way they control the reception of their
novels. Both writers employ energetic narrators and loquacious characters
to serve as their voice in the text, yet their ways of handling this aspect of
the novelist's art could not be further apart. Serious to the point of being
austere, Emin's authorial surrogates never overlook an opportunity to in-
doctrinate readers. From grandiose schemes of running a state or establishing the most effective system of education to the rigorous demands of leading a virtuous life, they never tire of making unequivocal moral judgments
in the self-assured tone of a teacher lecturing pupils. With the aid of such
figures Emin manages to touch on just about every important topic on the
Enlightenment agenda of eighteenth-century Russia over the course of his
six novels. In contrast, Chulkov's narrators take a laissez-faire approach to
their work. Although Martona and the anonymous monk of *The Mocker* also
frequently stop to analyze their stories for readers, their advice parodies the
learned and moral eloquence of their equivalents in Emin's oeuvre. With
absolutely no interest in making readers well-informed, morally sound sons
and daughters of the fatherland, they simply choose to overlook illicit behavior and frequently even encourage it. They pay little if any heed to rules
and moral judgments and view life as a freewheeling carnival that is to be
exploited for one's personal benefit and pleasure.

The ease with which Emin lectures readers on a variety of topics is
based upon the supposed knowledge of his surrogates in the text. From

traditional third-person narrators, to "epistolary narrators" like Ernest, to the image of author proffered in the prefaces to his novels, Emin endows virtually every authority figure with an understanding and experience of the world that is well beyond the ordinary. Emin sounds this theme in the preface to *Themistocles* when he compares himself to the great philosopher and teacher Plato. With feigned humility he declares: "I do not wish nor am I able to present myself to the world as a learned man; however, I must confess that over the years I have studied many subjects . . . in order that I might communicate my thoughts to the public" (xii–xiii). Common throughout Emin's prose fiction, the motif of the experienced observer of the world who wishes to share his knowledge for the benefit of humankind reaches its high point in his last novel, *Ernest and Doravra*. In the very first letter that he writes to Doravra, Ernest flatly states that he is a philosopher. Fate has been unkind to this noble-minded soul, and as a result of reflecting on the inequities in the world, he has been forced to adopt a philosophical attitude toward life (1:3). This bald statement is borne out by almost nine hundred pages of ruminations on every topic imaginable, from the public to the personal and from the sublime to the mundane. By part 3 the novel takes on the appearance of a philosophical tract: from the short, personal notes that dominate early in the work, the letters in the third part are routinely twenty, thirty, and even sixty pages long.[1] In addition to their encyclopedic treatment of the human condition, these letters also come with their own justification. As Ernest begins to withdraw from society, his friend Hippolyte encourages him to continue to contribute to it. After all, he asks, "Why have you studied the sciences? Why have you traveled so much? Certainly for no other reason than to be enlightened" (3:82–83). No matter which way they turn in this novel, readers are assured that Ernest's reflections are intellectually sound and worthy of emulation.[2]

Throughout Emin's six novels authorial surrogates are often called upon to bring their experience and erudition to bear on the problem of everyday morality. Without mincing words, they take every opportunity to reveal the workings of the world and guide readers along the difficult path of virtue. As with many aspects of Emin's art, the most explicit articulation of this philosophy occurs in *Ernest and Doravra*. In the preface the author proclaims that his goal is to teach young women how "to love virtuously, discern the faithfulness of their lovers, and know their dispositions so that, having joined with them, they may live together happily" (1:ii). Within the text itself Emin quickly pronounces this strategy a success through the character of Doravra. After just one letter from Ernest she confesses that "the description of your life is full of didactic arguments that reveal your intelligence, and for that reason I have read your letter two or three times" (1:7). Virtually every time he puts pen to paper in the four volumes of the novel, Ernest never fails to live up to this early promise as he harangues his correspondents on any number of topics dealing with ethics. In one letter he expounds at length on the need to punish evil (3:20–54), in another he evaluates the merits and liabilities of the major human emotions (3:126–44),

and in a third he rails against the bankruptcy of high society and court life
(3:156–73). Living by the maxim that there never was a topic that did not
deserve his attention, Ernest must be one of the most opinionated and un-
compromising figures in all of modern Russian literature.

As the narrator's closing comments in *Lizark and Sarmanda* clearly reveal,
the role of moral sentinel is so important in Emin's fiction that even unam-
biguously virtuous conduct must be thoroughly analyzed in order to avert
heterodox interpretations. Although the novel's heroine, the spotless Sarmanda, suffers many indignities (among other things, she is nearly raped,
drowned, and unjustly executed), she remains faithful to her idol Lizark,
eventually marries him, and then deservedly lives in "complete happiness"
for the rest of her days. Drawing what he considers the appropriate lesson
to be gleaned from Sarmanda's story, the narrator quickly proclaims that
her unflagging "love and tenderness can serve as an example for inconstant
hearts" (271). Just in case readers are not quite convinced of this assertion
by the events that have unfolded in the novel, Emin reinforces his message
with a source whose authority is on a much surer footing: the Bible. The
narrator likens Sarmanda's fate to the fable of the ancient Israelite who
served one master for fourteen years solely in order to win his daughter's
hand. Posing the question: "Is it possible to find vice in such a love?" he
immediately provides the answer and in effect puts words in the reader's
mouth. He confidently maintains that "we today are obligated to honor
[such fidelity]" and then closes the novel with the phrase: "To love that to
which we are drawn is a law of nature, but love ought to depend on prudence and constancy" (271). Forever playing the role of teacher, the narrators in Emin's novels guard the integrity of their texts right down to the final period.

Despite his carnivalesque orientation toward literature, upon occasion
Chulkov also makes use of an authoritative narrative voice. In *The Mocker*,
for example, Ladon indulges in the same sort of didactic commentary that
is Emin's stock in trade. He freely trumpets such platitudes as "misery
loves company" (4:57–58), assures us that misfortune inflicted upon the innocent can melt even the most bestial heart (3:3), and expostulates on the
dangers of forgetting the lessons of former misfortunes (3:124–25). As the
narrator of the more serious stories in the collection he also comes armed
with a satirical, rapier-like wit. In the opening pages of part 1 he offers caricatures of the pompous officer (14), the greedy priest (20), and the coquette,
a type he sardonically labels "the eighth wonder of the world" (50). Even
for the free-spirited and fun-loving Martona, the heroine of Chulkov's last
novel, there are limits that can be transgressed. Although she condones infidelity, lying, and greed, she finds corruption and hypocrisy to be repug-
nant. While working as a cook in the home of a Muscovite bureaucrat, Martona becomes familiar with the secretary's less than honest behavior. She
notes that he is a religious zealot who "did not go to bed without praying
to God, read aloud the appropriate prayers and washed his hands before
lunch and dinner, never missed a Sabbath, and always attended mass"

(*Comely Cook*, 165). In spite of this apparent religiosity, the secretary never fails to receive petitioners on church holidays, and when he happens to be praying, he lets his wife take over for him (165). Martona wryly remarks that the secretary judged all petitions according to the size of the bribe accompanying them and that his wife's fondness for spending the entire day drunk held no appeal for her (166). When she is forced out of the secretary's home, it is as though Martona were leaving an eighteenth-century version of Sodom and Gomorrah: she never looks back (167). Given that she finds redeeming value in virtually every sort of questionable character, from a conniving servant to the madam of a bordello, this is perhaps the most cutting commentary of all.[3]

Of all the self-confident pronouncements in the early Russian novel, none are made on a grander scale than those pertaining to civil administration. Operating within a fictional world that is animated by clear-cut lines of authority, Emin's surrogates in the text constantly reinforce the notion that hierarchies and order are the essential prerequisites of a harmonious society. The best introduction to this philosophy is provided by the title character of *Themistocles*, whose dominance of the novel is so complete that he effectively usurps the role of narrator. With his son Neocles in the role of eager pupil, Themistocles methodically outlines model organizational plans for the mayor's office (153–54), the police (59–63), and the judiciary (56–58, 63–66). In each instance officials are chosen owing to their wisdom and ability, and at each level of administration provision is made for internal review and a system of checks and balances. Covering an impressive range of governmental functions, Themistocles even expounds at some length on the proper manner in which to colonize new lands (109–14). This rather obscure aspect of a monarch's responsibility is touched upon as well by the narrator of *Inconstant Fate* (1:257–58), and in part 2 of the same novel Feridat adds to the survey of civil institutions by giving his thoughts on the concept of military leadership (170–71), a subject that Themistocles also broaches with King Xerxes of Persia (*Themistocles*, 139). Taken as a group, Emin's six novels read much like a primer on the ordering of the ideal society.

Emin's frequent reflections on politics were part of his contribution to the Enlightenment debate on the characteristics of the ideal monarch. He was so committed to this task that his novels are strewn with characters who openly advise the kings, queens, and sultans they serve on everything from a sovereign's rights and responsibilities to foreign policy decisions. The most overt example of this device occurs in the philosophical novel *Themistocles*, where the role of state counselor is formally inscribed into the text. Much as Diderot would do in real life for Catherine the Great some ten years later, Themistocles is given the opportunity to advise King Xerxes in a series of private audiences. Although Miramond, the hero of *Inconstant Fate*, cannot officially claim such an exalted station, he, too, frequently functions as a royal adviser. When leading the armies of Zhirie in a successful struggle against a neighboring aggressor, he provides in both word and deed an impeccable example for any enlightened monarch to follow.

He exhorts his troops to use no more force than necessary for, as he says, "neither political nor natural law permits the infliction of cruelty against those who have succumbed to our power" (1:255). When he captures the city, Miramond shows mercy, and in a letter to his monarch advises her on the best way to reestablish authority in the conquered land (1:259–61). Although the letter is executed with frequent expressions of profound humility, it reads like an instruction from teacher to student. In part 3 of *Inconstant Fate* this pedagogical relationship is reversed when the childless Prince Fetakh encourages Miramond to become his heir in order to save his realm from the chaos of a vacuum in leadership (3:149–50). With the assurance and authority of an omniscient narrator, he tells Miramond that a monarch must be virtuous, rational, self-critical, and somewhat aloof from his subjects if he is to succeed (3:169–70). Not content with this general counsel, Emin has the prince introduce Miramond to *The Book of Legal and Civil Regulations* (3:176–200). Underscoring its importance by noting that it is the only book in the prince's library, the narrator paraphrases its many chapters, which treat such diverse topics as faith, the monarch, ministers, judges, the military, education, the merchantry, and the common folk. Like a reflection of Emin's novelistic oeuvre in miniature, *The Book of Legal and Civil Regulations* confidently proposes the proper (and only) way to construct a society that will secure the peace and prosperity of all.[4]

Coupled with morality and politics, the theme of education serves as the third major vehicle for an authoritative voice in the early Russian novel. Following the approach that was so successful with the previous two topics, Emin's surrogates consider it a matter of conscience to share with readers their detailed (and completely inflexible) programs for educating the young. An excellent example of this device issues from the lips of the philosophical Themistocles, who contends that from their earliest years children must be trained to be strong, disciplined, and in full control of their passions (*Themistocles*, 223–25). Allowing no room for contradiction, he asserts that his system must be followed or disaster will result: children will never learn to harness their energies and will turn out to be emotionally and psychologically incapable of confronting life as adults (270–71). Feridat, the first-person narrator of much of part 2 of *Inconstant Fate*, intones the same warning in even greater detail. Using his own wayward youth as a counterexample, he sets out a basic course of studies for the successful student. Language, politics, and behavior are more important than math, physics, and other sciences (2:114); and because of its natural tendency to inflame the passions, history should only be taught after a pupil has learned temperance and prudence (2:116). Underscoring even more forcefully than Themistocles the social turmoil that results from incompetent teaching, Feridat declares: "As many unwise and vice-ridden people as there are in the world, all their dishonorable qualities arise from their upbringing" (2:117). In ever more impassioned tones he asserts that finding proper tutors for a child should be the parents' highest priority (2:117) and that if they are guilty of negligence in this area of family life, they will ultimately answer for it to God (2:118). With highly charged rhetoric and the presentation of a detailed plan of action Feridat leaves readers no choice: either they can agree with his assessment of life or join the ranks of the damned.[5]

Serving as a mock reader in *Ernest and Doravra*, Hippolyte embodies the predicament real readers must face in the authoritarianism of Emin's discourse. In one of the longest letters in the entire novel Ernest completely overwhelms his good friend with a fifty-page harangue on the proper way to raise children (3:190–243). Silencing Hippolyte with frequent reminders of the calamitous consequences of not following his system to the letter, Ernest answers what he considers to be every conceivable question regarding the proper development of the entire individual.[6] He contends that the body should be developed first lest frail minds be ruined by burdening them too early (3:191–93) and encourages parents to allow children the freedom to find and develop their own talents (3:196–97, 199–202, 209–14). Much like Feridat, Ernest also places particular emphasis on the selection of teachers. He warns that children should have more than one mentor so that they can realize their full potential (3:197–99) and strongly counsels against the employment of foreigners. The primary goal of education is to create willing and able supporters of the fatherland, a task that should be entrusted only to natives (3:239–43). As these cautionary examples imply, Ernest's discourse is inflexible in the extreme. From the general caveat that improper upbringing will ruin the individual (3:196) to specific warnings against such potential problems as lack of discipline in the educational process, Ernest overwhelms both Hippolyte and the readers of the novel. Caught between the encyclopedic nature of Ernest's proposal and the grave manner in which it is delivered, they are given little opportunity to do any more than simply nod their heads in agreement.

Whereas a didactic writer like Emin grounds each of his novels on a knowledgeable and authoritarian narrative voice, the carnivalesque mentality responds with textual anarchy. In Emin's six attempts at the genre his various surrogates strive to impress readers with the solidity of their credentials. As we have seen, Feridat's extensive travels and experience validate his frequent insights into the world *(Inconstant Fate)*, the depth and breadth of Themistocles's knowledge wins the ear of the great Persian king Xerxes *(Themistocles)*, and Ernest's difficult past and sensitive nature transform him into a self-proclaimed philosopher with a lengthy opinion on virtually any serious topic *(Ernest and Doravra)*. To these elevated voices carnivalesque prose fiction opposes the sort of motley social castoff personified by the first-person narrator of *The Comely Cook*. A prostitute and con artist, Martona uses a lingua franca culled from equal parts subterfuge and self-indulgence. Moral platitudes and high-minded theories about ideal government are ill suited to a woman who one moment robs an old man of his estate and the next threatens to tear the lover who has betrayed her to shreds. Coupled with the dubious quality of her associates and lovers—the madam of a Kievan bordello, a conniving servant and his unfaithful master, and the treacherous Akhal´—Martona's unorthodox behavior undercuts her ability to serve as the source of incontrovertible knowledge and judgments in the novel. She is simply too capricious to play such a part.

In addition to her marginal social status Martona's gender also parodies the use of erudite authorial surrogates in the first Russian novels. As Chulkov clearly points out in his earlier work *The Mocker*, women were generally considered unworthy of expounding on the wisdom and morality of the Enlightenment. Evening 7 of this rambling novel (1:181–96) finds the hero, Slavuron, forlorn over the death of his father and two close friends. When approached by an old woman who says that her brother wants to help him deal with his loss, Slavuron agrees to a meeting and spends the next day in the company of a mysterious philosopher (evening 8; 1:196–212). With the confidence of a Themistocles or Ernest, the aged and wise "brother" delivers a lengthy monologue on God, grief, virtue, and lasting happiness (1:198–202). During the audience the surprised Slavuron realizes that the supposedly aged counselor is in reality a "most charming and beautiful young woman" named Filomena (1:206). Revealing her disguise, Filomena explains that she had no choice but to deceive Slavuron for, if she had approached him as a woman, "without a doubt [he] would not have listened to [her]," thinking her to be either foolish or vain (1:208). While this sort of prejudice against a woman's intellectual abilities represents a significant obstacle to the aspirations of the forthright Filomena, it is nothing but an advantage for the whimsical Martona. Chulkov's carnivalesque heroine is not at all interested in joining the society of Enlightenment philosophers. Quite the contrary, the distance afforded by her gender, birth, and lifestyle not only exonerates her from having to create intricate theories of government, education, and morality, it also leaves her completely free to stand them on their head. Viewing the intellectual trappings of polite society as a comical sideshow, Martona abdicates responsibility and simply dances above the fray.

As colorful as Martona's past is, the two narrators of *The Mocker* come from the type of background that makes them even less qualified to play the role of moral philosopher. As he tells it himself, before he became a "religious" man, the monk made his living by swindling gullible people out of their savings and dallying with the wives of well-to-do landowners. When he crosses the line once too often, he is caught in the act and forced to enter a monastery (1:78–82). Apparently this experience does nothing to curb his illicit desires, for even in his new identity the monk has regular midnight trysts with the housekeeper of a nearby estate until he is unmasked yet again. As for Ladon, in the opening pages of part 1 he concocts a facetious autobiography that does anything but inspire confidence in his ability to draw edifying lessons from the stories he will soon begin to tell. Unfazed by questions of morality, he starts off by proudly proclaiming that his mother's promiscuity has made it impossible for him to identify his biological father. Gleefully lampooning his lineage even further, he also notes that his alleged father was a Jew and his mother a Gypsy, and thus, in his own words, he belongs to two groups whose biggest claim to fame is that they are masters of deception (1:1–2). Ladon follows these "facts" with the carnivalesque detail that he was brought to his christening by a drunken midwife who laughed all the way through the service (1:3) and then proceeds to fabricate a legend about himself. He boastfully insists that he was involved in many incredible happenings in his youth and that he was even able to talk with his mother while still in the womb (1:3–4). Together with his insistence that he is one of the world's most accomplished liars (1:97), Ladon's tongue-in-cheek autobiography makes it quite clear that his listeners will never be subjected to a fifty-page lecture on the nature of the ideal education.

The subversion of authority that lies at the heart of characters like Martona, Ladon, and the monk informs not just the narrators of carnivalesque novels but also the image of author in such works. Both Chulkov and Komarov take great pains to either belittle their creative abilities or at least cast them in a humorous and ambiguous light. In *Milord George* Komarov admits that he is uneducated and that he may be out of his depth in trying to write a novel (ii). Seven years later, in his next attempt at the genre, he reaches the same conclusion, only this time he is even more insistent. In a four-line poem placed directly after the title page and frontispiece of *Nevidimka*, he humbly writes:

> The reader will not be able to find in this book
> Either beautiful words or deep thoughts.
> Allow me to replace the merit of rare and elevated minds
> With the zeal of my soul.

> (Ni slova krasnogo, ni zamyslov glubokikh,
> Chitatel´ v knige sei ne mozhesh´ naitit´,
> Umov dostoinstvo i redkikh i vysokikh,
> Userdiem dushi pozvol´ mne zamenit´.)

Not satisfied with this blatant disclaimer of his skills, Komarov continues to denigrate his authorial persona in the six-page introduction to the novel. Among other things, he echoes the line first sounded in *Milord George* regarding his lack of education (*Nevidimka*, ii–iii), admits to having what he calls "a weak pen" (iii), and openly wishes that he possessed greater creative powers (v). As far as he can see, his only virtue as a writer is contained in the repeated promise to make up in zeal what he lacks in ability (v). Even at the end of his career when he compiled *Various Written Materials*, Komarov still did not seek the mantle of the esteemed man of letters. Despite a lengthy list of successful publications, including Russia's first best-selling novels, he maintained that he did not have the credentials to call himself an author (ii). A constant throughout his work, Komarov's literary insecurities made him more suited to the whimsicality of the carnivalesque than to the certitude of a more didactic view of his craft.

If Komarov unassumingly, yet quite seriously, refuses the title of enlightened literary despot in his three novels and one miscellany, Chulkov inflates this motif into one of the central comic concerns of *The Mocker* and *The Comely Cook*. Although he does not possess the stylistic genius of a

Rabelais, Chulkov fashions his image of the fiction writer from the type of ambivalent humor that was one of the great French Humanist's signature devices. As Bakhtin points out, the narrator in the prologue to book 2 of *Gargantua and Pantagruel* does not put himself above the crowd. While humorously chiding readers for not accepting the premise that his book is without equal, he also has the modesty to make even himself the target of his playful insults (*Rabelais*, 159–68).[7] Starting with his admission in the preface that he has introduced several foreign-sounding words into *The Mocker* so that "I may laugh at others, or so that others may laugh at me" (1:iii), Chulkov pointedly undercuts his authority in this text in much the same way. Eighteenth-century Russia's premier literary jester declares that he is "of little importance" (1:iii), the type of person who cannot afford to go around in a carriage (1:iv), and although he professes to lack nothing as far as humanity is concerned, he still admits that "my merits are just as low as my understanding is meager" (1:iv). Continuing in this vein, he starts off the body of the novel on the right foot by whimsically labeling chapter 1 "The Beginning of Idle Talk" and later confesses to being such an inveterate chatterer that unless someone stops him, he might very well carry on until he expires (4:250).[8] In another telling example, the preface to part 3 may be just one brief paragraph, yet its message is unmistakable. Lowering himself to the level of his audience, Chulkov encourages readers to alter his story as they see fit, for, as he puts it, "anyone can be the type of writer that I am" (3:i). More than just a disclaimer for the disadvantages of a humble birth, such self-deflating rhetoric is calculated to parody the dictatorial persona of the author cultivated in novels like *Inconstant Fate*.

Chulkov renews his assault on the inviolability of the author from the very first pages of *The Comely Cook*. In the first, or prose, preface to the novel he openly questions the value of his work (157) and in the second, or verse, preface admits to more than just an occasional imperfection. With large doses of gentle self-mockery he writes:

> Mistakes are innate in us, and weaknesses pleasant.
> All mortals are used to making mistakes.
> Although we have roamed about in the sciences
>   from the beginning of the century,
> We still have not found one wise man
> Who hasn't made at least one mistake in his life.
> I am not trained in dancing or the fife
> And therefore I can make a blunder.

> (Oshibki srodny nam, a slabosti prilichny,
> Pogreshnosti tvorit´ vse smertnye obychny.
> S nachala veka my khotia v naukakh brodim,
> Odnako mudretsa takogo ne nakhodim,
> Kotoryi by v ves´ vek oshibki ne imel,
> A ia ne pouchen ni v dudku, ni pliasat´,
> Tak, sledovatel´no, mogu i promakh dat´.)
> (158–59)

This irreverent attitude toward the profession of writing becomes even more pointed in the body of the novel when Chulkov introduces an outlandish crowd of literary poseurs. Masquerading as a patron of the arts, an uneducated merchant's wife organizes literary "salons" that in reality turn her boudoir into a bordello. Gold-digging gigolos court aged noblewomen, and young men try to impress their gracious sponsor with the "richness of their rhymes" (183). Very little, if any, literary discussion ever takes place at these soirees, and the only presumable motivation for them is the overinflated reputation of the hostess: she is known for writing novels containing prefaces in verse (183). Although Chulkov is satirizing the literary establishment in this scene, his words also intentionally reflect back on his own work. *The Comely Cook* contains a prominent verse preface and thus by association is lumped together with the sophomoric ramblings of a literary dilettante. By linking himself to this satirical fragment, Chulkov shows that, just like the narrator of *Gargantua and Pantagruel,* he does not put himself above the crowd.

RHETORIC: CLARITY AND REASON VERSUS AMBIGUITY AND PLAY

In the type of novels represented by Emin's six essays into the genre, the concept of the authoritative voice is supported by an equally rigid approach to the application of rhetoric. For an author focusing on such high-minded subject matter as the importance of preserving one's purity or the organization of the ideal state, multiple meanings and vague language are to be avoided at all costs. For this reason Chulkov's archrival views such devices as the metaphor, maxim, and monologue primarily as a means of shaping and severely limiting his readers' perception of the text. Almost without fail his rhetorical devices are direct, repetitive, and easily understood, and even such potentially ambivalent tropes as the metaphor tend to have just one readily accessible interpretation. On those occasions when he does resort to nonliteral language or lengthy digressions from the plot, Emin takes every precaution to make sure that readers do not need to penetrate beneath the surface of words to grasp their full meaning. In this manner he stays in total control of the text and ensures a serious and elevated reading of his novels.

Concerning the use of metaphor, Emin generally limits himself to socially accepted clichés—the tireless bee as ideal worker, the industrious ant as model citizen—with none occurring more frequently than the image of woman as priceless object. The commoner Lizark rhapsodizes about the "discovered treasure" he has found in the Egyptian princess Izida (*Lizark and Sarmanda,* 92), and Don Farina, one of the central figures of *The Marquis de Toledo,* claims as "his treasure" the beautiful young noblewoman Marianne (133). Not to be outdone, the hero of Emin's final novel, the emotional Ernest, professes that his love for Doravra "is a treasure . . . more valuable to me than the entire world" (*Ernest and Doravra,* 1:130) and on several occasions even imparts a metaphysical cast to this motif by praising her as "a sanctuary of virtue" and "a temple of propriety" (1:19, 104). Although Emin is not breaking any new ground with these comparisons, the manner in which he applies them from text to text stands him in good stead in two ways. First, by hyperbolizing his heroines, he constantly reinforces the high-minded ideals that supposedly inform his oeuvre. If his central characters can be compared to riches beyond measure, then it would seem to follow that his fiction as a whole, and in particular the altruistic philosophy it conveys, must also be of great worth. Second, by reprising the same metaphor from novel to novel, Emin leads his readers into a comfort zone. Doravra is essentially the same heroine as Marianne, who closely resembles Izida, who is really no different than Miramond's Ziumbiula. Given this sort of repetition, readers have no reason to suspect that there might be a hidden message or second meaning in Emin's discourse. If they have read one of his novels, they have read them all and can feel free to move through them just as fast as they can turn the pages. This of course plays right into Emin's desire to limit the perception of his texts. By utilizing just a few well-rehearsed code words, he can channel the interpretation of his novels into patterns of his own choosing.

The authoritarianism inherent in Emin's predilection for flat, predictable metaphors is further evidenced by the way he uses this trope as a means of clinching an argument. More than just a colorful comparison or stylistic embellishment, his metaphors often serve as "incontestable proof" of a debatable premise. Toward the end of part 3 of *Inconstant Fate* a young Indian prince falls in love with Miramond's sister, Agatha. When the prince is horribly disfigured by smallpox, Agatha reconsiders her feelings, and the prince becomes despondent. He eventually tries to commit suicide and is stopped only when his servant Belden pulls the dagger from his hand. Upon hearing the reason for his master's despair, Belden chastises him with the aid of several familiar metaphors. He rhetorically asks the prince: "What good is a crown if it weighs heavy on your head? Even though a person may be the ruler of the universe, unhappy is his kingdom if he cannot find in it his own pleasure" (3:289). According to Belden's logic, the humble shepherd who lives in harmony with nature has the more enviable fate. At first undaunted by this verbal onslaught, the prince immediately counters with a metaphor of his own. He cannot avoid a feeling of despair because until now he has never needed to learn patience, and after all, "it is impossible to bend a tree if it wasn't shaped in that direction as a sapling" (3:292). Fortunately for the prince his servant saves him from self-destruction by glibly outdueling him in the war of metaphors. Belden replies that if a blind man can avoid repeating his habitual missteps when he has a guide to lead him, the worldly prince should have no trouble learning how to nurture within himself the virtues of patience and self-restraint (3:292–93). Even though the prince does not respond immediately, his servant's words do strike home, and he eventually renounces his dark and desperate thoughts. The power of metaphor has fashioned an ironclad argument that he is incapable of contradicting.[9]

If metaphors represent the most colorful way of controlling the text in the early Russian novel, the most efficient as well as the most frequent means of accomplishing this task falls to the maxim. Especially in Emin's novels readers cannot progress more than five or ten pages without encountering one authoritarian voice or another—either a narrator or a morally upright character—that exploits this device. Brief and to the point, maxims comment on a broad range of issues dealing with human nature and the workings of the world, and taken as a whole, the maxims in a given novel form a sort of primer for everyday life. From love to fear and from skepticism to reason, they comment on just about every conceivable subject that could be of use to well-intentioned readers. Among these disparate topics there is, however, a common thread that holds them together: morality. No matter what issues particular maxims address, they always promote a virtuous code of conduct. Promising success and happiness to those who heed their lessons, they paint a frightening picture of life for those who would ignore them.

Considering no topic too banal, Emin and Komarov generally turn to the maxim to reinforce the eternal verities of life. For example, the narrator of Emin's *The Marquis de Toledo* warns that no matter how secure we might feel, we should always be on guard, for "as there is no rose without thorns so it is impossible to find a city without evildoers" (2). His counterpart in Komarov's *Vanka Kain* seconds this notion with the commonplace that "no family is without a black sheep" (117) and adds that we should avoid the company of corrupt individuals, for where there is one, there are usually many according to the saying "birds of a feather flock together" (rybak rybaka daleko v plese vidit; 74). Carrying this argument one step further, Emin cautions that in addition to fending off the evil machinations of others, we must also remain continuously vigilant against our own false desires. When Sarmanda realizes that she should squelch her feelings for Lizark because he is in love with another woman, she finds just the opposite temptation reigning in her soul. As the narrator puts it, this is a universal condition operating on the principle that "we find dearest of all that which makes us truly despair" (*Lizark and Sarmanda*, 104). The soundness of this maxim is so beyond question that even the Solomon-like Themistocles is powerless to forestall its implacable logic. The wise philosopher counsels his son to abandon his love for Xerxes's daughter because as a foreigner of lower birth he will never be allowed to wed the princess. Such sage advice falls on deaf ears, however, for Neocles, like all humans, desires nothing so much as forbidden fruit. Categorizing such behavior with the declaration "we usually want what is forbidden to us," the narrator clinches his argument with yet another, more visceral maxim. In his worldly opinion Neocles' hopeless love for the Persian princess can be summed up by the hunter's lament that "tastiest of all is the bird that saves itself from the arrow by taking flight" (*Themistocles*, 100).

Maxims are by nature a brief form of discourse, yet they need not be ambiguous. As the previous examples imply, Emin was fond of spelling out, sometimes at quite some length, his preferred interpretations. Such is the case early in part 2 of *Inconstant Fate* when, owing to a dazzling military victory, Miramond becomes so vainglorious that he considers himself a demigod. Soon after this grand accomplishment he is stricken by a devastating illness. He lies near death for quite some time and regains his health only after a lengthy convalescence. When he is lucid again, Miramond attributes his recovery to the beneficence of a Supreme Being, and right on cue, the narrator steps in to draw a heavy-handed lesson from the episode. He proclaims that "during times of danger we are extremely reverent and devout, but as soon as they pass, we once again cease to be pious" (2:31). Lest readers miss the full import of this maxim, Emin explains it with a nearly full-page story about a stereotypically greedy merchant. When overtaken by a storm that threatens to destroy not only his vessel and goods but himself as well, the merchant suddenly becomes a religious man. He swears he will give up his quest for riches and will content himself with whatever God deigns to provide him, but as soon as the danger passes, he forgets his hasty promises and begins to calculate exactly how much his next cargo will increase his fortune. By following a slim, one-line proposition with this lengthy exegesis, Emin intercedes to do the thinking for his readers.

In its three major subtypes—pathetic, philosophical, and moral—the monologue provided Russia's first novelists with an even more flexible means of manipulating reader response than the maxim. Usually lasting a page or two and often extending over five or ten pages, it accommodated a detailed investigation of a wide range of subjects, from the cruel vicissitudes of fate and the pleasures of friendship to the qualities of an ideal monarch and the rhythms of the natural world. No matter what the subject matter, however, virtually all serious monologues in the early Russian novel have one thing in common: the voice of authority. Monologues are almost exclusively reserved for heroes and heroines and thus come from the lips of characters who embody near perfection of intellect and emotion. Whether it be the heartrending sincerity with which it is delivered or the erudite nuances of its argument, this form of discourse overwhelms readers with an aura of infallibility. Caught in the throes of despair, characters like the Marquis de Toledo and Marianne appear incapable of uttering an untrue word, and the reclusive Ernest, who asks for nothing from the world, seems to possess the critical distance necessary for properly dissecting society's ills. Supported by a combination of self-righteousness and self-importance, the monologue often resembles nothing so much as an inspired sermon.

The key to the pathetic variant of the monologue is emotional intensity. Full of invocations to the gods, plaintive cries of pain and anguish, exclamations, rhetorical questions, and hyperbole, it gives the impression of being the direct and unembellished expression of a virtuous soul.[10] More often than not the impetus for such an impassioned speech is provided by the forced separation of young lovers, a situation that almost invariably leads the male character to question not just his own existence, but the very ordering of the universe. Sprawling over ten pages, Lizark's frantic diatribe against the gods serves as a primer of the device. Having been accidentally shot in a hunting accident, he believes his wound is a form of punishment for daring to love Princess Izida, a woman who is completely unattainable for a commoner such as he:

> O gods, who are envious of another's fate! Certainly when you are in our sphere you do not possess tenderness in your hearts, or else on Olympus there simply isn't any. Love must be unknown to you since you so unmercifully burden my heart. By what right should a tender heart be subjected to an admonition if not by the law of cruelty? O unbearable admonition! Your punishment exceeds the ferocity of the entire world. (Emin, *Lizark and Sarmanda*, 24–25)

Before long Lizark is so distraught that he begins to address himself in the third person, as though he were an objective observer of someone else's pain (33, 35). In this trancelike state he declares himself to be "the most unfortunate man in the world" (35) and claims that his passion exceeds the bounds of ordinary human nature (30). Referring to his love as though she were immortal—"O Izida!" "Worshipped Izida!" (25)—Lizark insists that death would be preferable to living without the object of his desire and that he views his end with joy for it would free the princess from the shame of a socially improper attachment (26, 29–30). Proving the sincerity of his words, Lizark actually attempts suicide by jumping into the Nile (37). That he is saved by fishermen does nothing to diminish the raw power of his discourse.[11]

Marked by the same pathos-filled denunciation of life's inequities as the outbursts of characters like Lizark, the monologues of female characters most often take society's sexual double standard as their target. A story from Emin's *Inconstant Fate*, wherein a widow decries the idea that a woman must give up her life to follow the wishes of the man she loves, typifies this approach. When her lover accuses her of having been unfaithful to him during his absence, the widow attacks his misplaced sense of possessiveness with a familiar set of rhetorical ploys:

> Do you really think that women ought to become your sacrifice? If we let you come into our company or show you a sign of regard, you already think that our obligation binds us to you to such a degree that we must obey you in everything. No, my friend, . . . don't think that I am so stupid as to be afraid of your reproaches. Go where you will, and I ask you not to appear at my home again. (2:277)

In another interpolated story in the final part of the novel a young woman lashes out even more severely at her husband for tracking her down as though she were his property. She has run away with her lover and feels not the least bit of guilt or regret for doing so:

Tyrant, do you really think that just because I became your wife I ought to be your slave? What's the difference between a husband and a wife? Of course there isn't any. We are only guilty, in your eyes, of not being as strong as you are! If this were true, then the powerful robber could freely take what he wanted from the weak noble simply because he is stronger. Oh, this advantage that you use against us is not natural. Nature gave one power to two united hearts: neither a husband without a wife nor a wife without a husband is able to bear fruit. Why does your ruinous guile separate us from you? And why has it come to such a pass that we must be your slaves? (3:137)

In passionate monologues such as these two, female characters add to the authoritative tenor of a text by exploiting the moral high ground for all it is worth.

In her tirade against a jealous and vindictive husband the young woman of the last-quoted passage touches upon another familiar motif of the early Russian novel: the hypocrisy of male sexual promiscuity. She angrily remarks that "[you] dally at will and satisfy your desires with various forms of voluptuousness. . . . Whatever you do is fine, but when we just look at someone else, you immediately become jealous and punish us" (3:138). This sentiment is picked up and expanded in a particularly poignant manner by Marianne, the heroine of *The Marquis de Toledo*. Having been raped by Bonveal and abandoned by her fiancé, Don Farina, Marianne is advised by the Marquis to begin her life anew. She rejects the Marquis's advice, but nevertheless takes the opportunity to lecture him (and Emin's readers) on the inconstant nature of his gender. She asserts that men "are only good on the surface, but even this cannot hide your inner stinginess: your flowery words are born of cunning, your humility is contrived, and your promises are false and hopeless" (60–61). Marianne compares men to spiders who entrap women like unwitting flies in the tender traps of their words. In her opinion men do not really love women but only use them to gratify their desires, and she finds their hypocritical attitude toward virginity repulsive. As she puts it, the same man who revels in his conquest of women looks down on them if they have lost their "wholeness" to another. When Marianne realizes that her fiancé has not abandoned her, she all but disavows these charges as she falls in love with not just one man, but two. At this point in the novel, however, her status as a wronged woman gives her the moral standing to harangue readers on a key theme of sentimentalist literature.

If the pathetic monologue employs the direct and stormy expression of deep-seated emotion to create an air of authority in the text, the philosophical variant relies on a pedagogic tone and thoughtful, detailed analysis. When Miramond reflects on the nature of court life, for example, he does so from the vantage point of the contemplative insider (*Inconstant Fate*, 1:302–6). As an adviser to two monarchs, he has the force of experience behind him, and his words seem to defy any attempt at rational contradiction. In a world-weary, yet self-assured manner he explains the rewards and liabilities of his position (1:302–3) and then, as in most philosophical monologues, ends his ruminations on a positive, functional note. With the directness and confidence so common among Emin's heroes, Miramond rhetorically asks: "What can I conclude from my reflections?" (1:304). Giving readers no opportunity to miss the message he has in mind, he immediately answers with two simple premises: while acting "rationally and carefully," courtiers should make the greater glory of the state their central purpose in life (1:304), and monarchs should always maintain the greatest circumspection when dealing with their advisers (1:305). As a final step, Miramond provides his own "proof" for these assumptions by excitedly proclaiming: "O happy are those European states where a peaceful disposition and a reciprocity of love reside! In such instances monarchs are satisfied with their subordinates, and subordinates serve their sovereigns with unanimous loyalty. There a golden spring of well-being produces complete satisfaction in human hearts" (1:305). With this seemingly incontrovertible statement based on long experience, Miramond not only validates his advice on politics, but also secures his credibility as an informed and trustworthy voice in the text.

Perhaps the most common way of introducing philosophical monologues into the first Russian novels involves the question of the ideal monarch. Such grave and erudite characters as Themistocles and Ernest spend considerable time discussing this topic, and it even occupies Chulkov's attention in the heroic tales of *The Mocker*. A particularly good illustration of the device occurs in the beginning of part 3 when an exiled king named Alim thoughtfully analyzes his reign for an interested listener. He explains that early in life the best teachers available instilled in him "a respect for God, a love of virtue, and a sensitivity for the people" while also enlightening him with "the laws of the state, military skills, and the way to restore the well-being of society—in short, everything that a sovereign needs to know" (3:4). When he ascended the throne, Alim protected the poor and helpless from those who would exploit them, promoted his subordinates solely on the basis of merit, and put the personal well-being of his subjects above his own. What is perhaps even more important, Alim realized the responsibility of his position and never allowed absolute power or a desire for self-aggrandizement to turn his head: "This high rank, which was an open door to splendor and vanity, did not in any way change my temperate desires. Such a great thankfulness to the people who had elevated me to the throne took root in my heart that I sincerely honored every citizen as my own father to whom I was obligated by birth, upbringing, and prosperity" (3:6). With these noble words and his cool, detached analysis Alim proves that he is a true son of the Enlightenment and in so doing gains the confidence of Chulkov's readers from his initial appearance in the novel. Sincere, reflective, and supremely competent, he turns out to be a reliable voice amid the dozens of characters inhabiting the fictional world of *The Mocker*.

In addition to politics, nature serves as the other stock theme of the philosophical monologue. Amid the chaos and uncertainty in novels like

Emin's *Inconstant Fate* it provides a universal standard for interpreting the world. Such at any rate is the lesson Miramond delivers as he ponders the abrupt change in his relationship with Queen Belilia of Zhirie. As the emissary of his Egyptian lord, Osman Bey, he was her equal, but now, after she has become betrothed to the bey's son, he must view himself as just another of her subordinates. Instead of railing against such a loss of status, Miramond takes comfort in the abundant precedents for such occurrences in the realm of nature.

> Time changes, and we conform with it. There has never been one disposition or being on earth that has been so constant that its existence has not been changed, and if we think about it deeply, there has also never been a constancy in things. The clear sun is eclipsed, stars change, clouds race off into other lands, fish shed their scales, animals living in their dens disguise themselves in various coats, and it would even be possible to say that the nature of man is change. (1:265)[12]

Ironically, even though Miramond rationalizes his new station in life by referring to the inconstancy of the natural world, his monologue reinforces at least two conventional hierarchies. On the one hand, it justifies the petrified sociopolitical relations of official society and, on the other, transforms the speaker into a voice of authority. By elevating himself to the position of a keen observer of life, Miramond encourages readers to see him as a worthy textual surrogate for Emin. From the first pages of *Inconstant Fate* to the last, nearly a thousand in all, this is a confidence he never breaks.

The third common type of monologue in the early Russian novel combines elements of the first two approaches. Melding the emotional intensity and intimate subject matter of the pathetic monologue with the deliberate analysis of the philosophical variant, the monologue of morality and manners focuses on such topics as constancy, friendship, infidelity, and the falseness of society. One of the rhetorical staples of Emin's prose fiction, it is particularly well suited to the ardent, yet intellectual, type of hero represented in his final novel. With the zeal of a social reformer Ernest utilizes this device to analyze methodically a series of moral questions. In a letter to Hippolyte, for instance, he sets out to prove that for any thinking person, a happy and satisfying life is out of the question given the way society is presently constituted. As though he were delivering a lecture, Ernest posits a range of relationships a person can strike with society and then shows how each one ultimately leads to the individual's downfall (*Ernest and Doravra*, 4:98–105). If you are rich and too approachable, your "friends" will turn out to be idlers and spongers who dissipate your fortune and then abandon you when you ask for help (4:98–99). If, in spite of such dangers, you do maintain a lofty station in life, there will always be those who envy your success and slander your reputation (4:99–101). On the other hand, the talented but poor man is fated to sacrifice his independence to serve the whims of the rich, thus opening himself up to the charge of toadyism, and intellectuals will always be looked upon as dangerous types who live to entrap others.

Even the dull-witted do not escape unscathed in this monologue for, as Ernest sees it, they will never be considered anything more than laughing-stocks and buffoons (4:101–3). Passionate, yet orderly and wide-ranging, this critique of society appears to be so logical as to preclude rational rebuttal.

Despite constructing what would appear to be an ironclad defense of the premise that it is better to remain aloof from society than to join it, Ernest is still far from finished with this particular monologue. In order to exploit his position of authority even further, he tackles the same problem one more time from a different, more personal perspective. Although he focuses on his own withdrawal from society, however, he maintains a sense of distance that allows him to speak as though he had an objective mastery of the topic. Referring to his hermitlike existence in the countryside, he condescendingly tells Hippolyte: "You call my life poor because I live on meager rations and forego many comforts. No, dear friend, I suffer from no shortcomings. What is necessary to maintain my life is not lacking. Abstention is the root of virtue, and excess is a most harmful worm that gnaws and devours that root" (4:103–4). From this opening salvo, which equates distancing oneself from the lure of society with the Enlightenment virtue of restraint, Ernest quickly resorts to the rhetorical ploy of "proving" his thesis by bombarding Hippolyte (and Emin's readers) with one irrefutable example after another. In rapid succession he asks: Whom would a country choose as military leader during time of war? Whom would you choose as the guardian of your children? Whom would you have as a servant in your own home? Of course, with each question there comes a brief, yet complete, answer that forces us to admit the only prudent course of action is to choose the person who exhibits the greatest self-control (4:104–5). Just in case we might have missed the point, Emin leaves nothing to chance when he closes this mono-logue by telling us exactly what we should have learned from it. Ernest writes that "a noble-minded person should not have an intemperate friend or servant, and the honest person should not only despise such people, but should eradicate the passion that harmfully forces him to collect without measure the great treasures of others" (4:105). Overwhelmed by examples and cajoled by Ernest's highly charged rhetoric, readers find themselves hard-pressed: they either accept his authoritative decrees or run the risk of being considered ignorant, imprudent, and even immoral.[13]

When devices such as the metaphor, proverb, and monologue are in-serted into a carnivalesque text, they usually enhance, rather than limit, our interpretive options. Unlike Emin, who tries to keep his readers sharply fo-cused on the didactic axioms forming the core of his work, Chulkov en-courages us to let our imagination run wild. He accomplishes this task by fostering the sort of ambiguity and multiple meanings that create the per-fect environment for parody. Although he employs the same rhetorical de-vices as Emin and at times duplicates some of his tropes almost exactly, his intent is to ridicule, rather than imitate, the serious side of the official liter-ary aesthetic. In Chulkov's prose fiction metaphors are laced with double

entendre, proverbs counsel a way of life that would lead even the most devoted moralist astray, and monologues are anything but sober-minded, rational analyses of the human condition. As the author of *The Mocker* self-
consciously admits, readers shouldn't waste their time trying to find deep
meanings in his work, for they simply aren't there (4:170–71). Only by
heeding this inside advice will we be able to fully appreciate the insistent
voice of mockery that animates Chulkov's approach to rhetoric.

Throughout his two major novels Chulkov directly challenges the hackneyed image of feminine purity advanced in works like Emin's *The Marquis
de Toledo*. As we have seen, Emin's tropes generally emphasize the spiritual
perfection of his heroines while ignoring their sexual appeal. When Don Farina compares Marianne to a treasure, readers are to interpret this metaphor
to mean that she is priceless, pure, and worthy of veneration. By extension
the elevated tone and imagery surrounding Marianne are also designed to
convince readers that the entire novel will appeal to the most high-minded
aspects of their nature. Chulkov's comely cook, Martona, deflates such ethereal fantasy by focusing on the material side of life and delights in using
metaphors to call a spade a spade. Caught after taking part in cheating an
aged client out of his estate, Martona languishes in prison until she is finally
rescued by the two dashing heroes, Akhal´ and Svidal´. Just as Don Farina
and the Marquis de Toledo strive to win Marianne's heart, both of Martona's liberators try to gain her favors as well. Instead of deifying her with
lofty metaphors, however, Chulkov chooses to emphasize the carnal motivations in this relationship. As opposed to the character in Emin's *Inconstant
Fate* who proclaims to a suitor that his daughter "is not some sort of mer-
chandise to be displayed to whomever asks to see it" (2:159), Martona playfully describes herself as "inherited wealth" and captured "booty" (*Comely
Cook*, 179). In her view of the world Akhal´ and Svidal´ have every right to
do more than just look her over. When she adds some time later that "I
found myself completely in Svidal´'s power, and he rejoiced more than a
vainglorious leader at the capture of an enemy fortress" (183), the implica-
tions of her words form a two-pronged assault on Emin's use of metaphor.
First, they act as a direct parody of the bloodless altruism that permeates
virtually every one of Emin's heroes and heroines. As opposed to the virtuous Marianne, for example, Martona would much rather be placed on a bed
than on a pedestal. Second, the bawdy cook's imagery is ambiguous enough to
pique our imagination. Unlike the narrow interpretive range of the vehicles
in Emin's metaphors (priceless treasure; unformed sapling), the suggestive-
ness of Martona's discourse encourages us to conjure up any number of images, each of them more provocative than the one before.

Besides attacking a type of writing that sought to appease the arbiters of
official literature, Chulkov's metaphors could also be quite sharply focused. For instance, when portraying the sensations of first love, Chulkov
draws on the very same image as his chief literary rival. In Emin's novel
Lizark and Sarmanda Princess Izida is flattered to find out that she has a devoted admirer. As she contemplates reciprocating his feelings, the narrator

tells us that "like a tender bee she selected a pleasant sweetness from her various newly blossomed thoughts and made up a pleasant honey in the delicate honeycomb of her heart" (26–27). Refined, innocent, and even somewhat removed, Emin's description of the newly announced love lacks even the slightest hint of the sexual energy that courses through an analogous situation in *The Comely Cook*. Almost as soon as she decides to become a prostitute, Martona is amazed at how easily she attracts a suitor. In the words of a simple woman from the countryside she rationalizes this state of affairs with the proverb: "A bee always flies to a pretty flower" (159). By comparing her suitor to a bee who plunders her nectar, Martona charges the pallid metaphor employed by Emin with layers of sexual innuendo. The image calls to mind the picture of an intimate rendezvous, and if it is pushed to its logical extreme—a bee making the rounds of many flowers— strongly implies the type of sexual promiscuity that Martona's entire narrative exalts as one of life's supreme pleasures. Moreover, the metaphor of the aggressive bee and the passive flower also seems to be a sly commentary on Emin's hypocritical depiction of sex. In all but two of his six novels Emin's heroines are threatened with rape, and in *The Marquis de Toledo* Marianne is sexually assaulted. Even though these scenes are recounted with an unflagging tone of moral indignation, the motivation behind them would appear to be more commercial than didactic. Then, as now, sex sold books. Emin exploited this fact, but tried to camouflage it behind a facade of high-sounding rhetoric. In *The Comely Cook* Chulkov whimsically exposes his duplicity and at the same time turns the theme of sex to his advantage.

Like the maxims so favored by Emin, Chulkov's folksy sayings and ambiguous proverbs are brief, expressive, and capable of transmitting the author's message on a variety of issues, but beyond these rather general grounds for comparison all similarity stops. As opposed to Emin, whose maxims cudgel readers into accepting a narrowly defined moral orthodoxy, Chulkov creates a promiscuous vision of the world. Right down to their frequently mocking bipartite presentation, the sayings and proverbs of the premier literary jester of eighteenth-century Russia function as a direct snub to Emin's rigid code of conduct. For example, when Martona's first lover begs her not to reveal their past relationship to the man who is both his master and her present "patron," he begins by saying that "money is iron and clothing perishable" (*Comely Cook,* 163). Up to this point it seems as though the servant were reciting a golden rule to live by that would conclude with an endorsement of knowledge, friendship, or some other Enlightenment virtue. As we have come to expect, however, Chulkov has something completely different in mind, for the jilted lover goes on to sarcastically proclaim, ". . . but our skin is our dearest possession." Maintaining that humans are more prone to selfishness than to altruism, this crafty proverb first teases readers with its didactic potential and then abruptly turns around and mocks it.

Whereas Emin's maxims portray nature, society, and human behavior in the starkest shades of black and white, Chulkov's proverbs and sayings can only find varying shades of gray in a world awash in relativism. Far from lamenting this fact, of course, carnivalesque discourse accepts and even champions it. When Martona suddenly finds herself living the high life just after she thought all was lost, she takes it in stride. All things are constantly being transformed, so you shouldn't be surprised when your luck changes in the blink of an eye according to the proverb: "Makar used to dig ditches, but now he's the governor" (*Comely Cook*, 162). Mirroring the capriciousness of her environment, Martona professes that she too is completely fickle. When the handsome Akhal´ announces his affection for her, she at first feels uneasy about deceiving her present patron, a septuagenarian colonel, but in virtually no time enters into an affair with Akhal´ without the slightest hint of remorse. As she sees it, her actions are in total accord with one of life's basic rules. Whereas Themistocles counsels his son to give up his pursuit of an unsanctioned union, Martona does not let anything stand in her way, rationalizing her conduct with the singsong proverb: "A sheep loves salt, a goat free reign, and a flighty woman new love" (Lakoma ovtsa k soli, koza k voli, a vetrenaia zhenshchina k novoi liubovi; 172). In pithy phrases such as this one Chulkov's heroine not only mocks the stifling morality of Emin's maxims, but also undercuts his propensity to dictate their meaning. Martona offers no commentary with her proverbs; either you accept them or you don't. She has supreme confidence that her laissez-faire approach to life will sell itself without any cajoling on her part.

Even at the most critical of times Martona refuses to enforce a punitive view of the world or dictate how readers should interpret the text. On the contrary, the more desperate the situation, the more she calls on a healthy sense of carnivalesque ambiguity to see her through. When Sveton's wife interrupts her husband and Martona in the act of making love, the young heroine is in danger of losing her life. Beaten and cast out on the road with nothing but the clothes on her back, she nevertheless makes light of the situation, saying simply, "The bear that ate the cow is guilty, but so is the cow that wandered into the forest" (165). With this wonderfully ambiguous proverb Martona completely obscures the notion of guilt and distances herself from its potentially devastating consequences. Just who is the bear in this episode and who is the cow becomes impossible to determine. Even if readers assume that Martona is the cow (*korova*, feminine) and Sveton the bear (*medved´*, masculine), the proverb still precludes any attempt at a seducer/victim interpretation. In this reading the two lovers share responsibility, and the affair is simply passed off as being part of the unavoidable cycle of life. Pushing this reasoning even further, a third interpretation, which associates Martona and Sveton with the cow and has Sveton's wife playing the role of the bear, suggests that Martona dismisses the notion of guilt altogether. In this scenario she confesses only to a lack of circumspection. Sveton and she have done nothing wrong; they are only to blame for not protecting themselves better from the malicious nature of respectable society as symbolized by the bear. Freed from having to defend anyone or anything, Martona can easily distance both herself and her readers from the often crushing burden of guilt that plays such a large role in Emin's novels.

Although the proverbs and sayings in Komarov's *Vanka Kain* do not counsel a life of complete promiscuity à la Chulkov's *The Comely Cook*, they do take aim at the restrictiveness of official society. When characters in the novel turn to these forms, they are usually intent on thumbing their nose at the sort of authority figures abounding in works like *Inconstant Fate* and *The Marquis de Toledo*. For example, having fallen in with a group of thieves in Moscow, Kain is introduced to the type of life they lead. In rhymed couplets known as *pribautki*, a staple comedic genre of the Russian carnival, one of the bandits tells him:

> Poverty and nakedness are all around,
> And we have barns full of hunger and cold.
> Living here, we rent out our rooms,
> And to those who pass by this bridge at night we give silent alms.
> To tell you the truth, we have nothing more than dust and soot,
> And sometimes there's not a thing to eat.

> (Nagoty, bosoty navesheny shesty,
> A golodu i kholodu polnye anbary stoiat.
> My, zhivuchi zdes´, pokoi svoi v naem otdaem,
> A prokhodiashchim po semu mostu noch´iu
>   tikhuiu milostyniu podaem;
> A pravdu tebe skazat´, tak u nas tol´ko pyl´ da kopot´,
> A inogda nechego i lopat´.)
> (13–14)

Colorful, witty, and even threatening, this brief discourse is saturated with a bitter commentary on the poverty, oppression, and violence experienced by Russia's lower classes. Devoid of the least bit of sympathy for official society, it brazenly, yet comically, depicts the carnivalesque antiworld that resides alongside the seat of power and privilege in the heart of the Russian capital.

It only seems fitting that the most irreverent sayings in Komarov's criminal "biography" belong to Kain himself. In one of his first lawless acts the rebellious serf sneaks into his master's bedroom and makes off with as many valuables as he can carry. As a final mark of disrespect he tacks the following *pribautka*-like statement to the merchant's door:

> Drink water like a goose,
> Eat bread like a pig,
> And let the devil work for you,
> 'cause I won't.

> (Pei vodu kak gus´,
> Esh´ khleb kak svin´ia,
> A rabotai u tebia chort,
> A ne ia.)
> (9)

Kain reprises the role of the defiant mocker later in the novel when he appears before a secretary of the Secret Commission. Asked to justify his request for an audience, he refuses to deal with the secretary, stating, "I don't know points or pounds or weights or overweights" (Ia ni punktov ni funtov, ni vesu, ni pokhodu ne znaiu; 20). Although he is beaten for this insolent response, Kain does get to deal directly with the count heading the commission and eventually wins his freedom by denouncing his master. For a time, at least, the jesting defiance encapsulated in Kain's carnivalesque sayings helps him break the bonds that keep him a helpless prisoner at the bottom of society.

Making a clean sweep of the salient rhetorical features of the early Russian novel, Chulkov treats the monologue with the same disregard he shows the metaphor and maxim. As practiced by Emin, this device supposedly conveys the unmediated expression of the most intimate feelings and supplies readers with practical solutions to a variety of problems they are likely to encounter in both their public and private lives. Moreover, the pathetic, philosophical, and didactic monologues in Emin's six novels carry with them the voice of authority: they must be true, given that they come from the mouths of characters who are paragons of intellectual and moral development. In carnivalesque fiction, on the other hand, such assumptions are mercilessly ridiculed. Whenever sentiment arises in *The Comely Cook* or the sections of *The Mocker* narrated by the monk, it is almost always shown to be a mere facade for a far more venal emotion. Martona, the monk, and even Ladon have seen it all and are not impressed. If a character engages in an effusive display of emotion, they know that he or she has most likely fabricated the scene for personal gain. This sort of skepticism also carries over to their treatment of intellectual pursuits. Following Rabelais's association of philosophizing with lying, the characters and narrators in Chulkov's novels view deep thinking not as a means of providing readers with greater insights into the meaning of life, but simply as a tempting target for their subversive wit. To top it off, the parodic monologues that appear in *The Mocker* and *The Comely Cook* come from characters who can claim a perverse sort of authority. As self-proclaimed charlatans, cheats, and rogues, they know of what they speak for they have extensive firsthand experience in exploiting the arts of subterfuge and insincerity. With this final ironic twist Chulkov negates his rival's approach to the monologue point for point.

As Akhal''s tearful farewell from Martona clearly indicates, the best that can be said about pathos in *The Comely Cook* is that it is misguided, or at the very least inappropriate. Falsely assuming he has killed his rival in a duel, Akhal' addresses his love for what he believes will be the last time. Using the exclamations, emotional intensity, and key words so common in the pathetic monologues of characters like Miramond and the Marquis de Toledo, he laments that "unmerciful fate has deprived [him]" of the pleasure of marrying Martona, has made him "an unhappy man who is subject to a cruel torture," and is forcing him to flee not just Moscow but the very borders of Russia in order to avoid the retribution of the law (181). When the tormented hero concludes with the declaration, "Farewell, my beautiful one, forever," he seems to have covered just about every element that is necessary for a successful pathetic monologue. Yet there is a catch: Svidal´ is not even wounded, and so Akhal´'s fine words are all for naught. Moreover, his leaving allows Svidal´ to win Martona's heart without a fight and makes his impassioned speech look like the blathering of a self-absorbed fool. Adding to the irony of this farcical scene is that Akhal´ is reprising the very role he forced another unwitting rival to play earlier in the novel when he worked his way into the home of Martona's seventy-year-old "patron" by masquerading as her sister. After overcoming his initial suspicions, the decrepit old man launches into an emotional speech on the "siblings'" virtuous conduct. He gushes: "I have never seen such a burning love between sisters. There's just no two ways about it: you could be considered lovers, and if one of you were dressed in men's clothing, no one would believe you were sisters. I praise your virtue and sincere hearts. You are close relations who are worthy of the greatest respect" (174). Of course, readers do know that one member of this couple is indeed a man and that the colonel is being hoodwinked. His beautiful phrases concerning love, respect, and virtue sound wonderful but are completely off the mark. Unbeknown to the misguided fool, he is encouraging deceit, promiscuity, and eventually larceny right under his own roof.

In addition to farcically imitating the pomposity of the pathetic monologue, Chulkov also provides a humorous running commentary on this device. In one metaliterary passage after another his narrators gleefully cut to pieces the false sentimentality underpinning the impassioned speeches of the Ernests, Lizarks, and Mariannes of the early Russian novel. Proving just how central this lighthearted jesting is to Chulkov's fiction, even Ladon, the narrator of the chivalrous tales in *The Mocker*, cannot pass up an opportunity to indulge in it. He sets the process in motion by putting on "the face of a desperate lover" (1:29) and approaching the object of his desire, the enchanting Alenona, with an emotional declaration of his feelings. Beginning with the phrases "Assemblage of benevolence! Font of beauty! Mistress of my sorrowful heart!" (1:29), he holds forth on bended knee for a page and a half trying to impress her with the unparalleled depths of his affection. In one of the most poignant moments in his monologue Ladon describes how the mere sight of Alenona overpowers him. Working himself into a frenzy, he tells her, "I forget myself, wonder takes possession of me, and I become immobile. . . . Passions shatter my understanding, confuse my thoughts, and take away the power of speech" (1:29). With the reverential attitude of a Miramond or a Feridat he speaks of his "lost peace" and "desperate life," beseeches his beloved to pity him, and claims that only death will make him forget her (1:30). Judging from Alenona's reaction, Ladon is indeed an effective practitioner of the pathetic monologue, for as soon as he finishes, she bids him to rise, promises to reciprocate his feelings, and the young pair kiss. Ladon's fine oration is so good that if the scene ended here, it would compare favorably with anything in Emin's oeuvre. As we have come to expect, however, Chulkov is never content to let well enough alone.

No sooner does Ladon realize that he has won Alenona's heart than he launches into a pointed metacommentary on what has just taken place. As if letting readers in on an inside joke, he says:

> I admit that the declaration of love I interjected for no reason at all proba-bly bored the reader more than the rest of the book combined. I myself had wanted to get up in the middle of this recitation because a pebble had got-ten under my knee, and it tickled me rather badly, but the pain resulting from this increased my passion, and so my lover thought that I was the most tender lover in the world. The reader . . . ought to forgive me, as a person who is subject to worldly weaknesses, for grabbing various phrases from tragedies and novels to express my passion and having woven [from them] this absurd declaration in which there is neither rhyme nor reason, for love is a waking delirium. (1:31)

In typical carnivalesque fashion Chulkov uses humor to dismantle the false premises and promises of the didactic fiction of his day. To his mind the pathetic monologues found in novels like *Inconstant Fate* have more to do with literary convention than with the unmediated expression of emotion. As Ladon demonstrates, a successful effort can be cobbled together out of clichés recycled from a variety of genres without once consulting your heart. Moreover, in addition to being shopworn and insincere this type of monologue can also be deceptive. Alenona may have thought that Ladon's blushing was the result of his feelings for her when it was in fact motivated by the far more mundane sensation of a stone digging into his knee. For-ever suspicious of any type of serious discourse, Chulkov lays bare the mo-tivation of the pathetic monologue and destroys the sense of solemnity and authority accompanying it in the work of a novelist like Emin.

From the presenters of the pathetic monologue to its recipients, Chulkov touches all the bases in his parody of this device. Although Alenona can be taken in by fine-sounding lies and airy promises, Martona is far too worldly to succumb to such blandishments. No matter how enamored she might become of a particular man, the skeptic in her always appraises him with a critical eye. Recalling the beginning of her relationship with the lusty Akhal´, she reflects:

> I knew that in the present age fidelity is the type of guest who says "hello" when he arrives yet has "farewell" ready and waiting on the tip of his tongue. A lover remains faithful as long as he doesn't see any sign of favor from the person he loves. Then he sighs and pines, pretends to cry, and vows the type of faithfulness that reigns only in the theater. But once he re-ceives everything from her, then, owing to the frailty of human memory, he forgets all his oaths in a minute and erases them from his mind. (*Comely Cook*, 175)

Instead of covering up an unseemly aspect of life in order to exhort others to an impossibly high standard of conduct, Martona simply calls a spade a spade. She warns that when a lover, even one as charming and dedicated as Akhal´, treats a woman to impassioned declarations of love, his motivation may well be less than pure. In her opinion exclamations, sighs, and promises to remain forever faithful are the currency of persuasion—just so many words designed to break down a woman's defenses. After all, as Ladon admits, these emotional outbursts basically consist of the regurgitation of tired formulas that owe more to the stage than to an ardent heart. Forever the pragmatist, Martona sees right through the sham motivations and unattainable expectations that are the very essence of the pathetic monologue.

Proving the solidity of her carnivalesque credentials, Chulkov's comely cook is also adept at parodying the philosophical variant of the monologue. In the early Russian novel this device is generally defined by a lofty choice of subject matter and a rigid method of argumentation: either you agree with the author's idealistic presentation or you are simply wrong. Openly laughing at such assumptions, Martona constructs a far more promiscuous view of both the world and the limits of rhetoric. As concerns constancy in love, for example, she asserts that change is the essence of life. Debating whether or not to overthrow one suitor in favor of another, she mockingly concludes:

> I have always been of the opinion that everything on earth is inconstant. When there is an eclipse of the sun, the sky is completely covered with clouds; seasons change four times a year, and the sea rises and ebbs; fields and mountains are at times green, and then turn white; birds shed their feathers, and philosophers change their systems. So how should it be possible that a woman, who is born to be whimsical, can love one man to the end of her life? . . . I was not a stoic and did not at all hold to their system and for that reason did not want to refuse the person who demanded my indulgence. (171)[14]

Open-ended and accommodating, Martona's monologue subverts the discourse of authority and morality on at least three levels. First, it banishes the vocabulary of condemnation and assumes true sexual equality. As a woman, Martona resides on the margins of society. Rather than submit to the brutalizing consequences of a judgmental discourse that demands an almost superhuman reserve of virtue, she simply circumvents this trap by redefining the world to suit her own particular tastes. In Martona's upside-down reasoning everyone enjoys the benefits of turning the entire year into one extended carnival. Second, her comparison of human fickleness to the wonders of the natural world functions as a carnivalesque Trojan horse to destroy the philosophical monologue from within. Instead of using nature to justify some grand intellectual scheme, Martona transforms the cyclical essence of the universe into a jeering denial of the efficacy and reliability of any system. As a parting shot, the comely cook thumbs her nose at the

entire enterprise. In contrast to her superficial imitation of the formal demands of the philosophical monologue (high-style rhetoric, syntactic paral-
lelism, a dense string of examples) in the first part of the passage, the directness and the matter-of-fact tone of the last sentence declare Martona's
complete independence in the matter. Flaunting a Rabelaisian brand of wisdom, she flatly refuses to acknowledge any standard of judgment other than
her own happiness. Playful and provocative, her monologue, like all carnivalesque rhetoric, consistently champions freedom and pleasure against the
more austere demands of constancy, authority, and truth.

Chapter

FIVE

THE SOCIAL ORDER

The fictional world of those early Russian novels that strove to win at least a modicum of legitimacy for their genre is circumscribed by a rigid combination of social and familial hierarchies. Within this system roles are defined, endowed with certain rights and responsibilities, and made virtually impregnable to the entrance of outsiders. Characters in any given station of life have power over the destiny of those below them, yet must totally conform their behavior and desires to the wishes of those above them. In Emin's novels and in Komarov's *Milord George* and *Nevidimka* the authors' focus is almost exclusively on characters of an aristocratic background. A benign God reigns over this world and vests His earthly power in a supreme monarch. The gentry in turn are subservient to their monarch, and within this social class sons and daughters must obey their father's word without the slightest hesitation. Given that Emin and Komarov generally focus on the theme of love, the literary impact of such a restrictive system usually results in the delayed union of the hero and heroine. Whether unequal social status or the insensitivity of an intolerant parent separates young lovers, the consequences are the same: individuals must surrender their personal independence to the collective wisdom and wishes of society.

HIERARCHIES

Respect for authority in the early Russian novel is justified by relying on ultimate causes. In a society structured around a distinct chain of command, the top rung is occupied by an all-powerful creator. Emin's living philosophical encyclopedia Themistocles flatly asserts that human beings must obey God owing to their great need for Him: "We must admit that God, not man, is the founder of the laws, without which people would be akin to animals and would not be even the slightest bit enlightened. For this reason, the primary law is to honor God and do everything that the most holy laws command" (*Themistocles*, 215). In the fictional world of Emin's novels unquestioning obedience to a set of divinely inspired rules serves as the foundation of a healthy society. No matter how characters like Miramond, the Marquis de Toledo, Lizark, or Sarmanda may suffer at the hand of fate, if they are true to the mores of their society, they will prosper in the end. Characters who remain faithful, honest, and virtuous can survive any number of shipwrecks, deceptions, and imprisonments. In this regard the artificially appended happy endings that so frequently accompany the novels of Emin and Komarov turn out to be an almost otherworldly, heavenlike reward for a life well lived. Conversely, it is just as important that the natural order of things eventually calls to account the perpetrators of evil. Kadyr admonishes the deceitful Gamlia for her machinations against the young lovers Kamber and Arisena. Confronting her, he rhetorically asks, "Can you set about your impudent intentions without fearing the power of the Almighty, who does not let scoundrels such as you go unpunished?" (Emin, *Kamber and Arisena*, 186). Events quickly provide a definitive answer to Kadyr's challenge when Gamlia's attempt to separate Kamber and Arisena is foiled, and she ends up committing suicide (192). As this episode in Emin's first novel clearly demonstrates, no punishment is too severe for those who defy the law.

The motivation for virtuous conduct does not come solely from a distant and abstract source in the fictional world of the early Russian novel. In addition to the righteous hand of God, characters can rely on the vigilance of a much more concrete and proximate entity: their monarch. Once again, it is Themistocles who lays down the philosophical basis for this aspect of life when he declares, "The gods hate unjust people, and monarchs, who are the gods' faithful deputies, ought to root them out of their domains" (Emin, *Themistocles*, 119). Divinely endowed with the role of lawgiver, a sovereign is entrusted with nothing less than the security and vitality of society. Hinting at the grim future awaiting any citizenry that does not honor legitimate authority, Themistocles explains to the Persian emperor Xerxes that "subversion of [the concept of] subordination destroys the civil obligation maintaining the harmony of society and leads to the state of jealousy that existed before there were order and political institutions among peoples" (207). In his next novel, *Lizark and Sarmanda*, Emin revisits this idea in more detail through the figure of the nobleman-turned-shepherd Amnon. Explaining why he has abandoned society for a life of solitude, he tells Sarmanda:

> As far as natural human rights are concerned, it would be fair to say that you are animals, or better yet, wild beasts. In your society sons hate their fathers, and mothers are never satisfied with their daughters. When you

see that someone has a piece of bread in his hand, you chase after him in order to steal it. This is what dogs do when they try to tear a bone away from one another. You are fortunate that foreseeing your fierceness and immoderation, the gods gave you sovereigns who can rein in your bestial passions to some degree. But if you didn't have them, your fury and immoderation would surpass the violence of animals, and then man would be called the most evil of beasts. (152–53)

In novel after novel Emin's message is clear: without the law and a strict social hierarchy society would degenerate into civil war.

Virtually without exception the rational, well-born characters of Emin's novels share Amnon's views on law and society and therefore deem state service as one of their primary responsibilities in life. As an episode in *Inconstant Fate* clearly shows, even when society turns against these selfless heroes, their sense of duty is still so great that they respond without hesitation whenever they are called upon. Unjustly banished from the capital by the woman he loves and the monarch he served, Miramond finds peace by living as a hermit in the countryside. When his presence is discovered by a local prince, he is forcefully reminded of the obligation that rests with his abilities and position in society. Prince Fetakh, who has no children of his own, wants Miramond to become his legal heir and admonishes him, "O Miramond, . . . what has become of your heroism? Don't you know that heroes care more for the general good than their own? . . . If not for me, then do this for my poor people, who, being left without a sovereign like a flock without a shepherd, will be subject to limitless violence" (3:149–50). Upon hearing these words, the conscientious Miramond not only agrees to succeed Prince Fetakh, but eventually even returns to Cairo, the city that spurned him, in order to save it from destruction.[1]

Going Miramond one better, Themistocles not only exhibits the sense of duty required of an educated man, but also the proper degree of humility. Despite his many accomplishments, such as saving Athens from foreign invasion and later providing King Xerxes of Persia with sage advice on topics ranging from the conduct of war to civil administration, Themistocles always takes care to lower himself before his monarch. He consistently downplays the significance of his position and, whenever he has an audience with Xerxes, addresses him on bended knee (Emin, *Themistocles*, 132–33). According to Themistocles, the hours and days he spends consulting with the king are insignificant. As he tells the Persian emperor, "In my former political conversations I only expressed my thoughts to Your Excellency and never uttered one word with the intention of offering advice, realizing that I am unworthy and incapable of such a task. I know that Your Excellency has no need of counsel and that your wisdom is able to satisfy everyone's needs" (252–53). Where duty is concerned, even the most talented person must be virtually without ego or individuality.

Just as monarchs serve as God's surrogates on earth, a father's rule is unquestioned within the family. In Emin's *The Marquis de Toledo* the title character falls in love with the novel's heroine after she is raped by one of

the most notorious libertines in the city. When the Marquis asks Marianne's grief-stricken father for his daughter's hand in marriage, he immediately agrees without so much as consulting her. Only after the fact does
Marianne's mother, Isabella, inform her that she has been betrothed to a
man she barely knows. Understandably, Marianne has no feelings for the
Marquis, for she had been formally engaged to her true love, Don Farina,
prior to the attack. Nevertheless, she consents, realizing that her parents
"would be extremely saddened by her failure to agree with their will and
would certainly force her to do that which she did not wish to do voluntarily" (33–34). In deferring to her parents' "right" to determine her future,
Marianne is hardly unique in the pages of the early Russian novel. In the
fictional world she inhabits children must fulfill their parents' every wish,
and nothing, not even the most exalted station in life, can exempt them
from this unwritten law. The heroic Prince Siloslav faces overwhelming
odds on the field of battle without flinching yet obeys his father's command to choose a wife without a second thought (Chulkov, *Mocker*, 1:102),
and Prince Alim temporarily abdicates his throne to search for his missing
parents, as any proper son would (4:98–99). An individual's free will is so
limited that even one of the greatest of all heroes, Achilles, must gain his
mother's approval before marrying the woman he loves (Chulkov, *Achilles*,
45). Thetis applauds her son's adherence to the decorum that structures
family life when she tells him: "Join yourself to [Princess Deidamiia] in
marriage. I permit you [to marry her], dear son, and praise your devotion
to your mother, because you did not begin without me that which children
do not begin without their parents' permission" (45).

Of course it is one thing to ask for parental consent when an affirmative
response is almost certain or to meekly accept a decision when it does not
seem to hold negative consequences. Yet, as Marianne's response to her
mother implies, hierarchical control is so firmly entrenched in the fictional
world of novels like *The Marquis de Toledo* that, whenever a parent demands it, characters are often more than willing to sacrifice their own best
interests. When Themistocles' son Neocles falls in love with Xerxes' daughter Pomena, his father counsels him to forget her: he is a foreigner and will
never be allowed to marry a member of the royal family. Neocles is torn
between giving up his love for Pomena—if he does, he will be "the unhappiest man in the world"—and the "eternal respect" he has for his father
(Emin, *Themistocles*, 288). In the end, self-interest is no match for filial responsibility. Neocles reasons: "How could I not be a criminal if I were to be
ungrateful to my parent and not obey his commands? But if I obey such a
virtuous parent, I will betray nature itself. No, cruel love! You are obliged
to yield to the duties of a son. I was born a son, not a lover, and innate law
ought to be justly preferred to all the measures of the universe" (290).[2] As
troublesome as this decision must be for Neocles, his example of self-
sacrifice pales when compared with the actions of a young woman named
Livona from Chulkov's *The Mocker*. In an interpolated tale Livona reveals
that she has been unjustly accused of wanton behavior. Believing that she

is indeed guilty of "losing her virtue," her father takes her to a lonely forest in the dead of night, pulls out a dagger, and tells her to kneel. It is apparent to Livona that her father is about to kill her in order to efface his imaginary shame, yet she does nothing to save herself. She kneels and takes the dagger in her chest without a word of protest (4:68–69). Moreover, when she survives and, after many years, is eventually reunited with her father, she harbors no ill will and joyfully returns home with him to play once again the role of loving daughter (4:74–79).

As opposed to a Miramond or a Livona, the heroes and heroines of *The Mocker, The Comely Cook,* and *Vanka Kain* inhabit the type of fictional world where authority figures are noticeably lacking. God plays absolutely no role in the last two novels, and in *The Mocker* the concept of a supreme being or a group of deities controlling human destiny is most often treated irreverently in the tales told by the anonymous monk. Earthly power also fares poorly in these works, with monarchs virtually nonexistent (except in Ladon's stories in *The Mocker)* and the law making its presence felt only as an entity to be avoided, circumvented, or deceived. Furthermore, the major characters in these three novels are orphans and outcasts who have no one to look after them and, what is even more important to a carnivalesque view of the world, no father figure to direct or command them. Neokh, Martona, and Vanka Kain are colorful vagabonds who do just about as they please and who think nothing of deceiving or betraying someone if it is to their benefit. On those rare occasions when they are forced to confront the power structure of their society—an army officer or the Moscow city government, for example—their initial response is not to express humility or a willingness to submit, but rather to turn the situation to their advantage. Given such a cast of characters, carnivalesque novels abound with comic turnabouts that, at least temporarily, raise even the lowliest of individuals above their former masters.

Contemptuous of the establishment and any form of legitimate power, the serf-turned-highwayman Vanka Kain never misses an opportunity to invert accepted social relationships. Just as a pauper or a fool reigned over the carnival, Kain manipulates, cajoles, and humiliates the authorities in such a manner that he temporarily gains ascendance over them. In order to pull off his impressive string of turnabouts, he runs the gamut of carnivalesque ploys, from simple jokes to pillaging polite society from within. While riding with Mikhail Zaria's gang, Kain comes upon the servant of a landowner named Shubin and facetiously remarks: "Is it really true that the general always goes around in a fur coat and therefore has the name Shubin [*shuba,* 'fur coat']? Well, tell him we're sending a tailor to sew him some summer clothes" (Komarov, *Vanka Kain,* 79). As Kain's thinly veiled threat implies, Zaria and his associates do "fleece" the general by returning to his estate when he is away and robbing it (84–85). From the verbal to the physical, Kain taunts official society even more blatantly when he uses his own gang to overpower a guard and free a thief from prison. Before he is finished with this episode, the rogue decides to turn the tables by putting the prisoner's shackles on the guard and then placing him in custody (144–45). On another occasion Kain unilaterally decides to give a young peasant who has just been conscripted into the military his unconditional release. When the manager of recruits objects, Kain marches him into the street, pours a bucket of tar over his head, and leaves him with the following piece of carnival doggerel *(pribautki):*

> I used to consecrate as monks
> People who didn't treat me honorably.
> Your archimandrite is a fool,
> You should have been made a monk long ago.
>
> (Ia i prezhde v takie startsy postrigal,
> Kto ne chestno so mnoiu postupal.
> Durak tvoi Arkhimandrit,
> Davno by pora tebe chernetsom byt´.)
> (138)

Of course Kain does not carry out these mocking inversions out of the goodness of his heart. On the contrary, with a hedonism reminiscent of the carnival, he only frees the two men after he has been promised substantial sums of money for the work.[3]

In addition to his jokes, tricks, and mercenary turnabouts Kain saves his most conspicuous carnivalesque behavior for direct confrontations with the authorities. While still a serf, he steals some valuable goods from his master, Filat´ev, is captured, and then is returned to the estate. As punishment Filat´ev chains Kain to a post along with a small bear and refuses to give him anything to eat or drink (15). The thief believes all is lost until one of Filat´ev's servants unexpectedly provides him with some valuable information: a police officer has been killed on the estate and the corpse thrown down a well (17). Kain declares *slovo i delo Gosudarevo* (Sovereign's word and deed; 18)[4] and is taken to the village of Preobrazhenskoe where he is given an interview with the governor of Moscow, Count Semen Andreevich Saltykov (20–21). The count determines that Kain should not be punished any further and escorts him back to the estate to conduct an investigation. When they arrive, Kain turns the tables by having Saltykov arrest the man who returned him to Filat´ev (22) and in short order leads the soldiers to the body, testifies against his master, and wins his freedom (22–23). Thus, right from the start of his life of crime Kain structures his activities on the model of the carnival: the rich merchant Filat´ev is found guilty and punished, the thief receives a pardon, and the entire affair is given a seal of approval by the authorities.

In perhaps the strangest turnaround of all in Kain's story the authorities themselves elevate the highwayman to a position of preeminence. Realizing that sooner or later his luck will run out, Kain decides to trade his intimate knowledge of the Moscow underworld for a fresh start. One day he simply barges into the home of the powerful senator Prince Kropotkin and

openly declares: "I am a robber and a thief . . . and know many other robbers and thieves not only in Moscow but in other cities as well. If my former crimes would be mercifully forgiven and a good team put at my disposal, I would be able to catch quite a few of them" (99). In order to prove
his sincerity, Kain is given a special unit of soldiers and responds by
rounding up 103 criminals in just one night (99–101). Impressed by Kain's
ardor, the entire senate not only pardons his by now rather lengthy life of
lawlessness but also names him the head of a forty-five-man special investigation unit and issues a decree ordering the Military College, Police
Chancellery, and Criminal Investigation Department to give him their full
cooperation.

For quite some time Kain does render the authorities a great service by
rounding up numerous criminals in Moscow and its environs, but he is
simply too much a creature of the subculture to play his newfound role
straight. Exploiting his freedom in true carnivalesque fashion, Kain works
both sides of the law. Like a character out of the Renaissance diableries
mentioned by Bakhtin, he prowls the streets of Moscow, plundering the
very society that has offered him refuge. Kain's reputation as a high liver
becomes legend among Moscow's lower classes, and a cadre of down-and-
out vagabonds and factory workers forms around him, eager to do his bid-
ding (101–2). At first they serve as extensions of the law, but soon find
ways to aggrandize both themselves and their boss.

> Going around Moscow, presumably as [police] spies, they found out
> through various means about many suspicious people and reported them
> to Kain. At the same time they themselves engaged in underhanded activi-
> ties, picking pockets of kerchiefs, watches, tobacco boxes, and whatever
> other things they could get their hands on, which they then brought to
> Kain. Out of these things he took part for himself and gave the rest to the
> thieves. Sometimes he returned stolen merchandise to its rightful owner,
> explaining that he found it with the help of his subordinates, and thus re-
> ceived a reward and hearty thanks. (107–8)

Just as the temporary antiworld of the carnival was sanctioned by the authorities, Kain the lowly serf exploits the good graces of official society in
order to crown himself king of the Moscow underworld.

Throughout his career Kain uses the wit and wisdom of the subculture
to free himself from one desperate situation after another, but, just like the
carnival, this way of life does have its limits. When carnival comes to a
close, the normal hierarchies of church and state are reestablished; when
Kain pushes his luck too far, no set of events, no matter how extraordinary, is able to save him. Late in the novel the narrator tells us that Kain
has become so intoxicated by his ability to perpetrate virtually any crime
with impunity that "one day he dared to kidnap and forcibly dishonor the
wife of Nikolai Budaev, a police official" (176–77). When the outraged Budaev files a formal complaint, Kain is called before the authorities. Threatened with torture, he tries to save himself by once again declaring *slovo i*

delo Gosudarevo. Unlike several occasions in the past, however, this time the ploy does not work, as both the police commissioner and the head of the Secret Chancellery are determined to make Kain submit to authority. Questioned under "merciless torture," he finally confesses not only to raping the police official's wife, but also to the many other crimes he committed while serving as a police informer (178). In virtually no time at all a commission is convened, Kain is found guilty, and the former lord of the subculture is flogged, branded, and exiled (178–79).[5] Perhaps because time has just run out for him or perhaps because his assault of an innocent woman went far beyond mere jesting and self-serving duplicity, carnival is over for Kain. In the 1890s the authorities closed down the carnival for fear it would exacerbate public unrest; in the 1740s they attempted to improve civil order by sentencing one of its most unruly exponents to a life of penal servitude.

The carnivalesque motif of the subversion of the upper echelons of society also plays a significant role in Komarov's novel *Nevidimka*, although in this work the deceit involved is more lighthearted and playful. In one interpolated tale a discharged army officer finds himself in a strange city where he is befriended by a local merchant who lures him to his house with the promise of free food and lodging (185–86). After a hearty meal and a night's rest the officer is ready to resume his travels when the merchant unexpectedly presents him with a bill (186–90). The officer has no choice but to pay what the merchant demands and is left without any money for the rest of his journey. When the story of this unfortunate traveler comes to the attention of a crafty servant, he immediately comes up with a plan to set the situation right. The very next morning the two allies make their way to the marketplace, and while patting the merchant on the shoulder (but looking at a shoulder of lamb), the officer asks, "How much?" When the merchant answers, the officer pays him and orders the servant to chop off the merchant's shoulder (195). Horrified at his mistake, the merchant is forced into giving the pair five times the amount of money he took from the officer in order to get out of this predicament, and the two merry mockers go on their way (196–98).

If the story ended here, the carnivalesque imperative of humbling the rich and powerful would have been satisfied when the conniving merchant was outsmarted by a mere servant. But this episode has yet another twist that underscores one more time the mocking nature of Komarov's final novel. When, as previously agreed, the time comes for the partners to split the money they extorted from the merchant, the officer tries to outwit the servant. He tells him to come to his house the next morning for a division of the spoils, but when the servant arrives with his master Polumedes, the officer feigns death (198–200). Realizing that this is a trick, the servant and Polumedes buy a coffin and line it in such a way that the tips of the nails poke through the fabric into the interior. When they lay the supposed corpse on this bed of nails, he winces in pain but refuses to betray himself, so the coffin is closed and taken to a deserted country church (200–201).

Placing themselves in hiding, Polumedes and his servant decide to observe the coffin and simply wait until the officer is finally ready to come out and give up the ghost, as it were. The officer remains firm in his resolve for quite some time until a gang of robbers suddenly storms into the church with a fresh haul of loot. Arguing over how to divide it, they decide that the person who can cut completely through the coffin with one stroke of his sword shall have it all (202–3). Hearing this and now really fearing for his life, the officer kicks the cover off the coffin, gnashes his teeth, and shouts: "Arise! Arise! Host of the dead" (204). Playing along with the game, Polumedes and his servant rush out from their hiding place, scare the startled robbers into making a mad dash for freedom and, along with the officer, split both the money they received from the merchant and the spoils left behind by their fleeing victims. Thus, by relying on their wits and the life-saving power of the trick, this unarmed threesome manage to overcome the representatives of greed and violence, with just a little help from the benign forces that shape a carnivalesque view of the world.

In addition to undercutting secular hierarchies, Chulkov and Komarov also focus their mocking sense of humor on the other basic target of the carnivalesque mentality: the clergy. For instance, early in his wanderings Neokh impersonates a man of the cloth so well that even the high priest who is out to kill him does not recognize the lusty vagabond (Chulkov, *Mocker*, 3:221–28). Taking advantage of the clergyman's inflated ego, Neokh serves as an accomplice in the unwitting hypocrite's self-immolation. When he is eventually sentenced to death for this "fun," as he calls it, Neokh uses the time-honored carnivalesque intermediary of wine to effect his escape. With the aid of a conniving peasant he gets his guards so drunk that "their inebriation dulled their boldness and vigilance, and they fell asleep so soundly that no fear or forthcoming misfortune had the power to rouse them" (3:228). In much the same fashion Vanka Kain also uses a dull-witted priest and the bounty of Bacchus to construct what the narrator calls a "comedy." After his wedding Kain dispatches the priest who performed the ceremony by tying his hands behind his back, draping two wine bottles around his neck, and pinning a sign to the back of his cassock that states: "Untie me when the wine hanging from my neck is completely gone" (Komarov, *Vanka Kain*, 133). The priest is so chastened by this experience, we are told, that when he crosses Kain's path some time later, he hikes up his skirts and makes a run for it so as not to reprise his starring role in the rogue's farcical attempt at street theater.

The carnivalesque motifs of the greedy merchantry and the lecherous clergy reach a climax of sorts in one of the most humorous episodes in *The Mocker*. When Neokh arrives penniless in the town of Vineta, a group of thieves and prostitutes take him under their wing and set him up with a merchant's wife. As the woman's gigolo, Neokh becomes so rich that her avaricious, yet gullible, husband wonders how the student has accumulated such wealth (4:211–21). To satisfy his curiosity, Neokh fabricates a story in which he serves as the go-between in a romantic affair featuring the high priest of the temple of Perun and a noblewoman named Minamila (4:223). He claims that the priest is so infatuated with this woman that no impropriety is beyond him and that he would be willing to turn his job as intermediary over to the merchant if only he would ask. To prove to the incredulous merchant the truth of his story, he invites him to observe secretly the couple's next meeting in the grove of the main temple. On the evening in question the playful trickster Neokh springs his trap by staging a bawdy, fully costumed "comedy," in which he stars as the high priest and the merchant's wife plays the role of Minamila. With the hapless, and still unsuspecting, merchant observing in the shadows, the union of the lovers is described in all its carnivalesque irony: a servant who is impersonating Neokh as go-between is called winged Mercury, Neokh becomes an august "earthly Jupiter," and the merchant's wife is a near goddess who "adorns all nature with her charms" (4:232). While the amorous couple desecrates the holy space of Perun's temple with their lovemaking, the sniggering merchant is given his own role to play: that of fool (4:233–35). Deceived by Neokh's charade, he finds it hard to conceal his glee. As the narrator tells us, "His joy kept increasing as the lovers came ever closer to their delight" (4:233). The cuckold's humiliation is complete when he returns home, greets his wife, who has made it home before him, and retires to his room to dream of all the wealth he will acquire as the new go-between. What he does not know is that, while he is conjuring up visions of riches that will never materialize, Neokh and his wife are in the next room "finishing up" what they have begun in the grove (4:234). Just as in the carnival, the rogue's sleight of hand has humbled the mighty and elevated the lowly to a position of preeminence—all to the accompaniment of a hearty belly laugh.[6]

SEXUAL (MIS)CONDUCT

Limiting personal freedom is a natural tendency in the more serious strain of early Russian prose fiction, and nowhere is this restrictive regime more evident than in affairs of the heart. From Emin's *Kamber and Arisena* to Ladon's tales in *The Mocker*, sexual conduct is circumscribed by a severe code. In the fictional world of novels like these an unmarried woman's virginity is synonymous with her virtue, and for any respectable, well-born heroine sex out of wedlock is "the vilest of crimes" (Emin, *Ernest and Doravra*, 4:84). Angelica, a young Maltese woman in Feridat's interpolated tale, speaks for all such heroines when she asserts that her chasteness is "everything that is of value to me" (Emin, *Inconstant Fate*, 2:309). If an unmarried woman has the misfortune to lose her virginity, even if against her will, she feels more disgraced than a gentleman who has lost his honor and all self-respect. When Sarmanda is in imminent danger of being raped, her first thoughts are not of her physical well-being or personal safety. Instead, she thinks of Lizark and of how she will not only be unable to love him fully but will also be undeserving of his affection (Emin, *Lizark and Sar-*

manda, 243). Like the heroines in every one of Emin's novels she instantly realizes that, in the world she inhabits, her virginity/virtue is a "priceless honor that even the heavens have no power to return" (Emin, *Kamber and Arisena*, 57).

In Samuel Richardson's classic novel *Clarissa* the steadfast heroine embraces a lingering, pathetic death as a means of escaping the disgrace she feels after being raped by the libertine Lovelace. When her end is imminent, she rejoices, certain in the belief that she will soon trade this vale of tears for eternal rest in Heaven (*Clarissa*, 393, 463). Although the refined, sensitive, and highborn heroines of Emin's novels are not looking for divine intercession to save them from the humiliation of losing their virginity, they are, to a woman, infected with the Clarissa complex. Without a moment's hesitation Arisena, Ziumbiula, Sarmanda, Marianne, and Doravra are willing to give up their lives to preserve their virtue. When confronted with either drowning at sea or being forced into a sexual liaison with the captain of her ship, Sarmanda considers the first option to be far more preferable. As the ship breaks apart after a six-day storm and the terrified Sarmanda is carried away by the driving waves, she "anticipate[s] her end," the narrator tells us, "with gladness, knowing that it [will] save her from the vile tyrant" (*Lizark and Sarmanda*, 245). In Emin's first novel Kadyr uses the same logic to comfort his best friend Kamber over the loss of his beloved Arisena. Deceived by false news of Arisena's death, Kamber is suicidally despondent, but at the graveside Kadyr assuages his grief with the thought that "it is better for you that she died yours rather than live and be someone else's" (*Kamber and Arisena*, 219). Needless to say, Arisena feels exactly the same way. The need to live within the boundaries set by society, especially those regulating sexual conduct, is so strong that the heroines of Emin's novels do not even need an evil outside influence to activate their suicidal impulses. Their own beloved will do if he should happen to insinuate anything improper. Believing that Ernest, who is married, has implied they should enter into a carnal relationship, Doravra rebukes him, saying: "I would sooner agree to death than give a place in my heart to an inclination that would be so opposed to my honor" (*Ernest and Doravra*, 2:112). Fortunately, Doravra never reaches such a desperate impasse, for no one is more committed to both the letter and the spirit of the law than her cerebral lover.[7]

Although early Russian prose fiction does have its Lovelace-like characters who are frequently overcome by "bestial desires," for the most part the noblemen heroes gracing its pages are nothing short of gallant. Ernest, for example, is just as concerned about preserving Doravra's reputation and virtue as she is. Moreover, even when temptation does cross their path, these heroes are careful to do everything in their power to avoid it. While shipwrecked and far from home, Lord George's resolve and faithfulness to his betrothed, Friderika Luisa, is put to the test in the court of the Moorish queen Musalmina. Taken by the stately Englishman, the queen attempts to seduce him by undressing and bathing naked in his presence (Komarov,

Milord George, 65, 70–71). If ever a man had reason to succumb to such blandishments, George does. As Musalmina's slave he should be persuaded not only by the queen's physical charms but also by the threat of punishment for failing to please his mistress. Fortunately for Friderika Luisa, George's head is not turned by this exotic woman's beauty. As a proper English gentleman he "courteously refuses the queen's declarations of love" and advises her to put her clothes back on lest she catch cold (71). In Chulkov's *The Mocker* the enlightened monarch Alim reacts to a similar provocation with the same sense of calm restraint. He is captivated by the unexpected apparition of the goddess Aropa, who descends from the heavens clad only in a sash wound about her "for the diversion of the gods and the pleasure of mortals" (3:14), but, being the good neoclassical character that he is, Alim dismisses the goddess's appearance as the product of a distorted imagination. After all, it would be unseemly to lust after her, and how could he hope to rule his kingdom effectively if he were to become obsessed with visions of a beautiful woman whose "clothing had been blown away by playful zephyrs" (3:14).

As the above examples imply, eroticism does have a place in those early Russian novels that depict a rigidly defined social order. On the rare occasions it does appear, however, it is almost always sterilized in one manner or another. The result of such an approach is that potential lovers do come together, yet they are never allowed to consummate their relationship. For instance, in Emin's *Kamber and Arisena* Gamlia pretends to seduce Kadyr solely in order to manipulate him. On one of his visits to her house she ushers the gullible officer into a sumptuously decorated room where he spies a painting depicting a naked Venus lying on a bed and beckoning Mars to the pleasures of love (92–93). Unbeknown to the credulous Kadyr, this is as close as he will ever get to sharing his passion with Gamlia, for she has absolutely no interest in him. Even when duplicity is not involved, chances are so slim that characters who feel a physical attraction for each other will actually engage in carnal love that they might as well be figures in a painting. In Emin's *Inconstant Fate* the inquisitive Egyptian princess Ziumbiula enters the room of a wounded and sleeping Miramond. At first her attention is drawn to his injured leg, but in no time at all she is captivated by Miramond's physical appearance. The princess cries out to heaven as she discovers the perfection of the unconscious hero's face, eyes, lips, and hands (1:138–40). When Miramond awakens, he apparently opens the way to their happiness by immediately confessing that he is just as attracted to Ziumbiula, but owing to the sexual code of conduct that governs their fictional world, the couple will not be allowed to experience the bliss of physical love for many years and hundreds of pages. In a similar incident the Marquis de Toledo comes upon a sleeping Marianne and marvels at her transcendent beauty. Clothed only in a light muslin shirt, she seems nothing short of a goddess with her ruby lips, pearly white face, and alabaster breasts (Emin, *Marquis de Toledo,* 204–5). For now, at least, Marianne is just about as accessible to the Marquis as if she were immortal. Married to another man, she will not be free to share her life with him for some time to come.

When men and women do confront their sexual desires openly in Emin's fiction, erotic tension is usually negated by not allowing it to progress beyond the verbal stage. Although impassioned and provocative talk is rather common in novels like *Inconstant Fate*, action is all but nonexistent. When Miramond is sent by Ziumbiula's father to a foreign court, he catches the eye of Queen Belilia. Without mincing words, she declares that Miramond may continue to love Ziumbiula and may even return to her, but first he "must satisfy the love and quiet the heart in which he has ignited a passion that engulfs my inner being" (1:281). Like Milord George, Miramond will not succumb to the queen's provocations even though he knows he will be tortured for opposing her wishes. In *Kamber and Arisena* Gamlia leads Kadyr to believe that his aid in helping her get acquainted with Kamber will be richly rewarded. She tells him: "I am extremely satisfied with you, . . . and rest assured that when heaven unites me with you, I will respond to your desires with the same amount of zeal" (108–9). Unfortunately for Kadyr, he is simply being led on, and physical bliss with Gamlia, wedded or otherwise, is not in his future. In an interesting twist on the "doomed to fail" approach to intimacy, Miramond becomes attracted to a stunning young woman yet for some inexplicable reason is unable to express his feelings to her. Even though we are told that Miramond's "blood began to become agitated, and it seemed as though it wanted to join with the blood of this beauty" (*Inconstant Fate*, 3:71), he refuses to give in to such impulses. As it turns out, Miramond's intuition is sound, for the woman who has captured his attention is none other than his long-lost sister Agatha. And so it goes, as one physical relationship after another is shortcircuited, if not forever, then at least until lawful wedlock is achieved.

When the heroes and heroines of novels like *Inconstant Fate* finally do express their desire in a physical manner, their actions resemble the behavior of moonstruck adolescents more than that of mature adults. Intercourse is obviously out of the question, but even touching and kissing are undertaken only with the greatest trepidation. Given the rare chance to be alone, Miramond and Agatha simply gaze at each other without speaking or touching; they are content to "satisfy themselves with the vision of [each other's] pleasantness" (Emin, *Inconstant Fate*, 3:81). When the brave Achilles, who is soon to become the hero of the Trojan campaign, expresses his love for Deidamiia, the pleasantries hardly rise above the level experienced by Miramond and his soon to be revealed younger sister. "Kissing his hand, Deidamiia bid him to rise, and so they enjoyed themselves with talk of love, which was as pleasant to them as they were sincerely in love with each other" (Chulkov, *Achilles*, 12–13). Superseding even these examples in its delicateness is the breathless love affair of Ernest and Doravra. With much effort and mental anguish the couple finally does graduate from wistfully looking at each other across a room to kissing, yet even this relatively innocent act is not without its drawbacks. Just recalling such an occasion almost incapacitates Ernest, who falteringly writes: "You took my

hand and pressed it. . . . Your lips so sweet . . . oh, the recollection of this
leaves me weak! . . . Your lips . . . united with mine. Then I was . . . Recalling this moment I am lost in my joy . . . . In your embrace" (Emin, *Ernest
and Doravra*, 1:120–21). Perhaps when a man can derive such pleasure from
simply kissing his beloved, greater physical intimacy is not required. Whatever his motivation, even when Doravra untypically agrees to enter into a
sexual relationship with him (4:17–18), Ernest reacts more like a timid
young virgin than an experienced man of the world by steadfastly refusing
to take advantage of her momentary weakness.[8]

On those rare occasions when sex out of wedlock does occur in the repressive fictional worlds inhabited by Miramond, Achilles, and Ernest and
Doravra, it is almost always presented in dark and threatening tones. Outside the bounds prescribed by society, sexual intercourse is transformed
from "the final pleasure on which love is based" (Emin, *Kamber and Arisena*,
95) into "bestial desire" and "animal passion" (Chulkov, *The Mocker*, 4:107,
5:103). Except for *Themistocles*, every one of Emin's novels includes a scene
in which a virtuous young heroine is either raped or threatened with sexual assault, with none extracting more pathos from this device than *The
Marquis de Toledo*.[9] No more than two pages go by before the innocent
young heroine, who is joyfully looking forward to her impending marriage, falls prey to the libertine Bonveal. Just as Lovelace lures Clarissa
away from the protection of friends and family, the smooth-talking Bonveal calmly plots his seduction and rape of Marianne. Ingratiating himself
with the young victim's family, he invites them to his residence for dinner
only to kidnap them as they return home late at night along deserted
streets (7–8). When Marianne is brought to him, she finds that Bonveal is
completely without conscience: no matter how much she implores, he will
not be dissuaded from his vile intent. The narrator describes the pathetic
scene: "Pale with fear, Marianne crawled along the ground near his feet
and, kissing them ceaselessly, begged the tyrant to have mercy on her and
spare her honor from his fury. But neither tears nor tender words could
reach Bonveal's barbaric heart, and this unfortunate woman was forced to
endure a severe beating and become a martyr to the barbarian's bestial passion" (11). Exhausted from her ordeal, Marianne drags herself home the
next day, knowing that her real test has just begun.[10]

If *The Marquis de Toledo* is the quickest of Emin's novels to accost readers
with the tragedy of unsanctioned sexual activity, *Inconstant Fate* sets the
record for the most frequent application of this motif. Early in his adventures Miramond manages to save a woman from a would-be ravisher who
has tied her to a tree (1:65–66), and shortly thereafter he meets another
woman who has experienced the horrors of being raped. She recounts how
she was drugged, stuffed in a trunk, and transported to another city where
she remained the sexual slave of a pirate captain for four years (1:90–95).
Much the same fate befalls the seventeen-year-old Sandra when she is kid-
napped by an aged lecher, who rapes her before selling her into slavery
(1:213–31), and Miramond's own sister and fiancée are also gravely threat-

ened with sexual assault. As a young woman Agatha is stalked by one of the beys of Cairo, who tries "to force her to satisfy his bestial lust" (3:249), and Ziumbiula makes it clear that even though she will agree to marry Hussein Bey in order to win her father's freedom, he will never freely enjoy the pleasures of the marriage bed. In a tearful farewell to Miramond she declares: "Don't think, my dear one, that I would entrust to your rival and my tormentor that which I have saved for you. . . . Death, the last refuge of the unfortunate, will save me from the violence of this tyrant" (3:326). In one final burst of tragedy Ziumbiula's father, Sultan Osman Bey, proves that even the mighty are not immune to such a cruel turn of fate. While recounting the story of his youth, Osman explains that he and his wife were once captured by pirates. Although they were eventually freed, it was not before his wife "was forced to submit to the coercion of her ravisher" (3:344), which no doubt had much to do with her dying shortly after being liberated. As this terrible litany suggests, when sex transgresses the limits ordained by society, it can only culminate in humiliation, suffering, and even death.

Reflecting on the proper ordering of personal relationships, the shepherd Amnon tells Sarmanda that "we begin to love women when we are joined to them in marriage, because loving a woman who isn't yours is the action of an ignoble man" (Emin, *Lizark and Sarmanda*, 154). Given his audience, the philosophical Amnon is preaching to the converted, for not only Lizark and Sarmanda but also every central couple in each of Emin's novels and in Komarov's *Milord George* and *Nevidimka* as well voluntarily end up in a state of lawful matrimony. Adherence to the law and to tacitly understood codes of conduct is so strong in these works that no self-respecting character would seriously consider a physically intimate relationship prior to the wedding ceremony. If any two persons had reason to transgress the sexual mores of their society, it would be the star-crossed Ernest and Doravra, yet neither of them will take this dangerous step. Realizing his responsibility to the married Doravra, Ernest tells her: "I . . . esteem the holy bonds that have bound your heart forever, . . . [and] a sense of justice and virtue has purged from my heart the violent passions that have tormented my entire nature" (Emin, *Ernest and Doravra*, 4:88). Marianne echoes this sentiment when she tells the Marquis that she cannot indulge her true feelings for him because she already has a "lawful husband": "It isn't hatred that gives rise to the coldness you notice in me, but a sense of duty that is laid upon us by the laws. You know that one is not permitted to love two hearts, and therefore it is necessary that one be excluded" (Emin, *Marquis de Toledo*, 209). The reflex to legitimize personal relationships is so deeply ingrained in this type of fiction that there is no way to express the overwhelming feeling of sudden passion. On first meeting it only takes a moment for Polumedes and Martemiana to become irresistibly attracted to each other, but instead of desiring some private time together, they both seek something more formal. Polumedes tells us that Martemiana "talked with me for a long time and came to love me so much that she made a solemn oath in her faith that she would marry me" (Komarov, *Nevidimka*, 74).[11]

Those early Russian novels that strive to promulgate an Enlightenment understanding of personal virtue generally end well for their central characters, yet there is a darker side to this veneer of happiness. Even when the most dedicated of lovers come together to share a life that turns out to be both long and prosperous, the goal of such marriages is not the personal pleasure of husband and wife, but rather the well-ordered running of the state. Doravra's confidant, Pulkheriia, makes this clear when she tells Ernest that "every time two hearts are united by the bond of the law, society ought to rejoice, because without this ritual we would not know who our relations are or what our rights are" (Emin, *Ernest and Doravra*, 2:225). What Pulkheriia sees as the obligatory foundation of the social edifice, however, is often perceived by others as an apparatus for the repression of women. Throughout his prose fiction Emin manages to work in what would pass for a feminist perspective even today. In *Kamber and Arisena*, for instance, Kadyr contends that women are radically altered upon entering a permanent union with a man. He sadly admits that after their wedding day "they are held in contempt, and so their former ardor cools" (165). This is also the opinion of Rukie, a widow in the novel *Inconstant Fate*, who launches the most forceful and articulate attack on the institution of marriage in all of Emin's oeuvre. She laments that "when they want us in marriage, [all men] kiss our hands, caress us with tender words, and promise to serve us eternally, but as soon as we marry them, [they] begin to rule over us and take away our freedom" (3:280). Spelling out the dismal future awaiting most women, she adds that wives have no choice but to obey their husbands and according to the law must endure every evil, including frequent beatings (3:279). Encouraged to marry into royalty, Rukie is not at all impressed, for as she sees it: "What sort of pleasure is it to ride together in a carriage and eat at magnificent tables if each piece of bread . . . must be mourned over with bitter tears?" (3:281). Even with their positive denouements the novels of Emin and, to a lesser extent, Komarov depict a world in which the personal satisfaction of the individual is relatively unimportant and in some cases impossible to achieve.

Early in Chulkov's *The Mocker* Ladon issues what he considers one of life's eternal truths, confidently maintaining that "any mature, unmarried woman would gladly agree to make love in a darkened bower where it is impossible to notice shame on a face" (1:43). With this statement, which is placed in the introductory section of his first original novel, Chulkov reveals a decidedly carnivalesque attitude toward the pleasures of the flesh. As opposed to the harsh code of sexual conduct restricting individual initiative in the novels of Emin and Komarov, any mores that might exist in Chulkov's prose fiction are there primarily to be flaunted. Characters are rarely, if ever, punished for their sexual promiscuity, and in several instances they reap tremendous benefits from it. For example, the wandering gigolo Neokh and the bawdy, gold-digging Martona both manage to secure lofty niches in society as a direct result of their loose sexual behavior. Moreover, what Emin sees as the darker side of sex is almost completely missing in Chulkov's fictional world. Since virtue is not an issue here, women do not find themselves in the sort of desperate situations that Emin's heroines always do. Abused wives and suicidal virgins simply have no place in *The Mocker* or *The Comely Cook*. On the contrary, Chulkov turns the tables and makes a promiscuous prostitute like Martona the benign ruler of just about any man who happens to cross her path. Martona need never worry about the terrors of rape; in her carnivalesque version of the world sex is not used for control, only for pleasure. Together with eating, drinking, and laughter it promotes a positive, festive image of life.

As Ladon's tale about two promiscuous noblemen makes abundantly clear (*Mocker*, 1:40–45), since sex has only positive connotations in the carnivalesque mentality, even the most grievous breech of decorum does not merit a punitive response. When the bachelor Milozor expresses an interest in one of his good friend Popal's female servants, Popal agrees to help out by arranging a tryst. He tells the woman that he is in love with her and orders her to meet him at midnight in a secluded arbor. Once she shows up, he plans to allow Milozor to take his place and have sex with her. The servant is not at all interested in such an arrangement and in her anxiety tells Popal's wife everything. Enraged, Popal's wife decides to revenge herself on what she thinks is her unfaithful husband by substituting for the object of Milozor's desire. When the appointed time arrives, Popal's wife meets Milozor in the arbor, and since it is so dark, neither of them knows who the other is. After they make love, they walk out into the moonlight and immediately realize their mistake. To make matters worse, Popal comes running up, having found out from the servant that her mistress has taken her place. The onetime lovers get down on their knees, fearing Popal's reaction, but anger and reproaches are completely lacking. Instead, Popal himself kneels and asks forgiveness from his wife and best friend. As Ladon's nonjudgmental "moral" emphasizes ("everyone was right, and everyone was wrong"; 1:45), there simply is no room for blame and retribution in the carnival. Popal is not humiliated, his wife does not even consider taking her life, and Milozor has not lost his honor over the affair. Ladon concludes the story with the facetious statement that "the friendship [of the two men] was not ended by this misunderstanding, and even though they became brothers-in-law, they died friends" (1:45). Beginning as an ignoble attempt to force a servant into an unwanted liaison, this episode is transformed into harmless farce by the life-affirming power of the carnival.

The story of Milozor and Popal reflects in microcosm the carnivalesque ethos of the almost one hundred pages that serve as an informal introduction to *The Mocker*. This nonpunitive spirit courses through virtually every episode in this part of the work and is especially important in motivating the appearance of the novel's second narrator, the anonymous monk. While staying at the estate of a retired colonel, the first narrator, Ladon, learns that the entire household lives in fear of a ghost that is supposedly stalking the premises. Attempting to find a rational explanation for this phenomenon, he follows the housekeeper late one night as she rushes to a clandestine meeting with the unwanted visitor. As we soon find out, far from being a spiritual encounter, the housekeeper's rendezvous is very much of this world, for as Ladon looks on, the young woman and the ghost make love in the colonel's cellar (1:6–8). Before long Ladon lays a trap, catches the pair, and exposes them to the colonel (1:47–55). Given the opportunity to tell his story, the ghost turns out to be a monk with a rich and ribald history on the fringes of society: for a time he fell in with a band of robbers, then worked as a confidence man, and finally was forcibly tonsured after having an affair with the wife of a rich and powerful noble (1:60–83). Considering his checkered background, the anxiety he has caused on the estate with his nocturnal visits, and the impropriety of making love with the colonel's housekeeper, the monk would seem to be in grave danger of being handed over to the authorities. The colonel, who as master of the estate and a representative of the official power structure should have no qualms about making the monk pay for his transgressions, has other ideas, however. Instead of punishing the monk, he not only forgives him (1:57–58), but even goes so far as to procure his freedom from the monastery (1:83), thus paving the way for the string of bawdy adventures the monk narrates in the last four parts of *The Mocker*. As a fitting end to this carnivalesque interlude the colonel also takes no punitive action against his housekeeper. After giving her a stern lecture on responsibility, he drops the matter altogether. In the lighthearted atmosphere that reigns on this estate, illegitimate sex is simply not a crime, even if it does upset the normal routine of the official world.

In Chulkov's two novels no one represents the pleasure principle of the carnival enunciated in the opening pages of *The Mocker* better than his capricious cook Martona and wayward student Neokh. Unlike Marianne, the scrupulous heroine of Emin's *The Marquis de Toledo*, who proclaims that one heart cannot love two persons, Martona has no problem being involved with more than one man at the same time. To recall just one of several examples, when Martona notices the lusty Akhal´ eyeing her in church, she almost instantaneously decides to hoodwink her seventy-year-old patron and take up with the much younger man. As soon as the occasion presents itself, she makes contact with Akhal´, and in practically no time at all they become lovers. In spite of the obstacle of carrying out their affair in the colonel's house, it proceeds so quickly that Martona concludes: "For his part Akhal´ considered himself quite fortunate in that without any trouble at all he received from me that which it is often impossible to attain with two years of constant effort" (*Comely Cook*, 175).[12] Taking the same approach, Neokh, the hero of *The Tale of the Taffeta Beauty Patch*, also uses the positive power of sex to make his way through life. A particularly good example of this philosophy occurs in an episode in which he falls in with a "shameless" crowd of thieves, confidence men, and prostitutes and finds that they are not at all like the stereotypes created by high society. These social pariahs willingly embrace the penniless student and eventually help him make his fortune by setting him up with a rich merchant's lonely wife

(*Mocker*, 4:214–15). In their indecorous antiworld, which is benignly governed by a jovial procuress, life is lived to the fullest, and sex is abundant. Every evening when the members of the gang reassemble at their flophouse, they divide the day's take and celebrate their good fortune. The dirty, grimy clothes of beggars and thieves are stripped away to reveal fine dresses and suits, food and drink abound, and when the evening comes to an end, "they all [go] off to lie down in pairs" (4:215). In this lighthearted assembly there are no rebukes, no demands of superhuman asceticism, and no threats of self-destruction. Unencumbered by the harsh and punitive social code of official society, the denizens of the underworld are, as the monk tells us, "more tranquil than any citizen" (4:216).

In novels imbued with the spirit of the carnival, not only are the characters ready and willing to follow the dictates of their desires, but eroticism itself is put on prominent display. As opposed to the longing looks and trembling kisses that pass for sensuality in Emin's novels, the depiction of sex in carnivalesque fiction is, if not always graphic, at least quite suggestive. For example, it seems as though whichever way he happens to turn, Milord George finds himself in the presence of women who are disrobing. The Moorish queen Musalmina undresses right in front of George before bathing in a fountain and then approaches him, clad only in a thin white sheet (Komarov, *Milord George*, 70–71). This incident follows closely upon her first striptease when the narrator tells us that "having bared her wonderfully shaped breasts, this beautiful woman said: 'Look, Milord, you certainly won't see such pleasant and tender forms as these in London, will you?'" (65).[13] Later in his travels George becomes enamored of the queen of Spain and with the help of a lady-in-waiting hides under her bed. Making good use of a strategically placed mirror, Komarov's stealthy hero watches as the queen undresses for the evening and "in this manner . . . was able to see not just her beautiful face but her entire body" (163). As is only fitting in carnivalesque fiction, conventional roles are often reversed, and a voyeur like George can easily become the object of a woman's amorous designs. During carnival time in Venice a mysterious dauphine takes an interest in the English lord. Although she does not want to reveal her identity, she wishes to find out if he would make a worthy suitor. When George takes ill, the dauphine decides to masquerade as a physician, telling his servant: "I will dress up as a doctor, go to him, and after having looked over his merits, if I find him pleasing, express my inclination through you" (202). When the dauphine conducts her examination, George's personal qualifications, both physical and spiritual, do pass the test. Instead of avoiding sex like the plague as Emin's characters do, the carnivalesque figures in *Milord George* seek out the pleasures of this world and revel in them.[14]

As might be expected, given her free-spirited appreciation of the world, some of the most provocative moments in the early Russian novel occur when the spotlight shines on the heroine of *The Comely Cook*. When Martona and her nobleman lover Sveton are consummating their affair, Sveton's wife catches them in the act. Openly, even proudly, proclaiming that their relationship has passed the stage of beautiful rhetoric and tearful promises,

Martona bluntly states that, as Sveton's wife barged into the room, "my lover jumped off [me], and I jumped up" (Chulkov, *Comely Cook*, 165). Finding escape to be the most prudent course of action, Sveton immediately slinks off, leaving his paramour behind to suffer his wife's wrath. When Chulkov's heroine pruriently adds that she was forced to "endure dozens of slaps on the cheeks" from Sveton's vengeful spouse (165), readers cannot help wondering if other exposed parts of her body were subjected to the same rude treatment. Later in the novel Martona recounts her first meeting with the young and handsome Akhal´, who has come to the retired colonel's estate disguised as her sister. From the description she gives of the scene, it is evident that her new lover is not at all shy about expressing his emotions. Unlike Ernest and Doravra, who simply cast longing looks in each other's direction or sneak off to steal a momentary embrace, Chulkov's characters take a much more direct approach. Martona lets us know that "pleasantry followed pleasantry, and kiss followed kiss. My sister pressed me to her heart and kissed me quite frequently on my breasts. I responded with such gratitude that, in short, even an industrious mathematician would not have been able to count all our kisses without making a mistake" (173–74).

Even when Martona's narration is not as graphic as the preceding examples, it remains quite suggestive and leaves little doubt as to what Chulkov's heroine has in mind. After she is sent packing by Sveton's wife, Martona finds a job as cook for a Muscovite bureaucrat. While in his employment, she is courted by a corrupt, ignorant, and unattractive scribe. In the only instance in the novel in which Martona turns down a suitor, she says of the scribe that "he did recognize love, but just didn't know which end to grab or how to hold on to it" (166). Immediately after this unexpected denial of the pleasure principle, Martona falls for the more desirable Akhal´, and her rhetoric returns true to form. In addition to being racy, it also acts as an aphrodisiac on her prospective lover. Despite the resistance he will undoubtedly meet from her jealous protector, the retired colonel, Martona encourages Akhal´ to continue his efforts to see her. She tells him that even without the colonel's approval "you can find the road to your prosperity" (171). As Martona's voluptuous reception of Akhal´ makes abundantly clear, this prognostication has little to do with material wealth.

As honest and appreciative as Martona is when it comes to the pleasures of sex, Ladon manages to go her one better. When he and Alenona decide to consummate their attraction for each other, his narration leaves little to the imagination. Rather coyly, as though they were acting out a passage from *Ernest and Doravra*, the couple begin by "kissing a bit" (*Mocker*, 1:38). The situation soon escalates far beyond this, however, as Ladon tells us that Alenona

> ordered me to undress her. Having unbuttoned her bodice, I touched with my trembling and sinful hand the delights of our life, both of which are called breasts, and immediately recognized that for men, women are an electric machine. I quivered, a chill ran up my spine, and if my skin

weren't so firmly attached to my body, my blood would have leapt out to freedom as though through a fine sieve. (1:38)

One thing leads to another, and Ladon concludes with what must be one of the most pointed descriptions of orgasm in mainstream Russian literature:

> I was on top of my well-being, and while being on top of it, I was not able to contain the joy within me, melted, became deprived of all my senses, and finally my limbs[15] became weak and I lay motionless. (1:39)

Portrayed both openly and honestly, eroticism is appropriately accorded a place of honor in those early Russian novels guided by the spirit of the carnival.[16]

Novels like *The Mocker, The Comely Cook,* and *Milord George* contain so many sexually graphic scenes because pleasure, and not responsibility or propriety, is the primary concern of the vagabonds, gold diggers, and adventurers inhabiting them. Characters invested with the Enlightenment virtues of restraint and self-control may pine away while the world around them celebrates, but Neokh, Martona, and Vanka Kain never pass up an opportunity to gratify their personal desires. A carnivalesque appreciation of sensuality pervades Chulkov's novels to such a degree that even Siloslav, a central character in one of the heroic tales in *The Mocker,* often delights in the bounty and beauty of the world. Even though he is on a sacred quest to recover his lost love, Prelepa, he is not one to close his eyes when temptation crosses his path. In one of his adventures he enters a magnificent temple and sees "a naked woman of indescribable beauty. Her body was so delicate that if the ephemeral Zephyr would have touched it with his wing, . . . this most tender creation would have been utterly destroyed" (1:140). Instead of running from this siren fearing that she might seduce him, Siloslav stops to admire her physical charms. Even when she proclaims, "My domain . . . is inhabited only by women, and you may receive in it every pleasure that you can imagine" (1:142), the honorable knight does not fear for his virtue and follows the mysterious woman as she gives him a tour of the temple. Later in his travels Siloslav is led to an earthly version of Paradise, and once again he refuses to shrink from the pleasures it proffers. Finding the primary virtue of this valley to be its state of complete sexual harmony, Siloslav looks on as

> the women adorned the men with flowers and, having done this, admired them, felt them, kissed, caressed, and showed them all those pleasures that nature gave to the tender sex. Cupid attended each couple and with each minute presented new diversions, increased the passion in their hearts, and tried to bring their love to completion. Joy, innocent games, and pleasant laughter reigned there. Rapture was portrayed on every face. (2:88)

To Chulkov's way of thinking at least, heaven looks a lot more like a carnival than the dry, formal, and hierarchical state of bliss depicted by Emin.

Chapter

SIX

CHARACTERIZATION

STEREOTYPES: OF GODDESSES AND ROGUES

Encamped at the grave site of his love, Arisena, Kamber pines away like a man who is already half dead. As he conducts his pensive vigil with tears streaming down his face, the narrator reveals his state of mind. Kamber is so tormented "because he reasoned that all people are happy in love, and that he alone, like a freak of nature, suffered misfortune in it" (Emin, *Kamber and Arisena*, 229). As excessive as this rhetoric might seem, it is far from unique. Virtually every serious, altruistic hero in the early Russian novel declares at least once that he is "the unhappiest man in the world" or "the most unfortunate creature under the sun."[1] The actions and feelings of characters like Kamber, the Marquis de Toledo, and Milord George acquire an intensity and importance that is surpassed only on Mount Olympus. Hyperbole serves as the foundation of characterization in the fictional worlds they inhabit as both negative and positive figures are inflated into caricatures of real human beings. Whether it is the cunning seductress Gamlia, who rivals the biblical Delilah in her appreciation of evil, or tearful, gentle souls like Kamber who seem to be copied directly from the pages of West European sentimentalism, virtually every character in novels attempting to mimic an Enlightenment approach to literature is structured around a narrow set of traits that is magnified until it becomes larger than life. While such an approach undercuts a thoughtful analysis of human nature, it does make for a potent pedagogical device. From the fearless *bogatyr'*-like brothers Arides and Polumedes to the despicable libertine Bonveal, hyperbolized characters function as powerful icons of the values sanctioned by the official literary culture of eighteenth-century Russia. Through them, virtue is portrayed in all its glory, the twisted nature of vice is revealed for all to see, and no room is left in the middle for speculation. On one of the many occasions when Polumedes is feted by royalty, he retires from the banquet and comes upon a "most beautiful maiden" (Komarov, *Nevidimka*, 115). Even though she turns out to be his long-lost love, Martemiana, this description almost damns her with faint praise. "Most beautiful" is hardly a sufficient epithet in the early Russian novel where virtually every woman who leads a virtuous life is a candidate for immortality. To the Marquis de Toledo Marianne is worthy of Olympus (Emin, *Marquis de Toledo*, 94), Milord George considers Friderika Louisa nothing less than a goddess (Komarov, *Milord George*, 9), and Ernest, as is typical for him, adds a note of religiosity to this motif by declaring Doravra the only idol in his temple of virtue and beauty (Emin, *Ernest and Doravra*, 1:185, 2:9). The convention of making women the repository of the sublime is so deeply ingrained in the eighteenth-century Russian novel that it even applies to transitory characters. While prowling the Mediterranean Sea as a privateer, the Marquis captures a ship carrying a Tunisian princess. Upon laying eyes on the young woman, he immediately decides that "she surpassed all the nymphs of Parnassus with her beauty" (Emin, *Marquis de Toledo*, 157), yet the princess is relegated to being just one more goddess in the pantheon of the times as she quickly exits both the Marquis's life and the pages of the novel.

As lofty as the preceding descriptions might seem, they hardly test the limits of the inflated rhetoric of perfection. Virtually no claim seems unreasonable to the heroes of novels like *Inconstant Fate* as they strive to elevate the objects of their love ever higher above the mundane sphere of flesh-and-blood human beings. For example, Miramond finds the Egyptian princess Ziumbiula more awe-inspiring than Juno, Minerva, or Venus and, overwhelmed by her physical presence, rhapsodizes that the gods would award her the golden apple before all others (Emin, *Inconstant Fate*, 1:300). Such is the logic in Emin's fictional world, however, that any given instance of hyperbole merely establishes a standard that is quickly destined to be broken. As it turns out, Ziumbiula is far from being the only woman who possesses transcendent beauty, even in Egypt. When Princess Izida, the heroine of a later novel, is introduced by the narrator, he exclaims that

> if Venus achieved the status of a deity in Greece owing to her great beauty, then Izida, who surpasses all the Greek goddesses with the fairness of her face, could justly be called the goddess of Egypt. . . . The pleasantness of her smiling gaze reveals the same joy that the gods revel in on Olympus. And the speech of the goddesses of Parnassus is not as pleasant as the satisfaction derived by those who hear the words spoken by Izida. (Emin, *Lizark and Sarmanda*, 8)

Later in the novel, when he dares to think about this princess, the page Lizark transforms her into his morning star and claims that the sweat from her face is heavenly dew sent to refresh the earth (17). In much the same manner Siloslav, a hero in one of Ladon's tales in *The Mocker*, also delights in investing women with supernatural powers. When he happens upon a mysterious castle inhabited solely by women, he is so overpowered by their beauty that he claims it even surpasses the magnificence of the natural world. He tells the mistress of the castle: "The air does not charm this place, but is itself charmed as it ripples over your fairness" (Chulkov, *Mocker*, 1:162). Depicted as though they come from a higher plane of existence, heroines like Ziumbiula and Izida serve as a constant reminder of the extreme and often unattainable standards that were promulgated by authors like Emin in an attempt to win the approval of the arbiters of literary taste.

Although figures like Miramond, Lizark, and Milord George have been favored by nature just as much as their female counterparts, the prime expression of their perfection of character is not through physical appearance. Instead, the transcendent nature of these virtuous heroes is revealed through their relationships with others. Disgusted by the vulgarity of both human nature and the society it has created, Ernest finds just one feeling to be utterly beyond reproach. In a letter to his confidant, Hippolyte, he writes: "Only friendship can be excluded from the vanities of society and be honored as a thing that is perfection itself" (Emin, *Ernest and Doravra*, 3:176). For Ernest, "a person's happiness is primarily based on a sincere and faithful friend. If I have one, then I have everything that I desire" (1:134). In his true friend Hippolyte Ernest does have a companion with whom he can share everything. Hippolyte counsels Ernest, restrains him when he is on the brink of acting rashly, and provides him with a sounding board for his schemes and plans. With the help he receives from Hippolyte, Ernest is able to withstand the shock of his enforced separation from Doravra and the attendant desire for self-destruction that regularly accompanies such situations. Like their counterparts in British sentimentalist fiction, Ernest and Hippolyte give each other unconditional support. No sacrifice would be too great; no request too difficult to fulfill. Given the great demands it places on an individual, true friendship is a rare commodity in the early Russian novel. Based on selflessness and altruism, it can only be achieved by those who possess an almost superhuman strength of character.

One of the greatest displays of friendship in the eighteenth-century Russian novel must certainly belong to Kadyr, a secondary character in Emin's *Kamber and Arisena*. When Arisena's father banishes Kamber for wishing to marry his daughter, he places him under house arrest and assigns Kadyr to serve as a live-in guard (71–73). At first antagonistic to one another, the two soon become the closest of friends. The reason for this dramatic turnaround is that Kadyr possesses the "greatness of soul" that is the essential prerequisite for any lasting friendship. While listening to the exile's sad tale, he is deeply touched. The narrator tells us that "they talked about their misfortunes for an entire day, and then Kamber expressed his situation in such a pathetic manner that tears began to well up in Kadyr's eyes" (117). Moreover, Kadyr is prepared to back up his emotional response with actions. Even though they are recent acquaintances, he trusts his new friend implicitly: "Kadyr's eyes poured forth bitter tears as he listened to Kamber's words. 'O my Lord!' he wailed, having come to deeply commiserate with him. 'I would gladly shed all my blood in your service, but it is a true misfortune that I am unable to render you any help'" (119). Later in the novel, when Kamber is so despondent over losing Arisena that he seriously contemplates suicide, Kadyr once again reveals that no sacrifice is too great to ask of a friend: "In the name of the friendship that you have sworn to me so many times, I beg you not to take the life that is joined to yours. Remember that if you take your life with your own desperate hand, you will also become [my] murderer" (220). When he cannot dissuade Kamber from wasting his life away at Arisena's grave, he does the only thing that his conscience will allow: he keeps the lonely vigil with him, proclaiming that "heaven united our hearts with an inseparable friendship so do not try to stand in the way of its decision" (224). As is most often the case with the virtuous characters of the early Russian novel, the many manifestations of Kadyr's friendship are eventually amply rewarded, but not before he reveals a degree of personal fortitude that virtually qualifies him for sainthood.[2]

In an age that placed a premium on the effusive display of sentiment, nowhere did the tears flow more freely than in the first Russian novels. Emotional outbursts by otherwise stalwart characters were thought to underscore their humanity, integrity, and sincerity and vindicate the moral code they espoused. Tears come so readily to Kadyr when he hears his new acquaintance Kamber tell him of his misfortune in love because he is a man with a good heart. He can be trusted not just as a confidant, but also as a living exemplar of the way to lead one's life. Milord George, Arides, and the Marquis de Toledo face murderous pirates on the open sea or incredible odds on land without flinching, yet these *bogatr´*-like heroes are easily brought to their knees should they be separated from the objects of their all-consuming desire. Arides loses control of his emotions when his promotion to the king's special counselor prevents him from pursuing a beautiful woman he has recently met. "Sitting in his room and finding himself lost in reflections of various kinds, he cried without reserve and, stretching his hands to heaven, pronounced the following words: 'O unfortunate Arides! How many misfortunes have found you in your lifetime, and now your life teeters between happiness and unhappiness. It would have been better had you not received any rank from the king and just lived your life in peaceful merriment'" (Komarov, *Nevidimka*, 280). In Emin's *The Marquis de Toledo* Marianne's fever and subsequent illness provoke such a torrent of tears from the otherwise imperturbable scourge of North Africa that he is unable to function. In fact, the Marquis's distress is so severe that Marianne's father worries more about him than about his own daughter, who has recently been raped (40). This deep-felt concern for the fate of a woman he hardly knows marks the Marquis as a man whose values are worthy of emulation.

Sometimes in Emin's novels tears alone do not serve as ample proof of character. When death or serious harm are immanent, heroes like Kamber and Miramond must reach new extremes of expressiveness in order to reveal the depth of goodness that lies in their heart. As Kamber stands at the grave of his love, Arisena, he provides a prime example of what such histrionics entail.

> While imagining to himself such an insufferable blow, a mortal tremor passed through his heart. . . . "O my God! I have perished forever," he cried. . . . Kamber's pathetic sighs, sobs, and tears were all that was heard. In a fit of madness he threw himself on the coffin of the former mistress of his soul and then, having lifted the lid, kissed the hands and feet of that terrible corpse. . . . He wanted to utter grievous complaints, but neither his reason, which had been eclipsed by this horrendous blow, nor his frozen tongue would obey his wishes. (*Kamber and Arisena*, 212–13)

Miramond, the hero of Emin's next novel, has much the same sort of tragic experience. When he realizes that Ziumbiula will sacrifice herself to the evil Hussein Bey in order to save her father's life, he faints and "takes leave of himself," speaking to his friend Feridat in a language that is totally incomprehensible (*Inconstant Fate*, 3:322). Upon hearing that Sarmanda has drowned at sea, Lizark also suffers what seems to be a seizure or stroke. In rather graphic terms the narrator recounts that Lizark "was no longer able to say even a single word, fell in a faint to the ground, and lumps of foam oozed from his mouth" (Emin, *Lizark and Sarmanda*, 256). After being attended to by a doctor and taken to his cabin, Lizark recovers, at least partially, with the aid of the sentimental hero's standard remedy—the lengthy, accusatory, and maudlin monologue cursing the vicissitudes of fate.

Tears are such an important part of the first Russian novels that their use is not restricted to moments of tragedy. In the novels of Emin and Komarov characters may also prove the tenderness of their hearts in positive situations. After numerous adventures and hardships, which include traveling to Constantinople, finding and then losing the love of his life, leading a gang of pirates, and eventually working as a merchant's helper, Polumedes stumbles across a long-lost relative. As soon as the two characters see each other, their reaction is both immediate and intense. Polumedes explains that "while watching him diligently, I recognized this aged gentleman as my uncle. Torrents of tears poured from my eyes, and having hugged and kissed me, my uncle also issued tears of joy" (Komarov, *Nevidimka*, 88–89). Although Polumedes is strong enough to survive one hardship after another as he wanders the Mediterranean world, this tearful reunion with his uncle proves that he is still sensitive to the essential matters of family and friendship.

In Emin's *Kamber and Arisena* Kadyr displays yet another function of tears by employing them as a silent expression of affection. Taken in by Gamlia's seductive words and actions, the good-hearted but gullible captain believes this deceiver is in love with him. Hence, when his feelings of joy become more than he can bear, he does what any proper sentimental hero would do: he throws himself at Gamlia's feet and "washes them with his tears" (89). Of the many characters in the first Russian novels who emulate Kadyr's seemingly contradictory behavior, none expresses the motivation behind it better than Ernest, the hero of Emin's final novel. When Doravra admits that she loves him, Ernest temporarily takes leave of himself, albeit in a positive manner. As he describes it in a letter to Doravra:

> O most pleasant raptures, joys, hopes, splendors, and wishes! You enervate my spirit more than sadness and ceaseless despair! . . . And so I cry about that which I so strongly and ceaselessly desire. Yet this crying doesn't burden my heart or unsettle my spirit, but rather fills my entire nature with a pleasant moisture of tenderness from which hope begins to grow and love matures. (*Ernest and Doravra*, 1:76)

More than just a delineation of character, the torrents of tears in novels like *Kamber and Arisena* and *Ernest and Doravra* act as an attestation of sincerity. Characters displaying such tenderness of heart certainly must be worth believing when they turn their thoughts to such weighty matters as marriage, education, and service to society.

Adding to the impression created by their ready tears, the heroes and heroines of the early Russian novel consistently prove the merit of their words and deeds by evincing an utterly selfless approach to life. At times even outdoing the most dedicated ascetic, characters like Lizark, Miramond, and Doravra simply refuse to consider their personal happiness, no matter what the cost. For example, while sailing to Italy, the young Miramond is caught in a ferocious gale. Even when he believes that he is about to die, he still cannot bring himself to contemplate his own feelings. It is as though any consideration of the self is somehow inappropriate, even when it is focused on the most basic concern of all: self-preservation. Clinging to a board in the middle of a raging sea, Miramond thinks first and foremost of his parents. He asks God to soften the blow that will come with the news of his death and to place all the calamities and misfortunes that his parents are to suffer on his head before it is sucked beneath the salty waves (Emin, *Inconstant Fate*, 1:11–12). This is the very approach that Ernest takes with respect to his love for Doravra. Fearing that their relationship can only cause her pain, Ernest outlines his course of action in the following words: "Ache, faint, tear yourself apart! It is better that you endure this agitation than torment the one whom you love and adore more than your entire nature. There is no other way. You must go away" (Emin, *Ernest and Doravra*, 1:30). For her part, once she realizes that Ernest is married, Doravra reciprocates these altruistic sentiments by encouraging him to love his wife and declaring that she will never give her hand to another man (2:54). In a type of fiction where the concept of self-interest rarely even makes it into a character's consciousness, Ernest naturally goes Doravra one better by promising to reconcile with his estranged (and manipulative) wife while at the same time encouraging Doravra to find a good man to marry (2:168). By offering to leave town and never contact Doravra again, Ernest displays the mind-set that places virtually everyone else's well-being before his own. With such a disinterested approach to life, how can readers fail to accept him as a trustworthy analyst of whatever he sets his sights on?

In the novels of Chulkov and Komarov the hyperbolized heroes and heroines so common in Emin's oeuvre are brought down to earth and mercilessly ridiculed as being false, pompous, and boring. Flesh-and-blood human beings possessing more vices than virtues are substituted for the lofty, unattainable caricatures of an Ernest or a Doravra. In the carnivalesque approach to literature blushing virgins are transformed into free-spirited prostitutes, and courageous adventurers become self-serving mercenaries. Moreover, the type of conduct that was used to underscore the worthiness of a foreign-inspired moral code is now exposed as nothing more than false sentimentality. Characters like Chulkov's comely cook Martona can manufacture a tear for any occasion, and virtually their every action is designed to mock the type of altruistic behavior that serves as the norm in novels like *Kamber and Arisena* and *The Marquis de Toledo*. When positive characters do make an appearance in carnivalesque fiction, they are usually pushed into the background. Such is the fate of two of Martona's lovers. Chulkov's heroine completely forgets Sveton, who is described as "an honorable man not without friends" (*Comely Cook,* 163), the moment his wife sends her packing, and the kind, thoughtful, and tender Svidal´ remains in the shadows from the time he is introduced to Martona until the very end of the story. Even though he is her preferred lover, his role in the novel pales when compared to the attention given to the man Martona eventually spurns, the rash and deceitful Akhal´.

As opposed to the superhuman Marquis de Toledo or the near goddess Marianne, who are so unchanging it is as though they were carved in stone, characters like Martona and Komarov's wily bandit Vanka Kain live in a constant state of flux. In their approach to life they epitomize the Bakhtinian conception of the individual as someone who is "existentially free, unique, and unpredictable, hence impossible to categorize or define in any fixed and immutable fashion" (Anchor, 239). Starting out as a serf, Kain becomes a member of a gang, a leader of his own group of thieves, a police informer, the head of a criminal syndicate, and finally a prisoner. Not even dimly aware of any sort of self-image, exalted or otherwise, that he needs to maintain, he simply shapes his personality to the demands of the moment. In the same manner Martona boldly declares that she is "one of that number of women who think they are not obligated to anyone in the world" (Chulkov, *Comely Cook,* 171). Like the pauper who crowns herself queen of the carnival, Martona blithely usurps whichever role appeals to her at the time. Starting out as the destitute widow of an army sergeant, she becomes, among other things, a prostitute, kept woman, cook, society lady, and eventually a landowner. Whether she is the philosopher who would contemplate a fickle lover or the respectable lady who would rob her aged benefactor of his last penny, Martona never fully assumes any one identity. She moves from role to role, from one position to the next, testing their possibilities, exposing their flaws, and eventually discarding them. Outdoing even Martona in the malleability of his personality, Neokh, the vagabond hero of Chulkov's *Tale of the Taffeta Beauty Patch*, confirms that inconstancy is the key to success in the subculture. Like an itinerant *balagur*, he moves from one community to the next until he irritates too many important people and is forced to leave. Quick-witted and silver-tongued, Neokh is willing to do just about anything to secure a place in the world. As he tells a mysterious woman in black who is willing to pay for his services: "I am the type of man with whom you can do whatever you want. I can be the tenderest Adonis, a crafty Mercury, or a clever attorney. I will look after your affairs so zealously that you would think they were my own. Just tell me what you need from me" (*Mocker*, 3:177). Among his rather long list of credentials as a subcultural antihero he can list liar, swindler, con man, gigolo, blackmailer, and impostor. In an ironic twist, the roguish Neokh is so good at doing what others want that he manages to pass himself off as a priest for quite some time before he is finally recognized and flushed from the cozy niche he has created for himself. Although a setback such as this would cause a Miramond to rail against the injustice of fate, it does not in the least perturb a charlatan who knows he is sure to land on his feet. Neokh's faith in the carnivalesque cycle is indeed well rewarded as in succeeding adventures he impersonates a doctor and blackmails the family of a retired government official (4:195–202), becomes the gigolo of a rich merchant's wife (4:218–34), and eventually wins the coveted prize of being named special advisor to the tsar (5:174–75).

Maintaining that "there is no well-being without virtue" (*Ernest and Doravra*, 4:94), Emin's straitlaced hero Ernest encapsulates into one brief expression the standard by which every positive character in the early Russian novel judges his or her behavior. In the type of fictional world that he inhabits, happiness and prosperity can only be found in the company of righteousness. On the other hand, a character like Martona takes a more carnivalesque view of such matters by turning this golden rule on its head. For her there can be no well-being where virtue is present. When Martona's husband dies in the battle of Poltava, she is destitute and without anyone in the world that she can turn to for help. As she wanders the streets of Kiev, she is spied by the madam of a bordello and brought under her protection. At first reluctant to become a prostitute, she soon realizes the direct connection between selling her body and achieving a state of material comfort. As her popularity with the clientele of her establishment rises, Martona is able to dress and even act like a noblewoman. She soon becomes a regular with the merchants of Gostinyi dvor, and her "personal property increases by the minute" (Chulkov, *Comely Cook*, 159). Following the adage that "from wealth comes honor" (160), Martona hires a servant and promenades daily throughout the city to showcase her newfound good fortune. Far from denouncing her way of life or harboring a subconscious self-hatred, she revels in the lifestyle that is open to her solely as the result of her less than proper occupation. Throughout the entire novel Martona never criticizes her life as a prostitute but, on the contrary, happily describes it in terms of a profitable business undertaking. Regarding one of her early clients, she says that "the first meeting was an auction, and we didn't talk about anything other than how to close the deal. He traded for my charms, and I ceded them to him for a proper price" (161).[3] As a result of this meeting Martona receives a present as a token of her would-be lover's goodwill, which leads her to joyfully proclaim that "Venus did not rejoice more about receiving the [golden] apple than I admired the tobacco box that was given to me" (161). Unlike the heroines of novels in which virtue becomes a crushing burden to bear, Martona simply lets go of it altogether in order to enjoy the material comfort such freedom brings.

As befits characters who must struggle for their very existence, the heroes and heroines of carnivalesque fiction have little time for such fine sentiments such as friendship. Unlike the tearful Kadyr, who is prepared to sacrifice the rest of his life mourning at the grave of a woman he has never met, the roguish Vanka Kain would never waste a moment's time thinking about anyone other than himself. After Kain bankrupts himself spending all his money on wine, women, and gambling, thoughts of self-sacrifice, or even hard work, are the furthest thing from his mind. Instead of tightening his belt for the sake of his comrades, he methodically carries out a plan to get rich at their expense. Understanding just how valuable his knowledge of the Moscow underworld would be to the authorities, Kain decides to trade it in for a cushy life. In fact, he is so determined to betray his friends that he refuses to be swayed from his mission even when some fairly stiff obstacles present themselves. At first the bandit waits outside the senate and hands one of its members, the powerful Prince Kropotkin, a note in which he says he has information the government would find useful (Komarov, *Vanka Kain*, 95). When the prince dismisses him as just another importunate petitioner and fails to respond, Kain finds out the location of the senator's home. Several days later he shows up at Kropotkin's doorstep only to be unceremoniously escorted from the premises by the prince's adjutant (96). As the narrator explains, "this unsuccessful attempt was not enough to sway Kain from the idea that was so pleasant to him" (97), and fortified with a bellyful of wine, the highwayman barges right into Kropotkin's home (98). On the third attempt he finally is successful and sets in motion the legal process that eventually gives him the power to incarcerate many of the people he worked and lived with just days earlier. Thinking only of himself in this affair, Kain proves to be guided by the carnivalesque rendition of an old adage: if at first you don't succeed in betraying your friends, try, try again.

As with many other aspects of a carnivalesque approach to life, when it comes to ingratitude and callousness, Martona provides some of the most forceful examples in all of early Russian prose fiction. Simply put, Chulkov's comely heroine finds no redeeming value in taking on the suffering of others. In her high-spirited, self-indulgent manner this creature of pleasure traipses through the world as though it were her own private garden, and thoughts about the welfare of others barely even register on her consciousness. When she moves into the retired colonel's household, she immediately sizes up the situation: although becoming the old man's lover is not to her liking, it offers the opportunity of a lifetime to improve herself materially. With few qualms and even less hesitation she quickly sets about taking control of the estate (*Comely Cook,* 168). Later, when the handsome Akhal´ comes along, she thinks nothing of carrying on a love affair right under the colonel's nose, even though he has confessed that her infidelity would kill him almost instantly (169). In a fitting finale to this part of her life Martona even contributes wholeheartedly to Akhal´'s plan to rob the old man and then run off with the spoils. When the colonel dies as a result of her treachery, she does shed a tear, but not for him. Unconscious of the irony of her actions, Martona cries solely because she has been betrayed by Akhal´ and must face the authorities alone. The old man's death means nothing to her compared to the indignity and material discomfort that results from being abandoned by her lover (176, 178).

Whereas Martona's callous behavior toward a decrepit Lothario who tries to purchase her affections might be understandable, she is just as indifferent to people who play a significant role in her life. Without friends or any form of support at the beginning of the novel, Chulkov's heroine almost certainly would have perished on the streets of Kiev if it had not been for the intercession of a kindhearted procuress. Under the madam's tutelage she is able to trade in the dismal prospects of a destitute sergeant's widow for the fancy dresses and haughty ways of a fashionable society lady. When she is ready to leave the bordello, however, she hardly recognizes the contribution her benefactress has made to her well-being. In her typically self-conscious yet indifferent way, Martona admits: "I parted from her without tears for I didn't know what gratitude was, had never even heard of it, and figured it was possible to live in this world without it" (*Comely Cook,* 164). Even more conspicuously, the same sort of ingratitude carries over into Martona's treatment of the very figures who make up the center of her life: her lovers. If she were to feel an allegiance to anyone, it would be to Sveton. Not only does this landed nobleman take her away from the bordello to an opulent life on his estate, he also acts as her savior when he stops his servant from carrying out a plan to destroy her. Nevertheless, when the servant returns with a scheme to ruin Sveton, Martona jumps at the opportunity. In a fictional world where loyalty is simply no match for self-interest, she unrepentantly admits that "no matter how conscienceless and vain I might be, the servant's zeal for his master seemed out of place to me; still, gratitude was unfamiliar to me even from a distance, and so in two words my former lover and I agreed to ruin his master" (163). Even though Martona never gets the chance to betray Sveton, her enthusiastic acceptance of the servant's proposal reveals her true nature.

Thoughts of leading a virtuous life are so unfamiliar to Martona because they have been crowded out of her mind by an almost obsessive materialism. Concepts such as love, friendship, and self-sacrifice are fine for the heroines of Emin's novels, but they are simply too airy to support her. Whereas Sarmanda, Marianne, and Doravra have the world at their feet if only they maintain their honor, Martona is defenseless without money. Realizing all too clearly that her station in life rests on a foundation of material wealth, she reacts as though her very life were in danger when a spurned lover threatens to confiscate the many gifts he has given her. With a sense of desperation born of the vulnerable position fate has bequeathed her, she exclaims: "I still didn't have enough confidence in my new lover not to believe that he would give me up if he saw that I was poor. Every presentiment seemed bad to me then, and I decided that I loved and admired my property so much that it would be better to die than part with it" (*Comely Cook*, 161–62). Even when it comes to Svidal´, the man for whom Martona reserves the greatest affection, her world view is so thoroughly materialistic that he has no choice but to appease it. Reflecting on their relationship, Martona recalls:

> My lover read somewhere that Cupid gilded his arrows and with this act of cunning conquered all mortals. For this reason, in the present age every heart wishes to be pierced with a golden arrow, because where there is poverty even beauty itself doesn't captivate. Therefore as a confirmation of our mutual passion he gave me an income of two thousand rubles, excluding gifts and other whims and fancies. In addition, he promised to give me a thousand rubles if I gave birth to a son who even looked like him. (183)

Though he once saved her life, Svidal´ knows that Martona's gratitude and affection will last only as long as his coffers remain full. As much as it is in her power, heroic asceticism will never interfere with this comely cook's sybaritic enjoyment of the world.

DECEPTION VERSUS MASQUERADE

In the six novels written by Emin, deception is painted in somber tones and almost always results in negative, if not tragic, consequences. Whenever truth is obscured, distorted, or only partially expressed in his fictional world, the innocent are sure to suffer. Writing to his friend Hippolyte, Ernest sums up Emin's attitude toward this type of behavior, proclaiming that "for me, pretense is the vilest of all vices because it is possible to save yourself from an openly evil person, but the covert evildoer can harm us the most because we do not sense impending misfortune and consider him our friend or benefactor" (*Ernest and Doravra*, 4:8–9). More than just abstract musing, the situation described by Ernest motivates the entire plot of Emin's first novel, *Kamber and Arisena*. When the commoner Kamber is banished by Bey Seidy Gamam for wishing to marry his daughter, Arisena seeks a confidant who will help reunite her with the man she loves. The rich noblewoman Gamlia willingly accepts the role, but, as soon as she sees the handsome Kamber, she does more to undermine Arisena's cause than support it. Gamlia convinces Seidy Gamam to stage a mock wedding for Kamber so that Arisena will think he has deserted her for another woman and then falsely accuses Kamber of fomenting insurrection so that he is placed under strict house arrest (134–40). With the aid of a false letter and some well-placed gossip Gamlia gets the despondent Arisena to believe that her love has left her and that he wants her to find another match (141–48). In reality, Gamlia has taken Kamber to the countryside, where she tells him that Arisena is responsible for his exile and tries to cajole him into proposing to her (156). Separated by Gamlia's machinations, the young lovers outdo each other in plumbing ever greater depths of despair. The tragedy of lives being wasted in eternal mourning is only averted when, through the intercession of trustworthy and honorable friends, this treacherous scheme is uncovered and brought to nil. Kamber and Arisena do eventually attain the rewards reserved for the heroes and heroines of Emin's novels, but not before Gamlia's clandestine behavior forces them to undergo an entire novel's worth of heartbreak and misadventure.

Exposing the evils of deception is such an important task in Emin's novels that interpolated tales are frequently employed to underscore the problem. A good example of this technique occurs when Miramond meets four men at an inn on his way home to Cairo after lengthy service in a foreign court. Even though he is only hours away from a long-awaited reunion with his love, Ziumbiula, he pauses to hear their unfortunate stories. Each of them has apparently fallen victim to a scheming and unfaithful wife, and the lessons that can be learned from their experiences are well worth Miramond's (and the didactic-minded reader's) wait. Among the tales of wives who falsely denounce, defame, and imprison their husbands, the third traveler's narrative stands out for the striking nature of the treachery involved (*Inconstant Fate*, 2:73–91). As the man tells it, he was happily married to a virtuous woman, who was outwardly pious and attended church faithfully. While at a party one night, he becomes attracted to a beautiful young dancer, who reminds him of his wife. Carried away by his emotions, the man promises to marry the woman, and the couple go to a house where they plan to make love. Before this can take place, he is arrested by the police and is only released when friends pay his fine. After this experience the man comes to realize that the dancer is his wife in disguise: on all those occasions when she was supposedly going to church, she was in fact performing at parties and soliciting young men. Determined to have his revenge, the next day he follows her to the house of a cleric and spies her sitting on a bed surrounded by imams. Losing his patience, the man rushes in and starts attacking his wife but is quickly captured and charged with attempted murder. Sentenced to death, he escapes only after bribing his guards and is destined to lead the unenviable life of an eternal fugitive. Lest readers miss the rather heavy-handed point of his tale, the man concludes by telling Miramond that "my accursed wife almost brought me to the gallows with her prayers" (2:90). This story, along with the three others that frame it, clearly points out the wisdom of Ernest's warning that deception is potentially the deadliest sin of all.

As the previous examples indicate, the harmful effects of deceitfulness frequently result from the machinations of a femme fatale. From Emin's *Kamber and Arisena* to Chulkov's *Adventures of Achilles*, just about every serious novel of the period utilizes the stereotype of the scorned woman out for revenge. In Miramond's case it is Queen Belilia who counterfeits a letter in which the object of her desire appears to be unfaithful to both his fiancée and his monarch (Emin, *Inconstant Fate*, 1:291–95). Completely taken in by Belilia's forgery, Ziumbiula and Osman Bey have no choice but to denounce the unwitting Miramond as a scoundrel and a traitor (2:1–11). In one of Emin's later novels the realization that Lizark has declared his feelings for Sarmanda sends the Egyptian princess Izida into a rage. Seeking nothing less than "a way to destroy the two unfortunate lovers" (*Lizark and Sarmanda*, 206), she has the ill-fated Lizark sent back to Cairo under arrest (230) while she plots the assassination of her unsuspecting rival (238–39). In Chulkov's *Adventures of Achilles* the role of the femme fatale is reserved for the princess Navpliia. Jealous of Achilles's love for Deidamiia, Navpliia swears that "you will be joined [in marriage] when I either kill the both of you or issue my final breath" (14). In order to have her vengeance, Navpliia falsely tells Deidamiia that Achilles and she have been lovers (24–27), tricks Achilles into writing a letter that can be used to confirm her story (28–31), and then lures Achilles into compromising Deidamiia by visiting her room at night (32–36). As a result of Navpliia's perfidy the high priestess of the temple of Diana declares that Deidamiia must be sacrificed or the city will be destroyed. Deidamiia's supposed liaison with Achilles has so angered the virgin goddess that she can only be assuaged by the transgressor's blood. Even though catastrophe is averted when Diana mercifully relents (42), Navpliia's deception is the cause of untold sorrow and leads an innocent young woman to the brink of death.

In the novels of Chulkov and Komarov deception is not regarded as negative conduct. Just as in the carnival, where a temporary change of identity liberates the individual from the restrictions of everyday society, fraudulent behavior in carnivalesque fiction improves the circumstances and enriches the lives of the characters who resort to it. More than any other quality, being able to bend the truth a bit is what allows vagabonds like Martona, Neokh, and Vanka Kain to turn the tables on polite society and insure themselves a good life. Moreover, even when it comes to affairs of the heart, deception almost always produces positive results. Unlike the crushing blow it brings to the tenderhearted characters in Emin's novels, within the carnivalesque mentality it usually expedites the cause of love. For example, even though she has yet to meet her young admirer Ludvig, a minor character in Komarov's *Nevidimka,* Epofradita, asks him to appear at the opera dressed in a masquerade costume. When Ludvig arrives in a French domino, Epofradita immediately falls in love with him without even seeing his face, and the two eventually wed (24–25). So brief as to seem out of place, this episode appears to have been inserted into the text for no other reason than to emphasize the life-affirming consequences attributed to a masking of identity in the literary subculture. Turning this motif around, yet maintaining the same positive outcome, a mask plays a more prominent role in Komarov's earlier novel, *Milord George.* When George ventures to Cartegena, he is captivated by the legend of the Spanish queen Ann. Apparently Ann is so beautiful that she must continually wear a mask in order to prevent men from committing suicide when they look at her (129–30). Even though George is told that the widowed queen has "an antipathy toward men" (129), the mere thought of her beautiful and mysterious personality draws him on. Before long he makes the queen's acquaintance, finds a way to see her without the mask, and wins her love (175). As opposed to an Achilles, Lizark, or Miramond, who are skeptical of any opacity of character, the English lord George finds the unknown to be both exciting and rewarding.

In addition to masking their outward appearance, characters in carnivalesque fiction frequently resort to a complete change of identity. Epitomizing this type of behavior, Polumedes, one of the heroes of Komarov's *Nevidimka,* ironically finds that cross-dressing provides an excellent means of securing a mate. In order to court Martemiana, the sequestered daughter of the Turkish sultan, drastic measures are called for. With Martemiana's blessing Polumedes dresses as a woman so that he may take up residence in her suite, thus allowing the couple to carry on their affair without arousing the sultan's suspicion (74–76). This ploy works so well that Polumedes uses it again later in the novel, only this time without the knowledge of his love interest. By dressing up as a young maiden, he becomes a lady-in-waiting in the court of Princess Revenza and spends virtually every day at her side (219–21). When, after two months, Polumedes reveals that he is really a man and in love with her, Revenza immediately proclaims, "What sort of gratitude may I show you?," embraces him, and accepts him as her secret fiancé (222). Unlike the fictional world portrayed in Emin's novels where disguises only produce dark and threatening situations, in the carnivalesque representation of life deception almost certainly leads to love.

As with most types of carnivalesque antibehavior, when it comes to artfulness and cunning, few can match the free-spirited Martona. Throughout her many adventures she delights in going beyond the occasional use of a mask or false identity to make deception a way of life. When Chulkov's heroine decides to sneak her lover Akhal´ into the household of the aged colonel by passing him off as her sister, the secretive and duplicitous nature of the liaison is almost as enticing to her as the promise of sexual fulfillment. Looking back on the affair, she readily admits: "I never rejoiced more than when I was able to deceive my unrelenting overseer so completely and successfully" (*Comely Cook*, 173). Martona is so used to deceiving others that even after Akhal´ runs off with the colonel's property and her treachery has been exposed for all to see, she has no compunction about reprising a role that everyone now knows to be false. Telling the colonel that "she left him only in order to test his fidelity to her, to find out whether or not being deprived of her would destroy him" (177), she slips right back into the doddering old man's good graces without so much as blushing. Moreover, Martona's commitment to the power of fraud and delusion forces those who are close to her to play the same game as well. In addition to Akhal´'s stint as her "sister," her first paramour, Sveton, conceals the comely heroine at a friend's house in order to hide her from his suspicious wife (163–64), and her last lover, Svidal´, is almost continually involved in one type of deception or another. The handsome officer feigns his death in a duel with Akhal´ so that he will no longer have to share Martona's love with him (182) and then stages a comedy in order to save an innocent man from a scheming and unfaithful wife. With the help of fake poison and a concocted tale that mirrors the treacherous wife's conduct toward her husband, Svidal´ and Martona save the innocent merchant from the madhouse and help him regain control of his life. In accordance with the laws of the carnival, deception is enrolled in the service of pleasure and freedom.[4]

Just as in Emin's novels, Russian carnivalesque fiction of the latter part of the eighteenth century also utilizes interpolated tales to investigate the depths of feminine cunning, but in contrast to the stories of the four men in *Inconstant Fate,* deception and trickery are not seen as being a character flaw. For instance, while in Toledo, Milord George makes the acquaintance of Ferdinald, Queen Ann's chamberlain and a man who is well versed in the ways of the world. Ferdinald cautions George to guard himself against the haughty queen, for like all women she is "cunning" and "insincere" (Komarov, *Milord George*, 137). To prove his point Ferdinald offers to tell George a chapter of his own life (137–61). Up until this point, it seems as though readers will be treated to a cautionary tale that bears a striking resemblance to the four stories of infidelity that were judged by Miramond in part 2 of *Inconstant Fate.* As soon as Ferdinald starts his recitation, however, it is quite clear that his tale has an altogether different "moral."

While in service in Genoa, Ferdinald falls in love with three married women: Geviia, Maremisa, and Filiia. When each one demands to be his sole companion, he is forced to make a choice. As a means of deciding this difficult question, the amorous diplomat proposes a rather unorthodox competition in which the winner will be the woman who shows the greatest imagination in deceiving her husband. For their part the contestants are certainly up to the challenge as they devise one inventive scheme after another. Geviia leads off by convincing everyone that her spouse is a madman, and then Maremisa drives her husband to distraction by pretending that he has just died. In order to get back into the good graces of their wives, the men must promise never again to question their actions, thus freeing the women for an affair with Ferdinald. Surprisingly, as good as these tricks are, Filiia's plan easily surpasses them. Ferdinald's third contestant drugs her husband and enlists him in the army. After three weeks, when he is convinced that he is a soldier, Filiia drugs him again and returns him to their home. The poor man swears up and down that he simply cannot be her husband, and it is only with a great deal of effort that she coaxes him into accepting that his "enlistment" was only a dream. Impressed by Filiia's skill in manipulating her spouse, Ferdinald declares her the winner and remains her faithful lover until he is recalled from his post six months later. Although he offers this tale as an example of feminine wiles, it is obvious that, at least from Ferdinald's perspective, deception often paves the way to a delightful outcome.

Like Komarov, Chulkov takes a much more whimsical view of the theme of infidelity than does his archrival Emin. Whereas a romantic triangle in a novel like *Inconstant Fate* inevitably leads to tragedy, Chulkov finds that this device lends itself more readily to comedy. For instance, in "The Goodhearted Cuckold" (*Mocker*, evening 29), a Rabelaisian type of merry devil intervenes behind the scenes in order to further the cause of love. A servant who has been entrusted with a money delivery is diverted by the devil to a rich woman's house. The servant offers her the money to make love to him, and the woman quickly agrees. For several days the couple enjoy each other's company in the woman's boudoir while the woman has her husband stay outside her locked door and play the violin for them (2:152–53). Not knowing that his wife has a lover in her bedroom, the husband believes he is making her confinement more pleasant. And in a way he most definitely is, as the narrator tells us that "during his playing she felt even greater pleasure" (2:152). After this amorous interlude concludes, the servant goes to church to expiate his sins and meets a man who asks him why he is alternately laughing and crying. The young man recounts his tale and soon realizes that he has told it to the cuckolded husband himself (2:153–54).[5] If this scene had taken place in one of Emin's novels, at this point in the story the interloper would have to die.[6] In Chulkov's fictional world, however, there is a completely different outcome. Rather than challenging the young man to a duel, the husband invites him home to dinner and even returns the money he paid his wife, less fifty kopecks for the lovemaking and music. The husband sends the young man on his way, asking only that he not tell a soul of his adventure, and thus all ends well for everyone concerned (2:154–56). Mirroring the dynamics of the carnival, the lovers' deception sets up a temporary moral and social antiworld. In this topsy-turvy entanglement the rich gentleman has been forced to play the servant, the young servant has partaken of the pleasures of polite society, and best of all this switch in roles has not created even the slightest hint of a dark and threatening situation. Love remains, as it should be, a strictly pleasurable experience.

SELF-IMAGES: DEBASEMENT VERSUS MOCKERY

Despite their privileged backgrounds and enviable destinies the heroes and heroines of Emin's novels spend a considerable amount of time engaged in self-inflicted character assassination. To these tormented souls no form of debasement seems too extreme as they conjure up one demeaning image of themselves after another. Believing that Arisena's marriage to another man is imminent, Kamber lays down the pattern for this type of behavior when he pathetically exclaims: "Oh, how I wish to be even the lowest slave of your spouse. I would be satisfied with being the servant of the one who is yours" (*Kamber and Arisena*, 86). As soon as they are separated from the person they love, whether it be by shipwreck, intrigue, or social stigma, characters like Kamber relinquish any sense of self-worth and willingly place their head under the oppressive heel of fate. Unlike the whimsical Martona or the opportunistic Neokh, who nimbly sidestep misfortune and move on, Kamber and his literary peers embrace misery as though it were one of life's supreme virtues. Metaphorically, and sometimes quite literally, the central figures in Emin's novels deliberately turn themselves into not only humble servants and slaves but also prisoners, criminals, and sacrifices. Always perversely derisive, this type of behavior at times even veers off into a masochistic enjoyment of self-annihilation. In addition to the privations and censure these high-minded characters endure for the sake of love, they also readily accept physical abuse, horrendous torture, and even death. As Miramond declares on the eve of Ziumbiula's wedding to another man: "My pain is extremely pleasant to me, and if it diminished for some reason, the medicine would be more vexing to me than the illness" (*Inconstant Fate*, 1:158).

Unlike characters in carnivalesque fiction, for whom pleasure and freedom go hand in hand, the heroes and heroines in Emin's novels are prepared to sell themselves into bondage without a second thought. Not long after they meet, Doravra openly proclaims her willingness to submit to Ernest when she bluntly writes: "I am completely conquered! . . . I surrender to you, fierce conqueror. Place on my heart the bonds of eternal slavery" (*Ernest and Doravra*, 1:66). Of course, in a literary aesthetic that puts a premium on self-abasement, there is no doubt that Ernest will match his love in the rhetoric of submissiveness. Denying that he even has a will of his own, he tells her: "For a long time I have chosen you as the possessor of my life, and at this very moment I cede to you power over my desires. Direct them as you see fit. Rule me like a person who can do nothing by himself and whose entire existence depends on yours" (2:143). In Emin's first novel the concept of bondage is made even more explicit in the narrator's description of Kadyr's state of mind. He is so taken in by the charms of the seductive Gamlia that it is as though "he were fixed to a chain of love that she had placed around his neck" (*Kamber and Arisena*, 106). Later in the novel, after the scheming Gamlia has been captured by Kamber and his men, this image is taken from a figurative level to a literal one. When a guard approaches Gamlia in order to unlock the shackles on her legs, she cries: "The cruel magnifier of my misfortune, the blacksmith of hell, has forged an unbearable chain around my half-dead heart, so let my legs bend under these heavy bonds" (189). Nor is Gamlia alone in wishing to be literally enslaved to the man she loves. In order to be close to Lizark, Sarmanda follows him abroad, disguises herself as a man of low social standing named Metafrast, and offers to indenture herself to the unsuspecting object of her desire. As the narrator explains, when Lizark accepts, Sarmanda is beside herself with joy: "Metafrast rejoiced in his soul because he was able to achieve such complete success, and if not with mutual love, he hoped to be satisfied with his service [to Lizark], for it is quite pleasant to be the slave of the one you love" (Emin, *Lizark and Sarmanda*, 126).

As the most sensitive of Emin's many tearful heroes it is only fitting that Ernest should come up with a metaphor for self-debasement that is uniquely his. After he has inappropriately revealed his love to Doravra and been scolded by her for such brazen conduct, he speaks of himself as a heinous criminal who deserves nothing less than the severest of punishments. At first he feels he should be banished from Doravra's sight and volunteers to become a man without a country whose sole goal in life will be to torment himself with the loss of his love. Referring to the letter Doravra sent him expressing her dismay, he reflects: "I will go to distant lands, bury myself in a primitive cave, and your letter, which I will never remove from my sight, will provide my standard of conduct" (*Ernest and Doravra*, 1:19). Typical of the self-lacerating behavior of Emin's heroes, Ernest is not satisfied with the severity of this penalty, and so he quickly escalates his rhetoric. Likening himself to a common murderer, he proclaims that he is unworthy of living: "Having realized his mistake, the condemned prisoner is crushed by the decision that will take his life away. He places his head beneath the fatal sword and without a murmur meets the death that will separate him forever from precious life" (1:19–20). Although Ernest is certainly indulging in hyperbole here, his words do not miss the mark completely. While Doravra does not wish to send him into exile and considers the death penalty out of the question, she does agree that some sort of punishment is in order as atonement for his presumptuous and improper behavior (1:22–23). With this response Doravra signals that, at least in a rhetorical sense, Ernest's psychic and emotional mortification is well deserved.

The oft-expressed desire in Emin's novels to make oneself subservient to another points to a leitmotif of masochism that runs throughout this type of fiction. For example, when Marianne unjustly denounces the Marquis de Toledo for contributing to her father's death, he is not the least bit daunted. To the contrary, when he confesses, "I will eternally love you because you hate me" (*Marquis de Toledo*, 63), he seems to be inspired rather than repulsed by Marianne's hostile behavior. Rejection and even outright punishment also have no deterrent force for the Marquis's immediate literary predecessor, Lizark. Izida falsely accuses Lizark of stealing her jewels and has him put under house arrest, yet the lovesick hero actually thrives on her ill will. Alone in his room, he confesses that he finds pleasure in her cruelty: "Every torment that comes from your hand is pleasing to me, and if my unhappiness brings you satisfaction, I am prepared to suffer every torment in the world for you. . . . Let me be the unhappiest person in the world if that is what would please you" (*Lizark and Sarmanda*, 59). Even Miramond, who as a former prisoner on the Isle of Malta knows all too well what it means to suffer, willingly embraces pain if it means gaining the respect of his beloved. Queen Belilia threatens him with torture, but Miramond is adamant in his refusal to betray Ziumbiula. He tells the queen: "Burden my heart with the cruelest torments, tear it into small pieces, cut my body into shreds. . . . For Ziumbiula's sake it is not only bearable but pleasing to suffer" (*Inconstant Fate*, 1:289). When Belilia imprisons the implacable Miramond with common thieves and robbers and parades him through the streets as a traitor, he proudly transforms his humiliation into a symbol of fidelity, proclaiming, "I kiss the heavy chain that Belilia's malice has laid across my tender neck. My slavery is pleasing to me when I understand that through my suffering I become worthy of Ziumbiula's love" (1:300).

As Miramond's rejection of the debauched Belilia indicates, the heroes and heroines of Emin's novels are willing to undergo more than just psychological torment for the sake of their beloved. Time and again they find themselves in grave physical danger as they pursue the object of their affections. Instead of prudently avoiding such potentially lethal situations, these high-minded characters gladly offer their lives as a sacrifice on the altar of love. Early in Emin's first novel Kamber and Arisena are stranded in the wilderness. When the starving couple comes upon a hermit, each one tries to convince him to care for the other first. Even though she is completely exhausted and on the brink of death, Arisena's first reaction is to exclaim, "I am more able to endure hunger than he is. Feed him, and I will manage without food" (*Kamber and Arisena*, 54). In a later novel the love-struck Lizark nearly loses his life, yet he finds his suffering to be cause for celebration because it draws him closer to the woman he longs for. While on a bear hunt, Princess Izida accidentally shoots him in the chest with an arrow. Rather than concentrate on his near mortal wound, the page can only think, "Oh! A hundred times sweeter is the death that comes from the hand of my sovereign than the life of grave complaints I would be forced to lead" (*Lizark and Sarmanda*, 21). When this unfortunate event gives Lizark the opportunity to profess his love, he is beside himself with joy. Almost losing his life means nothing as he ecstatically apostrophizes the arrow that nearly slew him: "O loving arrow! You have opened a wound in my heart so that it might be filled with joy and prosperity" (66–67). As self-sacrificing as Lizark is, however, the woman he will eventually marry outdoes even him in this regard. Seeing that Lizark is about to be executed for a crime he did not commit, Sarmanda quickly manufactures evidence to make it look as though she were guilty. Lizark is immediately released, but Sarmanda is arrested in his place and condemned to die for the crime in two days. Not in the least fazed by this turn of events, she reflects, "I am leaving this unhappy life with some satisfaction, knowing that by dying I am saving a life that is more valuable to me than the entire world or even ten worlds such as ours. I consider my death sufficient reward for my love" (170). While Sarmanda would never think of entering into a sexual relationship with Lizark out of wedlock, she does not have the slightest reservation about martyring herself for him. In novels infused with an Enlightenment understanding of virtue, it is almost as though suffering is the preferred state of being.[7]

Despite their many sufferings, characters like Kamber, Arisena, Lizark, and Sarmanda regularly survive their encounters with death unscathed and live to enjoy the positive denouements of their respective narratives; however, on one occasion, the terrible consequences of the masochistic mind-set underpinning the more serious strain of the early Russian novel are fully realized. Toward the end of his autobiography Miramond's friend Feridat includes what is undoubtedly one of the most striking examples of martyrdom in all of Russian literature. In heart-rending detail he recalls how Beliazen, a Turkish slave on the Isle of Malta, knowingly and willingly sacrificed his life for the woman he loved. Planning a revolt of his fellow slaves, Beliazen makes the fatal mistake of revealing the scheme to his Maltese mistress, Angelica. Overcome by a sense of patriotism, she informs the authorities, the plan is foiled, and Beliazen is captured. Almost immediately Angelica regrets her decision, but it is too late, and her lover is sentenced to a slow and painful death. In one of the most graphic passages in all of his novels Emin spares none of the horror in describing the torments inflicted on the poor Turk (*Inconstant Fate*, 2:314). Among other hideous tortures Beliazen is forced to endure, his fingers and toes are cut off one by one, his arms are burned off down to the elbow, and his arms and legs are cut into small pieces with dull saws. As he is about to expire, he asks to see Angelica. In a shocking, though perhaps not unexpected twist, when she arrives, she is not greeted with even one word of recrimination. Instead, Beliazen asks her to forgive him and apologizes for the shock she receives from seeing his dismembered body (315). With his last breath he tells her:

> I thank you, my lady, for coming to alleviate my great suffering with your presence. Please forgive the evil intention that I was about to undertake to the detriment of your society, for if I knew that you had still not forgiven me, it would be more unbearable than all the sufferings the executioners have inflicted upon my body. . . . Tell me that you forgive me. Let me hear just one more word from you before I die. (315–16)

Within the framework of novels like *Inconstant Fate* there are no grounds for censuring Angelica. According to the rules of the genre Beliazen's suffering ennobles his character far more than their illicit love affair ever could. In a perverse way his terrible death is actually an enviable fate.

In stark contrast to the type of characterization favored in Emin's novels, guilt, self-denial, and martyrdom have no place in the lives of antiheroes like Neokh, Martona, and Vanka Kain. Each of these rogues is so consumed by a madcap dash up the social ladder that thoughts of serving another person, much less of becoming a slave or sacrifice, never enter their head. Imbued with the spirit of the carnival, they are perpetually trying to turn the established hierarchy upside down so that they can, at least for a time, assume a position of power over others. In this vein Neokh exploits every opportunity until he finally becomes secretary to the tsar, Kain rises from the humblest beginnings to become the officially sanctioned king of the Moscow underworld, and Martona uses her physical attractiveness to gain control of her lovers. On those rare occasions when these carnivalesque figures do take a more circumspect look at themselves, they turn to the tongue-in-cheek humor of self-mockery rather than the vocabulary of condemnation. Instead of proclaiming their unworthiness or desire to perish, Neokh and Martona describe themselves with a gentle, burlesque-type humor that underscores their communality with all of humankind. In their eyes they are neither the most virtuous of beings nor incorrigible criminals deserving of the death penalty. Whatever their failings—and they are many—none merits the abusive language of self-contempt so prevalent among the Lizarks, Miramonds, and Ernests of the early Russian novel.

The self-deflating, yet gentle, brand of humor employed by Martona and Neokh is a natural manifestation of Chulkov's carnivalesque view of the world. Eighteenth-century Russia's premier literary jester had no interest in savagely denigrating anyone or anything, even if it were just one of his novelistic creations. As he would maintain over and over again, his cast of mind was more conducive to finding and devising a good laugh. Under the pseudonym of Rusak he asserts in the preface to *The Mocker* that he received his pen from Momus, the god of laughter (1:vi), and that he "knows how to dismiss something with a joke when the need arises" (1:vii). This is more than just a throwaway line, for Chulkov's alter ego sees laughter as the prime mover of human existence. Remarking upon the use of odd-sounding foreign words in the first volume of *The Mocker*, he says: "Man is an animal that is both funny and likes to laugh, that mocks others and serves as the object of mockery. We all are subject to laughter, and everyone laughs at others" (1:iii). In this rambling five-part novel humor is not a destructive force but a celebration, an acknowledgment of the universality of all human beings, and a temporary reprieve from the harsh realities of life, especially for those in the lower reaches of the social scale. Following this logic, Chulkov/Rusak does not exempt even himself from becoming the object of our merriment. He has no problem admitting that he is far from the world's most accomplished author and that much of what is to follow in *The Mocker* has been included "for the reason that it would allow you to make fun of me" (1:iii).

Chulkov keeps a gently humorous, self-effacing metacommentary running throughout *The Mocker* by means of his primary narrator, Ladon. From the first words of chapter 1, with its appropriately whimsical title "The Beginning of Idle Talk," Ladon convincingly demonstrates that he knows better than to take himself too seriously. With a twinkle in his eye he casually admits that his mother, who was a Gypsy, died in childbirth and that the man he called father always had reason to wonder whether he had a rightful claim to the title (1:1). Whereas any one of Emin's narrators would denounce such a questionable genealogy, Ladon proves the solidity of his carnivalesque credentials by finding in his family ancestry the grounds for a humorous and positive view of the world. According to his way of thinking the genes of his Gypsy mother and Jewish father have endowed him with extraordinary gifts. He proudly proclaims that people like his parents "are more skillful than others in trickery and deception" (1:2) and that through them he has acquired the traits allowing him to become a world-class raconteur and romancer of women. Ladon continues to regard himself in this tongue-in-cheek manner throughout the remainder of the nearly one-hundred-page introduction to *The Mocker* as well as intermittently in the five volumes of the body of the novel itself. He confesses that he tends to lie (1:97), implies that his stories are not all that impressive, because his auditors are always falling asleep on him (1:150), and even admits that if nobody stops him, he will just go on chattering indefinitely (4:250). As real as these shortcomings may be, they are worthy of a kindly guffaw rather than the life sentence that Emin would likely impose. Ladon often portrays his personality in a humorous light, but it is never with the intent of demeaning or belittling himself. As he proudly says of what others might consider a spotty family background, "A good tree puts out good branches" (1:2).

Even more so than Ladon, Chulkov's comely cook, Martona, rarely has a disparaging word to say about herself. Although she does understand that her behavior is considered immoral, she simply does not care. Shrugging off the opinions of polite society, she readily confesses to a lack of virtue (*Comely Cook*, 177), baldly defends her sexual promiscuity (160, 169), and flippantly dismisses her immodesty as a genetic imperfection beyond her ability to control (159). Although it is true that Martona is not above turning the critical spotlight on herself, she always does so in a jesting, self-indulgent manner. In her discourse the harsh condemnations and dire promises of Emin's characters are replaced by the affable tones of laughter. When Sveton saves Martona from a vengeful suitor, the last thing she has in mind is to define herself as his indentured slave. Instead, she casts him as the heroic Paris and claims for herself the role of the beautiful Helen of Troy (160). Not satisfied by reprising the story of mere mortals, Martona playfully elevates her rhetoric, naming Sveton her Adonis and designating herself "if not Venus, then at least a middle goddess" (160). While her self-conscious pomposity does set Martona up as the comic focus of this interlude, there is nothing derogatory or destructive about it. She may be presumptuous, naive, or even a bit silly in her recourse to mythology, but she can never be accused of harboring the sort of self-hatred that infects Emin's heroes and heroines. Later in the novel, when she actually compares herself to Venus (161, 164) and refers to Akhal´ and his servant, who appear at the colonel's doorstep in drag, as Jupiter and Mercury (172), she continues to indulge herself in a completely harmless type of self-parody. The images she conjures up become ever more ludicrous, yet they are not designed to degrade or harm. In her quest to enjoy life to the fullest, Martona is not above poking fun even at herself, but never with the intention of self-victimization.

In direct contrast to a heroine like Sarmanda, who abandons an enviable life at court to become Lizark's menial servant, Martona takes every precaution to avoid even the slightest hint of physical discomfort. As she puts it, she is a woman in search of *gulian'e* (carnival, merrymaking; 169) and more than willing to sacrifice anyone, even her current lover, to secure her own well-being. When Sveton's wife catches her in the act of making love with her husband and slaps her in the face, Martona shows just how little she is prepared to endure (165). Instead of fighting to keep Sveton, she surrenders him without a second thought and immediately takes to the road. Even if he did save her from the ugly threats of a jilted lover, no man can compensate for such pain and indignity. In a later escapade, when Martona is arrested for her part in swindling the retired colonel, she reflects on a philosophy of life that puts little stock in self-denial and suffering:

> They threw me in a stone cellar and didn't give me anything that I could use to rest on during the night. They served me food twice a day, but it consisted of bread and water so I was forced to observe a great fast, which is an idea that had never before even entered my head. This life of abstinence knocked any thoughts of love right out of me. I didn't think about my personal appearance or about attracting lovers and found myself in this situation for a little more than two weeks. (178)

Whereas a starving Arisena has the fortitude to calmly deny herself food if it means saving Kamber's life, Martona can only reflect on how miserable she is on her two meals a day. Describing her captivity as "hell" (178), she is never so happy and grateful as when Akhal´ and Svidal´ succeed in freeing her from the cellar.

Given that Martona has no tolerance for asceticism, she would never willingly become someone else's slave or sacrifice. In accordance with a carnivalesque view of the world she finds gaining the upper hand over those around her, even her closest associates, to be much more appealing. As though she were riding a carnival Ferris wheel, Chulkov's feisty heroine repeatedly allows the cyclical course of life that governs events in *The Comely Cook* to lift her above the fray. For example, when an ex-lover threatens to ruin her, Martona thinks all is lost. Just when she is at the nadir of despair, however, her world turns completely around, and she is quickly catapulted to the summit of power and prestige. Her former lover turns out to be the servant of her latest companion, Sveton, who puts his servant in his place and lavishes Martona with gifts. Elevated to the throne of her personal little kingdom, Martona revels in the coup that, as she says, in "one night made me the master and sovereign of my former commander" (163). Later, when Martona moves in as the kept woman of the retired colonel, life presents her with a golden opportunity to effect a reversal in the table of ranks. Owing to her aged suitor's infatuation with her, she has almost total control of both the man and his entire estate just a few short hours after their first meeting (168). When she brings the virile young Akhal´ into the old man's house as her live-in lover, the carnivalesque inversion of authority is complete: the representative of official society (the colonel) becomes the young couple's servant (175), while Martona crowns herself queen of all she surveys.

In the hearts of carnivalesque characters like Neokh and Martona there is little room for understanding. If someone puts them in a difficult situation, they immediately start thinking of how to get even. The Turkish slave Beliazen may be able to ask Angelica to forgive him even though she is responsible for the inhuman torture he is forced to endure, but such sentimental masochism is totally out of keeping with a carnivalesque mentality. When Vladimira walks away from her torrid love affair with Neokh to marry a rich nobleman, the poor student is at first heartbroken and depressed (*Mocker*, 5:159–60), but it does not take him long to contemplate a completely different type of emotion. Realizing that "his previous claims on Vladimira's benevolence will eventually be brought to the attention of her spouse" (5:162), he relishes the thought of the discord this news will soon create in the lives of the newlywed couple. When Martona finds herself in much the same situation as Neokh does, she is even quicker to vent her animosity. After Akhal´ absconds with the colonel's riches and leaves her to face the authorities alone, she has no inclination to stand back and wait for time to salve her feelings of vengeance. Comparing herself to the tolerant, long-suffering, and virtuous heroines of official literature, Martona declares: "The real Phillida did not bemoan Demofont's treachery but instead only felt sorry for it. I, on the other hand, was so evil that if he had been in my power, I would have agreed to tear him in half" (*Comely Cook*, 176). Confirming what she proves on so many different occasions, Martona leaves patience, understanding, and self-sacrifice to the fainting virgins and would-be martyrs of the early Russian novel. As a carnivalesque heroine, she is interested only in a life of pleasure and self-fulfillment.

Part

THREE

STYLIZATION:
A METALITERARY STRATEGY OF THE 1840S

Chapter

SEVEN

A THEORY OF STYLIZATION

STYLIZATION AND CARNIVAL

As in the first Russian novels of the second half of the eighteenth century, a strong metaliterary impulse runs through Russian prose fiction of the 1830s and 1840s. Gogol''s grotesquerie and linguistic nationalism, the self-consciousness of the young Dostoevskii, and even the word games, slapstick humor, and stylistic dissonance of a lesser figure like Jakov Butkov all reflect an ambivalent attitude toward the literary aesthetic of their day.[1] While taking West European romanticism and naturalism as their starting point, these authors undermine the norms and premises of the very works that serve as their models. In the metaliterary play of "The Overcoat," for example, the imitation of elements taken from the physiological sketch only serves as a broad target for Gogol''s particularly grotesque brand of parody. Unlike Chulkov and Komarov, however, Gogol' and Dostoevskii were not motivated by a carnivalesque mentality. Gogol''s vengeful demons, vacuous protagonists, and ultimately humorless laughter are simply too bleak to be associated with the good-natured trickery and hearty belly laughs of the carnival, and, Bakhtin notwithstanding, Dostoevskii's fiction also falls short of the mark in this regard. As René Wellek notes, "The term [*carnivalization*] seems to lose all meaning when applied to the general tone and attitude of Dostoevsky. . . . There is nothing in Dostoevsky of Rabelais's corporeality, of the lust for life in the ancient *saturnalia* or the *commedia dell'arte*. In every way Dostoevsky seems . . . to represent the opposite of the carnival spirit. He was a man of deep commitment, profound seriousness, spirituality, and strict ethics, whatever his lapses were in real life" (239). Concerned with probing the shortcomings and inconsistencies of the prevailing literary aesthetic yet eschewing the buffoonery of the carnivalesque, Gogol´ and Dostoevskii opted for the serious, more sophisticated metaliterary strategy of stylization.[2]

Although the two concepts are not synonymous, stylization does share common ground with Bakhtin's philosophy of the carnival. The regenerative power of the carnivalesque resides in its ability to use what Bakhtin calls a "merry deception" in order to subvert, at least for a time, the social and political status quo ("Discourse," 401–2). In the carnival, grotesque inversions ranging from the verbal to the situational smash the barriers between high and low, producer and receiver, thereby acknowledging the cocreative responsibilities of both entities. Stylization lacks the bawdy, disarming laughter so essential to the carnivalesque, yet it is predicated on a *serious* deception. Instead of comic inversion, stylization exploits the allure of a seemingly faithful reproduction of a given literary system in order to expose its weaknesses and conventionality. The result may be far less playful, but stylization obliterates the distinction between encoder and decoder just as successfully as the anarchic devilries of the carnival, in which spectators are transformed into performers. Bewildered by a decoding nightmare, readers of a stylization are forced to re-create and then dismantle the officially sanctioned view of literature they had previously accepted unquestioningly. Have we been satisfied with empty clichés? Are we too quick to elevate facile depictions of the world to the status of truths because they appease our vested interests in life? Do we, as Bakhtin writes, shun a healthy skepticism that acknowledges a multiplicity of meanings in favor of the self-serving lie of pathos (400–410)? These are the questions that stylization raises, and in every case the answer it demands is yes.

POSING THE PROBLEM: TYNIANOV AND BAKHTIN

Although he fails to apply it in a systematic way, Jurii Tynianov addresses the embryonic form of a theory of stylization in two articles: "Dostoevskii and Gogol´: Toward a Theory of Parody" ("Dostoevskii i Gogol´: k teorii parodii," 1919) and "On Parody" ("O parodii," 1929). As the former title implies, Tynianov was intrigued by the complex relationship between two of nineteenth-century Russia's most prominent authors. On the one hand, he viewed a work like "The Landlady" ("Khoziaika," 1847) as proof that Dostoevskii was an ardent admirer and imitator of Gogol´. The hyperbolic style, complicated syntax, church Slavonicisms, and rhythmic periods of this short story all struck him as reminiscent of a Gogolian approach to fiction writing (413–14).[3] On the other hand, Tynianov also believed that Dostoevskii was locked in a struggle with Gogol´. He concurred with the assessment of their contemporary—the poet, critic, and editor Petr Pletnev—who claimed that Dostoevskii "pursued Gogol´'" and "wanted to annihilate" him (413). From the complexity of character types to the employment of verbal masks, Tynianov considered much of Dostoevskii's fiction a parodic recombination of Gogolian poetics, with the high point of this critique being *The Village of Stepanchikovo* (*Selo Stepanchikovo*, 1859) (433–55).[4] Motivated by a desire to explain this apparent contradiction in Dostoevskii's attitude toward Gogol´, Tynianov ventured to hypothesize about the metaliterary nuances of a type of discourse he termed stylization.

In "Dostoevskii and Gogol´" Tynianov prepares the way for his musings on stylization by first examining the form and function of the larger strategy to which it belongs, namely parody. Keeping to a rather conventional definition of the term, he notes that parody consists of two planes: the first encompassing the fiction of the parody itself and the second reflecting the character types, themes, devices, and language of some other work that serves as the parodist's target. For this type of discourse to function efficiently, Tynianov emphasizes, it is essential that the two planes be clearly distinguished from one another. He writes that "parody exists as long as the second plane, the one that is being parodied, is visible in the work. The narrower, better defined, and more limited the second plane is, and the more all details carry a second shading and are perceived from a second point of view, the stronger the parody will be" ("Dostoevskii and Gogol´," 433). Like Foma Opiskin's misguided moral pronouncements, borrowed material placed in an unfamiliar context seems out of place and is readily identified as the target of the parodist's attack.

Closely bound up with the biplanar structure of parody, humor is the other essential component in Tynianov's theory of this mode of discourse. As a corollary to his dictum on the strict separation of planes he tersely asserts that "parody is the means and sign of the comic genres" ("On Parody," 294). In this strategy the discrepancy between the seriousness of the elements of the second plane and the new context, which fails to support them on the first plane, elicits laughter from the reader. Breaking no new ground in this regard, Tynianov's brief outline resonates with the more detailed analysis of later investigators. For example, in his wide-ranging book *The Anatomy of Satire*, Gilbert Highet writes: "[The parodist] takes an existing work of literature which was created with a serious purpose, or a literary form in which some reputable books and poems have been written. He then makes the work, or the form look ridiculous by infusing it with incongruous ideas, or exaggerating its aesthetic devices; or he makes the ideas look foolish by putting them into an inappropriate form; or both" (13). In other words, to flesh out Tynianov's laconic treatment of the subject, laughter is a means as well as an end: it is both our normal response to parody, something like an assurance that we are reading the text correctly, and also a highly efficient way of directing our attention to the proper target.

In "Dostoevskii and Gogol´" and "On Parody" Tynianov realized that the generally accepted definition of parody simply does not go far enough. Such a theory accounts for those instances when the discrete contours of a second plane are readily apparent in a given text, but it falls short when they fail to stand out and elude our perception. To account for this problem,

Tynianov expanded the boundaries of parody to include, as he called it, stylization. Like the broader category of discourse to which it belongs, stylization is a biplanar strategy, but it differs substantially from parody in that its second plane appears to merge with the first. Tynianov writes that "if the second plane diffuses into a general understanding of style, parody becomes one of the elements of the dialectical change of literary schools and borders on stylization" ("Dostoevskii and Gogol´," 433). Unfortunately, this line of reasoning is not satisfactorily developed in either of Tynianov's articles, thus leaving the more provocative part of his theory far too vague to be of any use. By extending it with the same parameters he used to define parody, however, we can begin to bring the full metaliterary power of stylization into focus. To rephrase Tynianov's statement on the structure of parody: stylization exists so long as a second plane is *not* visible in the text; the broader, less-defined the second plane is, and the harder it is to discern a second shading or second point of view, the stronger the stylization will be.

Like parody, stylization comes with a corollary regarding humor in Tynianov's theory. With the observation that "it is just one step from stylization to parody: stylization that is comically motivated or emphasized becomes parody" ("Dostoevskii and Gogol´," 416), Tynianov uncovers the most obvious, yet crucial, difference between these two closely related strategies.[5] Focusing on the prose and verse of Gogol´'s and Dostoevskii's less-talented contemporaries, he concludes that many works generally considered to be humorless parodies should be reclassified as stylizations.[6] Tynianov argues that in parody proper the author juxtaposes the two discrete planes of a text in such a way that the second one is made to look comical. On the other hand, laughter is *not* a prerequisite of stylization, because the two planes of this approach seem to merge with each other. Given that no target has been singled out for ridicule, a humorous response is generally not called for. In this respect, stylization looks very much like imitation. The writer Nikolai Polevoi, whom Tynianov regarded as a creator of humorless parodies (that is, stylizations), admitted as much when he remarked that "pleasing readers means closely following the basic principles of our literature, or imitation. We do not think of the beauty or gracefulness of verse or prose. On the contrary, we present exact imitations of the most fashionable and celebrated poets in those genres in which they pleased others and became famous" ("On Parody," 287). From scattered remarks such as these we may surmise that there is so little to laugh at in a stylization because, at least on the surface, it reveals hardly any critical distance from the most popular literature of its day.

In his article "On Literary Evolution" ("O literaturnoi èvoliutsii") Tynianov maintains that when one element of a literary system becomes less important, such as meter in a poem, other elements will take on a more prominent function (35–36). Once again, even though he never actually incorporates this particular theorem into his thoughts on stylization, his brief forays into the topic do support the conclusion that, as the role of humor and the separation of planes diminishes in this subtype of parody, the importance of intertextuality increases. For example, in "Dostoevskii and Gogol'" Tynianov notes that the goal of parody may be "the mechanization of a specific device" (430), but stylization envisions nothing less than "the dialectical change of literary schools" (433). Speaking more specifically about the fiction of his two subjects, he also claims that "Dostoevskii uses Gogol''s devices, but in and of themselves they are not necessary for him. This explains Dostoevskii's parody of Gogol': stylization, which is employed with definite tasks in mind, turns into parody when these goals are lacking" (428–29). Although these isolated statements are never properly developed, they do imply that stylization is a more unified and comprehensive strategy than parody. Whereas Dostoevskii's parody of Gogol' consists of a lighthearted mocking of certain character types and verbal games, a true stylization comprehends not just individual devices or even an entire work, but rather the literary aesthetic supporting a multitude of such devices and works. In short, just like the carnivalesque, the goal of stylization is nothing less than the subversion of the literary status quo.

Despite its promising beginnings, Tynianov's sketch of stylization in "Dostoevskii and Gogol'" and "On Parody" is simply too brief and disorganized to serve as a critical tool.[7] Moreover, from the time Tynianov first proposed his theory around 1920, the only critic to make a significant contribution to an understanding of this narrative strategy has been Mikhail Bakhtin, and even his insights leave several crucial questions unanswered. Bakhtin's best articulation of the problem occurs in *Problems of Dostoevsky's Poetics* (*Problemy tvorchestva Dostoevskogo*, 1929 [much expanded in the second edition, *Problemy poètiki Dostoevskogo*, 1963]), where he is especially helpful in stabilizing the critical paradigms used to define stylization. In addition, the discourse typology he proposes in this monograph clears up some of the ambiguities concerning the relationship of stylization to imitation and parody, two types of discourse with which it is frequently confused.

In Bakhtin's typology parody and stylization fit under the heading of double-voiced discourse, wherein "two contexts of enunciation, . . . two semantic orientations, two voices" are joined together (Todorov, *Bakhtin*, 71). In this type of discourse one of the voices belongs to an addresser (the author, the narrator, a character) who attacks, mocks, or manipulates the voice of a second addresser originating either within the same text or outside it. To quote Bakhtin, all forms of double-voiced discourse (other types include *skaz*, dialogue, and polemic) are "directed both toward the referential object of speech, as in ordinary discourse, and toward *another's discourse*, toward *someone else's speech*" (*Problems*, 185).[8] Parody and stylization can be distinguished from other types of bivocal discourse by the nature of their second voice. In polemic, for example, the authorial intent of the second speech act remains intact: its presentation in the text is complete and unambiguous in order to emphasize as clearly as possible the differences between opposing arguments. In contrast, parody and stylization also employ the discourse of a second voice, but rather than simply transmitting it intact, they reshape it, give it a new focus, and even distort it. "In stylization . . . and parody the other person's discourse is a completely passive tool in the hands of the author wielding it. He takes, so to speak, someone else's meek and defenseless discourse and installs his own interpretation in it, forcing it to serve his own new purposes" (197). It is precisely this ability to reshape the intent of a second voice that makes possible the unmasking of literary convention.

As Bakhtin points out through a simple, yet effective, terminological dichotomy, parody and stylization take different approaches to the manipulation of someone else's speech. On the one hand, parody is a "multidirectional" variant of double-voiced discourse, in which the authorial intentions of the two speech acts openly conflict with each other. Bakhtin writes that "having made its home in the other's discourse, [the parodic voice] clashes hostilely with its primordial host and forces him to serve directly opposing aims. Discourse becomes an arena of battle between two voices. . . . They are not only isolated from one another, separated by a distance, but are also hostilely opposed" (*Problems*, 193). To support this aspect of his theory, Bakhtin turns to Dostoevskii's early fiction, wherein the speech of characters like Makar Devushkin in *Poor Folk* (*Bednye liudi*, 1846) and Goliadkin in *The Double* (*Dvoinik*, 1846) is forever being reformed, refocused, and changed by the discourse of others. He notes that Devushkin's words consistently come from two points of view, "as he himself understands them and wants others to understand them, and as another might actually understand them" (208). In Dostoevskii's next work, *The Double*, this bifurcation of speech becomes even more pronounced. On occasion the narrator uses the very same words as the story's protagonist, but when he utters them, they are a stinging rebuke to the emptiness and ineptitude of Goliadkin's discourse. Bakhtin concludes that "this transferral of words from one mouth to another, where the content remains the same although the tone and ultimate meaning are changed, is a fundamental device of Dostoevsky's. He forces his heroes to recognize themselves, their idea, their own words, their orientation, their gesture in another person, in whom all these phenomena change their integrated and ultimate meaning and take on a different sound, the sound of parody or ridicule" (217).

As opposed to the multidirectional nature of parody, the intentions of the two voices in a stylization appear to merge. Bakhtin terms stylization a "unidirectional" variant of double-voiced discourse, for it "make[s] use of someone else's discourse in the direction of its own particular aspirations. Stylization stylizes another's style in the direction of that style's own particular tasks. It merely renders those tasks conventional" (*Problems*, 193). Although Bakhtin's comments on stylization are often incomplete and open to interpretation, his approach to this strategy suggests that it unfolds in two distinct phases. First, a stylization presents itself as a straightforward rendering of another's discourse that faithfully follows its intent. It does nothing to underscore any possible divergence from the other speech act and is crafted in such a way that readers can discern little or no distance between its two voices. In this regard, it overlaps with a conventional understanding of imitation. The second, and indispensable, aspect of stylization, which can only be inferred from Bakhtin's definition, centers on the dynamic, evolutionary role of this strategy. He writes that "stylization presupposes style; that is, it presupposes that the sum total of stylistic devices that it reproduces did at one time possess a direct and unmediated intentionality and expressed an ultimate semantic authority" (189). Most important, the stylizer's goal is not merely to imitate this intentionality, but rather to expose its conventionality by recontextualizing it: "Stylization forces another person's referential (artistically referential) intention to serve its own purposes, that is, its new intentions. The stylizer uses another's discourse precisely as other, and in so doing casts a slight shadow of objectification over it" (189). Although Bakhtin does not come out and say it, somewhere between a stylization's mimicry of the "particular tasks" of another style and its introduction of "a new intention" into this style lies its ability to function as an effective means of literary change.

Despite Bakhtin's succinct articulation of certain aspects of stylization his work in this area comes up short as a functioning theory of literary evolution. As in Tynianov's introduction to the topic too much must be assumed that is not explicitly stated. In particular, Bakhtin frequently fails to support theory with examples, generally leaves stylization in the shadows of parody, and tends to blur the distinctions between related forms of discourse (imitation, parody, stylization). More important than even these shortcomings is the question that neither critic ever raises: just *how* does the "dialectical change of literary schools" come about? To phrase it another way, using Tynianov's pronouncements as a starting point, if a stylization is *not* designed to elicit a humorous, mocking response from its readers, just how should we react to it? Before Tynianov/Bakhtin's rudimentary theory can be transformed into a productive approach to literary analysis, it is essential that the role of decoder be thoroughly understood. The following discussion, which defines stylization within the context of imitation and parody, concentrates precisely on this goal. The foundation of this analysis consists of the categories of planar structure, target, and motivation as sketched in by Tynianov and Bakhtin with more recent scholarship providing insights into the role of reader response, the all-important keystone that is missing from the original articulation of the problem.

IMITATION/PARODY/STYLIZATION: STRATEGIES AND GOALS

The absence of any critical distance from its target distinguishes imitation from parody and stylization. Of the three strategies under consideration here, it is the only one that is uniplanar. In an imitation there is no second plane or voice, because this type of discourse does not attempt to ridicule or uncover the flaws of another text. On the contrary, the sole motivation of an imitation is to faithfully reproduce the conventions of the material it selects as its target. Bakhtin concludes that "imitation does not render a form conditional, for it takes the imitated material seriously, makes it its own, directly appropriates to itself someone else's discourse. What happens in that case is a complete merging of voices, and if we do hear another's voice, then it is certainly not one that had figured in to the imitator's plan" (*Problems*, 190). Imitation capitalizes on the most successful literary models of the day. The recycling of contemporary character types, themes, and devices engenders yet another fictional world, but it is one that remains faithful to the original blueprint, avoiding anything that might call the soundness of its immediate predecessors into question.

Predicated on a sense of familiarity, imitation makes even fewer demands on readers than it does on writers. In this type of discourse readers are relegated to the role of passive observers. They remain outside the text and are not distracted by the task of tracking a second plane or voice, as they would be in double-voiced discourse. Their only responsibility is to sit back and follow the workings of the fictional world set out before them, and even in this rather limited endeavor they are given significant guidance. Walter Ong writes that all fiction coaches readers in the role they must adopt to decode the text successfully. An evocation of the muse tells them to prepare for the epic mode, and "once upon a time" places them in the land of fairy tales (12). No matter what role this may be in an imitation, one thing is certain: readers are familiar and comfortable with their position vis-à-vis the text. Writers of imitation seize upon a preselected approach to reading. The role they cast for their audience is one that both they and the reading public have accepted for quite some time. Readers never question what is demanded of them in an imitation, because they have practiced their roles so frequently and successfully in the past. They are much like veteran actors who have a set response for virtually every situation, so great is their experience. As readers of an imitation, we may be transported to distant ages and exotic cultures and can witness fantastic and even shocking events, yet we will never find anything to suggest that we ought to reassess our approach to decoding literature. On the contrary, successful imitations always manage to patronize our sense of security, comfort, and self-satisfaction.

When Gogol´ and Dostoevskii practiced their craft in the 1830s and 1840s, the passive approach to reading occasioned by imitation was well entrenched among the Russian public. A recent proliferation in the number of literary journals had greatly expanded the availability of belles lettres, yet the readership engendered by this process remained, in general, remarkably naive and undiscriminating. Virtually without experience in decoding literature, the legions of unsophisticated readers that flocked to journals like *Library for Reading* (*Biblioteka dlia chteniia*, 1834–1865) were forced to rely on the constant repetition of norms and the supposedly unrefracted representation of reality in order to maintain their bearings. Given such a context, editors frequently pitched their offerings to the lowest common denominator. Seeking to rescue people "'terrified by boredom'" and "'to pacify minds,'" Osip Senkovskii, the editor of *Library for Reading* from 1834 to 1847, considered the writer as nothing more than a "popular entertainer and purveyor of tranquilizers" (Fanger, *Gogol*, 44). Although he found such statements abhorrent, no less a firsthand observer than Gogol´ had to admit that there was more than a kernel of truth in them. Referring to those readers who made journal literature so popular, he complained about "how many people there are who judge, speak, and interpret because all their judgments have been presented to them ready made and who could not interpret, judge, or speak on their own" ("O dvizhenii," 156). No doubt Gogol´ had just such readers in mind when he drew up the character of the "significant person" in "The Overcoat." Despite the satisfaction he receives from dressing down subordinates, this self-consumed bureaucrat likes most of all to drop off "into that pleasant state that Russians love better than anything else, that is, when you don't have to think about a thing yourself and thoughts just crawl into your head, one more pleasant than the next, without even giving you the trouble of having to chase after or even search for them" (172). The frequent occurrence of unsophisticated or deluded readers like Poprishchin, Bashmachkin, and Goliadkin in the fiction of Gogol´ and Dostoevskii suggests that the topic of reading was a crucial issue for both authors.

As opposed to imitation, parody adopts a more discriminating attitude toward its target. Comprising two discrete planes, parodic discourse establishes a critical distance between the fictional world of the parody and the fictional world of the material being parodied.

> Parody-satire is commentary on *something else* and requires of the reader that this "something else" be construed as distinct from the text before him. Parody and satire can operate like fiction: that is, they may create fictitious worlds of their own; but these worlds and the texts that create them are parodic or satiric only if the reader himself constructs another world to place in direct comparison to the fictitious one. (Dane, 147)

In Bakhtinian terms the second world or plane of a parody consists of someone else's discourse and can include everything from the themes, types, and devices of another author to the words, tone, and gestures of a character or narrator in the parody itself. Whatever the target, parody brings these elements to our attention by turning the spotlight of humor on them. As the second plane emerges from behind the fictional world of the parody, readers are invited to join with the author in a critical evaluation of its characteristics. The emotional response generated by this technique— what Linda Hutcheon calls the ethos of parody—runs the gamut from ridicule to respect, from the bitter, scornful laugh to the knowing smile (*Parody*, 63–68), but in all cases, parody forces readers to see the target in a new light.

The motivation for parody has changed over time, but Robert Scholes's formulation of a "surgical response" to a target sums up the modern conception of this type of discourse.[9] In his succinct definition, "parody exists in a parasitic relationship to romance. It feeds off the organism it attacks and precipitates their mutual destruction" (103). Explaining this process on a tactical level, Peter Hodgson notes that from the eighteenth century to the present parody has generally been viewed as an attack "on specific literary practices which are judged censurable according to the commonly accepted standards of a serious community of letters" (*Gogol*, 26). As this comment implies, the quintessential requirement for parody is a well-defined set of literary norms. Hutcheon elaborates this point, saying that "parody posits, as a prerequisite to its very existence, a certain aesthetic institutionalization which entails the acknowledgment of recognizable, stable forms and conventions" (*Parody*, 74–75). No doubt one of the reasons why parody flourished during the age of neoclassicism was that both authors and readers subscribed to a rigid codification of norms, ranging from the linguistic and thematic to the structural and generic. In the "surgical" approach to parody, a work not meeting the agreed-upon standards becomes an easy and tempting target for the parodist's knife. Any competent attempt to ridicule it will find a large audience more than willing to delight in the unmasking of its every flaw.[10]

Even though parody establishes a more circumspect relationship to a second text than imitation does, the two strategies impose much the same sort of passive role on the reader. Hutcheon's conclusion that parody is an *overt* form of diegetic narcissism understates the case: *blatant* would be a more accurate description. On the one hand, it is true that in parody, as opposed to imitation, readers have the added burden of keeping track of two stories: the created fiction of the first plane and the re-created fiction of the second. The sort of double-entry bookkeeping demanded by this strategy does require a fairly sophisticated linguistic, generic, and ideological competence of its readers. To decode a parody successfully, readers must be able to recognize what is implied in a text as well as what is stated; they must be familiar with the rhetorical and literary norms of the canon in order to detect deviations from it; and they must have knowledge of the prevailing aesthetic and ideological values of their society (Hutcheon, *Parody*, 94–95). On the other hand, despite this rather complex list of requirements, the task of decoding a parody is simplified at every turn. Since parody is employed in defense of the canon, the literary and ideological norms that readers need to apply are the very ones they have already internalized simply by being familiar with the literature of their time. Moreover, parody always elicits some sort of heightened emotional response from its readers, if not outright mockery, then at least a smile of recognition. Humor illuminates the characters, themes, and devices that form the second plane of a parody, thereby giving readers a clear idea of where they should focus their attention. Readers must search for two orders of meaning in parody, but they are led every step of the way. The parodist tells them what their target is and then takes them to it, never demanding more than they can reasonably be expected to give.

As a result of having a highly visible, well-defined target, parody maintains a distance between its readers and the material under scrutiny. It "distinguishes between, on the one hand, the author and the audience (who are on the right side of the issue at stake) and, on the other hand, the target (who, or which, is on the wrong side)" (Hodgson, *Gogol*, 26). In this type of discourse readers are never asked to turn their critical powers inward for, as Peter Hodgson wittily reminds us, parody is "not directed at the audience any more than a satirical comedy like Molière's 'L'avare' was written to be performed before convocations of misers" ("Imitation/Stylization," 15). The parodist positions readers to apprehend a target, but takes pains to excuse them from any unpleasant association with it. Upon finishing a parody, readers never have any second thoughts about their relationship to literature but, on the contrary, feel enlightened, satisfied, and secure.

Like parody, stylization also fits under the rubric of double-voiced discourse, but, as Tynianov points out, there is a crucial structural difference between the two. Stylization resembles parody in that the devices, character types, and themes of its first plane allude to a second plane consisting of similar elements taken from other works of contemporary fiction. But as opposed to parody, stylization frustrates our attempt to attribute its target to a specific author or text. Instead, the elements constituting its second plane are culled from a large number of sources and represent what a formalist like Tynianov would call the dominant traits of the literature of the day ("On Literary Evolution," 41). Moreover, stylization eschews the humor that parody employs to highlight the discrete elements of its target. In a stylization the second plane initially recedes from our attention because it appears to merge with the first plane. Owing to a seemingly faithful and serious reproduction of the literary dominant, the question of a second plane simply does not arise until the decoding process is well under way.

Unaware of the frustrations and reversals they will eventually encounter, readers embarking on a stylization have no reason to suspect that the text before them is anything other than an imitation, for, as its first and absolutely essential task, a stylization must coax readers into deploying the type of decoding strategies that would be appropriate for uniplanar discourse. It does this by exploiting the dictum that a familiar stimulus from the author will evoke a familiar response from readers.

> The [literary] work has structure and meaning because it is read in a particular way, because these potential properties, latent in the object itself, are actualized by the theory of discourse applied in the act of reading. . . . To read a text as literature is not to make one's mind a *tabula rasa* and approach it without preconceptions; one must bring to it an implicit understanding of the operations of literary discourse which tells one what to look for. (Culler, 102)

Readers can always find what they are looking for in a stylization because recognizable character types, conventional themes, and a standard (if not shopworn) plot are the staples of this narrative strategy. To facilitate "the dialectical change of literary schools," a stylization must first set readers at ease by appearing to conform to the prevailing tastes in literature. Thus, at first glance, the stylized text always seems predictable and the decoding abilities of its readers more than sufficient for any challenge it may present.

In addition to using conventional genres, types, and themes, a stylization keeps readers on track by frequently encouraging them in their quest to find a familiar and comfortable interpretation. This task is accomplished with the aid of what Gerald Prince calls "reading interludes," a type of overt commentary that strives to make the text as accessible to readers as possible: "Reading interludes . . . are . . . an index of the stance taken by the narrative with regard to its own communicability and readability, as an indication of how it ostensibly wants to be read and a cue to the kind of program it considers most useful for its decoding, and as a factor determining to some extent the response of any reader other than itself" (237). In the imitative phase of a stylization the use of reading interludes puts readers into a state of intellectual torpor as the text openly acknowledges its devices and even explains the best way to interpret them. Readers are more or less guided through the initial stage of a stylization as every effort is made to lighten their burden and shield them from the unsettling test that lies ahead.

Once readers are convinced that the work before them is an imitation, they are vulnerable to the second, and final, part of the stylizer's plan. Having led readers into a comfort zone, a stylization slowly but surely transforms itself into something quite different. As this process unfolds, readers begin to realize that imitation and their well-rehearsed approach to decoding it will not lead to a satisfactory understanding of the story. If anything, they are suddenly overwhelmed by a redundancy of failure as the familiar becomes strange, the predictable veers off into the unknown, and all their confident assumptions about the text are engulfed in an ever-lengthening shadow of uncertainty. With the advent of new information that does not support the comfortable interpretation they have constructed, the entire story appears in a completely different light. Behind the first, and seemingly only, plane of a work like *The Double* an extremely bewildering second plane eventually reveals itself. This is not the second plane of parody, however, which is located outside the text. On the contrary, readers remain trapped within the fictional world of a stylization, and what is being questioned is not another author's work, but rather their approach to decoding literature.

Unlike imitation and parody, stylization makes readers the center of attention and demands that they take responsibility for constructing the text. Hutcheon writes that "metafiction . . . seems aware of the fact that it (like all fiction, of course) actually has *no* existence apart from that constituted by the inward act of reading which counterpoints the externalized act of writing" (*Narcissistic Narrative*, 28). Nowhere is this more true than in a stylization. Just when readers confidently internalize part of the story, the remainder of it becomes almost impossible to comprehend: devices contradict each other, a linear plot dissipates into a series of digressions and dead ends, and the apparent meaning of the work deteriorates into triviality or even complete insignificance. With nothing left to hold on to, readers have no recourse other than to ponder what has gone wrong. Since they have already committed themselves to the devices, types, and themes of the story, they are cut off from finding fault either with them or with the author. Instead, readers are compelled to question the validity of the literary aesthetic they supported not just on this occasion but so many times in the past as well. If they accepted a character who turned out to have no substance whatsoever as a convincing depiction of one of life's downtrodden "little people" or initially confused a superficial and saccharine fictional world for an insightful critique of society, they have no one to blame but themselves. Stylization is so disconcerting because it forces readers to admit that something is wrong with the way they read literature. Once they have come to this conclusion, they can begin to approach literary texts with greater circumspection. It is precisely by challenging us to become more sophisticated readers that a stylization like Dostoevskii's novella *The Double* promotes "the dialectical change of literary schools," a change that, in its own quiet manner, is every bit as effective as the comic subversion of the status quo in the carnivalesque.

Chapter

EIGHT

SLOWLY FADING INTO NOTHING

The Self-Effacing Stylization of *The Double*

In a February 1846 review of *The Double* for *Notes of the Fatherland (Otech-estvennye zapiski)* Vissarion Belinskii criticized the redundancy of Dosto-evskii's tangled web of dreams, impostors, and mirror images. While ex-pressing admiration for individual incidents, he declared that "there are far too many such wonderful places in *The Double,* and the same thing over and over again, however wonderful it may be, wearies and bores" (Fanger, *Dostoevsky,* 159). What Belinskii and others have failed to see, however, is that there definitely is a method to the madness of *The Double.*[1] Like the car-nivalesque fiction of Chulkov and Komarov, Dostoevskii's novel relent-lessly attacks Russia's thoughtless infatuation with foreign culture. Far from trying to appease the sensibilities of its age, it functions as a cleverly designed challenge to the Western-inspired literary aesthetic of the Natural School. With his great knowledge of both Russian and foreign prose fiction of the 1840s Dostoevskii knew quite well just what his readers could and would do. In a near flawless execution of the technique of stylization he first entices readers with the conventions they have come to expect from the Natural School and then, without warning, changes the way these are normally utilized. The premises readers have willingly accepted this time as well as so many times before gradually, disquietingly disintegrate before their very eyes. A protagonist who seemed to be a reliable literary type be-gins to act erratically; themes that had been clearly defined suddenly be-come ambiguous or disappear altogether; and confident predictions about the outcome of the work are shattered as the plot takes a series of confusing twists and turns. Confronted with a set of conventions that seem to be as empty as Goliadkin himself, readers are forced to reevaluate their allegiance to a type of literature they had previously embraced without reservation.

As in every stylization, the first part of Dostoevskii's strategy consists of lulling readers into a false sense of security by offering them an abundance of familiar material on virtually every page. To begin with, the story is set in the well-known environs of St. Petersburg, with much of the action taking place along the Fontanka and on Nevskii and Liteinyi Boulevards. Famous landmarks, such as the Neva River, the Semenovskii and Izmailovskii Bridges, and Gostinyi Dvor, also create an air of verisimilitude, and the merchants who cater Klara Olsuf´evna's name-day party are recognizable as the proprietors of St. Petersburg's largest food stores in the 1840s. Even more important than these reflections of a real city are the references to a living literary tradition that begins with Pushkin's *The Bronze Horseman* (*Mednyi vsadnik*, 1833). In *The Double* Goliadkin confronts the same "city-enemy" (Shklovskii, "O 'Dvoinike,'" 62) that claimed Evgenii's Parasha, and like Evgenii's tragedy his adventures unfold during November, a month when, we are told, "walking about isn't at all pleasant. The climate is just not good" (*The Double*, 116).[2] Like many characters before and after him, "Golyadkin is a creature of the putrid damp fog of Petersburg, a phantom living in a phantasmal city" (Mochulsky, 48). By the time Dostoevskii penned *The Double*, the aura of menace and grotesquerie associated with its subject had already been well established by Pushkin's *poèma*, Gogol´'s Petersburg tales, and a host of similar stories.

For readers well versed in Russian prose fiction of the 1840s the most familiar aspect of *The Double* is its hero. In this period of Russian literary history "the ill-used victim of one civil service department tended to be interchangeable with any number of other exploited inhabitants of the harsh Russian capital. In Golyadkin, the fledgling novelist was assumed to have contributed yet another exposé of the downtrodden little man whose fall could be attributed to a heartless bureaucracy" (Anderson, *Dostoevsky*, 12–13).[3] Goliadkin is better off, both materially and intellectually, than his immediate predecessor Devushkin (Terras, 168–70; Trubetsskoi, 140–41), yet he still represents "the most common type of Petersburg inhabitant, belonging to the middle rung of society" (Nechaeva, 154). Living a virtually anonymous existence in his cramped, dusty apartment, Goliadkin is an "insignificant" little person (*The Double*, 109), who labors with the faint hope of raising himself up another notch in the table of ranks. Like Gogol´'s Akakii Akakievich, what little standing he does have in society is solely owing to his official identity. When he arrives at the home of his superior in search of a protector, the servants want to admit him only if he is the bearer of official documents. After he gains an audience with the man known only by the condescending and distant title of His Excellency, Goliadkin is so overwhelmed that he is unable to look him in the eye. In a manner that recalls Bashmachkin's meeting with the "significant person," all he can do is stare at the medal on his superior's black dress coat (215).

Dostoevskii articulates the poor-clerk stereotype in even greater detail in his treatment of the mercurial Goliadkin Jr. Like his twin, the double is the epitome of the hard-working clerk whom both fate and the powers-that-be have treated less than kindly. At the office he can be found bustling about with a stack of papers, dutifully carrying out the orders of Andrei Filip-povich, the office manager. It is this side of his personality that leads a coworker, the sober Anton Antonovich, to dub him "a businesslike person" (*The Double*, 150). Later, when Goliadkin invites his double home for sup-per, the latter turns out to be a perfect example of the persecuted urban un-derman at the end of his rope. In describing this tête-à-tête, the narrator notes that "evidently, the guest was in extreme confusion: he was timid, submissively followed his host's movements, caught his glance, and, ap-parently, tried to guess his thoughts from them. Humiliation, oppression, and intimidation were expressed in his every gesture" (153). This "noble beggar" reinforces his martyr image with a tearful discourse about the in-trigues that cost him his position in another city, his vain attempts to find employment in St. Petersburg, and the abject poverty that drove him to borrow the very clothes on his back (155–56). As Bakhtin puts it, in this episode the double "is a characterization of the cringing and self-effacing Golyadkin"; he "speaks in Golyadkin's own words, bringing with him no new words or tones" (*Problems*, 215–16).[4]

As the number of stereotypes mounts in *The Double*, readers feel per-fectly at ease. The hero, setting, and apparent themes of this work offer nothing out of the ordinary and can therefore be processed without a sec-ond thought. Such a response would seem fully justified, for many of Dos-toevskii's literary contemporaries also found much that was familiar in the novel. Valerian Maikov and Nikolai Dobroliubov remarked that *The Dou-ble* was faithful to the prevailing creed that fiction ought to be a mirror of reality,[5] and Belinskii, the supreme arbiter of Russian literature in the 1840s, applauded it even before it was finished. Concerning a prepublica-tion reading of the novel given at the critic's home, Dostoevskii writes that "Belinskii found the three or four chapters I read to be extremely pleas-ing" (Dostoevskii, *Polnoe sobranie sochinenii*, 1:483). The writer Dmitrii Grigorovich, who was also present, describes Belinskii's reaction in the same glowing terms, claiming that he "greedily devoured every word and in places was unable to hide his delight" (Grossman, 73). Even after *The Double* was published and critics ceased to lavish praise on it, no one de-nied that Dostoevskii had been faithful to the poetics of the Natural School.[6] For K. S. Aksakov it was precisely a too slavish dependence on previous literature that made Dostoevskii's novel such a failure: "We don't even understand how such a story could have appeared. . . . It seems that this work is just phrases devoid of any life. It is just a naked imitation of the external features of the great works of Gogol´. . . . There is no sense, no imitation, no thought, nothing. Mr. Dostoevskii has sewn himself a coat out of the scraps of the shining clothing of the author and has boldly stepped before the public" (Bem, 140).[7] Even though *The Double* was a fail-ure, the consensus was that it contained the correct constituent parts and evinced an ideologically sound approach to literature.

Although readers are invited to place *The Double* in the literary canon of the 1840s for the first five or six chapters, eventually they are forced to reevaluate this notion as Dostoevskii springs the trap that is the second, and crucial, part of any stylization. Regarding the ability of a literary work to influence its reception, Gerald Prince explains that "many a narrative text presents, in part, one of [its] possible readings. It performs some of the reading operations that a given reader may perform. It specifically answers questions pertaining to the nature, the meaning, the role, the appropriateness of its constituent parts. It functions as a text reading itself" (230). If the first part of *The Double* celebrates an engaging familiarity, the second part, to paraphrase Prince, continually reads itself and finds its constituent parts to be sorely lacking. In the self-effacing stylization of *The Double*, the further readers move forward in the text, the less progress they make. As new and important facts come to light, they do not add to our understanding of the novel but on the contrary only leave us more and more confused. Eschewing the broad strokes of ribaldry and farce that mark the carnivalesque for a much quieter approach, Dostoevskii gradually transforms *The Double* into a grotesque reflection of the literary aesthetic of the Natural School. In this warped and convoluted work such concepts as temporal, spatial, and textual unity—the hallmarks of the mirror-of-reality approach to literature—simply do not exist. By the end of the novel exasperated readers come to realize that the decoding strategies that served them so well in the past with other "poor clerk" stories simply come up short in *The Double*. As the text disintegrates and finally fades into nothing, it takes our complacent attitudes toward literature along with it.

The first instance that forces us to question the veracity of the narrative occurs at the beginning of chapter 6. At this point in the story Goliadkin has just awakened on the morning after his initial meeting with the double. As he tries to recall the "unsettling encounter," we notice that the double, who had retired with his host just hours earlier, is surprisingly nowhere to be seen. A plausible explanation immediately presents itself when Goliadkin attributes the unexpected appearance of "his twin" to momentary hallucinations: "All of this was so strange, baffling, and wild, it all seemed so impossible, that it really was difficult to give any credence to the whole affair. Mr. Goliadkin himself was even prepared to recognize the entire thing as an unprecedented delirium, a momentary disorder of the imagination, a darkening of the mind" (*The Double*, 144). With this admission the demands of realism and credulity are satisfied. Upset by his blunder at Klara Olsuf′evna′s name-day party and sick from walking in the rain and snow of a November night in St. Petersburg, Goliadkin simply dreamed up the double. All the facts at our disposal fit into a pattern, and we can proceed with the story.

Everything does seem accounted for until we pause to think about one curious detail. In the first sentence of chapter 6 the narrator reports that Goliadkin awoke at *exactly eight o'clock* on what is supposedly day two of the story. Although this statement appears to connote nothing out of the ordinary, it is a perfect example of how a stylization forces us to move backward instead of forward and to question information that we accepted earlier without a second thought. The very first line of *The Double* tells us that the protagonist awoke *just before eight o'clock* on day one. In rereading this sentence and the one that follows, we also learn that "Goliadkin regained consciousness after a long sleep, yawned, stretched, and *finally* opened his eyes *completely*. For about two minutes, however, he lay on his bed without moving, like a man who wasn't completely certain whether he was awake or still sleeping" (109; emphasis added). Now the information given at the beginning of chapter 6 becomes both more important and more disturbing. On morning one Goliadkin has "awakened" from a *long dream*. It takes him quite a while to open his eyes, and he has trouble orienting himself. A comparison of the references to time and dreaming in the openings of chapter 1 (day one) and chapter 6 (day two) poses a startling question. Has Goliadkin imagined more than just his midnight meeting with the double? Up until chapter 6, has he ever left his bed and truly come to his senses, or are Klara's party and his shopping spree at Gostinyi Dvor, as well as the double's appearance, merely the result of ten minutes' worth of dreaming as he struggles to awaken from a deep sleep?

Dostoevskii supports this major attack on an orderly, natural progression of time with minor thrusts on just about every other page. Readers do not have to get very far into *The Double* before they accumulate a large inventory of the phrases "Goliadkin came to his senses" *(opomnilsia)* and "Goliadkin regained consciousness" *(ochnulsia).*[8] For example, when the double crosses his path along the Fontanka, Dostoevskii's incredulous protagonist is struck dumb and loses touch with everything around him. The narrator tells us that "whether Mr. Goliadkin's disbelief lasted a long time or a short one, whether or not he sat on the curb for very long, I'm unable to say, but having regained his senses a bit, he suddenly set off running and didn't look back" (142). Again and again Dostoevskii uses the device of his hero losing consciousness to challenge the temporal integrity of *The Double*. What, if anything, transpires during these blackouts? Is Goliadkin daydreaming? Do the events that follow these episodes actually take place in the streets and apartments of the northern capital or only in the mind of a deluded civil servant? Unfortunately for those readers seeking order, logic, and completion in Dostoevskii's novel, these questions are impossible to answer.

Dostoevskii's treatment of space in *The Double* serves as a visual analogue to the function of time. In this stylization, action is frequently carried forward only in order to be swiftly annulled. Of the many examples of the protagonist's self-effacing peripeteia in *The Double*, the most illuminating one occurs on the third evening of his adventures. Having sent a letter to the double via his servant Petrushka, Goliadkin is too impatient to wait for a reply so he dashes off to find some answers on his own (177). Half an hour of trudging through the mud and snow brings him to the doorstep of his imagined sweetheart, Klara Olsuf´evna, but then his resolution suddenly fails him, and he decides against ringing the bell. Rhetorically asking himself, "What am I doing here?"—by now we should have no trouble answering this question—Goliadkin sets off for work in order to pick up the trail of intrigues supposedly awaiting him there. As he approaches the darkened building, he once again falters, questioning his reasons for coming to the department in the first place. On the way home the befuddled hero finally admits the futility of his efforts, lamenting that "I have just wasted my time. . . . This is utterly absurd" (177). The wild-goose chase described above is an appropriate visual metaphor for the plot of *The Double.* Goliadkin has traced a closed loop through St. Petersburg in an effort to find the key to his problems only to end up right back where he started. In effect, he returns home without having done or found out a single thing. His wanderings are just as empty as a November night in St. Petersburg—could anyone really be about in weather like this?—and they represent just one of the many ways in which *The Double* slowly but surely "fades into nothing."[9]

As he does with the temporal black holes that dot *The Double,* Dostoevskii utilizes the technique of self-effacing movement virtually from the beginning of the novel. In chapter 1 Goliadkin takes a hired carriage up Liteinaia Street to Nevskii Prospect. When he spies the carriage of his superior, Andrei Filippovich, he immediately turns around and retraces his path down Nevskii to Liteinaia Street, where he visits his doctor. His interview with Krest´ian Ivanovich takes up all of chapter 2, and chapter 3 finds Goliadkin resuming his trip by again riding up Liteinaia and then along Nevskii. What Goliadkin has managed to do here—if that is the correct verb to use in a situation such as this—is to take his time getting nowhere. The trip to Dr. Rutenspitz is completely fruitless, for Goliadkin's disjointed conversation only perplexes the doctor, whose sole advice to the clerk is to keep taking the medicine he prescribed on a previous visit. In the end, all of Goliadkin's frenetic energy only serves to point out just how empty he and his concerns really are. It is as though the mercurial hero has performed yet another vanishing act by laying down a trail and then covering his tracks. What makes this episode so effective is its placement within the plot of *The Double.* Coming in the opening chapters, it does not obtrude, and readers have no reason to take special notice of it. On a first reading of the novel Goliadkin might seem a bit odd, but his actions do not appear to carry any symbolic significance. Moreover, as opposed to what would happen in a carnivalesque treatment of the same subject, the narrator's description of Goliadkin's wanderings is devoid of the sort of humor that would underscore the author's intentions for the reader. It is only after Dostoevskii unleashes the major challenges to time, space, logic, and textual veracity in the second part of *The Double* that readers are forced to return to episodes such as Goliadkin's visit to the doctor and to admit that they found some significance in a totally meaningless event.

As disconcerted as readers must be by the spatial and temporal black holes that cut up *The Double,* they no doubt find the five letters that appear in rapid succession near the end of the novel to be even more confusing. One by one each of these letters either cannot be found at a crucial moment or disappears altogether. As Bem writes, this is because they probably never existed in the first place: "This is not a genuine correspondence, but the delirium of Goliadkin's ailing imagination. The letters suddenly disappear—'yesterday's letter to Vakhrameev wasn't there' or 'the letter, to his surprise, turned out to be not in his pocket'—because Goliadkin didn't write or receive them in reality" (155). By introducing letters into the amalgam of elements that seems to dissolve into thin air in *The Double,* Dostoevskii adds a more directly metaliterary dimension to the technique of self-effacement that dominates this stylization. Now, not only the fixity of such concepts as time and space are challenged, but the credibility of verbal expression is undermined as well. After observing the shell game that haunts Goliadkin as he tries to keep track of the five letters, readers can no longer maintain any confidence in the text before them. In the treacherous narrative known as *The Double,* words turn out to be just as untrustworthy and empty as Goliadkin Jr.'s ingratiating smile.

The commotion surrounding Goliadkin's first letter to his twin epitomizes the illusory nature of written texts in *The Double.* Impatient for some sort of response, Goliadkin spends almost an hour rousing Petrushka from a drunken stupor in order to find out if the double has sent a reply. The answer the semiconscious servant finally comes up with is quite disturbing to his master, yet, in a way, expected by the reader. Petrushka brashly proclaims that Goliadkin's letter was never entrusted to his care, that he never went to Vakhrameev's lodgings (where the double is supposedly staying), and that indeed no such clerk exists (179). Thus we may conclude that the letter is just a figment of the hero's overheated imagination. Or can we? In rapid succession Petrushka maintains that he did drop off the letter—at Shestilavochnaia Street, which is where Goliadkin lives—recants and says he never saw the letter, and in the end once again admits delivering it. Exasperated at Petrushka's performance, Goliadkin exclaims: "What sense can you get from a drunkard! There's not a word here that isn't a lie" (180).[10] This absurd conversation between master and servant places readers in an impossible situation. They have no way of knowing whether or not the letter exists, because neither the unstable Goliadkin nor the drunken Petrushka is a dependable source of information. Bewildered by the text, all they can do is wonder how many other parts of this story are as incredible as Goliadkin's phantom letter to his nemesis.[11]

Those readers who are disturbed enough about the fate of Goliadkin's letter to go back and read it a second time will find that the text itself is totally unreliable. Concerned that he might be offending the addressee, Goliadkin pauses after completing the first two paragraphs to think about what he has just written. Searching for just the right tone and choice of words, he muses: "Won't this be too much? Isn't this too offensive, this hint at proper form, for example? Well, that's all right. I have to show him firmness of character, but to soften things, I can flatter him and butter him up in the end" (175). As this brief interlude clearly shows, Goliadkin believes that words are pliant and should be shaped to create the most favorable impression on their readers. From his point of view verbal discourse does not mirror reality—as Belinskii would have it—but rather shields us from it. Nowhere is Goliadkin's attitude more apparent than in his response to Goliadkin Jr.'s hostile reception of his second letter. The double had upbraided Goliadkin for the accusatory tone of the second missive, and its writer, by now desperate to win the goodwill of even his most hated enemy, implores him to see whatever he wants to in it: "I have erred in this unfortunate letter. Give me the letter, Jakov Petrovich, so that I may rip it up before your very eyes, or if this is impossible, then I implore you to read it just the opposite way, that is, with a purposely friendly intention, giving just the opposite meaning to all my words" (204).

As concerns the proliferation of unreliable letters in the latter stages of *The Double*, Dostoevskii's reworking of the 1846 (or journal) version of the novel helps to explain the modus operandi of his approach to stylization. Stung by the cold reception *The Double* received from readers and critics alike, the author longed to clarify his goals and intentions by revising the work. In 1859 Dostoevskii promised his brother to write a completely "new novel" (Dostoevskii 28, bk. 1:340), yet the final version falls far short of this goal. The revision comprises barely more than the deletion of a relatively small amount of material, mostly in three chapters near the end of the story, which does little to diminish the repetitious nature of the text. Tellingly, although these deletions do not transform *The Double* into a new novel, they do further the cause of stylization by bringing even closer together certain motifs and unreliable texts that undermine the credibility of what transpired earlier. For example, Dostoevskii took out about a page and a half from chapter 10 having to do with Goliadkin traveling from his apartment to the office. With the removal of this material Goliadkin's second phantom letter to the double is juxtaposed with his questioning of the drunken scribe Ostaf'ev, from whom he tries to solicit information concerning the state of affairs at work. In the shortened edition of 1866 readers are no longer distracted by Goliadkin's fragmented ruminations on chivalry and firmness of character, but instead, in rapid succession, confront an unreliable text (the letter) and an unreliable informant (Ostaf'ev). The proximity of these events makes them obtrude even more than in the journal version, thus accentuating the emptiness of the novel. If letters cannot be trusted and narrators cannot be trusted, what is there for readers to hold on to?

Although letters are an important means of establishing the unreliability of the text in *The Double*, on one occasion omitting a letter also serves to create this effect. In the original form of the novel (1846) a second communication to Goliadkin from a coworker named Vakhrameev clarifies certain matters that are better left vague if Dostoevskii's self-effacing technique is to work efficiently. Vakhrameev chastises Goliadkin for mistreating his former landlady, Karolina Ivanovna, and explains in some detail why he should expect to lose his job, apartment, credit, and good name as a result of such callous behavior. When this letter is included, the abuse Goliadkin suffers from those around him begins to make sense. When it is omitted, as in the 1866 version, readers are caught off guard. Why does Olsufii Ivanovich refuse to admit Goliadkin to his daughter's name-day party? Why do several characters make vague allusions to marriage and a certain "respected personage of the female gender"? Readers are unable to find answers to these questions in the revised version of *The Double*, because Dostoevskii's refractory text simply refuses to give them up.

The technique of self-effacement that dominates *The Double* completely upsets normal reading strategies. Instead of revealing more about the fictional world represented in the novel, each turn of the page leaves us more confused as to what, if anything, has really taken place. Despite repeated textual assurances to the contrary, by the time we get to the fourth and final day of Goliadkin's adventures, the experiences of the previous three days are all but erased. On day four Goliadkin's wanderings take him to the tavern he had visited after being kicked out of Klara's party at the beginning of the novel. During his first visit (day one) the dejected clerk ordered a meal, paced the room in agitation for quite some time, and then sat down to ponder his chaotic life. On day four, on the other hand, he orders nothing to eat since the only thing he wishes to devour is a love letter from Klara that miraculously materializes in his pocket. As Goliadkin finishes reading the letter, the narrator sets the scene: "The dishes from someone's dinner and a dirty napkin lay on the table, and a knife, fork, and spoon that had just been used were also scattered about" (208). Pressed to pay for a meal he cannot remember eating, Goliadkin reaches into his pocket (he seems to be wearing the same coat as on day one)[12] and, to his surprise, finds "a vial containing some sort of medicine that had been prescribed by Krest'ian Ivanovich four days ago" (208). Shaken by these events, Goliadkin runs from the restaurant shouting that his life is in danger, and at least in a literary sense, he is right. Goliadkin's actions firmly link day four with day one. No time has elapsed between the two visits because they are in fact one and the same. Goliadkin has never left the restaurant—if indeed he ever came there in the first place—and is being asked to pay for the meal he had ordered at the end of chapter 3 (day one). With this revelation, the "reality" of most of *The Double* simply vanishes. The credibility of Klara's declaration of love, the appearance of the double, and even Goliadkin's blunder at the party is shattered just as completely as the vial of medicine that breaks into pieces on the floor.

Dostoevskii's revision of the second scene in the restaurant for the final version of *The Double* accentuates the self-effacing nature of his narrative. In the 1866 edition he completely deleted Goliadkin's charge that the vial contains poison meant for him by his enemies. Although this alteration removes only about nine lines from the text, it changes the entire focus of the hero's frenzied claim that his life is in danger. With the reference to poison

included, as in the 1846 version, Goliadkin's exclamation reinforces the social motif of the little person as victim of an insensitive and repressive society. With the reference removed, the social motif is obscured, and the technique of self-effacement becomes even more prominent. In the revised
form of *The Double* readers have no reason to suspect that the dark red liq-
uid is poison. When Goliadkin finds the vial in his pocket, their first
thoughts are not about assassination, intrigues, and enemies, but rather of
the hero's meeting with Dr. Rutenspitz in chapter 2. Using this context to
evaluate the protagonist's actions, it would appear that Goliadkin does not
really believe that anyone is out to kill him; he experiences mortal terror
because he realizes this is still day one—the day he promised Dr. Rutenspitz he would get his prescription filled.

As befits a narrative strategy in which more equals less, the end of *The
Double* negates virtually the entire story. Sitting behind a woodpile in Olsufii Ivanovich's courtyard, Goliadkin wonders if this could possibly be the
night Klara appointed for their rendezvous (219). After all, why choose a
time when so many people are present to foil their elopement? The answer
to this question comes when the befuddled hero is escorted into the party
by his namesake. As Goliadkin Sr. surveys the scene, he finds that the same
people who were at the name-day party (day one) are also attending this
evening's ball. Olsufii Ivanovich, his daughter Klara, her fiancé Vladimir
Semenovich, and Andrei Filippovich are all guests that Goliadkin singles
out at both gatherings. What is even more surprising is that several minor
and insignificant figures are also present on both occasions. On day four
the narrator notes that "the youth, who at one time looked very much like
an important councilor" (225) as well as "the councilor wearing a wig on
his head" (226) are repeat guests at the Berendeevs' apartment. This information clinches the argument. Goliadkin was not to come on this particular
day, because Klara never wrote him the letter. Just as was the case with the
restaurant, two visits to the home of Olsufii Ivanovich are really one and
the same. Even without the sharply delineated targets found in the parody
and farce of the carnivalesque, disquieted readers slowly come to understand the breakdown in this fictional world: day four for Goliadkin is actually day one for everybody else.

Appropriately, the final scene of *The Double* forcefully punctuates the
motives of lost time and lost text that run throughout this novel. Just before
he is led away from Olsufii Ivanovich's apartment for the last time, Goliadkin struggles to recognize a new face in the crowd. He concludes that "he
knew this figure well. . . . He had seen it, had frequently seen it, had seen it
just today" (227). Even though it is soon apparent that the new arrival is
Dr. Rutenspitz, the clerk's hazy recollection of an earlier meeting lends itself to two completely different interpretations. If we still had faith in the
text, we would assume that "today" referred to day four and that Dr.
Rutenspitz was the person Goliadkin had seen just hours earlier at His Excellency's residence (216–17). This is what the mad Goliadkin would have
us believe. For those readers who are no longer as deluded as Dostoevskii's

miserable hero and who have watched the text dismantle itself chapter by
chapter and event by event, however, Goliadkin's use of "today" has an altogether different meaning: it can only refer to the meeting in Dr. Rutenspitz's office on the morning of day one. With this deft stroke Dostoevskii
connects the end of his novel with the beginning and thereby eliminates
the entire world of downtrodden clerks, maudlin love affairs, and hyperbolized social commentary that lies in between.[13]

As the fictional world of *The Double* gradually disintegrates, no one is
more dismayed than Goliadkin himself. Throughout the novel Dostoevskii's protagonist displays a broad knowledge of literature and a keen interest in using literary texts to analyze "real-life" situations. Whether it is
Komarov's *Milord George* (131) or Pushkin's *Count Nulin* (212), Goliadkin
frequently refers to literature in order to make sense of the difficult and
threatening situations confronting him. Moreover, even when he does not
rely on specific literary models, he acts just as though he were a reader. In
this respect he is what Tzvetan Todorov calls an *interpretant*: "Based on the
information he receives, every character must construct the facts and characters around him, thus he parallels exactly the reader who is constructing
the imaginary universe from his own information (the text, and his sense of
what is probable); thus reading becomes inevitably one of the themes of the
book" ("Reading," 78). Reading is indeed one of the central themes of *The
Double*, perhaps even the most important one. Goliadkin's strange actions,
the huge gaps in spatial and temporal unity caused by his hallucinations,
and the shifting, unsettling nature of the entire novel become much more
understandable if we see him as a mock reader. Try as he might, he can
find no refuge in a conventional reading of the events and circumstances in
which he is mired, and the more he insists on adhering to a sentimentalized literary view of the world, the closer he comes to his final rendezvous
with the madhouse. In *The Double* Goliadkin serves as a warning to all actual readers. To rephrase Naomi Schor's insight into Kafka's *The Trial*, via
the interpretant Dostoevskii is trying to tell the interpreter (reader) something about interpretation, and the interpreter would do well to listen and
take note (Schor, 170).

Seemingly forever on the outside of events and relegated to peering
through windows and craning around corners, Goliadkin struggles to make
sense of his world. After he is thrown out of Klara's name-day party (day
one), he ceases to participate in life and assumes instead the role of spectator or reader. As he huddles behind a screen on the Berendeevs' back
porch, he remains in the shadows, "following the general course of affairs
in the role of outside observer" (*The Double*, 131). When his pursuit of the
double takes him to the office, he hides behind a stove and observes the
movements of his coworkers from a distance. Unfolding beyond the closed
door of the entryway, the actions of his fellow clerks represent an in-
scrutable text that he cannot penetrate. Although he implores Anton
Antonovich to explain what has taken place (197), his superior's response
affords him little comfort, and the information he receives from two unreli-

able "narrators" (the scribes Ostaf'ev and Pisarenko) also does nothing to improve his predicament. Later in the same evening, just before he is led away to an insane asylum, Goliadkin resumes the role of "outside observer." From behind a woodpile in the Berendeevs' courtyard, he claims that "he himself could see everything decisively" (219), yet he understands virtually nothing of what is going on inside. Right to the bitter end Goliadkin remains a confused "reader" of events rather than a participant in them.

Like the overly credulous readers who are Dostoevskii's target in *The Double*, Goliadkin is able to make sense of a hopeless situation owing to his innate gullibility. Despite the many witch hunts he undertakes against various imaginary intriguers, it would be hard to envision a more accommodating interpretant than this nearsighted clerk. Since penetrating beneath the surface of a text raises frightening questions and leads to unwanted complications for Dostoevskii's hero, he always manages to find the meaning he is looking for. At first the double's maudlin, cliché-ridden autobiography rings false to Goliadkin, yet he eventually accepts it at face value because it sets his mind at ease. As the narrator describes it: "Mr. Goliadkin was moved; he was genuinely touched. Even though [the double's] story was the most empty sort of story, every word nourished his heart, like manna from heaven. The fact is that Mr. Goliadkin forgot his last worries, set his heart on a course for freedom and happiness, and, in the end, mentally called himself a fool" (156). If it says what he wants to hear, even the simplest, emptiest, and most overwrought discourse makes a deep impression on Dostoevskii's protagonist. Having been set up for more than three hours by the double's sad tale, Goliadkin signals his total capitulation when he is moved to tears by his visitor's vapid and blatantly self-serving doggerel:

> If you forget me,
> I won't forget you;
> Anything can happen in life,
> Don't forget me!
>
> (Esli ty menia zabudesh',
> Ne zabudu ia tebia;
> V zhizni mozhet vse sluchit'sia,
> Ne zabud' i ty menia!)
> (157)

In this pointed reference to the process of interpretation Dostoevskii underscores the danger of accepting clichés at face value. Persecuted petty clerks, cramped apartments, and office intrigues are a poor representation of reality, whether they appear in the double's autobiography or anywhere else in the prose fiction of the 1840s. Readers who fail to see this are just as blind as Dostoevskii's nearsighted hero.

Underscoring Goliadkin's role as an ineffectual mock reader, references to occluded vision are spread throughout *The Double*. From the hero's weak eyes to the frost-covered windows of his apartment, one image after another insists that he sees things far from clearly. The descriptions of Goliadkin's immediate environment suggest that some sort of opaque veil hinders the clerk's power of interpretation at every turn. The staircase of his apartment building is dark, damp, and muddy; his window is dingy; and even the weather that greets the sleepy civil servant on day one inhibits a proper view of things. The narrator tells us that "finally the gray, murky, and dirty fall day . . . glanced into the room at him through the dingy window angrily and with a sour grimace" (109). A sense of impaired vision intensifies as Goliadkin approaches his climactic first meeting with the double amid the worst of conditions: "The night was terrible, November-like: wet, foggy, rainy, snowy, fraught . . . in a word, with all the gifts of a Petersburg November" (138). The wind, rain, and snow lash Goliadkin's eyes so badly that they are almost glued shut. As a result, the poor clerk loses contact with his surroundings and is limited to squinting off into the murky distance of a pitch-black night (139). Just before he crosses paths with the double, Goliadkin completes his isolation by shutting his eyes altogether.

Despite his nearsightedness (both literal and figurative) and eventual madness, it is Goliadkin himself who exposes the stereotypical and unreal world he inhabits. As he stands in the Berendeevs' courtyard contemplating his elopement with Klara Olsuf'evna, the wretched clerk comes to understand that his plan will never work. In one of his rare insightful moments he reflects on the illusion of storybook romances: "Mr. Goliadkin recalled some sort of novel he had read a long time ago in which the heroine gave a prearranged signal . . . in just the same circumstances, having tied a pink ribbon to the window. But a pink ribbon now, at night, in the St. Petersburg climate, which is well known for its dampness and unreliability, could never enter into things and, in a word, was completely impossible" (219). Goliadkin is doomed to fail in *The Double* because his interpretations of reality as well as his reactions to it are based on literary clichés. At times he sees himself as the nearly perfect civil servant who wins accolades and promotions from grateful superiors. At others he casts himself as a persecuted urban underman constantly threatened by a hostile world full of malicious schemers. At all times he believes he is involved in an affair of the heart with Klara that is as saccharine as anything in Karamzin. Unfortunately, none of these personas can define a real human being, because they are all the stuff of literature, not life. At least in the peculiar air of St. Petersburg, they are an inadequate reflection of the human condition.[14]

Dostoevskii makes his strongest statement about the difference between literature and life just before his hero enters the Berendeevs' apartment for the last time. In an imaginary conversation with Klara Olsuf'evna, Goliadkin explains that certain outcomes are possible only in the realm of fiction:

> And now what, my young lady? What would you have me do? Do you order me, my young lady, in the manner of some stupid novels to approach on a nearby hill and melt into tears while looking at the bleak walls of your confinement and eventually die following the custom of certain nasty German poets and novelists? Is that what you want, my lady? Well, first of all,

permit me to tell you in a friendly way that things don't turn out that way, and second, I would heartily thrash you and your parents for having given you little French books to read. Because French books don't teach what is good. They contain poison. . . . Noxious poison. (221)

Goliadkin's critique of foreign literature blazes no new trails in the history of Russian letters; it simply follows the path laid down in the previous century by a wide array of sources, from the facetious metaliterary musings of Chulkov's *Mocker* to the condescending proclamations issued by Lomonosov (*Kratkoe rukovodstvo*, 223) and Sumarokov ("Pis´mo," 350). Yet Goliadkin's selection of both French and German writers as the target of his ire also reflects a specific moment in Russian literary history. In the 1840s foreign literature—especially French naturalism and German romanticism—cast a long shadow on Russian prose fiction. Given Dostoevskii's reliance on the literary material of his age and the total breakdown of the "reality" created from it, we can only suppose that Goliadkin's diatribe comprehends works that are far more modern than *Manon Lescaut*. In its own deceptive manner Dostoevskii's stylization in *The Double* underscores the inappropriateness of Russia's foreign-inspired literature of the 1840s just as successfully as the carnivalesque buffoonery of the subculture dismantles the pretensions of the age of Enlightenment.

Although *The Double* was written in the mid-1840s, it displays a twentieth-century approach to the problem of reader response. As Naomi Schor remarks in her analysis of Kafka's *The Trial* (1925), the novel's hero, Joseph K., is far from being the only one who is disquieted by his failure to decode the sign systems of his world: "It is at this juncture in literary history that the identification between interpretant [a character within the text] and interpreter [the reader] begins to produce diminishing narcissistic returns, and the interpreter feels compelled to work overtime lest he suffer the interpretant's sorry fate" (177). It is just such an experience of reader discomfort and alienation that lies at the heart of Dostoevskii's self-effacing discourse. If *The Double* is successful at no other level, it certainly entraps its interpreters into seeing themselves in the protagonist. Just as Goliadkin wanders the streets of St. Petersburg with his eyes sealed shut from the driving snow, readers react as though they were blind to what transpires before them. Dostoevskii tempts readers to accept, as they have many times in the past, the sentimental evocation of sooty apartments, simple yet good-hearted petty bureaucrats, and social injustice as being a valid representation of Russian cultural reality. But once they commit themselves to this familiar system of values, he plays with it, distorts it, and eventually totally effaces it. No matter how accommodating we are as readers, our attempts to make sense of a hopeless situation will prove just as fruitless as Goliadkin's. In Todorov's words, our constructions just will not tally. Thus, readers are the real target of *The Double*. Seduced, betrayed, and abandoned by the text, we are forced to admit to being just as nearsighted and deluded as Dostoevskii's little clerk.

Conclusion

Emin, Chulkov, and Komarov
and the Rise of the Russian Novel

Despite being overlooked by critics, Fedor Emin, Mikhail Chulkov, and Matvei Komarov have made a significant and long-lasting contribution to the literary and cultural life of Russia. Among their many accomplishments, this group of writers deftly exploited the literary opportunities of their age to become true pioneers in their field. Writing against the backdrop of an almost nonexistent tradition of native prose fiction, they borrowed from a wide array of sources to forge the first modern examples of the novel in Russia. In both content and world view works like *Ernest and Doravra*, *Comely Cook*, and even *Vanka Kain* brought Russia into the mainstream of eighteenth-century European novel writing. What is perhaps even more important is that Emin, Chulkov, and Komarov laid down a template that would influence later generations of Russians. From general themes to specific devices and approaches, they provided models for many aspects of the novelist's craft that would be developed in a more sophisticated way by the writers of the golden age. When viewed from this perspective, it becomes clear that Emin's fondness for detailed, documentary-like settings strikes a sympathetic chord in the fiction of Turgenev and Tolstoi, and Chulkov's and Komarov's reliance on the artistic milieu of the subculture calls to mind the metaliterary play of Gogol´ and the young Dostoevskii. In a variety of ways, the work of the first Russian novelists holds the key to fully comprehending some of the greatest achievements in Russian literature.

As the textual analysis in part 2 of this study emphasizes, imitation of the latest European models figures prominently in the genesis of the Russian novel. Although Emin, Chulkov, and Komarov frequently employed material that is associated with earlier periods of Russian literature, for the most part they strove to keep in step with the latest developments in the West. Emin, for instance, was able to move beyond the limitations of his literary milieu by following the lead of such prominent figures as Montesquieu, Voltaire, Lesage, Marivaux, Prévost, and Richardson. As I. Z. Serman notes, "these writers [provided Emin with] his spiritual food, circle of reading, source of ideas, [and] material for the programmatic utterances in his novels and satiric journals" ("Stanovlenie," 84). By making the most of these resources, Emin functioned as something like the Sumarokov of the novel genre. Just as the "Boileau of the North" established standards and goals for poetry and drama,[1] Emin, by virtue of his extraordinary output, transcribed the norms of the West European novel for a Russian audience. Starting with a popular mix of the adventure story and Eastern tale *(Kamber and Arisena, Inconstant Fate)*, he went on to write Russia's first philosophical novel *(Themistocles)* and then ended his career with a sentimentalist work *(Ernest and Doravra)*, which came out just five years after the publication of its model, Rousseau's *La Nouvelle Héloïse.* By staying close to Western sources of inspiration, Emin initiated the genre of the modern Russian novel by turning out six lengthy narratives in the brief span of three years.

The allure of Western models was so strong in eighteenth-century Russian culture that it even had a pronounced effect on the basically subcultural output of a writer like Matvei Komarov. Often called the first documentary novel in Russian literature, *Vanka Kain* might never have been published if it had not been for Komarov's infatuation with foreign literature. In the introduction to this narrative the serf-turned-writer openly acknowledges that he is out to prove that Russia can hold her own in the community of modern European nations. After proudly proclaiming that the reading of secular works is spreading throughout all layers of society, he confronts the myth that Russians have nothing interesting to write about. He recalls a conversation in which some young people commend a story about the French brigand Cartouche and then add that "it is as though here in Russia there aren't any scoundrels similar to him or, for that matter, any adventures worthy of curious note" (ii). Komarov immediately counters this argument with the assertion that since Russia is larger than all other European states combined, it must contain more than its fair share of courageous heroes, desperate rogues, and intriguing adventures (iii–iv). All that is presently lacking, he contends, is a sufficient number of writers who will turn their attention to such "historical" subjects. Komarov then explains that he is stepping forward to fill this void, and the story that follows fits the mold of the eighteenth-century criminal biography as popularized by works such as *Moll Flanders* and *Jonathan Wild*. Even at the very margins of the literary world Russian writers were able to internalize the conventions of Western literature and produce credible imitations of their own.[2]

Just as the first Russian novels were influenced by earlier works and trends, they also left their mark on the literary landscape of the following century. Schaarschmidt notes that Pushkin's personal library contained a copy of *Vanka Kain* (432), and in 1861 Tolstoi himself admitted that "the people, as in the old days, are reading not what we want them to read, but what they like: they are reading Dumas, the Čet´i Minei, Paradise Lost, Korobejnikov's Journey, Francyl Vencian, Eruslan, [and] The English Milord" (426–27). By the end of the nineteenth century Tolstoi was calling Komarov "the most famous Russian writer" (Shklovskii, *Komarov*, 16), and he even tried to emulate some of his practices. In order to reach the same broad base of readers as Komarov did, he helped found the publishing house Posrednik (Intermediary), which issued cheap, *lubok*-like editions, and also attempted to write an adapted version of *Milord George* (Schaarschmidt, 428). Even more compelling evidence concerning the legacy of early Russian prose fiction comes from one of its own, the author, fabulist, and journalist Aleksandr Izmailov, who is best known for his novel *Evgenii, or the Results of Bad Upbringing and Bad Company* (*Evgenii, ili pagubnye sledstviia durnogo vospitaniia i soobshchestva*, 1799–1801). Writing in the 1820s, Izmailov compiled a fictitious catalogue of the books that might be found in a typical landowner's library. According to this list, the reading habits of the time were strongly influenced by the subculture. Among the primers, adventure tales, *lubok* stories such as "Bova Korolevich," and collections of riddles, anecdotes, and dream interpretations that constitute this mélange, Izmailov singles out such classics of the early Russian novel as Komarov's *Milord George* and Emin's *Inconstant Fate* (Shklovskii, *Komarov*, 12–14). From testimonials such as this one it is clear that the pioneers of the Russian novel stand at the beginning of a literary tradition. Owing to their popularity with the masses, they helped to define the contours of Russian literature long after their careers came to a close.[3]

In addition to shaping the reading sensibilities of the nineteenth century, the first Russian novels also had a more direct impact on the development of a native tradition of prose fiction. From working out the complexities of plot construction and characterization to establishing an authoritative narrative voice, the eighteenth-century Russian novel served as a dress rehearsal for many important aspects of the genre. A good case in point concerns the question of mimesis. Although it would be incorrect to call Emin a protorealist, he did anticipate certain techniques commonly associated with major writers of the 1850s and 1860s. Referring to Chulkov's novel *The Comely Cook*, G. A. Gukovskii writes that "individual, externally observed facts, which are photographically recorded, make up the content of this book" (*Literatura*, 229). Ironically, while such a statement misses the mark with regard to Chulkov, it does seem appropriate when applied to his chief literary rival. As one means of reinforcing the historical nature of his fiction, Emin thought nothing of interrupting the flow of a narrative with a carefully chosen fact or evocative description. In addition to framing and evaluating the action of a given novel, his narrators are required to be sensitive observers of life. Whether they are commenting on ancient Egypt, the Middle East, or a contemporary European state, their insights into the physical, moral, and behavioral attributes of an area are every bit as important as the story itself. At times this technique obtrudes so much that it temporarily transforms the text into a documentary. Such is the case in *Inconstant Fate* when, already one hundred pages into his story, the narrator pauses for sixteen pages to introduce the city of Cairo, reflecting on everything from its weather patterns to its military history. Although Emin did not possess the same eye for detail and shading that can be found in Turgenev, Tolstoi, and Aksakov, his novels did provide a native inspiration for an approach to fiction writing that would flower in works like *Notes of a Hunter* (*Zapiski okhotnika*, 1852), *Childhood* (*Detstvo*, 1852), and *A Family Chronicle* (*Semeinaia khronika*, 1856).

Besides laying the groundwork for specific aspects of their craft, the pioneers of Russian prose fiction also worked out solutions to the larger problem of legitimizing the novel. From Komarov's insertion of a moralizing narrator into the raucous biography of an escaped serf to Emin's constant need to evaluate virtually any topic, no matter how mundane, the first Russian novelists helped to impart an aura of authority to their genre. As Emin never tired of demonstrating, this approach to the written word was based on the supposedly infallible judgment of a variety of authorial surrogates. Not just the narrators but also many of the central characters in novels like *Inconstant Fate* and *Ernest and Doravra* are endowed with the sort of experience and knowledge that makes them next to omniscient. Never allowing even the shadow of a doubt to creep into their pronouncements, Emin's surrogates are in total control of the story, and they offer readers no viable alternative to their interpretation of events. Either you agree with them, or you are labeled a fool, a scoundrel, or worse. In this regard they anticipate the authoritarian narration that sustains a novel like *Anna Karenina*. Despite Tolstoi's overwhelming intellectual and artistic superiority, even he cannot surpass Emin in his vigorous control of the text. The oft-quoted opening sentence of *Anna Karenina* ("All happy families resemble one another . . .") is certainly far more graceful than anything Emin ever wrote, yet, when judged strictly from the standpoint of function, Emin's oeuvre contains literally hundreds of similar statements that would fit seamlessly into Tolstoi's classic novel.

Peering through the transparent facade of his narrators and major characters, Emin manipulated a variety of devices in order to project an authoritarian voice into virtually every element of his fiction. At one end of this rhetorical spectrum are the lengthy monologues that treat such subjects as the structure of a proper education, governmental reform, and the lessons to be learned from the natural world. Covering at least a page or two and sometimes ranging up to ten pages or more, Emin's monologues preach a conventional Enlightenment philosophy of the world. At the other end of the spectrum, the smallest rhetorical devices are also efficiently utilized to extol the virtues espoused by official culture. When taken together, the numerous maxims in Emin's fiction form a primer of proper conduct for readers seeking the straight and narrow path of life, and even one-word metaphors reinforce the author's orthodox approach to questions of morality. In either case, whether a stalwart hero is holding forth at length about the rights and responsibilities of an enlightened monarch, or a hackneyed metaphor is employed to illuminate the wisdom of conforming to society's mores, Emin's goal is the same: to lead readers to his preferred conclusion. Throughout his six novels it is as though Emin is trying to convince his contemporaries that the novel is worthy of the same lofty status as the tragedy or the epic. By controlling the reception of his texts, by doing the thinking for his readers as it were, he enhances the seriousness and importance of his work. Emin's construction of an authoritarian voice and his insistence in having it permeate every page of his fiction provides ample evidence that the moral intensity evinced by the nineteenth-century Russian novel was an intrinsic part of the genre from its inception.

If Emin's six novels established the ability of the genre to treat weighty topics in a serious manner, they also served as the perfect target for a more lighthearted, whimsical, and parodic approach to literature. In the artistic reserve of the eighteenth-century Russian subculture would-be novelists found the perfect counterweight to the inflexibility and pretentiousness that defines works like *Inconstant Fate* and *Ernest and Doravra*. Consisting of pulp fiction *(lubok)*, folklore, translated miscellanies, and the genres of the carnival, the Russian subculture opposed anything that represented the literary status quo. The operating dynamic of this approach was informed by a carnivalized, mocking sense of humor. Like the irreverent, rapid-fire routine of a grotesquely costumed carnival *ded*, the discourse of the subculture turned the established order on its head: hierarchies were inverted, virtue was toppled from its pedestal of inviolability, and laughter became the openly acknowledged purveyor of truth. When serious literature did make its way into the subculture, the transformative powers of this milieu almost always guaranteed that it would not survive intact. Beginning with Sumarokov in the eighteenth century, a long list of famous Russian writers, including Pushkin, Lermontov, and Gogol´, had their work co-opted by the subculture. Cast into a completely different system that cared little for the high ideals of legitimate literature, the fables, poetry, and stories of these authors were often simplified and debased in order to appeal to the coarser tastes of a barely literate readership. With Emin's novels as their target and with the ethos of the subculture as their literary guide, Chulkov and Komarov challenged the very premises of their fledgling genre.

As long as Chulkov is categorized as a precursor of nineteenth-century realism, his prose fiction will always be considered stylistically inconsistent and far from graceful. The eroticism and slapstick humor of *The Mocker* and the crudity and bluntness of Martona's folksy narration in *The Comely Cook* do indeed obtrude if Chulkov must carry the burden of being the author who paved the way for Turgenev and the young Tolstoi. Given his role in the literary history of Catherine's empire, it would be much more appropriate to see Chulkov as something like the Russian Laurence Sterne. When he is viewed as a master parodist who used the wit and whimsy of the subculture to challenge the norms of official literature, his work makes perfect sense. For every attempt by an author like Emin to legitimize the novel genre with the discourse of enlightenment and morality, Chulkov has a comic, mocking rejoinder. While Emin offers readers heroes and heroines of unflinching virtue, Chulkov responds with prostitutes and con men; whereas Emin takes a puritanical approach to sex, his rival sees it as just another affirmation of the joyous abundance of life; and if Emin uses his position as author to preach from the bully pulpit, Chulkov revels in stories that challenge readers with their unorthodoxy and ambivalence. From the crafting of individual images and metaphors to the larger components of narration and plot, Chulkov proves on page after page of his major novels that he certainly deserves the title of eighteenth-century Russia's supreme literary jester.

Although Komarov was not as skillful as Chulkov at manipulating the artistic components of the subculture, his work provides even greater insight into the importance of this milieu for the rise of the Russian novel. While both writers relied heavily on *lubok*, carnival entertainment, folklore, and translated literature for the basic building blocks of their fiction, it is quite possible that without this rich reserve of comic inspiration Komarov would never have found his way into print. The author of such lowbrow classics as *Vanka Kain* and *Milord George* was able to become Russia's first commercially successful writer because he was adept at exploiting the carnivalized subculture of his day as a *system*. With his limited education and literary background Komarov's juxtaposition of opposing world views (such as an Enlightenment monologue on the well-being of society and a scene of erotic seduction) often seems accidental, but it is precisely the unselfconscious nature of his parody that is so revealing. Komarov may not have had a very clear idea of *how* he was undercutting the norms of official culture, but he certainly did have a definite plan of action. To compensate for a self-confessed lack of ability, he simply co-opted the themes, devices, and spirit of unvarnished playfulness that constituted the artistic sensibilities of the masses. The man whom I. R. Titunik calls a literary professional adapter ("Komarov," 353) was so successful in this endeavor that it would not be an exaggeration to say that the real author of *Vanka Kain* and *Milord George* was the subculture itself. Perhaps more than any other body of work, Komarov's output highlights the immense, yet far from completely understood, creative potential inherent in the Russian carnivalesque.[4]

The link between the artistic components of the subculture and the development of Russian prose fiction was not limited to the last decades of the eighteenth century. If anything, this connection became even more productive in the 1830s and 1840s when Pushkin, Gogol´, Lermontov, Dostoevskii, and Turgenev were writing the works that set the stage for the golden age of the Russian novel. As Gavriel Shapiro points out, Gogol´'s fiction is saturated with the devices, stereotypes, and ethos of the subculture. In addition to *vertep*, or the Ukrainian puppet theater, which has become a critical cliché in Gogol´ scholarship, Shapiro traces the influence of facetiae and *lubok*, two staples of the eighteenth-century Russian subculture, on Gogol´'s oeuvre.

From the puppet theater Gogol´ appropriated the models for many of his comic characters, including the heroes of "The Tale of the Two Ivans" ("Povest´ o tom, kak possorilsia Ivan Ivanovich s Ivanom Nikiforovichem"; 45) and Chichikov and Nozdrev in *Dead Souls* (*Mertvye dushi*; 48–49); the short, humorous, and witty narratives known as facetiae provided the inspiration for "The Nose" ("Nos"), "The Overcoat" ("Shinel´"), *The Government Inspector (Revizor)*, and *Dead Souls* (38); and the plots of "The Carriage" ("Koliaska"), *Dead Souls*, and the play *Marriage (Zhenit´ba)* as well as Gogol´'s general approach to satire are greatly indebted to *lubok* (76, 98–101). Moreover, just like Chulkov and Komarov more than half a century earlier, Gogol´ frequently channeled this rich reserve of comic material toward metaliterary ends. With the whimsical grotesquerie of "The Nose," the narrative and moral emptiness of "The Overcoat," and the sentimental fantasy of "Diary of a Madman" ("Zapiski sumasshedshego") he consistently undercut the literary and cultural stereotypes of his day. As he implies in the ending of "The Nose," he is just as interested in challenging our assumptions about literature as he is in uncovering the moral failings of his homeland (75). Following a path that was blazed by the pioneers of the Russian novel, Gogol´ marshaled the parodic impulses of the subculture to subvert the values of a foreign-inspired literary aesthetic.

Not long after Gogol´ published his first collection of tales, the artistic milieu of the subculture was enhanced by the phenomenal popularity of the vaudeville and *feuilleton*. Together with *vertep*, facetiae, *lubok*, and the carnival, the two new genres provided the perfect environment for the rise of stylization. In both subject matter and general orientation the new genres, like the older components of the subculture, frequently focused on literary rather than social or political concerns. Peter Hodgson writes that

> the vaudeville and feuilleton were mass produced, often collectively and anonymously: they took their material from their predecessors of the day or week before, incestuously generating their own progeny. The interrelation among the various subliterary genres was consequently a closed circuit, innocent of any reference to concrete, nonfictive reality. The residual impression left by the vaudevilles and feuilletons of the forties is that these forms are not concerned with urban reality, but that they are rather "about" themselves. Their metaliterary emphasis is the tendency toward self-parody. (*Gogol*, 59)

Churned out by the numerous literary hacks of the 1840s, the vaudeville and *feuilleton* often degenerated into nothing more than "a mindless preoccupation with the fabrication and reproduction of the form itself" (59). But when the parodic emphases of these genres were integrated into the work of writers with greater talent and literary circumspection, the results were far more enduring. In the hands of the "reluctant naturalists" (Evgenii Grebenka [1812–1848], Jakov Butkov [18??–1856], Ivan Kokorev [1825–1853]) and especially Gogol´ and Dostoevskii the metaliterary play of the subculture was frequently elevated into a sophisticated stylization of

Belinskii's demand that fiction be a "mirror of reality."

First sketched in by Tynianov and Bakhtin, the theory of stylization developed in part 3 of this monograph greatly enhances our understanding of the dynamics of Russian literary culture in the crucial period of the 1840s. By distinguishing stylization as a specific type of parody and clarifying its goals and modus operandi with insights from contemporary reader-response criticism, we can use it to unlock the previously overlooked significance of recalcitrant texts like *The Double*. From the time it was published in 1846, Dostoevskii's second novel has generally been dismissed as a convoluted and ineffectual work. Belinskii claimed that its repetitive structure could not help but bore readers, and twentieth-century critics have found it decidedly inferior to Dostoevskii's impressive novelistic debut *Poor Folk*. Declaring *The Double* part of the author's minor fiction, Joseph Frank states that "it was difficult at the time [the late 1840s] not to feel that, compared to the other young writers on the rise, [Dostoevskii] had simply lost his way" (296), and Konstantin Mochulsky insists that the skewed relationship between form and content in the novel is "outrageous" and makes "the tale cumbersome and tedious" (51). With the aid of a working theory of stylization, however, it soon becomes apparent that *The Double* is a far more productive and successful text than previously thought. To be sure, the author begins by pacifying readers with the themes, devices, and stereotypes of sentimental naturalism they have encountered numerous times before, and if this were the only goal of *The Double*, it would indeed be a failure. Dostoevskii's genius in this self-effacing stylization is that he then goes on to undermine the credibility of the very literary system he at first appeared to be defending. Saccharine love affairs, persecuted clerks, and even the possibility of achieving a detached, objective narration of events slowly fade into nonsignificance as the end of *The Double* cancels out its beginning. Taking his lead from the metaliterary preoccupation of the subculture, Dostoevskii traps readers into admitting the inappropriateness of an imported literary aesthetic they had previously endorsed without a second thought.

Besides uncovering the structural blueprint of *The Double*, a working theory of stylization can also be used to illuminate many other texts of the same period. The 1840s were a turbulent time in Russian letters when authors, critics, and publishers were consciously engaged in the process of self-definition. In such important works as "Diary of a Madman" and *Poor Folk* stylization made a substantial contribution to this debate. In the former tale Gogol´ implies that taking the literature of his age too seriously eventually leads to madness. Primed by what he reads in newspapers and miscellanies and what he sees and hears on the comic stage, Poprishchin, the poor-clerk hero of the story, concocts a fantasy life for himself in his diary. At first he harbors a futile love for Sofiia, the daughter of his superior at work, and later, when his dementia becomes full-blown, he fancies himself the unacknowledged king of Spain. By the time Poprishchin is carted off to an asylum, the fantastic musings that fill his diary manage to discredit everything from an unhealthy fascination with things foreign ("The

French need a good thrashing" [196]), to sentimental love stories ("What trash!" [204]), to the literary device of creating an aura of verisimilitude via lengthy descriptions of mundane occurrences ("As though there weren't anything more interesting to write about" [202]). Like the unfortunate copyist in "Diary of a Madman," Makar Devushkin, the central character in Dostoevskii's first novel, *Poor Folk*, also unwittingly parodies the conventions of the reigning trend in literature. Though he is well into middle age, poor, and balding, he sees himself as a possible suitor for his distant relative, the seventeen-year-old Varvara Dobroselova. As Devushkin pursues this relationship, he promotes any number of sentimental literary clichés and in the process reveals just how empty and outlandish they are. Among other things, he complains that Gogol''s parodic caricature of Akakii Akakievich in "The Overcoat" is directed at him (61–63), acknowledges that his life would make the perfect subject for a third-rate satirist (70), and by lauding the ineptitude of his writer friend Rataziaev, makes a mockery of the "mirror-of-reality" philosophy of literature (50–54).[5] As in "Diary of a Madman," the poetics of the sentimentalized prose fiction of the 1840s comes to naught in Dostoevskii's self-conscious epistolary novel.[6]

Of the many works in the 1840s that use stylization to undermine the prevailing literary aesthetic, "The Overcoat" comes closest to matching *The Double* in its systematic application of this strategy. From the very beginning of this tale to the end, every time Gogol´ introduces an idea, an image, or even a tone that invites us to sympathize with his hero as the innocent victim of a heartless society, he mercilessly ridicules such a response. On the one hand, he includes many scenes that appear to support a philanthropic approach to his subject. The narrator's description of a fashionable section of town where Akakii attends a party in the bright and festive apartment of one of his coworkers emphasizes how wretched the protagonist's existence really is (158–59), and when this poor clerk confronts his tormentors at the office with the famous lines "Leave me alone. Why do you offend me so?" (143), readers are no doubt intended to side with him. On the other hand, Gogol´ consistently negates this reaction by showing his hero in a completely different light. The very same character who arouses our pity when attacked by his coworkers is mockingly described at other times as "the eternal titular councilor" with the "hemorrhoidal" face (141), who, it would appear, "had been born into the world ready-made, in his frock coat and with a bald spot on his head" (143). Moreover, on his way to and from the office Akakii is generally so preoccupied with work that he never notices the garbage—a wisp of straw, a bit of thread, a melon rind—that is continually being thrown at him from every direction (145). Rather than arouse our indignation at the clerk's lowly position in life, "naturalistic" descriptions such as this one evoke such a ludicrous image that they underscore the conventionality of the device itself. Combined with frequent references to the process of reading (Akakii Akakievich is near-sighted [141], prefers to close his eyes when the world is not to his liking [161], and lacks the ability to appreciate irony or symbolism [145], the adversative style of "The Overcoat" puts readers in the center of the critical spotlight. By exposing one literary cliché after another, it traps us into admitting that at times we are just as blind as Gogol´'s unimaginative copyist.

Canonical texts like "The Overcoat," *Poor Folk,* and *The Double* confirm the importance of the pioneers of Russian prose fiction. Well before Gogol´ and Dostoevskii lampooned the Russians' often misguided attachment to a foreign-inspired literary system, Emin, Chulkov, and Komarov had already made this discussion a central concern of the novel genre. On the one hand, they assimilated the norms of Western literature well enough to write the first original novels in Russian. From establishing the poetics of the genre to exercising the moral power of the written word, their work represents a potent legacy for subsequent generations of Russian writers. On the other hand, Chulkov and Komarov were able to take a step back from the uncritical imitation of foreign culture and expose the shortcomings of such an approach. Inspired by the parodic impulses of the subculture, they deflated virtually every convention of the literature of their day. In this regard as well, then, their work is of lasting significance because it enhances our understanding of the crucial period of the 1840s, especially Gogol´'s and Dostoevskii's stylization of browbeaten copyists and mawkish love affairs. Given their historical and literary credentials, Emin, Chulkov, and Komarov deserve to be right in the middle of any thorough investigation into the history of the Russian novel. Or perhaps it would be more accurate to say, right at the beginning.

PLOT SUMMARIES

(Alphabetized by abbreviated title)

THE NOVELS OF FEDOR EMIN

Inconstant Fate (Nepostoiannaia fortuna, ili pokhozhdenie Miramonda):
Combining elements of the adventure story, Eastern tale, and travelogue, *Inconstant Fate* is a three-part work chronicling the far-flung exploits of Miramond, the son of a minister in the Turkish government. It opens with a series of catastrophes in which the young hero is shipwrecked, enslaved by the Maltese, captured by pirates, and enlisted as a seaman on an English ship before he finally makes his way to Cairo. It is here that he rises to the rank of general in the Egyptian army and wins the heart of Ziumbiula, the daughter of one of the many beys of Cairo. As in all of Emin's novels the young couple will not be able to enjoy a state of wedded bliss until they have overcome numerous obstacles that consume hundreds of pages in the telling. For example, in order to prove himself worthy of Ziumbiula's hand, toward the end of part 1 Miramond accepts a mission abroad. Serving as an adviser to Queen Belilia of Zhirie, he leads a successful military campaign against a neighboring aggressor and repeatedly displays his unflinchingly virtuous character by resisting the queen's numerous advances.

Early in part 2 Miramond is on his way back to Cairo and the life he has been dreaming of with Ziumbiula when he voluntarily stops to listen to a series of interpolated tales that take up the rest of the volume. By far the longest and most significant of these is the "History of Feridat," the figure with whom Emin associates himself in the preface to the novel. For 220 pages Feridat recounts his life, from his youth in Adrianople to his conversion to Orthodoxy many years later. In between, his lively narrative is full of intrigues, desperate love affairs, acts of vengeance, and military exploits that take him to more than a score of cities scattered throughout the Middle East and Europe.

As part 3 opens, Miramond returns to Cairo the triumphant hero, only to be falsely accused of treason and banished. Living the life of a hermit, he is reunited with the twin sister he never knew existed and is named the successor of a monarch who is without an heir. With this prince's help Miramond comes to the rescue of Ziumbiula's father, who is under attack by a hostile army. In the end, everything turns out well: the enemy is repelled (Ziumbiula dramatically kills the rebel bey with a dagger), Miramond and Ziumbiula marry, and Miramond ascends the throne of the prince who befriended him.

Kamber and Arisena (Liubovnyi vertograd, ili nepreoborimoe postoianstvo Kambera i Ariseny): Replete with tears and one deception after another, this tale portrays the arduous but—as is almost always the case in Emin—ultimately successful struggle of a pair of star-crossed lovers. Orphaned as an infant, Kamber is taken in by a Middle Eastern prince, who raises him and his daughter, Arisena, as brother and sister. Upon reaching adulthood, the "siblings" find out that they are not related and decide to marry. Uncertain of Kamber's bloodline—nobody knows that he belongs to the Egyptian nobility—Arisena's parents refuse their consent and in so doing put into motion a series of adventures that forms the plot line of the rest of the novel. The young couple run away but are captured and returned to the prince, who vows to execute Kamber should he ever set eyes on Arisena again. Desperate to be reunited with her beau, the heroine enlists the aid of the noblewoman Gamlia, but once she meets Kamber, Gamlia betrays Arisena's confidence and strives to win the affections of the handsome hero for herself. Among other treacherous acts, she forges a letter from Arisena to Kamber urging him to marry her, stages a mock wedding procession in the hope of convincing Kamber that Arisena has given her heart to another, and even fakes Arisena's death and burial. In spite of these efforts Gamlia is finally unmasked with the help of Kamber and Arisena's altruistic friends, and she eventually commits suicide. As the novel closes, the ever constant lovers marry, graciously forgive the near fatal opposition of Arisena's parents, and joyfully look forward to the day when the enlightened Kamber will inherit the throne.

The Letters of Ernest and Doravra (Pis'ma Ernesta i Doravry): The plot of this four-volume adaptation of Jean-Jacques Rousseau's epistolary novel *Julie, ou La Nouvelle Héloïse* centers around the breathless, and ultimately unsuccessful, love affair of the title characters. Even though they declare their feelings for each other early in part 1, Ernest and Doravra are forever prohibited form joining their lives together, first by Ernest's inferior social status and then, when this dilemma is overcome, by the unexpected reappearance of his wife, who had been presumed dead. These and the many other obstacles that crop up in the nearly nine-hundred-page novel provoke the star-crossed couple to indulge in the clichés of Emin's fiction: they rail against the cruelties of fate and express their love for each other in one overwrought declaration after another while steadfastly maintaining their virginity. Interwoven into this correspondence are the letters of their best friends, Hippolyte and Pulkheriia, who counsel the young pair to curb their emotional excesses and lead more reserved, rational lives. Not that Ernest is completely dominated by his emotions, for in addition to his role as the anguished lover he also plays the part of the keen analyst of life. Especially in part 3, which functions much like a philosophical novel, Ernest rarely misses an opportunity to lecture his correspondents on a wide array of Enlightenment commonplaces, from virtue, reason, and the value of our emotions to law, education, and the duties of a conscientious citizen.

Lizark and Sarmanda (Nagrazhdennaia postoiannost´, ili prikliucheniia Lizarka i Sarmandy) is another Emin novel set in Egypt featuring a peripatetic orphan/hero who is separated from the woman he desires by the barrier of class. When Lizark is sold as a slave to the king of Egypt, he eventually falls in love with his beautiful daughter, Izida. Although the princess returns his affection, the two are denied the opportunity to enjoy their budding relationship because Lizark is sent to Memphis on a diplomatic mission. To thicken the plot, Izida's lady-in-waiting Sarmanda falls desperately in love with Lizark and, disguising herself as Metafrast, a man from the lower classes, follows him to Memphis and becomes his servant. About a year later the two are captured by an enemy and sold into slavery, and Lizark is sentenced to death for a crime he never committed. Overwhelmed by love, Sarmanda willingly takes his place by falsely confessing to the crime and is saved from the executioner's blade only at the last instant. Just when he decides that he cannot marry Izida owing to his feelings of gratitude and love for Sarmanda, who has now revealed her true identity, Lizark receives a letter from the Egyptian princess explaining that her father has given them permission to marry. When Lizark balks, Izida becomes jealous and sets out to ruin the lovers. In what is the most convoluted ending of any of Emin's novels, the fortunes of the young couple fall from the height of happiness to the depths of despair and back again several times in the last forty pages. Among other things, Lizark is denounced as a traitor and sentenced to die at Izida's hand, Sarmanda is accosted and nearly raped, and Lizark almost loses his mind upon hearing that Sarmanda has perished at sea. Eventually all ends well when it is revealed that Lizark is Izida's brother and therefore part of the Egyptian royal family. Izida has no alternative but grudgingly to accept this turn of events, Lizark and Sarmanda marry, and we are told that the young couple lived happily for the rest of their days.

The Marquis de Toledo (Gorestnaia liubov' Markiza de Toledo) centers on the love triangle consisting of the Marquis, the noblewoman Marianne, and her fiancé, Don Farina. Early in the novel, the libertine Bonveal dupes Farina into leaving Spain for England, isolates Marianne from her parents, and rapes her. Deeply moved by this tragedy, the Marquis falls in love with the suffering heroine, who thinks that Farina has abandoned her, and proposes marriage. Marianne rejects the Marquis, because she incorrectly believes that he is in some way responsible for the death of her father, who was executed for killing Bonveal. Hearing that Marianne has fled to England to reunite with Farina, the Marquis follows her there, only to be greeted by the shocking news that Marianne has been captured by Moroccan pirates and forced into a harem. Much of the rest of the novel is devoted to the rivals' attempts to rescue Marianne: Farina by using his wits; the Marquis by plundering Moroccan ships as a privateer in the Mediterranean Sea. In the end, it is the Marquis's more direct approach that sets Marianne free, but in the sort of shocking plot twist that is so common in Emin, the Marquis, Farina, and Marianne are subsequently taken hostage by Algerians. During their captivity Marianne, who is now married to Farina, asks the Marquis to stay away from her lest she be tempted by her growing love for him, and he responds by selflessly smuggling the couple out of the country. When they return to Spain, Farina is slain by one of Bonveal's relatives, and Marianne is forced to take refuge with the governor of Gibraltar. Shortly thereafter, one of the Marquis's relatives becomes the chancellor of Spain and barters for his release from Algeria. When the Marquis returns to Gibraltar and is informed of Marianne's fate, he asks for her hand and is rewarded with the love and happy life that "he had so long deserved."

Themistocles (Prikliucheniia Femistokla i raznye . . . s synom svoim razgovory): Loosely modeled on the life of the ancient Greek statesman of the same name, *Themistocles* is the first philosophical novel in Russian literature. Expelled from an ungrateful Athens after leading its forces to victory against the Persians, the observant and encyclopedic Themistocles pauses frequently to hold forth on a broad range of political, civil, philosophical, and military matters as he passes through various foreign countries with his son, Neocles. When the unfortunate exile is eventually made a royal adviser by his former enemy Xerxes, he adds to this list a detailed analysis of the traits of the ideal monarch. In his capacity as advisor, Themistocles catalogues the duties of a king and the rights and responsibilities of subjects, quells the unrest in Xerxes's army, and even instructs the Persian monarch in colonizing new lands and dealing with conquered peoples. After a lengthy stay in Xerxes's court Themistocles is asked to return to Athens and provide leadership for a city wracked by civil disturbances. He agrees and serves his homeland for two years before being ostracized for a second, and final, time.

THE NOVELS OF MIKHAIL CHULKOV

Achilles (Pokhozhdenie Akhillesovo pod imenem Pirry do troianskoi os-ady) is an unrelentingly sentimental and didactic work that Chulkov lifted almost intact from Vasilii Trediakovskii's verse drama *Deidamiia* (1775). When the treacherous Navpliia realizes that Achilles—who is masquerading as a girl to foil the prognostication of his death at Troy—is actually a handsome young man, she declares her love for him and is rebuffed. Enraged, she vows to have her revenge by attacking the object of Achilles's affections, the princess Deidamiia. Using one ruse after another—lies, a forged letter, a staged scene that compromises the princess's honor—Navpliia succeeds in provoking the goddess Diana to call for Deidamiia's sacrifice. Just as the high priestess raises her knife above the innocent heroine's breast, Diana relents and pardons her. Having escaped this near tragedy, Deidamiia and Achilles become officially engaged, and their future seems bright indeed, until Navpliia manages to destroy their happiness once and for all by poisoning the unwitting princess. Upon rushing into Deidamiia's room and finding her discolored corpse lying on the bed, a distraught Achilles must be forcibly restrained from taking his own life. Some time later he exacts a measure of revenge by plunging a dagger into Navpliia's heart and then collapses, nearly mad with grief. Ulysses orders his men to carry the unconscious hero to his boat, which soon sets sail for Troy, and Deidamiia's father, King Lycomedes, dies of a broken heart the very next day.

The Comely Cook (Prigozhaia povarikha, ili pokhozhdenie razvratnoi zhenshchiny) opens with its destitute heroine, the nineteen-year-old Martona, being forced into prostitution after her husband is killed in the battle of Poltava. Displaying the resiliency that will stand her in good stead throughout the novel, she quickly adjusts to her new life and in virtually no time at all attracts a steady admirer, flaunts the baubles and clothes his attentions make possible, and even hires a servant. When her first client turns against her, Martona fears that all is lost, but given that her tale rests on a foundation of comic turnabouts, the situation brightens just when it seems the most bleak. The comely heroine is rescued by her irate lover's master, Sveton, who takes her in and makes her feel as though she were queen of the world. When Sveton's wife discovers the affair and sends Martona packing, she again lands on her feet as the cook for a Muscovite bureaucrat. Later, she becomes the mistress of a seventy-year-old retired colonel and with the help of a virile young lover named Akhal´ swindles the old man out of a substantial part of his fortune. Imprisoned for this offense by the colonel's relatives, Martona is rescued by Akhal´ and the dashing officer Svidal´, who then vie for her attentions. The two fight a duel in which Akhal´ believes he has killed his former friend, and he is forced to flee. Having only feigned death, Svidal´ settles in for a comfortable, sensual life with Martona, and together they help a merchant regain his respect and freedom by uncovering his wife's plan to humiliate him. The novel ends in the middle of a scene in which a repentant and still deluded Akhal´ returns to beg forgiveness for murdering Svidal´. Dramatically claiming to have taken a deadly poison, he shocks Martona with the announcement that she will soon inherit his entire estate.

The Mocker (Peresmeshnik, ili slavenskie skazki): Divided into five parts, *The Mocker* offers one hundred evenings of storytelling by two narrators: Ladon and a monk whose name is never given. As we find out from the informal introduction of about one hundred pages, Ladon earns his keep as something of a literary gigolo on the estate of a retired colonel by telling stories infused with comic exaggeration and ribaldry. During his stay he discovers that the monk is making nightly visits to the premises in order to carry on an illicit affair with the housekeeper. When he is brought before the colonel for this offense, the monk saves himself by humoring the landowner with his lighthearted autobiography, which includes a stint with a Robin-Hood-like gang of thieves, a merry funeral in which he is seduced by a none-too-grieving widow, and his dalliance with a married woman. Shortly thereafter the colonel dies, leaving his beautiful daughter, Alenona, an orphan. To alleviate her grief, the two visitors recite dozens of stories, with Ladon concentrating on the exploits of ancient knights and the monk brewing up a series of facetious and frequently bawdy adventures.

The ten evenings in part 1 are narrated by Ladon, who introduces us to Vineta, a mythical city located where Petersburg will one day stand. The plot is set in motion when Prince Siloslav (Strong Slav) ventures forth from Vineta to find his intended bride, Prelepa (Most fair), who has suddenly disappeared. Almost immediately he is involved in one incredible scene after another: he frees a naked sorceress entrapped in a rock, discovers that Prelepa's father has been turned into a stone idol, and watches in wonder as a fire-breathing serpent unexpectedly bursts out of an enchanted goblet. And this is just the beginning. Later in part 1 Siloslav is transformed into a raven and flies to the aerie of Chernobog (Black god), the underworld ruler of Chulkov's largely fabricated Slavic mythology. As will be the rule throughout Ladon's narrative, Siloslav's fantastic adventures are bolstered by the interpolated tales of various figures he meets along the way, such as the talking head of the decapitated King Roksolan and the unfortunate wanderer Slavuron, who, like Siloslav, searches for his missing love.

Part 2 begins with Slavuron recounting the major events in his life. As is often the case in the stories introduced by Ladon, the emphasis here is on personal tragedy: Slavuron's wife dies, he inadvertently kills his own son, and his only daughter commits suicide before he is falsely accused of treason and banished to the forest where Siloslav eventually finds him. Upon finishing this melancholy tale, Slavuron goes his own way, and the spotlight turns once again on Siloslav, who is swept up by a magical cloud and taken to a land of enchantment where he visits both paradise and hell. After this segment, the rest of Ladon's evenings in part 2 are devoted to the interpolated tale of Siloslav's archenemy Askalon, whose life of evil begins when he falls in love with his own sister. Ladon craftily suspends Askalon's story at the point where the villain encounters a groaning talking tree and finally gives the monk a chance to distract Alenona. He responds with five coarsely comic stories poking fun at greed, stupidity, and lust. Within this group, "The Generous Cuckold" ("Velikodushnyi rogonosets," evening 29) and "The Devil and the Desperate Lover" ("D'iavol i otchaian-nyi liubovnik," evening 30) are the most indicative of the monk's contributions to *The Mocker*. In the former, a young servant bribes a lady to have sex with him, and the woman not only agrees but also has her unwitting husband stand outside her chamber door and accompany them on the violin. In the latter, a benign devil helps a young man who has been swindled out of his inheritance by a con woman. Through a series of pranks the devil does away with the young man's competition and then transforms him into an enchanting Adonis, whom the woman cannot resist.

Far from bringing *The Mocker* to a close in parts 3, 4, and 5, Ladon proliferates the number of unfinished subplots. (At the end of evening 95 he implies that there will be a part 6 to the novel, but it never materializes.) In addition to following the exploits of the nefarious Askalon, he expounds at length on the fates of the deposed King Alim (the talking tree of part 2) and the unfortunate Prince Kidal, who is exiled for contemplating incest with his mother. As in the first two parts of *The Mocker*, Ladon's tales rely heavily on the use of fantasy. Among other things, Askalon sells his soul to the devil and is given a tour of the underworld, Alim makes love to an empress while in the form of an eagle, and Kidal traverses the seas on the back of a dolphin for over five years in search of his one true love. In the end, virtue is triumphant when Alim regains his rightful throne and restores order to a jubilant kingdom, and vice is punished when Askalon is transformed into the half man/half horse Polkan, who dedicates the rest of his life to performing good works.

When it is his turn to entertain Alenona in the last three parts of *The Mocker*, the anonymous monk concentrates solely on *The Tale of the Taffeta Beauty Patch (Skazka o rozhdenii taftianoi mushki)*, a labyrinthine novella recounting the bawdy adventures of the roguish student Neokh. In part 3 Neokh makes love with a beautiful masked woman named Vladimira and conspires with her to rob her father, the high priest of the temple of Chernobog. When the attempt is foiled, Neokh slips away, only to return disguised as a priest himself. While presiding with Vladimira's father at a religious ceremony, he kills the greedy cleric and is imprisoned, but eventually escapes by bribing a peasant to ply his captors with wine until they pass out. In part 4 Neokh ingratiates himself with a noble family by impersonating a doctor and then takes advantage of a gullible and greedy merchant. Falling in with a group of thieves and prostitutes, he is set up as the lover of the merchant's wife and enriches himself at the cuckold's expense. To add insult to injury, Neokh concocts a costumed farce in which he has the sniggering, but unwitting, merchant look on as he makes love to his wife. In part 5 the monk continues to chronicle Neokh's rise up the social ladder (he ends up as a special adviser to the tsar) and finally tacks on an explanation of the origin of the beauty patch in Western culture. (Although this motif is the ostensible motivation for the entire story, not a word has been said about it up to this point.) The monk facetiously assures us that one of Neokh's many lovers devised it to cover an imperfection on her face and in so doing started a fashion trend among her peers.

Forming something of an addendum, the last three stories of *The Mocker* are infused with a satiric, and at times even accusatory, tone that is generally lacking in the preceding ninety-seven evenings of the novel. The most caustic of these pieces is the propeasant exposé "A Bitter Lot" ("Gor´kaia uchast´," evening 98), which describes the bleak life of Sysoi Fofanov, a serf who labors under deplorable conditions for nothing more than bread and water. Exploited by rich peasants in his village, Sysoi is compelled to enter the army, where he serves bravely until he is discharged after losing an arm. Returning home on Christmas Day, he finds a horrific scene: his father's lifeless body hangs from a crossbeam in the courtyard, and inside the hut his mother has had her skull smashed in, his infant sister's throat is slashed open, and his four-year-old brother has been burned to death. To make matters worse, the authorities seem indifferent to this tragedy, and the crippled Sysoi, who was an inadequate farmer even with two good arms, is now left to his own devices. Far less poignant than "A Bitter Lot," "Gingerbread Money" ("Prianichnaia moneta," evening 99) and "The Precious Pike" ("Dragotsennaia shchuka," evening 100) are straightforward satires of greed. In the former, a nobleman circumvents the state monopoly on the sale of alcohol by encouraging local peasants to buy his gingerbread cakes and then trade them in for the real specialty of his estate: wine. The tale ends with the implied moral that the nobleman wrongly worried more about losing his money and material possessions because of his illegal activities than he did about losing his honor. In the last story of the novel the governor of a trading town enriches himself by demanding that petitioners purchase a certain fish from his personal dealer before he will hear their requests. Over the course of five years he raises twenty thousand rubles for himself, all the while ironically proclaiming that he took care of the town using the power of the law.

THE NOVELS OF MATVEI KOMAROV

Milord George (Povest´ o prikliuchenii aglinskogo milorda Georga . . .) intertwines the adventures of the enlightened Englishman mentioned in the title and a young Turkish expatriate named Martsemiris. After losing his way in a terrible storm, George enters a stone building located in an enchanted glade. The mistress of the house, the Brandenburg margravine Friderika Louisa, explains that she is in love with him and has invoked the power of the gods to lure him there. Unfortunately, in order to bring this about, she had to accept the condition that they would live apart from each other for the next three years. Despondent over this news, the lovesick George decides to see the world to alleviate his grief. During his travels he is abducted by pirates and eventually held captive by the Moorish queen Musalmina. She tries to seduce the Englishman, but he withstands her threats as well as her advances and finally escapes. Making his way to the sea, George is fortuitously rescued by a ship commanded by none other than the margravine Friderika Louisa. She proposes that they return to Brandenburg, where they can be married, and then sits down with George to lend a sympathetic ear to the sad tale of Martsemiris, the ship's captain.

In a life that includes being orphaned, raised by the Turks, and promoted to the rank of vizier, Martsemiris's adventures truly begin when he becomes head of the army and his troops are routed by the Persians. Fleeing the battlefield, he comes upon an enchanted building where the beautiful Sardinian princess Theresa has been held captive for three years. Martsemiris quickly frees her, for he possesses a magic ring that forces the spirit who imprisoned the princess to fall at his feet. The young hero has the genie transport Theresa and him back to Sardinia, but even though her parents are grateful for Martsemiris's intercession, they will not permit him to marry their daughter, citing his unknown parentage. On the verge of suicide, Martsemiris leaves the kingdom, only to be befriended by a strange boy and then reunited with Theresa, who has feigned death in order to elope with her beau. The boy turns out to be the genie in disguise, and he casts a spell that makes Theresa fall asleep whenever Martsemiris, who has lost his magic ring, looks at her. Seeing no way out of this predicament, Martsemiris is forced to part with Theresa, presumably forever, and eventually becomes the captain of Friderika Louisa's ship.

The morning after Martsemiris recites his story, the ship is destroyed by a fierce storm, which George assumes is the gods' revenge for his seeing Friderika Louisa before the three-year interdiction had expired. Believing that Friderika Louisa has drowned, he makes his way to Toledo, where he is charmed by the beauty of the queen. Gradually the queen's icy heart gives way to George's overtures, but her jealous sister has other plans. Using seduction, deceit, and eventually violence, Elena has the queen killed before the pair can be married. Distraught, George goes to Venice at carnival time. A mysterious dauphine, who has an uncanny resemblance to Friderika Louisa, makes his acquaintance and taunts the English lord. George confesses that he is still in love with the margravine of Brandenburg and that until he has incontestable proof that she is dead, he could never be attracted to another woman. Reassured by George's words, the dauphine takes off her mask to reveal that she is indeed the Margravine Friderika Louisa. Before the two return to Brandenburg, where they are married and beloved by their subjects, Friderika Louisa recounts the end of Martsemiris's tale. Making his way back to Sardinia after the shipwreck,

Martsemiris recovers his magic ring and is informed that the princess is being held captive by the genie in Copenhagen. Rushing to Theresa's rescue, he has the genie return them to Sardinia, where they are married and ascend the throne after the death of Theresa's parents.

Nevidimka (Nevidimka: Istoriia o fetsskom koroleviche Aridese i o brate ego Polumedese . . .) blends the episodic adventures of two brothers whose strength and courage recall the knights of Russia's oral epics with the interpolated tales of various unfortunate exiles they meet along the way. Arides' story begins when a snake transforms itself into a beautiful sorceress and presents him with a *shapka-nevidimka*, a cap that makes its wearer invisible. Using this cap to perform a series of playful tricks, Arides frees himself from prison, reunites the separated lovers Ludvig and Epofradita, and wins the heart of the beautiful Elizabeth before repulsing an attack by pirates who are led by none other than his long-lost brother, Polumedes.

After celebrating their unexpected reunion, Arides asks his brother to describe his life as a pirate, and he complies in a lengthy story loaded with adventure, magic, and many embedded tales. It begins happily enough with Polumedes dressing as a woman in order to court the Turkish princess Martemiana. When the sultan discovers that a man has been living in his daughter's chambers, things take a decided turn for the worse, and both Polumedes and Martemiana are hurled into a moat. Polumedes swims to safety, but the princess is swept away and presumed drowned. After several misfortunes Polumedes reaches the land of Lilliput, where he finds that Martemiana is indeed alive. She explains how she was saved by a stranger and then relates the tale of Abdel Dimers, an Indian prince who, with the aid of an Arab magician, wins the heart of the Persian princess Alzura, defeats a nine-headed monster, and foils the treachery of the duplicitous General Narkiz. When Martemiana finishes her narrative, Polumedes and she are married, but their happiness is short-lived, because the princess drowns just two months later. Traveling to Venice, Polumedes sets his sights on Princess Revenza, a woman who has sworn off the company of men. Disguising himself as a woman in order to become her lady-in-waiting, Polumedes does win Revenza's love, but his account of this phase of his life ends sadly when he recalls how he accidentally killed the princess while defending her against a gang of robbers.

In keeping with its genre, the fairy-tale-like adventure story of *Nevidimka* ends with the two brothers using their wits and physical prowess to secure a near perfect future. First they journey to Morocco, where they overcome the treachery and military might of the king and install Polumedes as monarch of a neighboring land. Having secured his brother's happiness, Arides then travels to Aragon, where he becomes a trusted aide to the king and falls in love with his daughter. After defeating all challengers in a tournament, Arides marries the princess and, when the king dies five years later, assumes the throne.

*Vanka Kain (Obstoiatel´nye i vernye istorii dvukh moshennikov: Pervogo
... Van´ki Kaina)* picks up the story of the serf-turned-bandit as he escapes
from his master, the merchant Filat´ev, and embarks on a life of crime in
Moscow. Using the cover of darkness to break into the homes of a priest,
doctor, tailor, merchant, general, and saddle maker, Kain quickly makes a
name for himself in the criminal underworld. When things get too hot, he
retreats to the countryside, where he pillages local fairs and hamlets in between leading occasional raids into the capital. After several years of avoiding and confounding the authorities, Kain comes to the conclusion that
sooner or later justice will catch up with him, so he decides to retire. In virtually no time at all he squanders his savings and is forced to find a new
source of income. Showing no sympathy for his former associates, Kain
volunteers to become a police spy and ends up supervising the capture of
hundreds of robbers, thieves, counterfeiters, and murderers in the Moscow
area. He is so successful in this new line of work that the authorities grant
him a pardon, place a squadron of soldiers at his disposal, and order all
governmental bodies to support his activities.

Kain leads a rich and riotous life as a police informer, but, true to his nature, he risks it all by playing both sides of the law. On the one hand, he
continues to round up criminals and political enemies, such as the more
than four hundred Old Believers who follow a false messiah named An-
driushka. On the other, he uses his position and power to aggrandize himself at the expense of the authorities. He thinks nothing of taking bribes to
free prisoners or using his network of spies to rob, swindle, and extort
money from the respectable citizenry of Moscow. Emboldened by his ability to do just about anything he pleases with impunity, Kain overreaches
himself when he abducts and rapes the wife of a police clerk. The enraged
husband files a petition, and Kain finds that his luck has finally run out.
Under merciless torture he confesses not just to the rape, but to all the
crimes he has committed after becoming an informer, and is sentenced to a
term of hard labor.

NOTES

INTRODUCTION

1. From 1981 through 1995 the *MLA Bibliography* contains roughly fourteen times more critical publications focusing on Russian literature of the nineteenth century than of the eighteenth century, and entries for twentieth-century Russian literature outstrip those of the eighteenth century by more than thirty to one. Even the category of Old Russian Literature (800–1699) contains twice the number of listings that appear under the heading Russian Literature, 1700–1799.

2. Other than dissertations, the only major studies that have one of these three figures as their central focus are by John G. Garrard, *Mixail Čulkov: An Introduction to His Prose and Verse* (1970), and Viktor Shklovskii, *Matvei Komarov: Zhitel´ goroda Moskvy* (1929) and *Chulkov i Levshin* (1933). Moreover, works that trace the development of the novel genre in Russia also tend to treat the eighteenth century with benign neglect. In *The Rise of the Russian Novel*, which begins with an in-depth analysis of Pushkin's *Evgenii Onegin* (1823–1831), Richard Freeborn asserts that only "the faint outlines of a novelistic tradition are discernible in eighteenth-century Russian literature" (1) and points to Karamzin as its most obvious source (2). In the introduction to the Academy of Sciences' *Istoriia russkogo romana* G. M. Fridlender notes in passing that eighteenth-century Russian prose fiction served as the foundation for the golden age of the novel yet claims that "to view the emergence and development of the Russian novel of the nineteenth century only as the direct continuation of the novel of the eighteenth century would be incorrect: after the events of 1825–26 and the creation of *Evgenii Onegin* the Russian novel began its historical path as a qualitatively new social and artistic phenomenon" (23). In one of the two articles in this collection dealing with material written prior to 1800, I. Z. Serman maintains that "for Pushkin, as the author of *Evgenii Onegin* and *The Captain's Daughter* [and] for Gogol´, the creator of *The*

Inspector General and *Dead Souls*, the living expression of Russian literature was the comedies of Fonvizin and the satiric odes of Derzhavin and not *The Comely Cook* or *The Adventures of Miramond"* (Moiseeva and Serman, 64).

3. It is interesting to note that the indifference shown by critics has not been endorsed by the reading public. During the past decade the novels of Komarov and Chulkov have experienced a sort of renaissance. This revival includes the publication of Komarov's *The History of Vanka Kain* (Moscow: Khudozhestvennaia literatura, 1992) and an edition that combines his *The Adventures of the English Milord George* (Moscow: Istoki, 1993) with yet another printing of *Vanka Kain*. Chulkov's *The Mocker* was issued by the Moscow publishing houses Sovetskaia Rossiia (1987) and Kul'tura (1994), and *The Comely Cook* has recently been published on three separate occasions by Kniga (1991), Lenizdat (St. Petersburg, 1992), and Istoki (Moscow, 1993).

CHAPTER 1: RELUCTANT IMITATORS

1. Lotman and Uspenskii write that "the image of a 'new Russia' and a 'new people' became a distinctive myth, which arose as early as the beginning of the eighteenth century and was bequeathed to the subsequent cultural consciousness" ("Binary Models," 53). They touch on Peter's role in the dissemination of the idea that Russia had been transformed by means of imitating the West and chart the reaction of prominent intellectuals of the era, from Feofan Prokopovich's claim that Peter had done more for Russia than the emperor Augustus had done for Rome to Antiokh Kantemir's assertion that the Russians had become "in a moment's time a new people" (53).

2. Lotman and Uspenskii survey this approach among the Russian intelligentsia up through the 1930s in "K semioticheskoi tipologii," 259–60.

3. Titunik surveys Emin's appropriation of Rousseau's classic text, which includes the reproduction of selected passages, the central characters, plot motivations, and the impassioned speech of distraught heroes and heroines ("Emin and Rousseau," 335–39).

4. This is also the case with most of Chulkov's oeuvre. While not denying the native bases of Chulkov's literary output, J. G. Garrard focuses on the foreign influences that he finds in virtually every genre Chulkov practiced. He maintains that the comedy *Call It What You Will (Kak khochesh' nazovi)* relies on a plot and character types that go back to the comedies of Menander, Terence, and Plautus (*Čulkov*, 21–23); sees the imprint of Ovid's *Metamorphoses* shining through the burlesque poem "Verses on a Ferris Wheel" ("Stikhi na kacheli," 77); and categorizes *The Comely Cook* as a first-person autobiography in the mold of *Gil Blas, Manon Lescaut, La Nouvelle Héloïse,* and *Moll Flanders* (123–25).

5. He writes: "There is no doubt that the multiple murder theme in 'A Bitter Lot' comes ultimately from the West. This agrees with the general conclusion of scholars that Chulkov drew primarily upon Western European sources along with some Russian manuscript tales that were themselves borrowings from the West" (580).

6. Staying closer to home, Garrard writes that the sympathetic treatment of peasants in "A Bitter Lot" seems to have been influenced by Radishchev's *A Journey from Petersburg to Moscow (Puteshestvie iz Peterburga v Moskvu,* 1790). Even though Radishchev published this celebrated work after Chulkov came out with part 5 of *The Mocker* (1789), Garrard notes that the two writers may have dis-

cussed their views on literature and society as early as the late 1770s when they were coworkers in the Department of Commerce ("Prose Fiction," 23–25).

7. Ironically, it is exactly the charge of not appreciating her own country's worth that M. M. Shcherbatov levels at Catherine. In the "Petition of the City of Moscow on Being Relegated to Oblivion" ("Proshenie Moskvy o zabvenii ee") he chides Catherine and her predecessor Elizabeth for abandoning the older of the two capitals: "Neither the assemblage of nobles, descendants of men who shed their blood in the service of their country, nor the multitudes of common folk whose joyful shouts testify to their loyalty and allegiance to their Sovereigns, nor the holy places famous for many miracles, where the saints beloved of God are buried, nor the tombs of their ancestors, nor the ancient buildings, where my former Sovereign, who laid the groundwork for Russia's might, used to dwell, nor my beautiful surroundings are able to attract and hold their hearts" (53).

8. Papmehl lists titles and publication dates for the works of these writers and collectors (33 n. 22).

9. Ironically, it was two areas that Peter stressed in his reforms, namely, science and the military, that encouraged the Russians to claim the superiority of their culture. The scientist, rhetorician, and poet Mikhail Lomonosov was championed as the equal of any Western thinker, and throughout the eighteenth century, Russian arms scored impressive victories over Sweden (Peter I), Prussia (Elizabeth), Turkey and Poland (Catherine II), and France (Paul) (Serman, "Rossiia i zapad," 57).

10. Although beyond the scope of this study, it should be noted that the Russians' spectacular failures in such areas as agricultural, social, and educational reform underscore just how great the gap between rhetoric and reality was in the latter part of the eighteenth century. For example, only 2 percent of the state budget was allocated to education, and by the time of Catherine's death in 1796 there were only 550 educational institutes in all of Russia (compared to over 8,000 in France), and only two out of every one thousand children received an education (Lentin, 110–11). Moreover, the curriculum of a gentry school would be just as likely to stress such nonacademic subjects as dancing, drawing, theatrical performances, fencing, and French as math, history, and political science (Rogger, 47). As for the serf question, Russian society was even more retrograde. After 1765 landowners could buy and sell serfs as they chose and had a de facto power of life and death over them (Lentin, 104–6; Richardson, 210).

11. Early in her reign Catherine fawned on Diderot. In 1762 she ordered the *Encyclopédie* published in Riga when license to do so was suspended in France (Diderot ultimately refused this honor) and in 1765 helped the philosophe out of his financial difficulties by purchasing his library and then paying him a stipend to act as its caretaker (Wilson, 166).

12. Years later, as the French Revolution drew near, Catherine took even stronger measures. She commanded her longtime confidant Baron Grimm to "acquire for me all the works of Diderot" and then cautiously added: *"Of course they will not get out of my hands and will not harm anyone"* (Oustinoff, 122).

13. De Madariaga covers the feelings of alienation and unhappiness that weighed on the philosophe during his visit to Petersburg (40–46). In a letter to Mme Necker (1774) Diderot wrote metaphorically about his Russian experience: "I will confess to you very much under my breath that we *philosophes*, who give the impression of best having known what despotism is, have seen it only through the neck of a bottle. What a difference there is between a tiger painted

by Oudry and a tiger in the forest" (Wilson, 197).

14. The author of the original play is given as Antonio Salvi with the added note that "the arias were translated from the French" (Lojkine, 87).

15. Lojkine gives a complete list of both the translated and the untranslated plays of Molière (91 n. 15).

16. This citation originally appeared in an article entitled "An English Stroll" ("Angliiskaia progulka") in *The Painter (Zhivopisets)* 1 (1772). Ironically, it was the French themselves who were responsible for the temporary diminution of their influence in Russian society. Overcome by the allure of English culture, they, more than anyone else, helped to popularize it among Catherine's subjects. Led by such ardent Anglophiles as Prévost, Voltaire, Montesquieu, and Diderot, the French became enamored of virtually every aspect of the intellectual and cultural life of Great Britain. Simmons writes that "from Bacon and Newton [the French] learned science, from Pope deistic philosophy, and Voltaire popularized English literature. Shakespeare, Milton, Pope, Addison, Young, Thomson, and the English eighteenth-century novelists were eagerly read and in many cases imitated in France. With no exaggeration Gibbon could write in 1763: 'Our opinions, our fashions, even our games were adopted in France; a ray of national glory illuminated each individual, and every Englishman was supposed to be born a patriot and a philosopher'" (81).

17. Russian admiration for this type of landscaping was so great that the Englishman Joseph Bush was given the task of designing the gardens and palace of Tsarskoe Selo (Cross, "The British," 248–49).

18. Levin (78) notes that *Historical, Genealogical, and Geographical Notes (Istoricheskie, genealogicheskie i geograficheskie primechaniia v vedomostiakh, 1728–1742)* was the first Russian periodical to include translations from British sources, but given the dates of its publication, it does not belong to the line of journals that would originate in the mid-1750s to help shape the rise of the Russian novel. Concerning this latter group of works, Levin estimates that "in one way or another more than two dozen English periodical 'essays' and monthly journals were translated into Russian. Over 300 separate issues or articles extracted from them served as material for more than 400 publications in 50 plus Russian periodical and nonperiodical editions. Approximately one-fifth of all English articles were published in Russian translation twice [and] one-tenth from 3 to 10 times" (75).

19. They are *Idle Time Put to Use (Prazdnoe vremia v pol'zu upotreblennoe,* 1759–1760), *The Industrious Bee (Trudoliubivaia pchela,* 1759), *Profitable Entertainment (Poleznoe uveselenie,* 1760–1762), *Harmless Exercise (Nevinnoe uprazhnenie,* 1763), *Free Hours (Svobodnye chasy,* 1763), and *The Good Intention (Dobroe namerenie,* 1764). Levin's index (100–101) lists all eighteenth-century Russian journals and collections that included translations from British sources.

20. Besides *The Spectator* other British journals that had a major impact on this area of Russian letters include the *Adventurer*, the *Guardian*, the *New Universal Magazine*, the *Rambler*, the *Tattler*, and the *Universal Magazine of Knowledge and Pleasure* (Levin, 96–100). Frequently the Russians simply published material from them without acknowledging the source (Levin, 5; Simmons, 111–12).

21. Publication data in this paragraph are from Simmons (139–52).

22. This opinion was seconded almost a decade later by the most famous of the Russian sentimentalists, Nikolai Karamzin (Martynov, 35–36).

23. When compared with the publication dates of the Russian translations of *Pamela, Clarissa,* and *Sir Charles Grandison,* the dates of these original Russian

works indicate that Emin, Lvov, and Karamzin read Richardson in a language other than Russian. For Karamzin this may have been English, but for the other two it was most likely French. This fact confirms that English novels were often accessible to educated Russians prior to appearing in their native tongue.

24. Brown calls *The Comely Cook* a "Defoeish novel" (64), and Garrard includes *Moll Flanders* as one of its many literary inspirations (*Čulkov*, 121). Segel places it in "the same tradition as Daniel Defoe's *Moll Flanders* (1722) and, to a lesser extent, *The Fortunate Mistress* (*Roxana*, 1724)" (*Literature*, 2:26). Whether or not Chulkov actually read Defoe's novel is open to question. He did not know English, but may have become familiar with the work through a French translation that appeared in Russia in 1761 (Garrard, *Čulkov*, 121).

25. See *The Comely Cook*, 159. Throwing over her first lover, who is a servant, for another, who turns out to be the servant's master, Martona muses: "From the very first moment he [the master] seemed so tender that in order to please him I would have gladly dumped the servant, and when he made me a gift of the snuffbox, it seemed vulgar to me to have anything to do with a serf" (160–61).

26. In at least one listing of Chulkov's work, *The Comely Cook* is given the subtitle of "a satiric novel" (see Garrard, "Narrative Technique," 556, especially n. 9).

27. Watt notes that in Defoe's age the mixing of sex and morality was completely acceptable and not perceived as ironic or even sensationalistic. He notes that Pepys "bought a pornographic work and read it in his office on Sundays, commenting 'a mighty lewd book, but not amiss for a sober man to read once over to inform himself in the villainy of the world'" (128).

CHAPTER 2: THE CARNIVALESQUE SPIRIT
OF THE EIGHTEENTH-CENTURY RUSSIAN NOVEL

1. Bakhtin traces the noncarnival components of the cult of folk humor in *Rabelais*, 67–90. They include, among many others, the feast of fools, feast of the ass, ironic Christmas songs, and parodic literature, such as the fifth-century *Cyprian's Supper*, which turns all sacred history from Adam to Christ into a fantastic, clownish banquet. Analyses of specific comic banquets and feasts can be found on pages 286–300.

2. Although Bakhtin's theory provides an excellent analytical framework for the study of the early Russian novel, his tendency to stress only the positive, liberating effects of the carnivalesque is a bit skewed. The revelry and dynamism associated with this ethos also had a darker side, which I discuss in the upcoming section on carnival in Russia.

3. Bakhtin points out that the folk considered the places the Lord defecated and urinated worthy of veneration (*Rabelais*, 145–50).

4. This is not to say that the literary aesthetics of neoclassicism and sentimentalism did not have their lighter moments. The satire, comedy, mock epic, and lyric poem all provided opportunities for the use of humor, though often not without a substantial dose of moralizing. Moreover, further investigation may well reveal a carnivalesque motivation for the humor in such neoclassical works as Ivan Barkov's obscene odes and Vasilii Maikov's mock epic *Elisei, or Bacchus Enraged* (*Elisei, ili razdrazhennyi Vakkh*, 1771) which, among much other riotous behavior, depicts the carnivalesque mass fistfights known as *kulachnye boi.*

5. Nicknamed the uncalled *skomorokhi*, they played without invitation and often were accused of criminal behavior. The situation was serious enough to warrant their frequent expulsion and even permanent banishment from some communities (Kuznetsov, *Iz proshlogo russkoi èstrady*, 24–25).

6. The importance of these rides was reflected in the popular names for the carnival. In summertime it was known as "under the Ferris wheel" *(pod kacheliami)* and in winter months it was referred to as "under the mountains" *(pod gorami).*

7. For an artist's rendition of the *ded* see Atkinson and Walker, vol. 1, plate 30.

8. In the eighteenth century the *dedy* were known by the foreign term *paiatso* (clown). This was no doubt the result of the great influx of foreigners into the ranks of entertainers at Russia's carnivals and fairs. Nevertheless, the *dedy* maintained a decidedly Russian look and relied on a Russian sense of humor and subject matter in their routine. Kuznetsov notes that the role of the *ded*, like that of the strolling comics known as *raeshniki*, was reserved for Russians, who "did not travel abroad for their humor" (*Iz proshlogo russkoi èstrady*, 43).

9. Firsthand accounts of the construction and operation of the ice hills can be found in Kuznetsov, *Gulian'ia*, 25–26; Atkinson and Walker, vol. 1, plate 9; and Shoberl, 1:105–6. Ice mountains and the carnival were such an important and ubiquitous part of Russian life that they even make an appearance in Tolstoi's decidedly uncarnivalesque novel *War and Peace* (*Voina i mir*, see p. 362).

10. Detailed descriptions of different types of swings used at fairs and carnivals can be found in Miege, 55. In addition to written accounts Atkinson and Walker include artistic reproductions of these rides (vol. 1, plate 30; vol. 3, plate 16).

11. Atkinson and Walker give an artistic rendering of a late eighteenth-century *zbiten'shchik*, or *zbiten'* hawker (vol. 2, plate 3), and Sytova provides a mid nineteenth-century *lubok* drawing of this type (137).

12. Collins is even more direct in his description of the frightening and often tragic consequences of such behavior: "These drinking bouts are commonly attended with quarrels, fightings [*sic*], and murthers [*sic*]. Some of these going home drunk, if not attended with a sober companion, fall asleep upon the snow (a sad cold bed) and there they are frozen to death" (23). He adds that during Lent two to three hundred unfortunate revelers are found frozen to death on the roads around Moscow (24).

13. Atkinson and Walker provide brief descriptions and pictures of the *golubets* (vol. 3, plate 18) and the Polish dance (vol. 3, plate 28), two other favorites of the carnival.

14. Even in the middle of the eighteenth century it was not unusual for owners to walk bears around the carnival grounds. "Not infrequently they escaped from their leashes and caused grievous damage and alarm amongst the surging mob" (Burgess, 100). Decrees in 1744 and 1752 enjoining bear owners to muzzle their animals and restrain them with adequate chains failed to eradicate the practice (Burgess, 100–101).

15. In part the diatribe reads: "The devil seduces people by turning them away from God with various temptations. We have seen places that have been trampled down for celebrations. A great multitude of people gathers, and there is a crush [of bodies] when the spectacle, which has been incited by the devil, begins. And when prayer starts, you won't find many of these same people in church" (Kuznetsov, *Gulian'ia*, 4).

16. The term *lubok* is derived from the Russian word *lub*, which designates the first, soft layer of wood under the bark of a tree.

17. Ovsianikov describes the process of producing broadsides from carved wood boards (10–13), and Rovinskii details the later use of metal plates, which enabled a simple peasant operation to turn out almost five hundred pictures per day (338–39).

18. Sytova presents nineteenth-century *lubok* renditions of "Eruslan Lazarevich" (76, 145), "Peter of the Golden Keys" (78), and "Bova" (100).

19. In the first half of the nineteenth century works by Krylov, Lermontov, Gogol´, and Pushkin were also co-opted by *lubok,* and the demand only increased as the century came to a close (Schaarschmidt, 428).

20. Ovsianikov notes that *lubok* editions of religious topics usually sold for between three to six kopecks whereas Trediakovskii's *Journey to the Island of Love* (*Ezda v ostrov liubvi,* 1730) cost sixty kopecks (24). Most books were so expensive that they were regarded as something akin to a personal treasure. In the seventeenth century books ranked in value only behind icons in an inventory of one's personal wealth (Baklanova, 168–70).

21. The tale of Bova Korolevich was so adaptable that it even made its mark in official literature, albeit in a suitably carnivalesque manner. In the late 1790s Aleksandr Radishchev wrote an epic poem in eleven cantos based on this story (only the introduction, first canto, and a prose description of the poem have survived). Often ironic, satiric, and bawdy, Radishchev's "Bova" is a heavy-handed travesty in the manner of Maikov's *Elisei* (Brown, 488–90, analyzes the formal innovations and content of this work). Reyfman develops the interesting thesis that this poem is a parody, in the Bakhtinian sense, of one of the major figures of Russian neoclassicism, Vasilii Trediakovskii (185–90). She claims that the ambivalent humor of "Bova" gently ridicules yet also validates Trediakovskii's attempts to use folk meters as a means of invigorating the orthodox system of Russian versification.

22. The works in question are Chulkov's *Short Mythological Lexicon* (*Kratkii mifologicheskii leksikon,* 1767) and Popov's *A Short Description of Ancient Slavic Pagan Mythology* (*Kratkoe opisanie drevnego slavianskogo iazycheskogo basnosloviia,* 1768). Gukovskii discusses the fictional quality of these works and also notes that right up to Pushkin's day they were still regarded as reliable sources by Levshin, Derzhavin, Radishchev, and "dozens of other masters of literature" (*Literatura,* 224–25).

23. As the tsarist era of Russian history drew to a close, popular literature enjoyed a tremendous surge in reader interest. The first decade of the twentieth century saw the emergence of two *gazety-kopeiki* (kopeck papers) in St. Petersburg and Moscow. Sold for just one kopeck, or at least 50 percent less than their closest journalistic rivals, these papers "were the first regular Russian dailies to focus on the world of the urban poor and working class" (Brooks, 85). Brooks analyzes the contents of these papers, which include reflections of such *lubok* classics as *Vanka Kain* (93) and *Milord George* (94).

24. His case in point is Voltaire: "In spite of his popularity with Catherine II and her court, Voltaire's ideas played only a small role in shaping the public mind and culture of the Russian educated elite. Voltarianism became synonymous with mockery of the Church, but for this there was a healthy native tradition in the satirical tales of the seventeenth century, to which Voltaire only gave a more attractive and modern form" ("Enlightenment," 38).

25. This is not to say that some collections of the *Facetiae* did not take on a decidedly moralistic cast. "An ambivalent plot, which permitted various under-standings and evaluations, often became flat and predictable *("odnoplanyi")* under the influence of a Russian editor who, in the traditional manner of the Christian Middle Ages, interpreted all the lively and improper situations of the facetiae. [Thus] the novella was transformed into a didactic story" (Kukushkina, 185).

26. Adrianova Peretts has strung these quotations together from the title pages of several collections ("Gorodskaia novella," 13).

27. Berkov (27–28) and Guberti (3:607) discuss the publication history of this work. Adrianova Peretts believes that it circulated in manuscript as early as the 1750s (Berkov, *Russko-pol´skie literaturnye sviazi,* 32).

28. Gary Cox convincingly shows how the folktale plot as outlined by Propp functioned as a template for stories like "Bova Korolevich" and "Vasilii Koriotskii" (85, 88–91). Although this influence waned before the emergence of the first Russian novels in the latter half of the eighteenth century, other aspects of folklore—motifs, legends, and devices—did have a significant impact on the prose fiction of Chulkov, Komarov, and at times, even Emin.

29. Shklovskii analyzes the folkloric basis of *Milord George* (77–131) and *Ne-vidimka* (*Komarov,* 152–216).

30. Although Russia's first novelists were from lower- and middle-class mi-lieus, this does not mean that every writer who came from such an environment brought a carnivalesque approach to his calling. Emin, for instance, was in many ways a staunch defender of the values of official society; and one of the greatest Russian enlighteners of the eighteenth century, Mikhail Lomonosov, was born into a peasant family in the far north of Russia near the White Sea. Social class no doubt influenced the writings of Emin, Chulkov, and Komarov, but it was far from being the sole determinant of their work.

31. Guberti cites an advertisement in the *Moscow News* stating that "Ko-marov was the manor serf and house manager of Count Ivan Nikitich Zotov, who had his residence in Moscow on Mokhovaia Street" (1:25). Shklovskii traces Komarov's lineage from what the author says about himself in the introductions and dedications in his works and their announcement in newspapers (*Komarov,* 17–31). He concludes that Komarov gained his freedom sometime between the publication of *A Description of Thirteen Ancient Weddings (Opisanie trinattsati starinnykh svadeb . . .)* in 1785 and *Ancient Letters of the Chinese Emperor to the Rus-sian Sovereign (Starinnye pis´ma kitaiskogo imperatora k rossiiskomu gosudariu . . .)* in 1787 (148–49).

32. The precise meaning of the term *raznochintsy* (people of various ranks), which was first used officially around 1720, changed dramatically and often over time. By the mid–eighteenth century, when Chulkov entered the gymnasium, it designated a person from any class other than the gentry (Becker, 63–67). De-rived from circumstantial evidence, the consensus of scholars is that Chulkov was most likely the son of a clergyman or merchant. (Biographical data in this paragraph come from Garrard, *Culkov,* 14–24; Shklovskii, *Chulkov i Levshin,* 5–6; and Gukovskii, *Literatura,* 222.)

33. Once again, social status does not guarantee a particular approach to writing but merely acts as one of the factors determining the course an author will take. Coming from the same background as Chulkov, Trediakovskii, the son of an Orthodox priest, developed into one of the prime proponents of the Rus-sian Enlightenment despite many personal and professional disappointments.

34. Another one of Chulkov's burlesque poems, "Verses on Semik" ("Stikhi na semik"), is also full of direct references to the carnival (*semik* is a celebration of the seventh Thursday after Easter in the Orthodox rite). In true Rabelaisian manner feasting, drinking, and merrymaking are everywhere. Chulkov lovingly recites the long list of culinary delights that are offered at the celebration; a drunken *skomorokh* collapses in the mud, and the *golubets* and *bychok* are danced with wild abandon (440–42). As though directly justifying Bakhtin's rose-tinted analysis of the carnival, the narrator cheerfully constructs a world of "happy and satisfied drunks" (442) in which people eat and drink their fill and negative consequences are nowhere to be seen.

35. In his *Pantheon of Russian Authors* (*Panteon rossiiskikh avtorov*, 1802) Karamzin remarks that "Emin's most curious novel is his own life, as he told it to his friends" (171).

36. Beshenkovskii covers each of the four biographies in detail (186–88).

37. Interestingly enough, this "unauthorized" change in Emin's biography occurs in a version of *The Path to Salvation* published by Schnoor, the same firm that put out Komarov's *lubok* classic *The Adventures of the English Milord George*.

38. This fact was certainly not lost on Emin's contemporaries, especially Chulkov. In week 36 of *Both This and That* (1769) an Emin-like character named "the Slanderer" is forced to admit that he writes only for glory and profit (Garrard, *Čulkov*, 69–70). As Beshenkovskii notes, Emin was able to use his writing as a guarantee in order to borrow twenty-five hundred rubles from Catherine to pay off his debts (194). By the end of his career he was so famous he even managed to receive advances on his work (195).

39. Some fifty years later Karamzin would confirm Shishkin's assessment of the Russians' intense and often reckless attachment to books. He noted that there were noblemen "with a yearly income of not more than five hundred rubles who, in their own words, collect *small libraries,* rejoice over them, and as opposed to us who toss around expensive editions of Voltaire, . . . will not let a speck of dust fall on *Miramond.* They read each book several times and reread them with new pleasure" ("O knizhnoi torgovle," 178).

40. By the beginning of the eighteenth century newspapers had caught on to such an extent in Russia that they even had a following among those who could not read. Karamzin writes that "the poorest people subscribe [to newspapers], and even illiterates want to know *what is being written from foreign countries.* One of my acquaintances happened to see several pie sellers who, having surrounded a reader, were listening to a description of a battle between the Austrians and the French with rapt attention. He asked and found out that five of them pool together and take Moscow newspapers. Although four of them can't read, the fifth can make out the letters, and the others listen" ("On the Book Trade [O knizhnoi torgovle]," 177).

41. As the experience of the trading peasantry implies, reading had become the rage even in the countryside. In "On the Book Trade" Karamzin reports that "there are already bookstalls in just about all our provincial cities, and, along with other goods, the riches of our literature are brought to every fair. Now, for example, rural noblewomen at the Makar´evskaia fair stock up not just on caps, but on books as well" (178).

42. Chulkov makes the same admission in the introduction to *The Mocker,* writing that he is addressing himself to those "uneducated people who have only studied grammar" (1:iii).

43. Watt maintains that Robinson Crusoe and Clarissa Harlow were so well received as literary characters in eighteenth-century England primarily because there were so many self-made men and determined young women struggling to find a niche in society in the readership of the time (57–59).

44. The actual number is probably significantly higher since the concept of copyright was not honored in the eighteenth and nineteenth centuries, and unauthorized versions of many writers were frequent. As Guberti admitted in the last decades of the nineteenth century, "*Vanka Kain* is being reprinted even in our time in the form of thin pamphlets" (1:114).

45. Though not quite as tragic, the fate of Bogdanovich reveals the same inability to make the publishing of official literature pay for itself, much less make a profit. Bogdanovich had to sell his press because he had run up huge debts with the Academy of Sciences. In order to protect him from further losses, the senate banished him to his father's estate in Poltava (Marker, 112–13).

46. *Tilemakhida, or the Wanderings of Telemachus, the Son of Odysseus (Tilemakhida ili Stranstvovanie Telemakha syna Odysseeva)* is an original experiment in hexameter, the rough Russian equivalent of the meter of classical Greek poetry (Brown, 65–66). Although *Tilemakhida* turned out to be one of the most frequently ridiculed works of eighteenth-century Russian literature, what Trediakovskii himself labeled its "fabulous flow of discourse" (Reyfman, 38) did merit at least one favorable comparison with the language and style of Homer's epics (Reyfman, 164–65).

47. Kheraskov's *Numa, or Flourishing Rome (Numa, ili Protsvetaiushchii Rim*, 1768) and M. M. Shcherbatov's *Journey to the Land of Ophir (Puteshestvie v zemliu Ofirskuiu*, 1784) were also influenced by the Masons' ideology, but to a far lesser degree than Kheraskov's two later novels. (For Kheraskov, see Baehr, 100; for Shcherbatov, see Baehr, 258–59 n. 106, 260 n. 115.)

48. The architectural symbols Masons used to express the essence of their ideology contrast markedly with the reality of the carnival. The flimsy, temporary structures of the carnival are the direct opposite of the permanent stone temples and pyramids that represent the Masonic ideal of perfection and completion.

49. In his "Introduction to the Use of Church Books in Russian" ("Predislovie o pol'ze knig tserkovnykh v rossiiskom iazyke," 1758) Lomonosov states that the middle style of Russian should be used for prose works that contain "memorable events and noble teachings" and that the third, or lowest, style suits prose that "describes everyday occurrences" (589–90). Presumably he has in mind that translations of novels like *Don Quixote* should be rendered in the middle style, whereas writers like Chulkov and Komarov ought to employ the low style, but nowhere does he mention the genre by name. In this regard the pioneers of the Russian novel share the same fate as the author of *Gargantua and Pantagruel*, the seminal work of Bakhtin's theory of the carnival. When a hierarchy of genres began to coalesce in sixteenth-century France, Rabelais was pushed beyond the bounds of "serious" literature and considered irrelevant or simply amusing (Bakhtin, *Rabelais*, 64). Two centuries later Rabelais's mixing of the ideals of Humanism with a voluptuous imagery of food, drink, and sex led Voltaire to label him a "drunken philosopher."

50. This is not to say that the novel did not have its supporters among the representatives of official literature. By the beginning of the nineteenth century Karamzin, arguably the most prominent figure in Russian sentimentalism, would give his seal of approval, albeit grudgingly, to the genre. In "On the Book Trade"

(1802) he declares that "it is good that our public is reading novels" (180) and even encourages less-educated layers of society to take up works like *Unfortunate Nikanor* (*Neshchastnyi Nikanor* [179]). In the same year in his journal *Messenger of Europe* (*Vestnik Evropy*) he ambiguously endorses what he calls "the most stupid of Russian novels": "I do not know what others think; but I would not want to blame a person even for 'Milord George.' . . . A stupid book is no great evil in the world" (Hammarberg, 264).

51. Garrard categorizes the various aspects of the narrator's persona with the terms "self-conscious," "coy," "recalcitrant," and "partially informed" (*Čulkov*, 101–4). Titunik catalogues Chulkov's assault on such conventions as motivation, authorial omniscience, moralistic digressions, and narrative flow ("Chulkov," 40–42).

CHAPTER 3: APPROACHES

1. Emin's name appears on the title page as the author of the work, yet in the preface (which is unsigned) and throughout the body of the novel he encourages readers to identify him with Feridat, a kindred soul with whom Miramond shares many adventures. When Emin uses the first-person singular in the preface to *Inconstant Fate*, he is no doubt referring to Feridat.

2. The narrator again pleads ignorance as to the fate of a woman Kain rescues from two would-be murderers. Kain and Kamchatka turn all three over to the authorities, but the narrator then adds: "What happened to them after this is unknown, and therefore we will leave them in Lefortovo Prison" (83).

3. A list of the places that Feridat visits in part 2 includes Adrianople, Constantinople, Bosnia, Damascus, Persia, Tunis, Carthage, the Gulf of Messina and Mount Etna, Rome, Florence, Naples, Frescata, the Moselle and Rhine Rivers, Venice and Tuscany, Savoy, Turin, Monte Cristo, Portsmouth, and London.

4. Sometimes, however, the narrator's judgments are so superficial that they seem to undermine his authority in the text. Among many questionable observations, Feridat, the narrator of part 2, claims that Florentine youths—all of whom are poets—do not respect their elders (2:227), the impoverished Neapolitan nobility is relegated to earning money mostly by fencing (2:239), and the French just do not have the patience to read books (2:295).

5. At times Chulkov is even more direct in stating his willingness to explore the boundaries of literary expression. In the introduction to *The Mocker* he unashamedly admits to being a liar (1:i), and "Verses on a Ferris Wheel" opens with the following homage to "creativity": "Tell me, O muse, how a writer ought to begin / When he wants to lie about something / So that he can pass off a tall tale as the truth / And make by chance a maiden out of a widow" (414).

6. Titunik comments on the "spoof" of delaying the publication of the fifth part of *The Mocker* by two decades ("Chulkov," 35).

7. The narrator devotes evening 71 to a discussion of literature and the topic of women and money, and evening 72 is a satire of contemporary writers in the figure of the eighty-year-old, hunchbacked dwarf Kuromsha. Titunik explores Chulkov's use of digressions in this tale in "Chulkov," 41–42.

8. Sterne sketches the roundabout nature of his plot on pages 453–54. If Sterne's method of graphing could ever be deciphered, the pictorial representation of the plot of *The Mocker* would most likely bear a striking resemblance to Shandy's doodling.

9. Levitsky argues that the story does come to a proper end when Martona acquires Akhal´'s estate, because this action fulfills her quest for material security that began with the death of her husband in the second paragraph of the novel (109–10). He deftly points out, however, how Chulkov uses elements that nullify each other to turn *The Comely Cook* into a hoax (108–9). When Akhal´ mistakenly believes he has killed his friend Svidal´ in a duel, he initiates a mock tragedy complete with maudlin rhetoric and staged scenes (*Comely Cook,* 180–81). This tragedy is interrupted by a mock comedy featuring a merchant and his wife (185–89), which is in turn neatly balanced by another mock tragedy when the plot closes with Akhal´ lying on his deathbed (190–92).

10. In the immediately preceding episode Svidal´ and Martona help free a merchant from his manipulative and sadistic wife by, among other things, giving him fake poison. Moreover, the phrases used to describe the two poisoning "victims" seem uncannily similar. The narrator tells us that when Akhal´ saw Svidal´ enter his sickroom, he "beat and tore at himself, screamed as much as his strength would allow, and looked entirely like a madman" (192). When the merchant is given fake poison, Martona recalls that he "became enraged and rushed at his servants" (186), and "everyone considered him to be mad" (187). Perhaps the poison that Akhal´ has taken is no more real than the poison Goliadkin's enemies have supposedly planted on him in *The Double.* (See chapter 8 of this study.)

11. A concise survey of the spread of Christianity in Europe from the eleventh through the fifteenth centuries can be found in Hardwick, 206–16 and 312–15.

12. See *Nevidimka,* 19, 84, 101, and 102. In another twist on the subversion of the principle of historicity, Chulkov does not seem troubled by the profusion of myrtle, laurel, and cypress—all plants that thrive in warm, southern climates—in the northern fortress city of Roksolan's kingdom (*Mocker,* 1:135).

13. Moiseeva seconds this opinion, especially as it concerns the representation of the novel's heroine, Martona ("Mesto povestei," 185–87), and Sipovskii offers the opinion that Chulkov created a true history by simply embellishing the actual confession of a "fallen woman" with the devices and tone of the rogue's novel (1:640).

14. Gukovskii notes that many of the descriptions in *The Comely Cook* are recorded with the realist's meticulous attention to detail and that this is a raison d'être of the novel: "Individual, externally observed facts, which are photographically recorded, make up the content of his book" (*Literatura,* 229).

15. Concerning Martona's speech, critics also focus on her frequent recourse to proverbs. Serman concludes that "folklore in Chulkov's novel is one of the means he uses to make *The Comely Cook* a Russian novel about Russian people" ("Stanovlenie," 95), and Stepanov writes that Martona's use of proverbs "acquired a form that corresponded to her nationality, class, and cultural level, and the character of her entire image" (238).

16. Garrard notes the literary precursors of this scene, including the Russian apocryphal story "The Descent of the Virgin into Hell" ("Khozhdenie Bogoroditsy po mukam"; Čulkov, 52).

17. In the first four pages of the next evening's tale (2:99–102) Siloslav's tour continues, and the torments suffered by the inhabitants of this grim valley are briefly depicted in grisly detail. It is interesting to note, however, that with the exception of just one of these unfortunate creatures, the sins that have led to

their damnation are not revealed. Once again, the opportunity to pass judgment is downplayed in favor of pictorial intensity and inventiveness.

CHAPTER 4: THE LIMITATIONS AND POSSIBILITIES OF VOICE AND RHETORIC

1. The record is held by letter 4, in which Ernest touches on everything from Adam in the Garden of Eden, to the philosophy of John Locke, to the need for personal discipline and good health.

2. Titunik sounds an appropriate note of caution concerning the authoritative nature of Ernest and Hippolyte's correspondence. Between them, they drop the names of more than twenty great thinkers ranging from Socrates to Locke, yet the content of the statements attributed to these figures is often quite banal ("Emin and Rousseau," 338–39).

3. The concluding stories of *The Mocker*—"A Bitter Lot," "Gingerbread Money," and "The Precious Pike"—also provide an excellent example of Chulkov's sporadic flirtation with an authoritative narrative voice. As several scholars have noted, Chulkov abandons his facetious tone in these three tales for a more serious, and at times even caustic, view of the world. Garrard considers these stories a foreshadowing of the type of social satire written by Saltykov-Shchedrin in the nineteenth century (*Čulkov*, 146–51), and Oinas calls Chulkov's sympathy for the peasantry and implied critique of society a "complete reversal" from his approach in the previous chapters of the sprawling novel (577).

4. In the early Russian novel abstract discussions of the ideal monarch are supported by characters who are the embodiment of such a figure. Xerxes is more than just an avid listener; he is also a wise and energetic ruler (*Themistocles*, 253) who actively solicits information from the knowledgeable Themistocles. (See also the image of the prudent and magnanimous Malla Agmet [*Kamber and Arisena*, 200–202].) In Ladon's stories in *The Mocker* lessons are drawn not only from the lives of enlightened monarchs like Alim (3:4–11), but also from cautionary tales of evil tyrants who were the undoing of their people (3:87–88, 5:135–53).

5. Feridat follows this lecture with a description of his own worthless education that led to his unfortunate love affair with the beautiful but treacherous Nartsiza, his lengthy exile and wanderings, and his near constant unhappiness right through the end of the novel.

6. Since this letter is the last entry in part 3 and the discussion is not renewed in part 4, the inference is that Ernest's program is totally unassailable.

7. Nonexclusive laughter forms the core of the carnivalesque mentality. Comparing the openness of this approach to the stinging rebuke of satire, Bakhtin writes: "The satirist whose laughter is negative places himself above the object of his mockery, he is opposed to it. The wholeness of the world's comic aspect is destroyed, and that which appears comic becomes a private reaction. The people's ambivalent [carnivalesque] laughter, on the other hand, expresses the point of view of the whole world; he who is laughing also belongs to it" (*Rabelais*, 12).

8. Just whom this voice represents is unclear but hardly problematic. The monk has just finished an episode in *The Tale of the Taffeta Beauty Patch*, and it seems as though a different voice is responsible for the final paragraph in part 4, although this is never made clear. Perhaps Ladon, as the narrator/overseer of the entire novel, has once again reasserted his prerogative, or it is quite possible that Chulkov is addressing readers directly. Although we cannot determine who is speaking, it really does not matter. All three voices are carnivalized to one extent

or another, and the ambivalence of the voice at the end of part 4 serves as a crafty symbolic reminder of the carnivalesque foundation of the entire novel.

9. Still in a state of shock after leaving Belden, the prince is counseled by Agatha's confidante, Rukie. During the course of a lengthy monologue she finally gets the prince to acknowledge that his despair is both foolish and cowardly (3:296–304). Just as in Belden's speech, figurative language provides the justification for Rukie's argument. Her shrewd recourse to the metaphors of the absolute monarch unable to control his own destiny (3:298), the prisoner condemned to death (3:303), and the injured man in need of an amputation to save his life (3:303) finally convinces the prince to accept Agatha's rebuff with equanimity.

10. Sipovskii labels this technique, which he notes is employed by Emin's model Rousseau to depict a character's "elevated and agitated mental state," *bavardage de la fièvre.* Quite frequently it is broken up into fragments through the use of ellipses, which further reflect the speaker's torment and disordered state of mind (2:438). (See also Titunik, "Emin and Rousseau," 337.)

11. For other examples of the pathetic monologue see Kamber's funeral lament (Emin, *Kamber and Arisena,* 214–16), Miramond's denunciation of the gods (Emin, *Inconstant Fate,* 1:151–53), Ernest's appeal to nature (Emin, *Ernest and Doravra,* 1:93), and George's frequent attacks on the cruelty of fate (Komarov, *Milord George,* 60, 67, 187). Titunik sees Hippolyte, Ernest's confidant in *Ernest and Doravra,* as an exception to the type of overwrought hero represented by the above-mentioned characters. He rightly characterizes Hippolyte and Pulkheriia, the woman he eventually marries, as "cool, collected sensible people [who] strongly disapprove of Ernest and Doravra's emotional excesses" ("Emin and Rousseau," 340). It should be noted, however, that the motif of the despairing unrequited lover is so ingrained in Emin's fiction that even the rational Hippolyte, who continuously praises the virtues of moderation, succumbs to it. Believing he has been spurned by Pulkheriia, Hippolyte dashes off a letter in which he passionately discusses the most efficient means of ending his life (2:20–23).

12. Other philosophical monologues expressing this idea can be found in Emin's *Inconstant Fate,* 3:84–85, *Lizark and Sarmanda,* 185–86, and *Ernest and Doravra,* 1:113.

13. Other particularly good examples of this approach appear in *Ernest and Doravra,* 1:109–11 and 1:134–36. Monologues of morality are also quite common in Emin's *Adventures of Themistocles.* See 28–29 (on happiness), 30–33 (constancy), 45–53 (friendship), and 136–48 (warfare).

14. With her reference to an eclipse of the sun and birds shedding their feathers, Martona appears to be irreverently spoofing a specific monologue from *Inconstant Fate.* See page 102 of this study for an analysis of how Miramond employs similar imagery in the service of a far more altruistic argument.

CHAPTER 5: THE SOCIAL ORDER

1. From one of his first novels to the last Emin's philosophy remains constant. Hippolyte, Ernest's confidant in *The Letters of Ernest and Doravra,* counsels his friend to leave his isolation and become a useful member of society. He boldly states that there simply is no rational alternative: "Being subjects of the monarch and reasoning in a political manner, we are not free. We have strength in order that we might serve our sovereign and society" (*Ernest and Doravra,* 3:153).

2. Doravra echoes this sentiment. She rejects the idea of marrying Ernest because she believes (wrongly, as it turns out) that her father would be disgraced by such a union. She considers herself a daughter first and a young woman in love second (*Ernest and Doravra*, 1:34–35, 67–70, 163–65, 195, and 2:136–38). Titunik argues that this unwarranted sacrifice functions as a parody of the love affair in Emin's source, Rousseau's *La Nouvelle Héloïse*. Given that Ernest and Doravra could have joined their fates together, Titunik reasons, the agony and tears they expend over their far from hopeless situation is "a total, and totally unnecessary, waste" ("Emin and Rousseau," 341). In the context of this study, however, the lovers' passionate, yet needless, torment is viewed as just another plot device employed to increase the pathetic tension in a novel that takes the guiding principles of sentimentalism quite seriously.

3. As for Kain's tendency to mock the church, it is interesting to note that he and his band of fugitives frequently hide out at monasteries, where they receive food, drink, and shelter from the peasants. For a short time, at least, a carnival mentality is established as sacred space is profaned by Kain's presence (27, 91).

4. This phrase is the rough equivalent of the French *lèse majesté* and was uttered by individuals claiming to have evidence of treason against the tsar. (My thanks to Nancy Kollmann and the Eighteenth-Century Russian Studies Association for their insights into this matter.) Komarov explains this practice in a footnote: "At that time [the mid-1700s] this was considered so important that if an actual thief or robber was caught in a distant city and said these words, no one dared punish him, and they were obligated to send him to Moscow to the Secret Chancellery. No small number of delays took place in these investigations, which gave robbers time to find a means of escaping" (18).

5. The brief description of Kain's downfall in the last three pages of the novel (177–79) underscores the irreverent nature of the story as a whole. Over 95 percent of the book is given over to Kain's tricks, thievery, and mocking of authority, whereas less than three full pages register his final defeat.

6. Unfortunately for the merchant the turn of the carnival cycle has not yet brought him to its nadir. The next morning he decides to ask Minamila herself to let him act as go-between, believing that she has been prepared for this request by Neokh. Since the entire affair was Neokh's invention, the widow is shocked at the merchant's improper suggestion and has her servants throw the "madman" into the street. They happily oblige their mistress, but not before taking the opportunity to pummel the poor wretch thoroughly (4:242–43).

7. In a letter to his friend Hippolyte, Ernest writes that "to murmur against laws [*opredeleniia*] and decrees I consider the gravest sin. . . . No matter how unjust a law might seem to us, we must always obey it without complaint. It is better to think that our opinion is unjust rather than the law" (*Ernest and Doravra*, 3:27–28). Although Ernest is talking about the legal system, these words also characterize his attitude concerning the sexual mores of gentry society. He will live in misery married to a woman he does not love rather than transgress the unwritten laws regulating interpersonal relationships.

8. Another excellent example of the prudery inherent in Emin's last novel concerns a meeting between Ernest's best friend, Hippolyte, and Doravra's confidante, Pulkheriia. Hippolyte surprises Pulkheriia while she is swimming and inadvertently sees her knees. Even though they will soon marry, the chance encounter produces an immediate reaction of mutual embarrassment. As Hippolyte tells it: "I saw you in the pond. . . . You ran from me, and I moved far away from

you" (2:35). Titunik rightly points out that in general Hippolyte and Pulkheriia "conduct their courtship in jokes and light-hearted sexual innuendo" and that they are destined to "live a life together of utmost agreeableness and mutual satisfaction" ("Emin and Rousseau," 343). In writing of this incident, Hippolyte even chides Pulkheriia for her modesty: certainly such a beautiful woman should not be ashamed of baring her legs before the man she loves (2:35–36). In the midst of this amicably teasing discourse, however, Hippolyte sounds a serious note when he hints at the dire consequences that unchecked carnality can have in his world. He explains to Pulkheriia that upon seeing her in the pond, he immediately retreated in order to avoid repeating the actions of the unfortunate Actaeon, who was turned into a stag and killed by his own dogs after stumbling upon the naked Diana while she was bathing (2:35).

9. It should be noted that the heroes of Emin's and Komarov's novels are often put in the same predicament. As we have already seen, Miramond and Milord George are tortured when they do not submit to the sexual demands of women more powerful than they are. This motif is also used in Emin's *Kamber and Arisena* when Gamlia imprisons Kamber with the hope of forcing him to love her (160) and once again in *Milord George* when George is put through a mock execution by a scorned Spanish princess (186–91).

10. Marianne underscores the social stigma that attaches to the victims of rape in novels like *The Marquis de Toledo* when she beseeches Bonveal: "Have mercy, O sir, on one as unfortunate as I. . . . If you do not tame your rage, having found out about my misfortune, society will forever shun me, my fiancé will abandon me, and I will be eternally condemned to a miserable fate" (9–10).

11. Even powerful despots are subject to this unwritten law. When Malla Hasan, the bey of Morocco, is told of a beautiful widow, he has her brought to the palace with the intention of using her to "satisfy his bodily weaknesses" (Emin, *Marquis de Toledo*, 113). Even though he directly tells the woman that he "wants her to make [him] happy" (116), she is able to forestall the absolute monarch's advances until he legitimizes their relationship by marrying her.

12. Martona knows of what she speaks, for in a novel like Emin's *Inconstant Fate* two years seem like a rather brief courtship. When Ziumbiula and Miramond meet for the first time, they take up eleven full pages just to express their feelings for one another (1:138–49). Moreover, even with this lengthy introduction, everything is left up in the air. Both are troubled more than comforted by their nascent love, and Miramond wonders aloud how he, being a commoner, could have the bad fortune to fall in love with a princess (1:148). Three volumes, hundreds of pages, and many years lie ahead of the unfortunate couple before they have the chance to enjoy the carnal pleasures that Martona and her lovers experience almost within minutes of the first handshake. In just eleven pages in *The Comely Cook* Martona has not only met Akhal´ but has become his lover, been deceived and abandoned by him, rescued by him, and finally left for good when Akhal´ mistakenly believes he has killed Martona's next lover, Svidal´, in a duel (170–81).

13. This passage clearly shows the clash of ideologies that runs throughout the novels in this study. As noted earlier in this chapter, George, the well-educated and proper gentleman, calmly turns down the queen's invitation and walks away. This is certainly a reflex of the didactic side of Komarov's oeuvre. On the other hand, the blatant depiction of Musalmina's naked body reveals the side of Komarov that is guided by a carnivalesque mentality. Although it is unusual to have

both ideologies come together in the same scene, they do coexist in a given work, whether it be a novel by Komarov, Chulkov, or Emin.

14. In all fairness it should be noted that Emin's novels are not completely without eroticism. For example, toward the end of *The Marquis de Toledo* there is an interpolated tale reminiscent of the Russian story of Karp Sutulov, in which three figures of authority (a field marshal, a vizier, and a patriarch) attempt to blackmail a faithful wife into having sex with them. Strong-willed and resourceful, the woman eventually outsmarts them, but not before putting up with a significant amount of ill treatment. On one of his visits the vizier has dinner with the young woman and then "wipes his lips" against hers and beckons her to bed (198). Despite the aggressive nature of this behavior the woman adeptly rebuffs it, for she has already had a run-in with the patriarch. When the woman first meets him, he kisses her, and from the way he does it, she concludes that "not having strong teeth, the bearded ones [the clergy] like soft meat" (194). During his next meeting with the virtuous wife the patriarch again makes improper advances, which leads the woman to say that "he had such a thick beard that when he kissed me, clumps of hair crawled into my mouth, and I had to spit out all his kisses" (200). Although each of these passages conjures up an erotic image, it is important to note that, unlike similar episodes in carnivalesque fiction, sex has a negative connotation: it is threatening to the woman (she repeats several times that if her nocturnal visitors are seen by the neighbors, she will be ruined) and in each case never consummated.

15. To top off the salacious nature of this passage, the Russian word for "limb" *(chlen)* also refers to the male sexual organ.

16. The striking sensuality of Ladon's narrative does not end when his body goes limp. After the couple make love, Ladon tells Alenona a story. When he finishes, he notices that she is sleeping. As Alenona rests beside him, a grateful Ladon takes in the sight: "My beauty had already fallen into the sweetest sleep. Her excellent figure was in a beautiful position. Her right hand lay on my knees, and the left was pleased to circle her head. My friend Morpheus, as a favor to me, uncovered her breasts, which rose and fell most pleasantly and attracted my eyes to them. The thin bedspread and my penetrating gaze presented all the parts of her body as though they were uncovered" (1:46).

CHAPTER 6: CHARACTERIZATION

1. For just a few examples of such emotional outbursts see Emin, *Themistocles*, 283, *Lizark and Sarmanda*, 55, *Marquis de Toledo*, 92, *Ernest and Doravra*, 2:58; Komarov, *Milord George*, 83; and Chulkov, *The Mocker*, 3:2.

2. At the end of this narrative Kamber marries Arisena, ascends the throne, and then makes Kadyr, who has wed the beautiful Rossolana, his chancellor (251–52).

3. The way Martona uses commercial terminology to describe her activities recalls Fanny Hill, the heroine of Cleland's unabashedly erotic novel. After her initial reservations Fanny comes to appreciate the opportunities that a life of vice can bring her. Moving from one liaison to the next in a businesslike and even joyful manner, she greatly improves her position in society. For examples of Fanny's commercial jargon see pages 44, 54, 89, 123, and 180.

4. Of course, not every character is affected in a positive manner. Sveton's wife and the merchant's spouse are humiliated, and the colonel is so shaken by

Martona's temporary flight from him that he dies shortly thereafter, but in each of these cases the carnivalesque principle remains intact. Sveton's wife is a shrew, whom he married not out of love but because the match was arranged by their parents (164), and therefore she shares at least part of the blame for her husband's behavior. Moreover, in the end she uncovers the affair, throws Martona out of the house, and reclaims Sveton for herself. The merchant's wife treats her spouse even worse: she turns their house into a bordello, humiliates and imprisons her husband, and even plots his death right before his friends' eyes (183–88). Cast in this role, she becomes a figure of repression and therefore worthy of being toppled from her pedestal of power. As for Martona's aged lover, he never rises above the level of a cartoon character, a "toothless Adonis" (170), for whom readers develop little emotional attachment. When he passes away in his sleep, he evokes no sympathy and the episode maintains its comic coloring.

5. When thinking about his liaison with the rich woman, the young man uses the appropriately carnivalesque term of "feasting" or "banqueting" (*pirovanie;* 2:154).

6. When Feridat finds that his love, Nartsiza, has had a child by another man, he immediately seeks him out and kills him (*Inconstant Fate,* 2:201–17), and Gamlia's punishment is to commit suicide for trying to come between Kamber and Arisena, even though her plan was never consummated (*Kamber and Arisena,* 192).

7. Although Sarmanda just barely escapes this execution, her close brush with death does not make her hold her own life any dearer. When Izida suspects that Lizark and Sarmanda have been having an affair behind her back, she seeks revenge against both of them. Proving once again the utter selflessness of her love, Sarmanda implores Izida to punish only her and let Lizark go free. On her knees, she pleads with the princess, "Take your vengeance against me alone. I am prepared to meet the cruelest death just in order that Lizark will be happy and free from any misfortune. . . . Thrust this dagger into my breast; tear my unhappy heart to pieces" (236).

Chapter 7: A Theory of Stylization

1. In his groundbreaking study *From Gogol to Dostoevsky* Peter Hodgson analyzes Butkov's work as an example of what he terms the "reluctant naturalism" of many Russian writers in the 1840s. For an introduction to this problem, see 37–71.

2. Despite a general lack of life-affirming humor in Dostoevskii, modern critics have applied Bakhtin's theory of the carnival to his works. For example, Roger Anderson ("Carnival") finds a carnivalesque mentality animating the repeated transgression of behavioral norms in *The Brothers Karamazov.* These infractions range from the sexual excesses of Fedor Karamazov and his son Dmitrii to the monk Zosima's paganlike appreciation of nature. There is no denying, however, that it is virtually impossible to find in Dostoevskii the sheer delight in carnal excess and roguery that is the hallmark of writers like Chulkov and Komarov.

3. Tynianov found that even specific incidents in "The Landlady" reveal an indebtedness to Gogol´. For example, he argues that the comparison of Ordynov's attack to a storm in "The Landlady" mimics the metamorphosis of black frock coats into flies buzzing around sugar loaves in chapter 1 of *Dead Souls.*

4. In this novella Dostoevskii goes beyond an attack on Gogol''s penchant for verbal play to lampoon the author himself. Gogol´ is humorously depicted in the figure of the short, shabby, wrinkle-faced Foma Opiskin, an unsuccessful writer, who dreams of composing the one work that will shake his native land to the core. Opiskin's pitiful reflections on the peasantry, landowners, lyric poetry, and virtue are modeled after similarly titled entries in Gogol''s *Selected Passages from a Correspondence with Friends* (*Vybrannye mesta iz perepiski s druz´iami*, 1847), and at times Dostoevskii even directly quotes from this work (Tynianov, "Dostoevskii and Gogol´," 446).

5. Although parody is usually associated with a humorous response from the reader, there are some critics who do not insist upon such a connection. See, for instance, Linda Hutcheon's *A Theory of Parody* and Joseph Dane's "Parody and Satire: A Theoretical Model." Dane writes: "That the effect of satire and parody is often comic is undeniable, but that what we would regard as satire or parody is necessarily so is dubious" (146). It is interesting to note, however, that neither critic taps the rich possibilities implied in Tynianov's conception of stylization.

6. His case in point is Konstantin Aksakov's *Oleg at Constantinople* (*Oleg pod Konstantinopolem*, 1858). Aksakov himself called this drama a parody, but Tynianov, as well as a reviewer who was Aksakov's contemporary, did not agree. They both found large sections of serious, first-rate poetry in it that go far beyond mere mockery ("On Parody," 284–86). Moreover, Tynianov maintains there were many other works written in the mid–nineteenth century that were labeled parodies in their day yet lacked the humor generally associated with this mode of discourse. Among those he names are Karolina Pavlova's "Everywhere and Always" ("Vezde i vsegda," 1850), Ivan Panaev's verse parodies written under the pseudonym of the New Poet, and the literary output of a host of minor figures ("On Parody," 286n). In "On Parody" Tynianov uses the terms "parody of form" (*parodichnost´*) and "parody of function" (*parodiinost´*), but they are for all intents and purposes synonymous with "parody" and "stylization."

7. Inconsistency is yet one more shortcoming that can be added to the list. In the passage in "Dostoevskii and Gogol´" that is most often quoted, which occurs just two sentences before the assertion that comically motivated stylization is actually parody, Tynianov writes: "A comedy is the parody of a tragedy . . . [and] a tragedy is perhaps the parody of a comedy" (416). Since tragedy is not a comic genre, Tynianov seems to be saying that parody can be humorless as well. Two solutions come to mind to explain this apparent contradiction. On the one hand, the addition of the modifier "perhaps" in the second clause suggests that Tynianov was only speculating here. On the other, he may have been trying to equate tragedy with stylization (that is, the humorless subtype of parody). Unfortunately, we can never be sure since neither conclusion is supported by the limited evidence available in Tynianov's two articles on this topic.

8. The other two categories in Bakhtin's typology are referential discourse, which "recognizes only itself and its object, to which it strives to be maximally adequate" (*Problems*, 187), and objectified discourse, which is most often found in the direct speech of characters (186–87). Unlike double-voiced discourse, which contains the words, ideas, and tone of a second speaker, referential and objectified discourses are univocal and therefore devoid of the potential ambiguities and conflicts that could arise from a clash of separate voices. See Hammarberg, 18–21, for a brief but cogent overview of these two parts of Bakhtin's tripartite typology.

9. Markiewicz plots the fluctuating terminology and definitions associated with parody. The chart on page 1267 and his comments on page 1269 are especially helpful.

10. Although a definition of parody that stresses its penchant for mockery has prevailed for the last two hundred years, the alternative posed by a contemporary critic like Hutcheon is appealing because it accounts for a greater number of works that have actually been deemed parodies. In her understanding of the term Hutcheon stresses the mutual illumination of texts while downplaying the aggressive and derisive nature of the process. Although she admits that parody frequently does expose and exploit the aesthetic weaknesses of a second text, she asserts that this is not its essential characteristic. What really distinguishes parody is its ability to be "both a re-creation and a creation, making criticism into a kind of active exploration of form" (*Parody*, 51). The incorporation of another's discourse into a parodic text provides it with a new background and casts it in a new light, but this tactic does not presuppose an attack on the worthiness of the model. Our perception of the incorporated material will almost certainly change when we see it in a new context, but our response, as well as the parodist's intention, could be admiration or indifference just as well as scorn. It is important to note, however, that even Hutcheon's expanded definition of parody directs our attention to another text and not, at least primarily, to ourselves or our approach to decoding literature.

CHAPTER 8: SLOWLY FADING INTO NOTHING

1. Most twentieth-century critics maintain that Dostoevskii's novel is shapeless and needlessly repetitive (see Frank, 295–96, 310, and Mochulsky, 51). Konrad Onasch's claim (23) that *The Double* is a well-rounded masterpiece exhibiting a complete formal and aesthetic unity definitely represents the minority opinion.

2. The term *nynche* directly preceding this quotation could refer to a short period of time surrounding Goliadkin's visit to his doctor. Then again, it could be translated as "nowadays" and refer to the 1840s, a period in Russian literary history when a character in a work of fiction might meet someone as "unpleasant" as the oversized, coat-stealing ghost of an abused civil servant on the streets of the northern capital.

3. Chizhevsky calculates that there were over two hundred such stories in Russian literature of the 1830s and 1840s (310), and Gippius lists works by Ushakov, Bulgarin, and Grebenka as general and specific models of "The Overcoat" (108–9), yet another tale that, at least in its own time, was an unacknowledged stylization of the "little man" *(malen'kii chelovek)* motif in Russian literature.

4. Beginning with Belinskii, many critics have noted the merging of voices in *The Double*. Wolf Schmid's article on text interference is most helpful for sorting out the parameters and subtypes of this phenomenon.

5. Nechaeva, 156. Joseph Frank agrees, writing that *The Double* is a "portrayal of a consciousness totally saturated with the formulas and slogans of its society" (308). In addition, M. S. Al'tman offers the idea that *The Double* reflects reality in yet another way. He contends that Jakov Petrovich Goliadkin is modeled after Dostoevskii's contemporary, the writer Jakov Petrovich Butkov (198–99).

6. Although his opinion of the novel changed somewhat after its publica-

tion, Belinskii always maintained that Goliadkin was a character taken straight from life. In the March 1846 issue of *Notes of the Fatherland* he wrote, "Mr. Goliadkin is one of those touchy, ambition-crazy people who are so frequently found in the lower and middle classes of our society. . . . If you look around more attentively, how many poor and rich, stupid and intelligent Mr. Goliadkins will you see!" (Dostoevskii, *Polnoe sobranie sochinenii,* 1:489–90).

7. For a brief survey of the intertexts, Gogolian and otherwise, that apply to *The Double,* see Harden, xxiv–vi, and Dostoevskii, *Polnoe sobranie sochinenii,* 1:486–88.

8. As noted in the preceding paragraph, the first example of Goliadkin "regaining consciousness" occurs in the first line of the novel.

9. Dostoevskii defines the verb *stuzhevat´sia* as meaning "'to disappear,' 'to be annihilated,' . . . 'to come to naught.' But not to be annihilated suddenly, as though having fallen through the earth to the accompaniment of thunder and lightening, but, so to speak, sinking into nothingness delicately, smoothly, imperceptibly" (Dostoevskii, *Polnoe sobranie sochinenii,* 26:66). The author applies this term to Goliadkin, but it just as appropriately describes the novel as a whole.

10. These are interesting words coming from Goliadkin. Both he and the double were pleasantly inebriated when the latter recounted his clichéd "life story" (155–58).

11. We are already aware that Goliadkin is fond of mixing fantasy and reality. During his dinner conversation with the double earlier in the novel he gives an expansive description of St. Petersburg that is a cheerful combination of fact, anecdote, and imagination (156–57).

12. See pages 199 and 208. On this evening Goliadkin surprisingly retains yet another article of clothing from the first day of his adventures. When he encountered the double for the first time, Goliadkin lost both of his galoshes chasing after him (142), but on night four he is wearing them once again (199, 211). Although he could have procured a new pair, this odd detail implies that he never lost them in the first place. Moreover, in his notebook for the years 1862–1864 Dostoevskii returned to the importance of the galoshes. A long list of one-line ideas for the revision of *The Double* includes the following: "The director on Nevskii at night. Galoshes, a fantastic scene" (Dostoevskii, *Polnoe sobranie sochinenii,* 1:435). Although the brevity of this statement makes it impossible to determine the author's exact intention, it does support the theory that Goliadkin's galoshes function as something more than a realistic detail.

13. In *The Young Dostoevsky* Victor Terras states that the long interval between Dr. Rutenspitz's two appearances "interrupts the natural course of the narrative" and that "once introduced, he should have stayed in the novel" (194). When viewed within the context of Dostoevskii's self-effacing stylization, this peculiarity, which at first appears to be a structural defect, becomes one of the text's many strengths.

14. The "literature" from which Goliadkin creates his version of reality is a subcultural mix of *lubok* adventure novels, romances, and material from the mass-oriented journal *Library for Reading* (1834–1865) and the newspaper the *Northern Bee* (*Severnaia pchela,* 1825–1864). For an introduction to Goliadkin as a parody of the heroes of sentimental and romantic fiction see Neuhäuser, especially sections 5 ("Idealisten und Romantiker") and 19 ("Der Doppelgänger: Ein Interpretationsmodell"). In the chapter "Reluctant Naturalism" (*Gogol,* 37–71)

Peter Hodgson surveys the broader topic of the parody of Russian naturalism in the literature of the 1840s.

CONCLUSION

1. In addition to a prolific career in the fable, ode, tragedy, and comedy Sumarokov also made one of the first significant theoretical contributions to modern Russian literature. In his *Epistle on Poetry* (*Èpistol o stikhotvorstve*, 1748) he identified which foreign authors were worthy of emulation, circumscribed what he considered to be the proper subject matter of Russian neoclassicism, and established a hierarchy of genres.

2. Komarov's life is such a mystery that we will never know whether he ever read *Jonathan Wild*, but it is interesting to note that his *Detailed and Reliable Histories of . . . Vanka Kain* has more in common with Defoe's *True and Genuine Account of . . . the Late Jonathan Wild* than just the similarity of its title. Both texts claim to be documentaries that use reliable written sources and firsthand testimony to describe and analyze the life of a notorious felon. Just as Defoe compiled his account from documents written by Wild himself as well as the experience he gained from an encounter with the outlaw, Komarov asserts that his novel is based on Kain's autobiography and an interview he had with the "thief and scoundrel" some years earlier (iv–vii). In addition, both novels recount strikingly similar tales in which a celebrated outlaw manages to procure official protection for his activities. Wild won the epithet of "Thief-Taker General" by turning over to the police any member of his pickpocket syndicate who refused to play by his rules. In exchange for this service the authorities were more than willing to turn a blind eye to his illegal transactions. With a senate *ukaz* (decree) of 1744 making him immune from prosecution, Kain also played both sides of the law. Using his position to inform on and eliminate his major criminal competitors, he became the officially sanctioned king of the Moscow underworld. Beyond these compositional similarities, Defoe and Komarov also seem to agree on the larger goals of their work. Both writers emphasize the educational and social inadequacies of the early years of their subjects' lives, frequently pause to analyze the moral and social consequences of their criminal deeds, and express a grim satisfaction when the judicial system finally brings the brigands to account.

3. The influence of Russia's first novelists may once again be on the rise with the republication of their work beginning in the late 1980s (see my introduction).

4. In addition to the formative role it played in the prose fiction of Chulkov and Komarov, the subculture also significantly influenced many other writers of the late eighteenth century. For example, Nikolai Kurganov (1725?–1790) compiled a wide-ranging miscellany entitled *Pismovnik* (1769), which consisted of a grammar and various readings aimed at the broadest possible audience; Vasilii Levshin (1746–1826) published *Russian Folk Tales* (*Russkie skazki*, 1780–1783), a mixture of satirical stories and knightly tales based on the heroes of Russia's oral epics; and Aleksandr Izmailov (1779–1831) closed out the century with his *Evgenii, or The Results of Bad Upbringing and Bad Company* (1799–1801), which blends didacticism with provocative scenes of vice.

5. The younger, yet more worldly and sophisticated, Varvara underscores the folly of Devushkin's veneration of Rataziaev when she calls his overblown stories nothing but nonsense (55).

6. Hodgson adds Jakov Butkov to the list of writers who stylized the literary aesthetic of the 1840s. In his monograph he examines how Butkov used a Gogolian sense of humor to parody the trendy genre of the physiological sketch. Modeled after the French *physiologie,* the sketches of, among others, Vladimir Dal´, Vladimir Sollogub, Ivan Panaev, Nikolai Nekrasov, and Dmitrii Grigorovich focus on the sights, sounds, and character types of the lowest reaches of Russian society. Infusing his work with the tone, style, and technique of the *feuilleton* and vaudeville, Butkov consistently deflates the supposedly objective manner of narration that served as the justification of this genre. See Hodgson, *Gogol,* especially chapters 3–6.

Works Cited

Primary Sources

Fedor Emin

Liubovnyi vertograd, ili nepreoborimoe postoianstvo Kambera i Ariseny [The Garden of Love, or The Insuperable Constancy of Kamber and Arisena]. St. Petersburg: Sukhoputnyi kadetskii korpus, 1763.

Nepostoiannaia fortuna, ili pokhozhdenie Miramonda [Inconstant Fate, or The Adventures of Miramond]. 3 parts. St. Petersburg: Sukhoputnyi kadetskii korpus, 1763.

Prikliucheniia Femistokla, i raznye politicheskie, grazhdanskie, filosoficheskie, fizicheskie i voennye ego s synom svoim razgovory . . . [The Adventures of Themistocles and Various Conversations with His Son on Political, Civil, Philosophical, Physical, and Military Matters . . .]. St. Petersburg: Sukhoputnyi kadetskii korpus, 1763; Moscow: N. Novikov, 1781.

Nagrazhdennaia postoiannost´, ili prikliucheniia Lizarka i Sarmandy [Constancy Rewarded, or The Adventures of Lizark and Sarmanda]. St. Petersburg: Akademiia nauk, 1764.

Gorestnaia liubov´ Markiza de Toledo [The Sorrowful Love of the Marquis de Toledo]. St. Petersburg: Sukhoputnyi kadetskii korpus, 1764.

Pis´ma Ernesta i Doravry [The Letters of Ernest and Doravra]. 4 parts. St. Petersburg: Akademiia nauk, 1766.

Mikhail Chulkov

Kak khochesh´ nazovi [Call It What You Will]. Literaturnoe nasledstvo, nos. 9–10, 226–42. Moscow: Institut literatury Akademii nauk SSSR, 1933. This play was probably written in the mid-1760s but never published until it was issued in the above-mentioned series.

Peresmeshnik, ili slavenskie skazki [The Mocker, or Slavic Tales]. 5 parts. St. Petersburg:

Ponomarev, 1789. The first four parts of this work were originally published in 1766–1768; part 5 was published in 1789 along with a reissue of parts 1–4.

Pokhozhdenie Akhillesovo pod imenen Pirry do troianskoi osady [The Adventures of Achilles under the Name of Pyrrha before the Siege of Troy]. St. Petersburg: Sukhoputnyi kadetskii korpus, 1769.

"Stikhi na kacheli" ["Verses on a Ferris Wheel"], "Stikhi na Semik" ["Verses on *Semik*"], and "Plachevnoe padenie stikhotvortsev" ["The Lamentable Downfall of the Poets"]. In vol. 1 of *Poèty XVIII veka*, ed. G. P. Makogonenko and I. Z. Serman, 414–71. 3d ed. Leningrad: Sovetskii pisatel´, 1958. (These three mock heroic poems were originally published in Chulkov's journal of 1769, *I to i sio [Both This and That]*.

Prigozhaia povarikha, ili pokhozhdenie razvratnoi zhenshchiny [The Comely Cook, or The Adventures of a Debauched Woman]. In vol. 1 of *Russkaia proza XVIII veka,* ed. A. V. Zapadov and G. P. Makogonenko, 157–92. St. Petersburg: Morskoi kadetskii korpus, 1770; Moscow: Gosudarstvennoe izdatel´stvo khudozhestvennoi literatury, 1950.

Matvei Komarov

"Pis´mo ego siiatel´stvu kniaziu Alekseiu Vasil´evichu Khovanskomu" ["A Letter to His Excellency Prince Aleksei Vasilievich Khovanskii"]. In Komarov, *Raznye pis´mennye materii [Various Written Materials],* 176–80. Originally published in Moscow: Senatskaia tipografiia, 1771.

Obstoiatel´nye i vernye istorii dvukh moshennikov: pervogo rossiiskogo slavnogo vora, razboinika i byvshego moskovskogo syshchika Van´ki Kaina so vsemi ego syskami, rozyskami, sumazbrodnoi svad´boi i raznymi zabavnymi ego pesniami . . . [The Detailed and Reliable Histories of Two Scoundrels: The First Being the Famous Thief, Bandit, and Former Moscow Police Spy Vanka Kain with all of His Investigations, Inquests, Madcap Wedding, and Various Humorous Songs . . .]. St. Petersburg: Senatskaia tipografiia, 1779; Moscow: Reshetnikov, 1794.

Povest´ o prikliuchenii aglinskogo milorda Georga i o brandeburgskoi markgrafine Friderike Luize [The Story of the Adventures of the English Milord George and of the Brandenburg Margravine Friderika Louisa]. St. Petersburg: Shnor, 1782.

Nevidimka: Istoriia o fetsskom koroleviche Aridese i o brate ego Polumedese s raznymi liubopytnymi povestiami [Nevidimka: The History of the Fetsskian Prince Arides and His Brother Polumedes with Various Curious Stories]. Moscow: Reshetnikov, 1789.

Raznye pis´mennye materii, sobrannye dlia udovol´stviia liubopytnykh chitatelei [Various Written Materials, Collected for the Pleasure of Curious Readers]. Moscow: Reshetnikov, 1791.

Other Authors

Cleland, John. *Fanny Hill, or Memoirs of a Woman of Pleasure.* Harmondsworth, England: Penguin, 1985.

Defoe, Daniel. *Moll Flanders.* Harmondsworth, England: Penguin, 1972.

———. *The True and Genuine Account of . . . Jonathan Wild.* In Fielding, *Jonathan Wild*, 221–57.

Dostoevskii, F. M. *Bednye liudi [Poor Folk].* In vol. 1 of *Polnoe sobranie sochinenii,* 13–108.

———. *Dvoinik [The Double].* In vol. 1 of *Polnoe sobranie sochinenii,* 109–229.

———. *Polnoe sobranie sochinenii [Complete Collected Works].* 30 vols. Leningrad: Nauka, 1972–1986.

Fielding, Henry. *Jonathan Wild*. Harmondsworth, England: Penguin, 1982.

Fonvizin, D. I. *Brigadir* [*The Brigadier*]. In vol. 1 of *Sobranie sochinenii* [*Collected Works*], 45–103. Moscow: Khudozhestvennaia literatura, 1959.

Gogol', N. V. "O dvizhenii zhurnal'noi literatury v 1834-m i 1835-m godu" ["On the Situation in Journal Literature in 1834 and 1835"]. In vol. 8 of *Polnoe sobranie sochinenii*, 156–77.

———. "Nos" ["The Nose"]. In vol. 3 of *Polnoe sobranie sochinenii*, 47–75.

———. *Polnoe sobranie sochinenii* [*Complete Collected Works*]. 14 vols. Moscow: Akademiia nauk, 1937–1952.

———. "Shinel'" ["The Overcoat"]. In vol. 3 of *Polnoe sobranie sochinenii*, 139–74.

———. "Zapiski sumasshedshego" ["Diary of a Madman"]. In vol. 3 of *Polnoe sobranie sochinenii*, 191–214.

Karamzin, N. M. *Izbrannye sochineniia* [*Selected Works*]. 2 vols. Moscow: Khudozhestvennaia literatura, 1964.

———. "O knizhnoi torgovle i liubvi ko chteniiu v Rossii" ["On the Book Trade and the Love of Reading in Russia"]. In vol. 2 of *Izbrannye sochineniia*, 176–80.

———. "Panteon russkikh avtorov" ["The Pantheon of Russian Authors"]. In vol. 2 of *Izbrannye sochineniia*, 156–73.

Lomonosov, M. V. *Kratkoe rukovodstvo k krasnorechii* [*A Brief Introduction to Rhetoric*]. In vol. 7 of *Polnoe sobranie sochinenii*, 89–378.

———. *Polnoe sobranie sochinenii* [*Complete Collected Works*]. 10 vols. Moscow: Akademiia nauk, 1952.

———. "Predislovie o pol'ze knig tserkovnykh v rossiiskom iazyke." ["Introduction to the Use of Church Books in the Russian Language"]. In vol. 7 of his *Polnoe sobranie sochinenii*, 585–92.

Pushkin, A. S. *Evgenii Onegin*. In vol. 4 of *Sobranie sochinenii* [*Collected Works*], 7–166. Moscow: Khudozhestvennaia literatura, 1975.

Rabelais, François. *The Histories of Gargantua and Pantagruel*. Trans. J. M. Cohen. Harmondsworth, England: Penguin, 1955.

Richardson, Samuel. *Clarissa, or The History of a Young Lady*. Ed. George Sherburn. Boston: Houghton Mifflin, 1962.

Sterne, Laurence. *The Life and Opinions of Tristram Shandy*. Harmondsworth, England: Penguin, 1967.

Sumarokov, A. P. "Pis'mo o chtenii romanov" ["A Letter on the Reading of Novels"]. In vol. 6 of *Polnoe sobranie vsekh sochinenii* [*Complete Collected Works*], 350–51. Moscow: Universitetskaia tipografiia u N. Novikova, 1787.

———. *Two Epistles, the First Treating of the Russian Language, the Second of Poetry*. In Segel, *Literature*, 1:221–38.

Tolstoi, L. N. *Anna Karenina*. In vol. 18 of *Polnoe sobranie vsekh sochinenii*.

———. *Polnoe sobranie vsekh sochinenii* [*Complete Collected Works*]. 90 vols. Moscow: Khudozhestvennaia literatura, 1930–1958.

———. *Voina i mir* [*War and Peace*]. In vol. 10 of *Polnoe sobranie sochinenii*.

CRITICAL WORKS

Adrianova Peretts, V. P. "Novellisticheskie siuzhety v fol'klore i russkoi literature XVIII veka." In vol. 10 of *Russkaia literatura XVIII veka i ee mezhdunarodnye sviazi*, ed. I. Z. Serman, 12–17. Leningrad: Nauka, 1975.

———. "Zapadnoevropeiskaia gorodskaia novella v russkoi literature XVIII veka." In *Russko-pol'skie literaturnye sviazi*, ed. P. N. Berkov, 13–17. Moscow: Nauka, 1966.

Al'tman, M. S. "Iz arsenala imen i prototipov literaturnykh geroev Dosto-evskogo." In *Dostoevskii i ego vremia*, ed. V. G. Bazanov and G. M. Fridlender, 196–216. Leningrad: Nauka, 1971.

Anchor, Robert. "Bakhtin's Truths of Laughter." *Clio* 14 (spring 1985): 237–57.

Anderson, Roger B. *Dostoevsky: Myths of Duality*. Humanities Monograph Series, no. 58. Gainsville: University of Florida Press, 1986.

———. "The Meaning of Carnival in *The Brothers Karamazov*." *Slavic and East European Journal* 23, no. 4 (winter 1979): 458–78.

Atkinson, John Augustus, and James Walker. *A Picturesque Representation of the Manners, Customs, and Amusements of the Russians in One Hundred Coloured Pictures, with an Accurate Explanation of Each Plate in English and French*. 3 vols. London: W. Bulmer, 1803.

Baehr, Stephen Lessing. *The Paradise Myth in Eighteenth-Century Russia*. Stanford, CA: Stanford Univ. Press, 1991.

Bakhtin, Mikhail. "Discourse in the Novel." In *The Dialogic Imagination*, trans. Caryl Emerson and Michael Holquist, 259–422. University of Texas Slavic Series, no. 1. Austin: Univ. of Texas Press, 1981.

———. *Problems of Dostoevsky's Poetics*. Ed. and trans. Caryl Emerson. Theory and History of Literature, 8. Minneapolis: Univ. of Minnesota Press, 1984.

———. *Rabelais and His World*. Trans. Hélène Iswolsky. Cambridge: MIT Press, 1968.

Baklanova, N. A. "Russkii chitatel' XVII veka." In *Drevnerusskaia literatura i ee sviazi s novym vremenem*, ed. O. A. Derzhavina, 159–93. Moscow: Nauka, 1967.

Bartlett, R. P., A. G. Cross, and Karen Rasmussen, eds. *Russia and the World of the Eighteenth Century*. Columbus, OH: Slavica Publishers, 1988.

Becker, Christopher. "*Raznochintsy*: The Development of the Word and Concept." *American Slavic and East European Review* 18 (1959): 63–74.

Bem, A. L. "'Nos' i *Dvoinik*." In *U istokov tvorchestva Dostoevskogo (O Dostoevskom)*, ed. A. L. Bem, 139–63. Prague: Petropolis, 1936.

Berkov, P. N. "Ivan Shishkin—literaturnyi deiatel' 1740 godov." In *Voprosy izucheniia russkoi literatury XI–XX vekov*, ed. B. P. Gorodetskii, 49–63. Moscow: Akademiia nauk, 1958.

———. "Russkaia literatura XVIII veka i drugie slavianskie literatury XVIII–XX vekov: V poriadke postanovki voprosa o literaturnyh kontaktakh." In *Russkaia literatura XVIII veka i slavianskie literatury*, ed. Berkov, 5–39.

———. *Russko-pol'skie literaturnye sviazi v XVIII veke*. Moscow: Akademiia nauk, 1958.

———, ed. *Russkaia literatura XVIII veka i slavianskie literatury*. Moscow: Akademiia nauk, 1963.

Beshenkovskii, E. B. "Zhizn' Fedora Emina." In vol. 11 of *XVIII vek: N. I. Novikov i obshchestvenno–literaturnoe dvizhenie ego vremeni*, ed. G. P. Makogonenko, 186–203. Leningrad: Nauka, 1976.

Brockhaus Enzyklopädie, 19th ed.; s.v. "Brandenburg."

Brooks, Jeffrey. "The Kopeck Novels of Early Twentieth Century Russia." *Journal of Popular Culture* 13, no. 1 (summer 1979): 85–97.

Brown, William Edward. *A History of Eighteenth Century Russian Literature*. Ann Arbor, MI: Ardis, 1980.

Budgen, D. E. "The Concept of Fiction in Eighteenth-Century Russian Letters." In Cross, *Great Britain and Russia*, 65–74.

———. "Fedor Emin and the Beginnings of the Russian Novel." In Cross, *Russian Literature*, 67–94.

Burgess, Malcolm. "Fairs and Entertainers in Eighteenth-Century Russia." *Slavonic and East European Review* 38, no. 90 (December 1959): 95–113.

Chizhevsky, Dmitry. "About Gogol's 'Overcoat.'" In *Gogol from the Twentieth Century,* trans. and ed. Robert A. Maguire, 295–322. Princeton, NJ: Princeton Univ. Press, 1974.

Collins, Samuel. *The Present State of Russia. In a Letter to a Friend at London; Written by an Eminent Person Residing at the Great Tzar's Court at Mosco for the Space of Nine Years.* London: John Winter, 1671.

Cox, Gary. "Fairy-Tale Plots and Contemporary Heroes in Early Russian Prose Fiction." *Slavic Review* 39, no. 1 (March 1980): 85–96.

Cross, Anthony G. "The British in Catherine's Russia: A Preliminary Survey." In Garrard, *Eighteenth Century,* 232–63.

———, ed. *Great Britain and Russia in the Eighteenth Century: Contacts and Comparisons.* Newtonville, MA: Oriental Research Partners, 1979.

———, ed. *Russia and the West in the Eighteenth Century.* Newtonville, MA: Oriental Research Partners, 1983.

———, ed. *Russia under Western Eyes, 1517–1825.* New York: St. Martin's Press, 1971.

———, ed. *Russian Literature in the Age of Catherine the Great.* Oxford: Willem A. Meeuws, 1976.

Culler, Jonathan. "Literary Competence." In *Reader-Response Criticism: From Formalism to Post-Structuralism,* ed. Jane P. Tompkins, 101–17. Baltimore, MD: Johns Hopkins Univ. Press, 1980.

Dane, Joseph A. "Parody and Satire: A Theoretical Model." *Genre* 13 (1980): 145–59.

Dukes, Paul. "The Russian Enlightenment." In *The Enlightenment in National Context,* ed. Roy Porter and MikuláS Teich, 176–91. Cambridge: Cambridge Univ. Press, 1981.

Fanger, Donald. *The Creation of Nikolai Gogol.* Cambridge: Harvard Univ. Press, 1979.

———. *Dostoevsky and Romantic Realism.* Cambridge: Harvard Univ. Press, 1965.

Frank, Joseph. *Dostoevsky: The Seeds of Revolt (1821–1849).* Princeton, NJ: Princeton Univ. Press, 1976.

Freeborn, Richard. *The Rise of the Russian Novel.* Cambridge: Cambridge Univ. Press, 1973.

Fridlender, G. M., ed. *Istoriia russkogo romana.* Vol. 1. Moscow: Akademiia nauk SSSR, 1962.

Garrard, J. G. *Mixail Čulkov: An Introduction to His Prose and Verse.* The Hague: Mouton, 1970.

———. "Narrative Technique in Chulkov's *Prigozhaia povarikha.*" *Slavic Review* 27, no. 4 (December 1968): 554–63.

———. "The Portrayal of Reality in the Prose Fiction of M. D. Chulkov." *Slavonic and East European Review* 48, no. 110 (January 1970): 16–26.

———, ed. *The Eighteenth Century in Russia.* London: Oxford Univ. Press, 1973.

Gippius, V. V. *Gogol.* Ed. and trans. Robert A. Maguire. Ann Arbor, MI: Ardis, 1981.

Goodliffe, J. D. "Some Comments on Narrative Prose Fiction in Eighteenth-Century Russian Literature with Special Reference to Chulkov." *Melbourne Slavonic Studies,* nos. 5–6 (1971): 124–36.

Grossman, L. *Dostoevskii.* Moscow: Molodaia gvardiia, 1962.

Guberti, N. V. *Materialy dlia russkoi bibliografii. Khronologicheskoe obozrenie redkikh i zamechatel'nikh knig XVIII stoletiia napechatannykh v Rossii grazhdanskim shriftom, 1725–1800.* Moscow: Universitetskaia tipografiia, 1878–1891; Leipzig: Zentralantiquariat der Deutschen Demokratischen Republik, 1980.

Gukovskii, G. A. "Emin i Sumarokov." *XVIII vek* 2 (1940): 77–94.

———. *Russkaia literatura XVIII veka.* Moscow: Gosudarstvennoe uchebno-pedagogicheskoe izdatel'stvo, 1939; Ann Arbor, MI: University Microfilms, 1966.

Hammarberg, Gitta. *From the Idyll to the Novel: Karamzin's Sentimentalist Prose.* Cambridge: Cambridge Univ. Press, 1991.

Harden, Evelyn. "Introduction." In *"The Double": Two Versions,* by Fyodor Dostoevsky, trans. Evelyn Harden, ix–xxxvi. Ann Arbor, MI: Ardis, 1985.

Hardwick, Charles. *A History of the Christian Church.* London: Macmillan, 1872.

Highet, Gilbert. *The Anatomy of Satire.* Princeton, NJ: Princeton Univ. Press, 1962.

Hodgson, Peter. *From Gogol to Dostoevsky.* Munich: Wilhelm Fink Verlag, 1976.

———. "Viktor Shklovskii and the Formalist Legacy: Imitation/Stylization in Narrative Fiction." In *Russian Formalism: A Retrospective Glance. A Festschrift in Honor of Victor Erlich,* ed. Robert Louis Jackson and Stephen Rudy, 195–212. New Haven, CT: Yale Center for International and Area Studies, 1985.

Hutcheon, Linda. *Narcissistic Narrative: The Metafictional Paradox.* Waterloo, Canada: Wilfrid Laurier Univ. Press, 1980.

———. *A Theory of Parody: The Teachings of Twentieth-Century Art Forms.* New York: Methuen, 1985.

Jackson, Robert Louis, and Stephen Rudy, eds. *Russian Formalism: A Retrospective Glance. A Festschrift in Honor of Victor Erlich.* New Haven, CT: Yale Center for International and Area Studies, 1985.

Kukushkina, E. D. "Perevodnaia novella v rukopis'nykh sbornikakh XVIII v." In vol. 14 of *Russkaia literatura XVIII veka-nachala XIX veka v obshchestvenno-kul'turnom kontekste,* ed. A. M. Panchenko, 180–92. Leningrad: Nauka, 1983.

Kuznetsov, Evgenii. *Iz proshlogo russkoi èstrady: Istoricheskie ocherki.* Moscow: Iskusstvo, 1958.

———. *Russkie narodnye gulian'ia.* Leningrad: Iskusstvo, 1948.

LeBlanc, Ronald D. *The Russianization of Gil Blas: A Study in Literary Appropriation.* Columbus, OH: Slavica, 1986.

Lentin, A. *Russia in the Eighteenth Century.* New York: Barnes and Noble, 1973.

Levin, Iu. D. *Vospriiatie angliiskoi literatury v Rossii.* Leningrad: Nauka, 1990.

Levitsky, Alexander. "Mikhail Chulkov's *The Comely Cook:* The Symmetry of a Hoax." *Russian Literature Triquarterly* 2, no. 21 (1988): 97–115.

Likhachev, D. S. "Predposylki vozniknoveniia zhanra romana v russkoi literature." In Fridlender, 26–39.

Lincoln, W. Bruce. "Western Culture Comes to Russia." *History Today* 20, no. 10 (1970): 677–85.

Lojkine, A. K. "Molière in Russia in the XVIII Century." *AUMLA (Australasian Universities Modern Language Association)* 39 (1973): 85–93.

Lotman, Iurii, and Boris A. Uspenskii. "Binary Models in the Dynamics of Russian Culture (to the End of the Eighteenth Century)." In *The Semiotics of Russian Cultural History,* by Iurii Lotman, Lidia Ia. Ginsburg, and Boris A. Uspenskii. Ed. Alexander D. Nakhimovsky and Alice Stone Nakhimovsky, 30–66. Ithaca, NY: Cornell Univ. Press, 1985.

———. "K semioticheskoi tipologii russkoi kul'tury." In *Khudozhestvennaia kul'tura XVIII veka: Materialy nauchnoi konferentsii, 1973*, ed. I. E. Danilova, 259–82. Moscow: Sovetskii Khudozhnik, 1974.

Madariaga, Isabel de. "Catherine and the *Philosophes*." In Cross, *Russia and the West*, 30–52.

Marker, Gary. *Publishing, Printing, and the Origins of Intellectual Life in Russia, 1700–1800*. Princeton: Princeton Univ. Press, 1985.

Markiewicz, Henryk. "On the Definitions of Literary Parody." In vol. 2 of *To Honor Roman Jakobson*, 1264–72. The Hague: Mouton, 1967.

Martynov, I. F. "English Literature and Eighteenth-Century Russian Reviewers." *Oxford Slavonic Papers*, n.s., 4 (1971): 30–42.

Miege, Guy. *A Relation of Three Embassies from His Sacred Majestie Charles II to the Great Duke of Muscovie, the King of Sweden, and the King of Denmark . . . in the Years 1663 and 1664*. London: John Starkey, 1669.

Mochulsky, Konstantin. *Dostoevsky: His Life and Work*, trans. Michael A. Minihan. Princeton, NJ: Princeton Univ. Press, 1973.

Moiseeva, G. N. "Mesto povestei pervoi treti XVIII veka v russkoi literature." In *Russkie povesti pervoi treti XVIII veka*, 160–88. Moscow: Nauka, 1965.

Moiseeva, G. N., and I. Z. Serman. "Zarozhdenie romana v russkoi literature XVIII veka." In Fridlender, 40–65.

Nechaeva, V. S. *Rannii Dostoevskii*. Moscow: Nauka, 1979.

Neuhäuser, Rudolf. *Das Frühwerk Dostojewskis: Literarische Tradition und gesellschaftlicher Anspruch*. Heidelberg, Germany: Carl Winter, 1979.

Novikov, Nikolai Ivanovich. "On Man's High Estate." In Raeff, *Russian Intellectual History*, 62–67.

Oinas, Felix J. "The Transformation of Folklore into Literature." In vol. 2 of *American Contributions to the Eighth International Congress of Slavists*, ed. Victor Terras, 570–604. Columbus, OH: Slavica, 1978.

Onasch, Konrad. *Dostojewski als Verführer: Christentum und Kunst in der Dichtung Dostojewskis, ein Versuch*. Zürich: EVZ-Verlag, 1961.

Ong, Walter J. "The Writer's Audience Is Always a Fiction." *PMLA* 90, no.1 (January 1975): 9–21.

Oustinov, Pierre C. "Notes on Diderot's Fortunes in Russia." *Diderot Studies* 1 (1949): 121–42.

Ovsianikov, Iurii. *Lubok. Russkie narodnye kartinki XVII–XVIII vekov*. Moscow: Sovetskii khudozhnik, n.d.

Papmehl, K. A. "The Quest for the Nation's Cultural Roots in Russian Historiography before Karamzin." In Bartlett, Cross, and Rasmussen, 22–35.

Prince, Gerald. "Notes on the Text as Reader." In Suleiman and Crosman, 225–40.

Raeff, Marc. "The Enlightenment in Russia and Russian Thought in the Enlightenment." In Garrard, *The Eighteenth Century in Russia*, 25–47.

———, ed. *Russian Intellectual History: An Anthology*. New York: Harcourt, Brace and World, 1966.

Reyfman, Irina. *Vasilii Trediakovsky: The Fool of the 'New' Russian Literature*. Stanford, CA: Stanford Univ. Press, 1990.

Rice, James L. "The Memoirs of A. T. Bolotov and Russian Literary History." In Cross, *Russian Literature*, 17–43.

Richardson, William. "The Slavery of the Russian Peasants." In Cross, *Russia under Western Eyes*, 208–11.

Rogger, Hans. *National Consciousness in Eighteenth-Century Russia*. Cambridge: Harvard Univ. Press, 1960.

Rovinskii, D. *Russkie narodnye kartinki.* Vol. 5. St. Petersburg: Akademiia nauk, 1881.

Schaarschmidt, Gunter. "The Lubok Novels: Russia's Immortal Best Sellers." *Canadian Review of Comparative Literature* 9, no. 3 (September 1982): 424–36.

Schmid, Wolf. "Die Interferenz von Erzählertext und Personentext als Faktor ästhetischer Wirksamkeit in Dostojewskis *Doppelgänger.*" *Russian Literature* 4 (1973): 100–13.

Scholes, Robert. "Metafiction." *Iowa Review* 1 (1970): 100–115.

Schor, Naomi. "Fiction as Interpretation, Interpretation as Fiction." In Suleiman and Crosman, 165–82.

Segel, Harold B. "Classicism and Classical Antiquity in Eighteenth- and Early-Nineteenth-Century Russian Literature." In Garrard, *The Eighteenth Century in Russia,* 48–71.

———. *The Literature of Eighteenth-Century Russia.* 2 vols. New York: Dutton, 1967.

Serman, I. Z. "Rossiia i zapad." In Cross, *Russia and the West,* 53–67.

———. "Stanovlenie i razvitie romana v russkoi literature serediny XVIII veka." In *Iz istorii russkikh literaturnykh otnoshenii XVIII–XX vekov,* ed. S. V. Kastorskii, 82–95. Moscow: Akademiia nauk, institut russkoi literatury, 1959.

Shapiro, Gavriel. *Nikolai Gogol and the Baroque Cultural Heritage.* University Park, PA: Pennsylvania State Univ. Press, 1993.

Shcherbatov, Mikhail M. "Petition of the City of Moscow on Being Relegated to Oblivion." In Raeff, *Russian Intellectual History,* 50–55.

Shklovskii, Viktor. *Chulkov i Levshin.* Leningrad: Izdatel'stvo pisatelei, 1933.

———. "Dvoiniki i o 'Dvoinike.'" In *Za i protiv: zametki o Dostoevskom,* 50–63. Moscow: Sovetskii pisatel', 1957.

———. *Matvei Komarov: zhitel' goroda Moskvy.* Leningrad: Priboi, 1929.

Shoberl, Frederic. *Russia: Being a Description of the Character, Manners, Customs, Dress, Diversions, and Other Peculiarities of the Different Nations Inhabiting the Russian Empire.* Vols. 19–22 of *The World in Miniature.* 39 vols. London: Ackermann, 1822.

Shreder, Kh. "Laroshfuko v Rossii." Trans. R. Iu. Danilevskii. In vol. 10 of *Russkaia literatura XVIII veka i ee mezhdunarodnye sviazi,* ed. I. Z. Serman, 184–89. Leningrad: Nauka, 1975.

Simmons, Ernest J. *English Literature and Culture in Russia (1553–1840).* Harvard Studies in Comparative Literature 12. Cambridge: Harvard Univ. Press, 1935.

Sipovskii, V. V. *Ocherki iz istorii russkogo romana.* Vol. 1. St. Petersburg: Trud, 1909–1910.

Sokolov, Iu. "Lubochnaia literatura (russkaia)." In vol. 6 of *Literaturnaia èntsiklopediia,* 595–606. Moscow: Sovetskaia èntsiklopediia, 1932.

Stepanov, V. P. "Chulkov i 'fol'klornoe' napravlenie v literature." In *Russkaia literatura i fol'klor (XI–XVIII vv),* ed. V. G. Bazanov, 226–47. Leningrad: Nauka, 1970.

Suleiman, Susan R., and Inge Crosman, eds. *The Reader in the Text: Essays on Audience and Interpretation.* Princeton, NJ: Princeton Univ. Press, 1980.

Sytova, Alla, ed. *The Lubok: Russian Folk Pictures.* Leningrad: Aurora, 1984.

Terras, Victor. *The Young Dostoevsky (1846–1849).* The Hague: Mouton, 1969.

Titunik, I. R. "Fedor Èmin's *Pis'ma Èrnesta i Doravry* and Jean-Jacques Rousseau's *Julie, ou La Nouvelle Héloïse.*" *Russian Literature* 34 (1993): 333–50.

————. "Matvei Komarov's *Van'ka Kain* and Eighteenth-Century Russian Prose Fiction." *Slavic and East European Journal* 18, no. 4 (1974): 341–56.

————. "Mikhail Chulkov's 'Double-Talk' Narrative: *(Skazka o rozhdenii taftianoi mushki) (The Tale of the Origin of the Taffeta Beauty Patch)*." *Canadian-American Slavic Studies* 9, no. 1 (spring 1975): 30–42.

Todorov, Tzvetan. *Mikhail Bakhtin: The Dialogical Principle*. Trans. Wlad Godzich. Theory and History of Literature, vol. 13. Minneapolis: Univ. of Minnesota Press, 1984.

————. "Reading as Construction." In Suleiman and Crosman, 67–82.

Trubetskoi, N. S. "Rannii Dostoevskii." *Novyi zhurnal* 61 (1960): 124–46.

Tynianov, Iurii. "Dostoevskii and Gogol: Toward a Theory of Parody [Dostoevskii i Gogol' (k teorii parodii)]." In *Arkhaisty i novatory*, 412–55. Leningrad: Priboi, 1929; Ann Arbor, MI: University Microfilms, 1962.

————. "On Literary Evolution [O literaturnoi èvoliutsii]." In *Arkhaisty i novatory*, 30–47. Leningrad: Priboi, 1929; Ann Arbor, MI: University Microfilms, 1962.

————. "On Parody [O parodii]." In *Poètika. Istoriia literatury. Kino*, 284–309. Moscow: Nauka, 1977.

Watt, Ian. *The Rise of the Novel*. Berkeley: Univ. of California Press, 1957.

Wellek, René. "Bakhtin's View of Dostoevsky: 'Polyphony' and 'Carnivalesque.'" In *Russian Formalism*, ed. Jackson and Rudy, 231–41.

Wilson, Arthur. "Diderot in Russia, 1773–1774." In *The Eighteenth Century in Russia*, J. G. ed. Garrard, 166–97. London: Oxford Univ. Press, 1973. Citations used by permission of Oxford University Press.

Zapadov, A. V. "Zhurnal M. D. Chulkova 'I to i s'o' i ego literaturnoe okruzhenie." *XVIII vek* 2 (1940): 95–141.

INDEX

Academy of Sciences, 54, 57, 57–58, 60
Addison, Joseph, 21
Adversative style, in *The Double*, 182, 183; in "The Overcoat," 196–97; in stylization, 177, 178
Aelianus, Claudius, 13
Aksakov, K. S., 229n.6
Aksakov, Sergei, 191
Amusing Philosopher, The (Zabavnyi filosof), 21
Andersen, Hans Christian, 48
Anglomania: in eighteenth-century Russia, 4–5, 20–21, 214n.16
Authorial surrogates: in Chulkov, 91–92; in Emin, 86, 86–88, 89–91, 191, 223nn.1–2. *See also Inconstant Fate*
Authority, subversion of: in Chulkov, 93, 108, 117; in Komarov, 117, 118–20, 146, 153–54
Authority, voice of: in Chulkov, 88–89; in Emin, 86–88, 100, 102, 108, 113–17, 223n.2
Autobiography: *Comely Cook* as, 62, 188, 212n.4; *Inconstant Fate* as, 54; *Moll Flanders* as, 62, 189, 212n.4; parody of, in Chulkov, 92; parody

of, in *The Double*, 185; *Vanka Kain* as, 12, 32, 48, 63, 232n.2

Bakhtin, Mikhail: on authoritarian discourse, 32; on carnival, 6, 29, 30–31, 47, 140, 223n.7; carnival, theory of, 34, 36, 162, 215n.2, 219n.34, 228n.2; on cult of folk humor, 6, 215n.1; "Discourse in the Novel," 29, 30; discourse typology of, 165–66, 229n.8; and Dostoevskii, 29, 30, 161, 176; and Gogol´, 29; on imitation, 167–68; and novel, theory of, 29–30, 65; and parody, theory of, 165–67, 169, 176; *Problems of Dostoevsky's Poetics*, 29, 165; on Rabelais, 6, 29, 94; on satire, 223n.7; and stylization, theory of, 165–67, 167
Balagany, 33–34, 35, 36
Balagur: in *The Mocker*, 141
Barclay, John: *Argenis*, 60, 64
Barkov, Ivan, 215n.4
Bavardage de la fièvre, 138, 139, 224n.10
Belinskii, Vissarion: and critique of *The Double*, 174, 176, 195, 231n.6; on imitation of Western literature, 11;

on literature as mirror of reality, 195

Belles lettres, 23, 42–43, 56, 57, 168, 192, 217n.21. *See also Lubok*

Berynda, Pamva, 39

Bogatyri: as heroes in *Nevidimka,* 134, 137

Bogdanovich, Petr, 58, 220n.45

Boileau, Nicolas: *L'Art poétique,* 4, 18

Bolotov, A. T., 19

Book market: influence of, on publishing, 58

Books, value of, 217n.20

Booksellers, eighteenth-century Russian, 23, 54

"Bova Korolevich": and belles lettres, 56, 217n.21; and Emin, 56; folktale plot of, 218n.28; and French novels, 64–65; and *lubok,* 39, 40, 41, 217n.18

Burlesque, 51

Butkov, Jakov: discourse in, 161; as model for Dostoevskii's Goliadkin, 230n.5; and reluctant naturalism, 228n.1; stylization in works of, 233n.6; and the subculture, 194–95

Carnival, Russian: admission price of, 36; alcohol and, 131, 216nn.11–12; attendance at, 34; and Bacchus, 36; *balagany,* 33, 33–34, 35, 36; behavior at, 30–31; carousels at, 35, 216n.10; censorship of, 38, 216n.15; in Chulkov, 51–52, 219n.34; comic inversions at, 35, 36, 65, 117, 141, 154, 162; commedia dell'arte and, 34, 36, 161; cycles of, 35, 36; dancing at, 35, 36, 37, 216n.13; in Emin, 65; eyewitness accounts of, 33, 36, 37; Ferris wheels at, 33, 36, 51, 216n.6; foreign elements of, 34–35; grotesquerie of, 34–35, 35–36, 36–37; Harlequin and, 34–35; history of, 32–33, 38, 120; humor of, 30, 216n.8; ice mountains at, 17, 33, 36, 216n.9; identity, change of, at, 34, 146; *karusel´nyi ded* and, 35, 36, 38, 46, 192, 216n.7; in Komarov, 107, 118, 119, 120; *kulach-*

nyi boi and, 52, 215n.4; liberating forces of, 6, 30, 36, 37, 119, 129, 146; *pribautki* at, 107, 118; *raeshniki* at, 38, 216n.8; religion and, 38, 133, 225n.3; satire and, 34, 35; *saturnalia* and, 161; sensuality of, 35, 37, 129; *skomorokhi* and, 32, 38; tricks at, 36

Carnivalesque mentality: alcohol and, 121; antiauthoritarian discourse of, 67, 91, 106; comic inversions and, 38–39, 107, 142, 156–57; and Dostoevskii, 161–62; devices of, 30, 161; and eighteenth-century Russian novel, 5, 31–32, 65; and the Enlightenment, 187; and eroticism, 131, 131–33; in *Gargantua and Pantagruel,* 31; humor of, 223n.7; in Komarov, 29, 31, 107–8, 117, 119–20, 133, 142, 225n.3; liberating forces of, 38–39, 108; and Masonry, 61, 220n.48; and masquerade, 146–49; merchantry as target of, 120–22, 130–31, 225n.6; religion as target of, 118, 121–22; rhetoric of, 103–4, 112, 132; servant as hero in, 120–21, 121, 122, 149; sex in, 78, 119, 122, 128–31, 133, 148–49; stylization and, 162, 165, 173, 177, 179, 183, 187, 189. *See also* Chulkov; Folklore

Catherine the Great: *All Sorts and Sundries (Vsiakaia vsiachina),* 15–16, 21; and Diderot, 18, 89, 213nn.11–12, 213n.13; and Emin, 52, 219n.38; empire of, 3–4, 17, 213nn.7, 9, 10; and Free Press Law of 1783, 54, 58; literature in reign of, 19, 192–93; publishing in reign of, 54, 57; and The Society for Translating Books, 58; and the West, 4, 15–16, 28

Censorship: and carnival, 38, 216n.15; of *lubok,* 43

Cervantes Saavedra, Miguel de: Bakhtin and, 29, 30; *Don Quixote,* 60, 64, 220n.49

Characters in the eighteenth-century Russian novel, 134, 191; carnivalesque view of, 140; hyperbole and, 134, 135–36, 227n.1; mythology and, 135; neoclassical, 124;

religion and, 135; tears and, 134; and self-debasement, theme of, 150–53, 156, 228n.7; and social hierarchies, 113, 115, 116, 224n.1, 225n.2. *See also* Kain, Vanka; Martona; Neokh

Chulkov, Mikhail: authoritative voice in, 88–89; authority, subversion of, in, 93, 108, 117; biography of, 5, 15, 50, 50–51, 54, 218n.32; carnival in, 51–52, 219n.34; carnivalesque mentality in, 29, 32, 51, 76, 106, 120–22; characters in, 80, 104, 137, 142, 193 (*see also* Martona; Neokh); critics and, 3; and Dostoevskii, 29, 30, 161, 174; and Emin, 193, 219n.38; eroticism in, 105, 124, 130, 131–33, 192, 226n.12, 227nn.15–16; folklore in, 16, 47, 52, 105–7; and Gogol', 29, 161, 194; humor, self-inclusive, in, 51, 66, 78, 154, 154–56; as journalist, 50; as literary jester, 25–26, 78, 83, 94, 154, 193; literary persona of, 50, 54, 71, 78, 93–94, 94–95; and Lomonosov, 50, 220n.49; metaliterary commentary in, 77–78, 109–10, 110, 154–55, 187; metaphor in, 104, 104–5, 228n.4; money, motif of, in, 50–51, 105, 124, 141–42, 144, 156–57; monologue, parody of, in 108–11, 111–12; and mythology, Slavic, 41–42, 50–51, 84, 122, 217n.22; narrators in, 88–89, 91–93, 109 (*see also* Martona); and neoclassicism, relationship to, 49–50, 51; and nineteenth-century Russian prose fiction, 4, 6, 7; and the novel, rise of, 7–8, 30, 192; as parodist, 5, 17, 66–67, 95, 192; as poet, 50; and Rabelais, 66, 94, 95, 212n.6, 219n.34; readers and fiction of, 78, 80, 105; realism in, 78, 82–83, 190, 192, 222nn.13, 15; satire in, 51, 88–89, 95, 217n.22, 223n.3; sex in, 122, 128–31, 131–33, 141–42, 143, 149, 193 (*see also* Comely Cook, The; Mocker, The); and Sterne, 79–80, 192–93, 221n.8; and the subculture, 5, 30, 66; and Western literature, influence of, 4, 13, 21, 82, 212nn.4–5. Works: *Achilles, The Adventures of (Pokhozhdenie Akhillesovo pod imenem Pirry do troianskoi osady)*, 146; "A Bitter Lot" ("Gor'kaia uchast'"), 13; *Both This and That (I to i sio)*, 50, 50–51, 66; *Call It What You Will (Kak khochesh' nazovi)*, 212n.4; *A Short Mythological Lexicon (Kratkii mifologicheskii leksikon)*, 50–51, 217n.22; *The Trinket Dealer of Parnassus (Parnasskii shchepetil'nik)*, 66; "Verses on a Ferris Wheel" ("Stikhi na kacheli"), 51–52, 212n.4, 221n.5; "Verses on Semik," 219n.34. *See also Comely Cook, The; Mocker, The; Tale of the Taffeta Beauty Patch, The*

Cleland, John: *Fanny Hill*, 227n.3

Comely Cook, The (Prigozhaia povarikha): authorial surrogates in, 91–92; as autobiography, 62, 188, 212n.4; comic inversions in, 76, 80, 92, 106; critics and, 82–83, 212n.2; cross-dressing in, 76–77, 109; deception in, 109, 140, 147–48, 148, 222n.10, 227n.4; and *The Double*, 222n.10; eroticism in, 105, 130, 131–32, 226n.12; folklore in 47, 105, 106; humor, self-deprecating, in, 66, 76, 94–95, 155–56, 222n.9; love, parody of, in, 109, 110–11, 143, 156; Lomonosov in, 83; metaphor in, 228n.4; and *Moll Flanders*, 24–28, 215n.24; money, motif of, in, 105, 141–42, 144, 156–57; morality, parody of, in, 111–12; mythology, travesty of, in 142, 144, 155, 228n.4; narrator of, 192 (*see also* Martona); and official literary culture, 28, 157; popularity of, 212n.3; reader, role of, in, 25–26, 106; realism in, 82–83, 190, 222nn.13, 15; satire in, 88–89; sex in, 26–28, 88, 91–92, 95, 104, 105, 105–6, 129, 130, 131–32, 155, 157; unfinished nature of, 79, 80; virtue, parody of, in, 109. *See also* Martona

Comic inversions: in *The Comely Cook*,

76, 80, 92; in *Vanka Kain*, 107, 142.
See also Carnival; Carnivalesque
mentality
Commedia dell'arte, 34, 36, 161
Corneille, Pierre, 4, 57
Cross-dressing: at carnival, 34; in *The
Comely Cook*, 76–77, 109; in *Nev-
idimka*, 147; and self-debasement,
151
Custine, Marquis de, 17

Dance: at the carnival, 35, 36, 37,
216n.13; and the carnivalesque, 78,
145, 219n.34; in Chulkov, 78,
219n.34
Dashkova, Catherine, 16
Decameron, 45
Deceit (deception): as carnivalesque
virtue, 93, 146–47, 155; in
Chulkov, 120–22, 146, 147, 149; in
Emin, 114, 144–46; in Komarov,
73, 120–21, 142, 146, 147; and love,
131, 155; and the pathetic monologue, 110; and religion, 145–46;
and sex, 129, 132; tragic consequences of, 144–46, 146, 150–51.
See also Comely Cook, The
Deeds of the Romans (Rimskie deianiia),
44, 45
Defoe, Daniel: *The Fortunate Mistress*,
215n.24; *Jonathan Wild*, 189, 232n.2;
publication of, in Russia, 4, 22;
Robinson Crusoe, 44, 220n.43. See
also Moll Flanders
Delirium: in *The Double*, 178, 180,
231n.10
"Descent of the Virgin into Hell, The"
("Khozhdenie Bogoroditsy po
mukam"), 222n.16
Destouches, Philippe: *Dissipateur*, 46
Dickens, Charles, 30
Diderot, Denis: as Anglophile, 214n.16;
and critique of Russian society, 17,
18; and Catherine the Great, 18,
89, 213nn.11–13
Discourse typology, 167–73; Bakhtin's,
165–66, 229n.8
Dobroliubov, Nikolai, 176
Documentary: in Emin, 188, 191; in
Vanka Kain, 72–73, 189, 232n.2

Dostoevskii, F. M., 7, 161, 166; and the
carnivalesque, 161–62; and
Gogol´, relationship to, 162–63,
165, 176; and readers of the 1840s,
169, 174 (see also Double, The:
reader's predicament in); and the
Russian novel, rise of, 6, 193; stylization in, 7, 172, 173, 174, 177–87,
195; and the subculture, 194–95;
Tynianov on, 162–65. Works: *The
Brothers Karamazov (Brat´ia Kara-
mazovy)*, 228n.2; "The Landlady"
("Khoziaika"), 162, 228n.3; *The
Village of Stepanchikovo (Selo Stepanchikovo)*, 163, 229n.4. See also
Double, The; Poor Folk
Double, The, 4, 174, 186; adversative
style of, 182, 183; autobiography
in, 185; critical views of, 174,
176–77, 181, 195, 230nn.1, 4,
231n.6; delirium, hero's, in, 178,
180, 231n.10; disappearing text in,
183–84, 195; drunkenness in, 180,
231n.10; "fading into nothing,"
179, 231n.9; and foreign literature,
186–87, 187; and Gogol´, 175, 176;
grotesquerie in, 175; intertexts of,
184, 231nn.7, 14; letters, disappearing, in, 178, 180, 181; litera-
ture-life nexus in, 184, 185, 186–87;
and literature of the 1840s, 175,
185, 187; medicine, motif of, in,
179, 182; metaliterary commentary
in, 180, 182, 186–87; and mirror of
reality, literature as, 176, 181,
230n.5, 6; misinformation in, 180,
231n.11; mock reader, Goliadkin
as, in, 169, 184–87; narrator of, 176,
178, 179, 184–85; and Natural
School, challenges to, 174–75,
176–77; parodic discourse in, 166,
175–76; Petersburg as setting of,
174, 177, 179, 186, 230n.2, 231n.11;
poison, motif of, in, 222n.10; "poor
clerk" motif in, 175–76, 177, 183,
186, 187, 195; reader's predicament in, 174–75, 177, 179, 183–86,
187; realism in, 177, 182, 185, 187;
revision of, 181–83; on Russian
novel, rise of, 186; satire in, 183;

self-effacing movement in, 178–79; sentimental discourse in, 185, 186–87, 187, 195; servant, role of, in, 178, 180; stereotypes in, 175, 176, 186; stylization in, 7, 172, 173, 174, 177–87, 195; tears in, 176, 185, 186; time, problem of, in, 177–78, 182, 183, 231nn.12–13; unreliable text in, 178, 180–81, 181, 184–85

Double-voiced discourse: definition of, 165; parody as, 165–66; stylization as 165–67, 171; types of, 165–66

Eastern tale, 21, 56, 189

Education, theme of, 5, 32; dangers of improper, 223n.5, 232n.2; in Emin, 90, 91, 115

1840s, Russian literature of, 161, 175, 185, 187, 194, 195, 232n.14, 233n.6; fantasy in, 230n.2; foreign literature, influence of, on, 187; and novel, rise of, 6–7; readers of, 168–69, 174; stereotypes in, 195; and stylization, 194–95, 195; the vaudeville and, 233n.6

Elizabeth I, 213nn.7, 9; carnival in reign of, 36–37; imitation of foreign models in reign of, 4; *lubok* in reign of, 43; novel in reign of, 44

Emin, Fedor: biography of, 52, 52–54, 75; carnival in, 65; and Catherine the Great, 52, 219n.38; characters in, 103, 113, 128, 136, 191; critics and, 3; documentary style of, 188, 191; and earlier Russian literature, 56; and the Eastern tale, 189; and eighteenth-century Russian novel, development of, 7–8, 188, 189; emotional outbursts in, 138, 139; endings in, 114; and Enlightenment philosophy, 52, 62, 191; eroticism in, 124–26, 225n.8, 227n.14; feminism in, 128; femmes fatales in, 134, 138–39, 146; folklore in, 65; and foreign literature, appropriation of, 4, 6–7, 12, 13, 15, 21, 52, 189; as historical figure, 75–76; historicity in, 71–72, 73–75, 77, 80, 190–91; and legitimizing the novel, 66; literary persona of,

48, 53–54; maxims in, 88, 97, 97–98, 105, 191; metaphor in, 95–96, 96–97, 100, 135–36, 191–92, 224n.9, 227n.14; monologue in, 62, 66, 98–103, 108, 111, 112, 139, 224nn.11–13; narrators in, 75, 87–88, 190–91, 191, 221n.4; and nineteenth-century Russian literature, 4, 188, 191, 192; and official literary aesthetic, 62; readers, limiting interpretive options of, in, 86, 87, 88, 90, 91, 95, 96, 101, 145–46, 192; readers, morality of, in, 104, 145; and the reading public, 56, 100; realism in, 190–91; religion in, 99, 113, 113–14; rhetoric of, 95–103, 191–92; sentimentalism in, 52, 225n.2; sex in, 100, 105, 111, 122–28, 129, 131, 149, 153, 225n.7, 228n.6; society, hierarchies of, in, 102–3, 113, 115, 128, 224n.1, 225n.2; subculture, relationship to, 52, 62; and Sumarokov, 62, 189; travelogue in, 75; and Western thinkers, 75, 87, 223n.2. Works: *A Brief Description of the Ottoman Porte (Kratkoe opisanie drevneishego i noveishego sostoianiia Ottomanskoi Porty)*, 53; *Hell's Post (Adskaia pochta)*, 21, 62; *The Path to Salvation (Put' k spaseniiu)*, 53, 63. See also *Ernest and Doravra, The Letters of; Inconstant Fate; Kamber and Arisena; Lizark and Sarmanda; Marquis de Toledo, The; Tale of the Taffeta Beauty Patch, The; Themistocles*. See also Authority, voice of; Self-debasement; Selflessness; Tears

Emin, Nikolai: *Roza: A Half-True Story (Roza, poluspravedlivaia original'naia povest')*, 22

Encyclopédie, 57, 213n.11

English novel, the, 22–24, 215nn.23–24

Enlightenment, the: and carnivalesque mentality, 187; and eighteenth-century British journals, 21; and eighteenth-century Russian literature, 19, 134; in Emin, 52, 62, 191; Russians' reception of, 14–15, 15,

17–20, 21, 43–44, 57; values of, 31, 103, 133. *See also* Monarch, Image of the ideal; Russian novel, eighteenth-century

Epistle on Poetry (Epistol o stikhotvorstve), 20, 232n.1

Ernest and Doravra, The Letters of (Pis'ma Ernesta i Doravry): Emin on author's high calling, 62; authorial surrogates in, 78, 91, 223nn.1–2; *bavardage de la fièvre* in, 224n.10; didacticism of, 87; education, theme of, in, 91; as epistolary novel, 62–63; eroticism in, 225n.8; and *La Nouvelle Héloïse*, 12, 189, 225n.2; love in, 125–26, 224n.11; maxims in, 88; mock reader of, 91; mythology, classical, in, 226n.8; as parody, 221n.51, 225 n.2; and readers, limiting interpretive options of, 103, 223n.6; sex in, 132

Eroticism: in carnivalesque fiction, 131; in Chulkov, 105, 124, 130, 131–33, 192, 226n.12, 227nn.15–16; sterile depiction of, in Emin, 124–26, 225n.8, 227n. 14; in Komarov, 123–24, 131

"Ersh Ershovich," 40, 45

"Eruslan Lazarevich," 39, 217n.18

Facetiae, 44, 45, 218n.25

Fantasy: in the eighteenth-century Russian novel, 77, 82, 83, 84–85, 129, 222n.17; in Gogol', 194, 195, 230n.2

Fate: in the eighteenth-century Russian novel, 114, 150

Feminism, 128

Femme fatale: in carnivalesque fiction, 146–49; in Emin, 134, 138–39, 146

Fénelon, François: *Télémaque*, 60, 64

Ferris wheels, 33, 36, 51, 216n.6

Feuilleton, 194, 233n.6

Fielding, Henry: Bakhtin and, 29; novels of, 22, 44; publication of, in Russia, 4, 22, 56; and Smollett, 23, 24

Folk humor, cult of, 6, 7, 30, 31

Folklore: and "Bova Korolevich," 218n.28; carnivalesque spirit of,

43, 46–47, 47–48, 52, 67, 105–6; and eighteenth-century Russian novel, 47, 49; in Emin, 65; in *Milord George*, 48, 218n.29; in *Nevidimka*, 48, 83; and Russian national identity, 16; in *Vanka Kain*, 12, 16, 48, 97, 107–8, 218n.29; and "Vasilii Koriotskii," 218n.28

Fonvizin, Denis: *The Brigadier*, 17, 64; *The Minor (Nedorosl')*, 16

Free Press Law of 1783, 54, 58

Friendship, motif of: as defense against deceit, 145; parody of, in carnivalesque fiction, 142; rewarding, 137, 227n.2; and sentimentality, 136; as supreme male virtue, 102, 105, 136, 137

Garrard, J. G., 62, 66; on Chulkov's biography, 50, 218n.32; on Chulkov's polemic with Emin, 219n.38; on eighteenth-century Russian novel, 211n.2; on motif of money in Chulkov, 50–51; on narrators in *The Mocker*, 221n.51; on realism in *The Comely Cook*, 82; on satire in Chulkov, 212n.6, 215n.26, 223n.3; on sources of Chulkov's novels, 12–13, 212n.4, 215n.24, 222n.16

Gay, John: "The Fan," 13

Gender: and the parody of authoritative discourse, 92

Gibbon, Edward, 21

Goethe, Johann Wolfgang von, 56

Gogol', N. V.: characters in, 194; facetiae in, 193–94; fantasy in, 194; grotesquerie in, 161, 194; laughter in, 161; and *lubok*, 43, 192, 193–94, 217n.19; metaliterary commentary in, 194; on readers of the 1840s, 169; and the Russian novel, rise of, 6, 193; stylization in, 7, 195–96, 196–97; and the subculture, 193, 193–94, 194–95. Works: "The Carriage" ("Koliaska"), 194; *Dead Souls (Mertvye dushi)*, 3, 194, 211n.2, 228n.3; "Diary of a Madman" ("Zapiski sumasshedshego"), 195–96; *The Inspector General (Revizor)*, 194, 211n.2; *Marriage*

(*Zhenit'ba*), 194; "The Nose"
("Nos"), 194; *Selected Passages from
a Correspondence with Friends (Vy-
brannye mesta iz perepiski s
druz'iami)*, 229n.4; "The Tale of the
Two Ivans" ("Povest' o tom, kak
possorilsia Ivan Ivanovich s
Ivanom Nikiforovichem"), 194.
See also "Overcoat, The"
Goldsmith, Oliver, 22
Great Mirror, The (Velikoe zertsalo), 44, 45
Grebenka, Evgenii, 194–95
Grigorovich, Dmitrii, 176, 233n.6
Grotesquerie: in the carnival, 34–35,
35–36, 36–37; in Chulkov, 85; in
Dostoevskii, 175; in Gogol', 161,
194; in Komarov, 49; in literature
of the 1840s, 161; in *lubok,* 39

Harlequin, 34–35
Heroes, 123–24; in Chulkov, 104, 137,
193; and desire, 125, 135; hyperbole surrounding, 134; parody of,
140, 142; and rhetoric in Emin,
138, 212n.3; selflessness of, in
Emin, 103, 104, 115, 133, 138,
139–40, 193; sentimental, 138. *See
also* Neokh: as antihero
Heroines: in Chulkov, 80, 142, 193; and
desire, 125; as goddesses, 135,
135–36, 140; in official literature,
157; parody of, 140; rhetoric of,
212n.3; virtues of, in Emin, 104,
129, 130, 139–40, 144, 193. *See also*
Martona: as antiheroine
Heteroglossia: in the eighteenth-century Russian novel, 65–67, 226n.13
Historicity, 71; in Emin, 72, 73–75, 77,
80, 190–91, 221n.1; in Komarov,
73, 75–76, 81, 189; subversion of,
81, 222n.12
Hume, David, 21
Hyperbole: and Emin's heroines, 96;
and characterization, 134, 135–36,
227n.1; and official literary culture,
134–35; and self-debasement, 151

Ice mountains, 17, 33, 36, 61, 216n.9
Identity, change of, 140–41. *See also*
Cross-dressing

Image of author, 31, 63
Imitation: 168–69; motivation of,
167–68; readers and, 168–69; reading interludes and, 168; and Russian prose fiction of the 1840s,
168–69; structure of, 167, 167–68;
and stylization, 164, 166–67,
171–72, 174–77; of Western culture, 4–5, 8, 11–13, 60, 188–89
Inconstant Fate (Nepostoiannoe fortuna):
authorial surrogates in, 78, 91,
101, 102, 125; as autobiography,
54; characterization in, 135; critics
and, 212n.2; deception in, 145–46;
documentary form in, 191; as
Eastern tale, 56, 189; education,
ideal system of, in 90–91; Enlightenment theorizing in, 52, 62; historicity of, 72, 74–75, 221nn.1, 3;
love, depiction of, in, 124, 226n.12;
maxims in, 98; metaphor in, 96;
monologues, pathetic, in, 96; popularity of, 56, 190, 219n.39; rape,
theme of, in, 126–27, 226n.9; religion in, 98, 145–46; sex, depiction
of, in, 99–100, 104, 125, 153;
sources of, 12, 65; women in, 128,
145
Intelligentsia, Russian, 3–4, 15
Interpolated tales, 75–76, 82; and
theme of deception, 120–21, 145,
148–49
Interpretant: definition of, 184
Intertextuality; in *The Double,* 184,
231nn.7, 14; stylization and 165
Izmailov, Aleksandr: on eighteenth-
century Russian prose fiction, 190;
Evgenii, 190, 232n.4

Jokes: in Chulkov, 154; in Komarov,
117, 118
Journals, eighteenth-century British:
impact of, on eighteenth-century
Russian journals, 21–22, 214nn.18,
20; *The Spectator,* 21
Journals, eighteenth-century Russian:
*All Sorts and Sundries (Vsiakaia vsi-
achina)*, 15–16, 21; *Both This and
That (I to i sio)*, 50, 50–51, 66;
British writers in, 21–22; and the

Eastern tale, 21; and eighteenth-century British journals, 21–22; *Historical, Genealogical, and Geographical Notes (Istoricheskie, genealogicheskie i geograficheskie primechaniia v vedomostiakh),* 214n.18; *Idle Time Put to Use (Prazdnoe vremia v pol´zu upotreblennoe),* 66; *The Industrious Bee (Trudoliubivaia pchela),* 66; list of prominent, 214n.19; *Monthly Writings and News about Learned Affairs (Ezhemesiachnye sochineniia, k pol´ze i uveseleniiu sluzhashchie),* 21, 66; *The Painter (Zhivopisets),* 214n.16; selecting literature for, 23; *Society for Lovers of the Russian Word (Sobranie liubitelei rossiiskogo slova),* 49; *The Trinket Dealer of Parnassus (Parnasskii shchepetil´nik),* 66; *The Twaddler (Pustomelia),* 49; *Various Written Materials, (Raznye pis´mennye materii),* as sources of, 12, 42, 49

Kafka, Franz: *The Trial,* 184, 187
Kain, Vanka: and authority, subversion of, 117–19, 146, 153–54; autobiography of, 12, 32, 48, 63, 232n.2; carnivalesque behavior of, 107–8, 119, 120, 133, 142, 225n.3; deceit of, 73, 142; downfall of, 119–20, 225n.5; jokes of, 117, 118; as Komarov's subject, 72–73, 232n.2; and religion, mockery of, 121, 225n.3; and *slovo i delo Gosudarevo,* 118, 119–20
Kamber and Arisena (Liubovnyi vertograd, ili nepreoborimoe postoianstvo Kambera i Ariseny): deception in, 144–45; as Eastern tale, 189; femme fatale in, 134, 146; friendship, theme of, in, 136–37; rape, theme of, in, 226n.9; self-sacrifice of characters in, 152; sex in, 124, 125; tears, function of, in, 138, 139; as translation, 71–72; women in, 128
Kantemir, Antiokh, 18, 212n.1
Karamzin, Nikolai, 186; on books, love of, in Russia, 219nn.39–41, 220n.50; on Emin's biography, 219n.35; and *lubok,* 40, 42; as Mason, 21, 61; on *Milord George,* 221n.50; on the novel, 211n.2, 214n.22, 220n.50; "The Pantheon of Russian Writers" ("Panteon russkikh avtorov"), 219n.35; as pioneer of Russian prose fiction, 3; "Poor Liza" ("Bednaia Liza"), 22
Karusel´nyi ded, 35, 36, 38, 46, 192, 216n.7
Kheraskov, Mikhail: as Mason, 21, 61; and Moscow University Press, 57; novels of, 61, 220n.47
Khmelnitsky, N. I., 20
Kiprianov, V. A., 39
Kochanowski, Jan, 45
Kokorev, Ivan, 194–95
Komarov, Matvei: authority, subversion of, in, 117, 118–20, 146, 153–54; biography of, 5, 48, 49, 218n.31; carnival in, 118, 119, 120, 131, 219n.34; carnivalesque mentality in, 29, 31, 107–8, 117, 119–20, 133, 142, 225n.3; characters in, 113, 140 (*see also* Kain, Vanka); and critics, 3; and Dostoevskii, 29, 161, 174; endings in novels of, 114; eroticism in, 123–24, 131; fantasy in, 83; folklore in novels of, 12, 16, 48, 49, 83, 97, 107–8, 218n.29; foreign culture, relationship to, 4, 6–7, 12, 13, 21, 189; and Gogol´, 29, 161, 194; historicity and, 73, 75–76, 81; image of author in, 63; literary persona of, 13, 49, 63, 93; and Lomonosov's theory of three styles of the Russian language, 220n.49; and *lubok,* 40, 41, 49; narrators in novels of, 191; and neoclassicism, 49; and nineteenth-century Russian prose fiction, 6, 7, 188; and novel, Bakhtin's theory of, 30; as parodist, 5, 192; popularity of, 49, 212n.3; and Rabelais, 66; readers of, 55; religion in the novels of, 113, 121, 225n.3; and sentimentalism, 49; and subculture, relationship to, 5, 30, 66, 193; and *The Thousand and One Nights,* 12;

Tolstoi on, 43, 190, trickery in, 117–18, 120–21, 149. Works: *Ancient Letters of the Chinese Emperor to the Russian Sovereign (Starinnye pis´ma kitaiskogo imperatora k rossiiskomu gosudariu . . . .)*, 218n.31; *Thirteen Ancient Weddings (Opisanie trinattsati starinnykh svadeb . . . .)*, 218n.31. *See also* Milord George; Nevidimka; Vanka Kain; Various Written Materials

Kopeck papers *(gazety-kopeiki)*, 217n.23

Krylov, Ivan, 217n.19

Kulachnyi boi, 39, 52, 215n.4

Kurganov, Nikolai: *Pismovnik*, 47, 54, 232n.4; and popular culture, 16

La Rochefoucauld, François, 19–20, 21

Laughter: and truth, 192; as universal celebration, 154

Lermontov, Mikhail: and *lubok*, 192, 217n.19; and the Russian novel, rise of, 6, 193

Lesage, Alain René: Bakhtin and, 30; and eighteenth-century Russian prose fiction, 189; *Gil Blas*, 55, 62, 82, 212n.4

Lèse majesté, 225n.4. *See also* Slovo i delo Gosudarevo

Levitsky, Alexander, 78–79, 82–83, 222n.9

Levshin, Vasilii: and popular culture, 16, 40; *Russian Folk Tales (Russkie skazki)*, 232n.4

Liars: in carnivalesque fiction, 93, 155, 221n.5; Martona as, 76–77, 147–48; Neokh as, 121, 122, 141

Libertines, 123; in *The Marquis de Toledo*, 116, 126, 134

Library for Reading (Biblioteka dlia chteniia), 168, 231n.14

Literacy: in eighteenth-century Russia, 54; and *lubok*, 40

Literary appropriation, theory of, 44

Lizark and Sarmanda (Nagrazhdennaia postoiannost´, ili prikliucheniia Lizarka i Sarmandy): didacticism in, 88; foreign cultures in, 74; love in, 104–5, 152; monarch, ideal, in, 114–15; narrator in, 73, 104–5; religion in, 88

Locke, John, 21, 223nn.1–2

Lomonosov, M. V., 50, 83, 218n.30; as arbiter of literary taste, 15; grammar of, 54; "Introduction to the Use of Church Books in Russian" ("Predislovie o pol´ze knig tserkovnykh v rossiiskom iazyke"), 220n.49; and the novel, 60, 64–65; compared to Western thinkers, 213n.9

Lotman, Iurii, and Boris A. Uspenskii: binary model of Russian culture, 13–15; on imitative interpretation of Russian culture, 212n.2; on the "new" Russia, 212n.1

Love: carnivalesque depiction of, 111, 111–12, 131; and despair, 99, 134, 150; and the law, 127; and marriage, 127–28, 226n.11; pallid descriptions of, 123, 124–26, 226n.12; parody of, 109, 110–11, 143, 156; and religion in Emin, 99; and sex in Chulkov, 104–5, 132–33; and social hierarchies, 113, 116–17, 225n.2; and suicide, 114, 123, 136, 137, 147; and virtue in Emin, 88, 124, 138, 139–40, 152

Lubok: audience of, 40–41; and belles lettres, 39, 40, 42, 61, 189–90, 192, 217n.19; broadsides, 40, 43; and censorship, 43; demand for, 39, 40; derivation of word, 217n.16; distribution of, 41; eclecticism of, 39–40, 41, 45, 46–47, 217n.18; and the eighteenth-century Russian novel, 40, 41, 49, 59, 60; and farce, 39; and the folk tale, 43; foreign influences in, 39; and Gogol´, 43, 192, 193–94, 217n.19; grotesquerie of, 39; history of, 39; *kulachnyi boi* in, 39; lack of standards in, 41; and literacy, rise in, 40; and nineteenth-century Russian prose fiction, 194, 217n.19; price of, 217n.20; printing of, 39, 40; publishing of, 39, 40, 59, 217n.17; and Rabelais, 39; religious, 39; and satire, 39; Tolstoi and, 43, 190, and translated literature, 45

Lukin, Vladimir: as Mason, 61; on Russian reading public, 19

Lvov, Pavel: *A Russian Pamela (Russkaia Pamela ili istoriia Marii, dobrodetel′noi poselianki),* 22

Mably, Gabriel Bonnot de, 57

Macartney, Lord, 17

Maikov, Valerian, 176

Maikov, Vasilii: *Elisei (Elisei, ili razdrazhennyi Vakkh),* 215n.4, 217n.21; as Mason 61

Malherbe, François de, 19

Malinovskii, A. F., 19

Marivaux, Pierre Carlet de Chamblain, 189

Marker, Gary: on Academy of Sciences press, 58; on *lubochnaia literatura,* 59; on merchant publishers, 58; on publishing and censorship, 54

Marquis de Toledo, The (Gorestnaia liubov′ Markiza de Toledo): eroticism in, 124–25, 227n.14; familial hierarchies in, 115–16, 117; historicity in, 74; libertines in, 116, 126, 134; maxims in, 97; metaphor in, 100, 227n.14; rape, theme of, in, 126; sex in, 100

Marriage: and civic responsibility, 128; and love, 226n.11; and society, 127, 128; and violence, 128

Martona: as antiheroine, 106, 140, 141–42, 144, 153–54, 155, 157; as authorial surrogate, 91–92; as authoritative narrator, 88–89; as carnival comic, 76; as conventional heroine, 80; and Fanny Hill, 227n.3; and folklore, use of, 47, 67, 106; humor of, 155–56; as liar, 76–77, 147–48; and Moll Flanders, 24, 26–28; parodic roles of, 52, 76, 80, 111–12, 117, 128, 141–42; as promiscuous philosopher, 111–12; as prostitute, 141–42; as queen of the carnival, 52, 140; realism of, 82; as rogue, 80, 82; and sex, parodic attitude toward, 104, 106, 129, 130, 131–32; as skeptic, 110–11; unpredictability of, 140–41

Masonry, Russian: and carnivalesque

mentality, 61, 220n.48; and eighteenth-century Russian novel, 61, 220n.47; and English model, 21; and Russian literati, 21, 61, 220n.47

Masquerade, 146–49

Maxims: of La Rochefoucauld, 19–21; in Emin, 88, 97–98, 105, 191; in Komarov, 97

Merchantry: carnivalesque mockery of, 120–22, 130–31, 225n.6

Metaliterary commentary: in *The Double,* 180, 182, 186–87, 187; in the literature of the 1840s, 161, 194, 196, 232n.5; in *The Mocker,* 77–78, 109–10, 154–55, 187

Metaphor: in Emin, 95–97, 100, 135–36, 191–92, 224n.9, 227n.14; parody of, in Chulkov, 104–5, 228n.4

Milord George (Povest′ o prikliuchenii aglinskogo milorda Georga . . . .), carnival in, 131; devices in, 148–49; didacticism in, 226n.13; and Emin, 75–76; eroticism in, 123–24, 131; exoticism in, 81; fantasy in, 83; folklore in, 48, 218n.29; foreign sources of, 12; heteroglossia of, 226n.13; historicity in, 73, 76, 81; Karamzin on, 221n.50; in kopeck papers, 217n.23; marginalia in, 55; masquerade in, 147; mythological dictionary in, 55–56; popularity of, 56, 190, 193, 212n.3; rape, theme of, in, 226n.9; Tolstoi and, 190; tricks in, 149

Mirror of reality, literature as: Belinskii and, 195; and *The Double,* 176, 181, 230n.5, 230n.6; elements of, 177; parody of, 196

Mocker, The (Peresmeshnik, ili slavenskie skazki), 12–13; author's prerogative in, 77–78; autobiography, parody of, in, 92; *balagur* in, 141; deceit in, 121–22, 149; eroticism in, 124, 132–33, 192, 227nn.15–16; familial hierarchies in, 116–17; fantasy in, 82, 84–85, 129; and *Gargantua and Pantagruel,* 78; grotesquerie in, 85; historicity, subversion of, in, 222n.12; interpolated tales in, 82;

liars in, 155, 221n.5; love in, 109,
116–17, 133; metaliterary commentary in, 77–78, 109–10, 154–55, 187;
monarch, image of ideal, in, 89,
89–90, 90, 101, 124, 223n.4; money,
motif of, in, 124; monologue, pathetic, in, 109; mythology, classical, in, 88, 133, 154, 227n.16;
mythology, Slavic, in, 122;
mythology, travesty of, in, 122,
141; popularity of, 56; prostitutes
in, 130–31; readers and, 84, 85, 94,
104, 110; religion, parody of, in 92,
121–22, 130; satire in, 88; sex, ethos
of, in 129, 129–30, 132–33, 149; sex,
illicit, in, 130, 149, 157; sex, positive treatment of, in 121, 128, 130,
133; sources of, 12–13; unfinished
nature of, 71, 221n.6; women in,
92, 128, 133, 136
Mock readers: in *The Double*, 169,
184–87; in Emin, 88, 91; in "The
Overcoat," 169, 196–97
Molière: reception of, in Russia, 4, 20,
21; translations of, 57, 214n.15
Moll Flanders, 82; authoritarian voice
in, 27; as autobiography, 62, 189,
212n.4; and eighteenth-century
Russian novel, 5, 24–28,
215nn.24–25; sex, illicit, in, 26–27
Monarch, image of the ideal: in Komarov, 117; in *The Mocker*, 89,
89–90, 101, 124, 223n.4; and the
public welfare, 113, 114–15
Money, motif of: in Chulkov, 50–51,
105, 124, 141–42, 144, 156–57; in
Komarov, 120–21
Monologue, 62, 66; authority of, 108;
parody of, in Chulkov, 108, 110;
structure of, 98
Monologue of morals and manners: in
Emin, 102, 103, 224n.13
Monologue, pathetic, 96, 98–99, 138,
139; of female characters, 99–100;
of male characters, 98, 224n.11;
parody of, in Chulkov, 108–11
Monologue, philosophical, 111; authority of, 102; parody of, in
Chulkov, 111–12; structure of,
101–2, 112; subject matter of,

101–2, 191, 224n.12
Montesquieu: as Anglophile, 214n.16;
impact of, on eighteenth-century
Russian prose fiction, 189; *The
Spirit of the Laws*, 18, 57
Morality: in eighteenth-century Rus-
sian novel, 87, 88, 92, 114, 148–49,
192, 225n.5; parody of, in
Chulkov, 111–12. *See also* Mono-
logue of morals and manners
Moscow News (Moskovskie vedomosti),
23, 40, 54
Moscow University Press, 56, 57, 58
Mythology, classical: in carnival, 36; in
Chulkov, 84, 88, 133, 146, 154,
227n.16; in Emin, 135, 226n.8; in
Komarov, 55–56; travesty of, in
Chulkov, 122, 141, 142, 144, 155,
228n.4
Mythology, Slavic, 41–42, 217n.22; in
The Mocker, 84, 122; *A Short Mytho-
logical Lexicon (Kratkii mifologich-
eskii leksikon)*, 50–51, 217n.22

Narrators: in Chulkov, 88–89, 91–93,
109, 192 (*see also* Martona); in *The
Double*, 176, 178, 179, 184–85; in
Emin, 73, 75, 87–88, 104–5, 190–91,
221n.4; in Komarov, 191
Nationalism: and eighteenth-century
Russian novel, 15–16; and prose
fiction of 1840s, 161
Natural School, the: conventions of, 30;
The Double and, 174–75, 176–77,
177; parody of, 196, 232n.14; readers of, 174; and Russian prose fiction of the 1840s, 161
Naturalists, Reluctant, 194
Neoclassicism, French: and eighteenth-century Russian literature,
4, 7, 13, 46, 170; and the subculture, 46
Neoclassicism, Russian: Chulkov's relationship to, 49–50, 51; humor in,
215n.4; Komarov and, 49; and the
novel genre, 59–60, 62, 64, 187;
popularity of, 19; values and
norms of, 19, 64, 170
Neokh: as antihero, 79, 117, 153–54,
157; as fictional character, 77–78;

as liar, 121, 122, 141; sexual conduct of, 78, 79, 128, 130, 141
Nevidimka: bogatyri as heroes of, 134, 137; carnivalesque behavior in, 120–21; cross-dressing in, 147; deceit in, 120–21, 147; fantasy in, 83; folklore in, 48, 83; footnotes in, 55; foreign sources of, 12; historicity, subversion of, in, 81, 222n.12; interpolated tales in, 120–21; money, motif of, in 120–21; readers of, 93; tricks in 120–21
Northern Bee (Severnaia pchela), 231n.14
Notes of the Fatherland (Otechestvennye zapiski), 174, 231n.6
Novikov, Nikolai: as editor, 21, 58; *Kalisfen*, 60; as Mason, 21, 61; and the novel, 60; *The Painter (Zhivopisets)*, 214n.16; as publisher, 56, 57, 59; on Russian Anglomania, 20; and skepticism of the West, 16, 28; *The Twaddler (Pustomelia)*, 49; and the Typographical Company, 20, 58

Ovchinnikov, Matvei, 58
"Overcoat, The" ("Shinel'"), 4; adversative style of, 196–97; facetiae, influence of, on, 194; metaliterary play in, 161; mock readers in, 169, 196–97; naturalism, parody of, in, 196; physiological sketch and, 161; "poor clerk" motif in, 196, 230n.3; readers as target of, 196–97; stylization in, 196–97

Panaev, Ivan, 229n.6, 233n.6
Parody: and authorial intention, 166; biplanar structure of, 163, 169, 170; as double-voiced discourse, 165–66; history of, 229n.9; humor, role of, in, 163, 169, 170, 229n.5; motivation for, 169–70, 230n.10; and prevailing literary aesthetic, 170; reader's role in, 170, 170–71, 230n.10; target of, 163, 169, 170, 171. *See also* Stylization
Patriarch Nikon, 13
Paul I, 213n.9

Pavlova, Karolina, 229n.6
Pepys, Samuel, 215n.27
"Peter of the Golden Keys" ("Petr zlatykh kliuchei"): and Emin, 56; and *lubok*, 39, 40, 41, 217n.18; as translated work, 44
Peter the Great: and imitation of the West, 4, 11, 212n.1; as new Prince Vladimir, 15; reforms of, 16, 213n.9
Petersburg, St.: carnival in, 33; Diderot's view of, 17, 18; Emin's arrival in, 52–53; legend of, in Russian literature, 175; and "poor clerk" motif, 175; as setting of *The Double*, 174, 177, 179, 186, 230.2, 231n.11
Petrine tales, 59
Physiological sketch, 161, 233n.6
Physiologie, 233n.6
Picaresque, 46, 47
Pioneers of Russian prose fiction: critics and, 3, 188; and creation of unique novelistic voice, 28; legacy of, 188, 197; and West European literary models, 48–49
Plato, 87
Pletnev, Petr, 162
Poland: as literary intermediary for Russia, 44, 45, 46
Polevoi, Nikolai, 164
"Poor Clerk" motif in Russian literature: in *The Double*, 175–76, 177, 183, 186, 187, 195; in Gogol', 195–96, 230n.3; history of, 230n.3; stylization and, 173
Poor Folk (Bednye liudi): metaliterary commentary in, 196, 232n.5; and "The Overcoat," 196; parody in, 166, 196; reception of, 195; stylization in, 195
Pope, Alexander, 22
Popov, Mikhail: and popular culture, 16; and Slavic mythology, 41–42, 217n.22
Prach, I., 16
Prévost, L'Abbé Antoine François: as Anglophile, 214n.16; influence of, on eighteenth-century Russian prose fiction, 189; *Manon Lescaut*, 62, 212n.4

Pribautki, 45, 107, 118
Prokopovich, Feofan, 15, 212n.1
Propp, Vladimir, 218n.28
Publishers, eighteenth-century Russian, 54, 55, 58; Academy of Sciences, 54, 57, 57–58, 60; Akhmet´ev, 40; Artillery and Engineering Corps, 56–57; backgrounds of, 58; and belles lettres, 23, 57; Bogdanovich, Petr, 58, 220n.45; increase in, 56; Infantry Corps, 56, 57; and *lubok,* 39, 40, 59, 217n.17; Moscow University Press, 56, 57, 58; Naval Corps, 56, 57; and the novel, 56, 59; Novikov, Nikolai, 56, 57, 59; Ponamarev, 40, 58, 59; profitability of, 57–59; Reshetnikov, Andrei, 40, 58, 59; Schnoor, Johann, 58, 59, 219n.37; Weitbrecht, Johann, 58
Pushkin, A. S., 189–90; *The Bronze Horseman (Mednyi vsadnik),* 175; *The Captain's Daughter (Kapitanskaia dochka),* 3, 6, 211n.2; *Count Nulin (Graf Nulin),* 184; *Evgenii Onegin,* 33, 211n.2; and imitation of Western literary models, 11; and *lubok,* 189–90, 192, 217n.19; and the novel, rise of, 6, 193

Rabelais, François, 60; Bakhtin on, 6, 29; and carnival, 6; Chulkov and, 66, 94, 95, 212n.6, 219n.34; *Gargantua and Pantagruel,* 30, 31, 39, 78, 94, 95, 220n.49; image of author in, 31; on philosophizing, 108; on wisdom, 112
Racine, Jean, 4
Radishchev, Aleksandr: "Bova Korolevich," 217n.21; *A Journey from Petersburg to Moscow (Puteshestvie iz Peterburga v Moskvu),* 212n.6; as Mason, 21, 61
Raeshniki, 38, 216n.8
Raznochintsy: Chulkov as member of, 50; definition of, 218n.32
Reader-response criticism, 195
Readers, eighteenth-century Russian, 19, 54–56, 81; lower-class origins of, 55; numbers of, 54; and popularity of novel, 52; simplicity of, 219n.42; tastes of, 57. *See also* Chulkov; Emin; Komarov
Reading in eighteenth-century Russia, 189, 219nn.39–41
Reading interludes, 172, 177
Realism: in Chulkov, 78, 82–83, 190, 192, 222nn.13, 15; in *The Double,* 177, 182, 185, 187; in Emin, 190–91
Religion: and the carnivalesque, 38, 92, 118, 121–22, 130, 133, 225nn.3, 6; in eighteenth-century Russian novel, 88, 113, 114–15, 117; in Emin, 88, 98, 99, 113–14, 145–46; in Komarov, 113, 121, 225n.3
Reshetnikov, Andrei, 58; and *lubok,* 40; and the novel, 59
Rhetoric: carnivalesque, 103–4, 112, 132; of despair, 137, 212n.3; of feelings, 62; of perfection, 135; of submissiveness, 150–53
Richardson, Samuel: *Clarissa,* 22, 123, 220n.43; *Pamela,* 44; popularity of, in Russia, 4, 22, 189; rhetoric of feelings in, 62; Russian imitators of, 22
Rousseau, Jean-Jacques: *La Nouvelle Héloïse,* 12, 189, 212nn.3–4, 225n.2; Russian editions of, 57
Russia, eighteenth-century: foreign accounts of 216n.12. *See also* Carnival: eyewitness accounts of
Russian novel, eighteenth-century: as antibehavior, officially sanctioned, 15; carnivalesque recycling in, 5, 31–32, 65; critics and, 5–6; and eighteenth-century British literature, 24; Enlightenment skepticism of, 16, 59–60, 64–65; first-person narration in, 62–63; heteroglossia of, 65–67, 226n.13; history of, 44, 211n.2; and imitation of foreign literary models, 4–5, 8, 12–13, 60, 188–89; legacy of, 189–93, 197; legitimizing, 61–64, 66, 136, 191, 192; letters, function of, in, 62; *lubok* and, 40, 41, 49, 59, 60; and Masonry, 61, 220n.47; and nineteenth-century Russian prose fiction, 6, 8, 211n.2; popularity of,

4–5, 19, 52, 54, 59; profitability of, 53; and Russian literary tradition, 3; sentimentalism and, 7, 49, 52, 60, 136, 211n.2, 214n.22, 220n.50, 225n.2; stereotypes in, 134–40; and the subculture, 5, 30, 42, 52, 62, 66, 119, 193, 232n.3; and translated literature, 43–47, 71–72; and translation, 72

St. Petersburg News (St. Peterburgskie vedomosti), 54–55
Saltykov-Shchedrin, Mikhail, 223n.3
Satire, 39, 45, 232n.4; Bakhtin on, 223n.7; in the carnival, 34, 35; in Chulkov, 51, 88–89, 95; in The Double, 183; in Komarov, 64
Saturnalia, 161
Scarron, Paul, 66
Schnoor, Johann, 58, 59, 219n.37
Self-debasement, theme of, 150; criminality, images of, and, 151; martyrdom and, 153, 228n.7; masochism and, 151–53; slavery, images of, and, 150–51, 156
Selflessness, theme of: in Emin's fiction, 103, 104, 115, 133, 138, 139–40, 193
Senkovskii, Osip, 168–69
Sentimental discourse: in The Double, 185, 186–87, 195; in Gogol´, 196
Sentimentalism, 13; British, 136; and eighteenth-century Russian novel, 7, 49, 52, 60, 136, 211n.2, 214n.22, 220n.50, 225n.2; humor in, 215n.4; and lubok, 42
Servants: as hero, 120–21, 122, 149; subverting masters, 143, 149, 178, 180
Sex: and the carnival, 35, 37; carnivalesque approach to, 78, 119, 122, 128–31, 133, 148–49, 193; and death, 127, 149, 228n.6; denied in Emin, 125, 126, 132, 154; hypocritical attitude toward, 99–100, 105, 111; and marriage, 127; and morality, 104, 129, 154, 217n.27; as means of social advancement, 128–29, 130, 141–42, 143, 149; and suicide, 129, 131; and virtue, 127,

133. See also The Comely Cook, Martona; The Mocker
Sexual code of conduct: in Emin, 122–28, 153, 225n.7
Shakespeare, William, 22
Shapka-nevidimka, 83
Shcherbatov, M. M. 16, 213n.7, 220n.47
"Shemiaka's Court" ("Shemiakin sud"), 40
Shishkin, Ivan, 54
Shklovskii, Viktor: on Komarov, 12, 55, 218nn.29, 31; on social origins of novel readers, 55
Skomorokhi: censorship of, 38; in Chulkov, 219n.34; reputation of, 32, 216n.5
Slovo, 64
Slovo i delo Gosudarevo, 118, 119–20, 225n.4
Smollett, Tobias: Bakhtin and, 29; novels of, 23, 33, 44; reception of, in Russia, 4, 23
Social hierarchies: and love, 113, 116, 225n.2; and state service, 115, 224n.1; subversion of, 120–22
Society: and the individual, 102–3, 113; and the law, 128; and morality, 114
Society for Translating Books, the, 58
Socrates, 223n.2
Sorel, Charles, 66
Sovest-Dral, The Adventures of, (Pokhozhdeniia . . . Sovest-Drala), 46–47, 218n.47
Steele, Sir Richard, 21
Stereotypes: in The Double, 175, 176, 186; in eighteenth-century Russian novel, 134–40; in literature of the 1840s, 195
Sterne, Laurence: Bakhtin and 29, 30; and Chulkov, 79–80, 192–93, 221n.8; publication of, in Russia, 4, 22
Stylization: adversative style of, 177, 178; and authorial intention, 166; biplanar structure of, 164–65, 171, 172; and the carnivalesque, 162, 165, 173, 177, 179, 183, 187, 189; as double-voiced discourse, 165–67, 171; and 1840s, 7, 194, 195–96, 196–97, 233n.6; and humor, lack

of, 164, 179, 229n.6; and imitation, relationship to, 164, 166–67, 171–72, 174–77; intertextuality in, 165; and literary schools, change of, 164, 165, 167, 171, 173; and parody, relationship to, 7, 164–65; planes, merging of, in, 164, 166–67; and "poor clerk" motif, 173; and prevailing literary aesthetic, 162, 164–65, 173; reader as target of, 7, 162, 167, 171–73; and reader-response criticism, 195; reading interludes and, 172; vaudeville and, 194; and Western literature, 7. See also The Double

Subculture: audience of, 38–39; belles lettres, distortion of, in, 39, 40, 42–43, 61, 189–90, 192, 217n.19; discourse of, 35, 36, 38–39, 66; and the eighteenth-century Russian novel, 5, 30, 42, 52, 62, 66, 119, 193, 232n.3; elements of, 38, 46, 65, 192, 194; humor of, 5, 6, 7, 30, 66, 85, 192; and nineteenth-century Russian literature, 193–95; readers of, 190, 192. See also Carnival; Carnivalesque mentality; Folklore; Lubok; Translated literature

Suicide: and love, 114, 123, 136, 137, 147; and sex, 129, 131

Sumarokov, Aleksandr, 50; and Emin, 62, 189; epistles of, 18, 20, 232n.1; and lubok, 40, 42, 192; as Mason, 21, 61; and Molière, 20; and the novel genre, 59–60, 60, 64, 187; plays of, 56; as theorist, 15, 19, 232n.1

Swift, Jonathan, 4, 22

Tale of the Taffeta Beauty Patch, The (Skazka o rozhdenii taftianoi mushki): dancing in, 78; drinking in, 78; hero of, 141; metaliterary commentary in, 77; sex in, 78; sources of, 13; unfinished nature of, 79–80. See also Neokh

Tears: in carnivalesque fiction, 140; in The Double, 176, 185, 186; motivation of, 139; and self-pity, 143; virtues of, in Emin, 134, 137, 138–39, 225n.2

Themistocles (Prikliucheniia Femistokla . . . .), 89; authorial surrogates in, 91; as first Russian philosophical novel, 62, 189

Thousand and One Nights, The, 12

Till Eulenspiegel, 46

Titunik, I. R.: on Emin's appropriation of La Nouvelle Héloïse, 212n.3; on Ernest and Doravra, 212n.3, 223n.2, 224n.11, 225n.2, 226n.8; on image of author, 63; on Komarov, 193; on the "new" prose fiction and the neoclassical canon, 61–62; on parody in The Mocker, 221n.51

Tolstoi, Lev: Anna Karenina, 191; Childhood (Detstvo), 6, 191; and lubok, 43, 190; and the novel, rise of, 6; War and Peace (Voina i mir), 216n.9

Translated literature: and carnivalesque mentality, 45; and eighteenth-century Russian novel, 43–47, 71–72; humor of, 45; and lubok, 45; popularity of, 45, 59

Trediakovskii, Vasilii: biography of, 218n.33; Journey to the Island of Love (Ezda v ostrov liubvi), 217n.20; as target of parody, 217n.21; Tilemakhida, 220n.46; as translator, 20, 60

Trickery: as carnivalesque virtue, 155; in Komarov, 117–18, 120–21, 149. See also Carnival; Joke

Turgenev, Ivan: Notes of a Hunter (Zapiski okhotnika), 191; and Russian novel, rise of, 6, 193

Tynianov, Iurii: "Dostoevskii and Gogol´," 7, 162–65; on Dostoevskii's relationship to Gogol´, 165; "On Parody" ("O parodii"), 162–65; parody, theory of, 163–64, 165; stylization, theory of, 7, 162–65, 165, 167, 229n.6

Unfortunate Nikanor (Neshchastnyi Nikanor), 221n.50

Uspenskii, Boris A. See Lotman, Iurii

Vanka Kain: attempts to legitimize, 63–64; authority, subversion of, in, 117, 118–20; carnivalesque turnabouts in, 107, 142; carnival in, 118,

119, 120; didacticism in, 225n.5; as
documentary, 72–73, 189, 232n.2;
and folklore, 12, 16, 48, 97, 107–8;
footnotes in, 73; high society, critique of, in 107–8; historicity in, 73,
75–76, 81, 189; image of author in,
63; jokes in, 117; and *Jonathan Wild*,
232n.2; and Kain's autobiography,
63; in kopeck papers, 217n.23;
maxims in, 97; as modern novel,
188; Moscow underworld in, 118,
118–19, 120, 232n.2; narrator, reticent, in, 221n.2; *pribautki* in, 107,
118; popularity of, 56, 193, 212n.3,
220n.44; in Pushkin's library,
189–90; religion, subversion of, in,
113, 121, 225n.3; satire in, 64; self-
sacrifice, parody of, in 142; sex in,
119; subculture in, 119; tricks in,
117–18
*Various Written Materials (Raznye
pis´mennye materii . . . .)*: as cap-
stone of Komarov's career, 93;
footnotes in, 56; grotesquerie of,

49; sources of, 12, 42, 49, 63
"Vasilii Koriotskii," 56, 218n.28
Vaudeville, the, 194, 233n.6
Vertep, 193, 194
Villon, François, 66
Virginity: consequences of losing, 123;
as supreme virtue in Emin's nov-
els, 100, 122, 123
Virtue: in Chulkov, 146; in Emin, 88,
95–96, 100, 103, 122, 123, 124, 127,
133, 138, 139–40, 141–42, 144, 152;
parody of, in Chulkov, 109, 155.
See also Friendship; Selflessness
Voltaire: *Candide*, 57; influence of, on
eighteenth-century Russian cul-
ture, 19, 189, 214n.16, 217n.24

Watt, Ian, 55, 56
Weitbrecht, Johann, 58
Women: role of, in Chulkov, 92, 128,
129, 133, 136; role of, in Emin, 128,
145; and suicide, 114, 123. *See also*
Femme fatale